MW01251206

NIGHT+DAY
LONDON

By Claire Gervat and
Francesca Gavin

PULSE GUIDES

Pulse Guides' **Night+Day London** is an independent guide. We do not accept payment of any kind from events or establishments for inclusion in this book. We welcome your views on our selections. Please email us: **feedback@pulseguides.com**.

The information contained in this book was checked as rigorously as possible before going to press. The publisher accepts no responsibility for any changes that may have occurred since, or for any other variance of fact from that recorded here in good faith.

No part of this book may be reproduced in any form without permission in writing from the publisher, except by a reviewer who wishes to quote brief passages for a published review. This publication is a creative work fully protected by all applicable copyright laws, as well as by misappropriation, trade secrets, unfair competition, and all other applicable laws. The authors and editors of this work have added value to the underlying factual material herein through one or more of the following: unique and original selection, coordination, expression, arrangement, and classification (including the itineraries) of the information.

Distributed in the United States and Canada by National Book Network (NBN). First Edition. Printed in the United States. 30% postconsumer content. Copyright © 2006 ASDavis Media Group, Inc. All rights reserved. ISBN-10: 0-9766013-7-0; ISBN-13: 978-0-9766013-7-1

Credits

Executive Editor	Alan S. Davis
Editor	Christina Henry de Tessan
Authors	Claire Gervat, Francesca Gavin
Contributor	Sejal Sukhadwala
Copy Editors	Gail Nelson-Bonebrake, Elizabeth Stroud, Kelly Borgeson
Maps	Chris Gillis
Production	Jo Farrell, Samia Afra

Photo Credits: (Front cover, left to right) Les Byerley (martini), courtesy of Brown's Hotel (Brown's), Wing Tang (City Hall); (Back cover, left to right) courtesy of One Aldwych, courtesy of Pearl (Pearl), Ian Heide (River Cafe), courtesy of Visit London (London Eye); (Inside cover, top to bottom) courtesy of Cocoon Restaurant (Cocoon Bar), Andrea Cellerino (Bistrotheque), Jon Spaull (Ronnie Scott's); (p.4) Mary Lou D'Auray

Special Sales

For information about bulk purchases of Pulse Guides (ten copies or more), email us at bookorders@pulseguides.com. Special bulk rates are available for charities, corporations, institutions, and online and mail-order catalogs, and our books can be customized to suit your company's needs.

NIGHT+DAY
The Cool Cities series from **PULSE**GUIDES

P.O. Box 590780, San Francisco, CA 94159
pulseguides.com

Pulse Guides is an imprint of ASDavis Media Group, Inc.

The Night+Day Difference

The Pulse of the City

Our job is to point you to all of the city's peak experiences: amazing museums, unique spas, and spectacular views. But the complete *urbanista* experience is more than just impressions—it is grown-up fun, the kind that thrives by night as well as by day. Urban fun is a hip nightclub or a trendy restaurant. It is people-watching and people-meeting. Lonely planet? We don't think so. Night+Day celebrates our lively planet.

The Right Place. The Right Time. It Matters.

A Night+Day city must have exemplary restaurants, a vibrant nightlife scene, and enough attractions to keep a visitor busy for six days without having to do the same thing twice. In selecting restaurants, food is important, but so is the scene. Our hotels, most of which are 4- and 5-star properties, are rated for the quality of the concierge staff (can they get you into a hot restaurant?) as well as the rooms. You won't find kids with fake IDs at our nightlife choices. And the attractions must be truly worthy of your time. But experienced travelers know that timing is almost everything. Going to a restaurant at 7pm can be a very different experience (and probably less fun) than at 9pm; a champagne boat cruise might be ordinary in the morning but spectacular at sunset. We believe providing the reader with this level of detail makes the difference between a good experience and a great one.

The Bottom Line

Your time is precious. Our guide must be easy to use and dead-on accurate. That is why our executive editor, editors, and writers (locals who are in touch with what is great—and what is not) spend hundreds of hours researching, writing, and debating selections for each guide. The results are presented in four unique ways: The *99 Best* with our top three choices in 33 categories that highlight what is great about the city; the *Experience* chapters, in which our selections are organized by distinct themes or personalities (Hot & Cool, Hip, and Classic); a *Perfect Plan* (3 Nights and Days) for each theme, showing how to get the most out of the city in a short period of time; and the *London Black Book*, listing all the hotels, restaurants, nightlife, and attractions, with key details, contact information, and page references.

Our bottom line is this: if you find our guide easy to use and enjoyable to read, and with our help you have an extraordinary time, we have succeeded. We review and value all feedback from our readers, so please contact us at **feedback@pulseguides.com**.

In Berkeley Square

From the Publisher

I've had the travel bug ever since my first summer job during college—escorting tour groups around Europe to evaluate them for my parents' travel company. When I retired from the paper business ten years ago I set out on a journey to find the 100 most fun places to be in the world at the right time. The challenge of unearthing the world's greatest events—from the Opera Ball in Vienna to the Calgary Stampede—led me to write a guidebook.

The success of *The Fun Also Rises*, named after Ernest Hemingway's *The Sun Also Rises*, which helped popularize what has become perhaps the most thrilling party on earth (Pamplona's Fiesta de San Fermín, also known as the Running of the Bulls), persuaded me that there were others who shared my interest in a different approach to travel. Guidebooks were neither informative nor exciting enough to capture peak experiences—whether for world-class events or just a night on the town.

My goal is to publish *extraordinary guides for extraordinary travelers*. **Night+Day**, the first series from Pulse Guides, is for Gen-Xers to Zoomers (Boomers with a zest for life), who know that if one wants to truly experience a city, the night is as important as the day. **Night+Day** guides present the best that a city has to offer—hotels, restaurants, nightlife, and attractions that are exciting without being stuffy—in a totally new format.

Pulse Guides abides by one guiding principle: *Never settle for the ordinary.* We hope that a willingness to explore new approaches to guidebooks, combined with meticulous research, provides you with unique and significant experiences.

I've been fortunate enough to have lived in London for two years, and it is a rare year when I haven't spent some time in this incredible city. Nearly four decades ago I worked a college summer helping to manage arrangements for visiting tour groups. In those days, the only reason to visit London was for its history. Things have changed dramatically, and I'm excited to show you today's **Night+Day London**.

Wishing you extraordinary times,

Alan S. Davis, Publisher and Executive Editor
Pulse Guides

P.S. To contact me, or for updated information on all of our **Night+Day** guides, please visit our website at **pulseguides.com**.

TOC

INTRODUCTION 9
  Night+Day's London Urbie 12

THE 99 BEST OF LONDON .15
  Al Fresco Dining 16
  Always-Hot Restaurants 17
  Aristocratic Mansions 18
  Bar Interiors 19
  Bars with a View 20
  Celeb Haunts 21
  Cocktails 22
  Dance Clubs 23
  Famous Chefs 24
  Fine Dining 25
  Fresh Air Experiences 26
  Gastropubs 27
  Gay Bars and Clubs 28
  Green Spaces 29
  Hotel Bars 30
  Indian Restaurants 31
  Late-Night Haunts 32
  Live-Music Venues 33
  Markets 34
  Modern Art Spaces 35
  Oriental Restaurants 36
  Power Lunches 37
  Pubs 38
  Rainy Day Activities 39
  Restaurant Lounges 40
  Romantic Dining 41
  See-and-be-Seen Spots 42
  Shopping Streets 43
  Singles Scenes 44
  Small Museums 45
  Spas 46
  Sushi 47
  Trendy Tables 48

EXPERIENCE LONDON 49
Hot & Cool London 50
The Perfect Plan (3 Nights and Days) 51
The Key Neighborhoods 55
The Shopping Blocks 56
The Hotels 57
The Restaurants 62
The Nightlife 74
The Attractions 85
Hip London 92
The Perfect Plan (3 Nights and Days) 93
The Key Neighborhoods 97
The Shopping Blocks 98
The Hotels 99
The Restaurants 102
The Nightlife 111
The Attractions 121
Classic London 126
The Perfect Plan (3 Nights and Days) 127
The Key Neighborhoods 131
The Shopping Blocks 132
The Hotels 133
The Restaurants 139
The Nightlife 155
The Attractions 163

PRIME TIME LONDON 173
Prime Time Basics 174
Eating and Drinking 174
Weather and Tourism 174
National Holidays 175
The Best Events Calendar 176
The Best Events 177

HIT THE GROUND RUNNING 185
City Essentials 186
Getting to London: By Air 186
Getting to London: By Land 191
London: Lay of the Land 192
Getting Around London 192

Other Practical Information (Money Matters; Metric Conversion; Safety; Numbers to Know; Gay and Lesbian Travel; Traveling with Disabilities; Print Media; Radio Stations; Attire; Size Conversion; Shopping Hours; Drinking; Smoking; Drugs; Getting into Clubs; Time Zone; Additional Resources for Visitors) 195

Party Conversation—A Few Surprising Facts 200

The Cheat Sheet (The Very Least You Ought to Know About London) (Neighborhoods, Thoroughfares, Performing Arts Centers, Influential Architects, Landmarks, Central Parks, Markets, Department Stores, Mayors, Singular Sensation, and Coffee) . .201

Just for Business and Conventions 206

London Region Map 208

LEAVING LONDON 209
   Overnight Trips
      Bath 210
      Cornwall 212
      The Cotswolds 214
      Edinburgh, Scotland 216
      The Lake District 218
      Suffolk 220
   Day Trips
      Brighton 222
      Middle Thames Valley 223
      Oxford 224
      Whitstable 225
      Winchester 226

THE LONDON BLACK BOOK 227
   London Black Book 228
   London Black Book by Neighborhood 248
   London Unique Shopping Index 253

London Action Central Map 254
London Neighborhoods Map 255

About the Authors

 **Claire Gervat** was born and raised in London and aside from her college years has never lived anywhere else. She writes about London and further-flung places for a range of national magazines and newspapers, including *Condé Nast Traveller*, the *Daily Mail,* and the *London Evening Standard*. She is also the author of *Elizabeth: The Scandalous Life of the Duchess of Kingston*, about a woman who knew all about having fun in London. Find out more at claire-gervat.com.

Francesca Gavin is a features writer and editor based in London. She regularly contributes to international magazines and newspapers from *Dazed & Confused*, BBC online, and *The Times* in London to *Citizen K* in Paris and *Soma* in San Francisco. She is also the associate editor of *Marmalade* magazine. She is a passionate Londoner who knows the city better than most taxi drivers.

Sejal Sukhadwala is a London-based food writer and restaurant critic. She writes for *Time Out, The Guardian, The Daily Telegraph, The Times, The Independent, Caterer & Hotelkeeper,* and bbc.co.uk/food.

Acknowledgments

Thank you to all the enthusiastic gallery owners, spa types, and museum gurus who gave up so much of their time to talk to me, and to the kind people who made my visits out of town such an experience. A big cheer, too, for Alison C, without whom this book, and the last, would have been that much harder to do; for Christina Henry for being the world's most patient editor; and for Alexander and Perkins, just because.
Claire Gervat

Thanks to Andrea Thompson and Ruby Warrington for joining me on 1001 nights out; to Seana, Bianca, and Paola for softening the hangovers.
Francesca Gavin

Introduction

Welcome to London. By that we mean the glorious, sprawling, beautiful, maddening, exciting, bewildering, bewitching capital of Great Britain, the city where skyscrapers have Roman ruins in the basement, where 300-year-old houses can contain anything from displays of classical antiquities to an achingly hot nightclub, where there are streets that still follow the same route they did a millennium ago and plenty that don't. We mean the London that is home not only to seven million people, more than a third of whom belong to nonindigenous communities and speak more than 300 different languages, but also to six million trees. We mean the city (actually, two cities and 31 boroughs, if you want to get technical about it) that attracts 27 million visitors every year, in spite of the reputation of its weather. Yes, that London.

This glorious, sprawling, beautiful, maddening, exciting, bewildering, bewitching capital has skyscrapers with Roman ruins in the basement, 300-year-old houses that are home to hot nightclubs, and so much more.

London: What It Was

The story of this world-class city begins nearly 2,000 years ago. The invading Romans, never slow to spot a strategic site for a city, took one look at the River Thames and the fertile land around it and promptly constructed a frontier town of wooden houses and boardwalks on its banks. Unfortunately, it didn't last long. Local heroine Queen Boudicca and her Iceni tribesmen burned it to ashes ten years later, but by then the Romans were too entrenched in the area to consider leaving. This time they built more solidly, and Londinium soon established itself as the glamorous capital of the province of Britannia, its defensive walls containing all the temples, bathhouses, and villas worthy of an important Roman town.

But in the early fifth century, the Roman Empire went into terminal decline. Londinium was abandoned and a new wave of invaders, this time from what is now northern Germany, arrived to fill the void. The country-born Anglo-Saxons had little interest in city living—in fact, they found the half-deserted Roman town rather creepy—and Londinium was left to crumble. Within 300 years, however, the new rulers had discovered the joys of urban life, establishing their prosperous trading town of Lundenwic a little upstream from the Roman town, where a convenient beach (or strand) made it easier to land their goods.

Success breeds envy, however, and soon yet another band of invaders had their beady eyes on London's riches. This time the intruders were from even further north, fearsome Vikings from Scandinavia, and their series of devastating raids in the early ninth century wiped out the settlement yet again. That could so easily have been the end for London, but it proved instead to be a beginning. By the final decades of the century, the far-sighted king of the southern provinces had re-established the city at its former site within the old Roman walls, from where it was to prosper and grow in the succeeding centuries.

There was just one more invasion to come, the Norman Conquest in 1066, which heralded a long spell of peace and prosperity. Within its sturdy walls, London soon became a cosmopolitan center of trade, industry, and government, widely acknowledged as one of the greatest cities in Europe. It acquired its first parliament, first mayor, and first printing press, along with major landmarks such as the first London Bridge (the only bridge over the Thames until 1750) and the first St. Paul's Cathedral, as well as a slew of smaller churches and grand palaces. The population grew to 100,000, all crammed within the city walls, which meant that when the plague arrived in 1348 it spread quickly. Thousands died, some fled to the countryside; the net result was that the population halved and stayed that way for more than a hundred years.

After the intermittent disturbances of the civil Wars of the Roses through much of the 15th century, the new Tudor dynasty brought a period of political stability, though not without changes (and religious upheavals). Expansion was the keyword now, whether that meant exploring new lands overseas, building more and grander palaces and aristocratic mansions, or exporting more and more luxurious goods from the thriving port to eager overseas buyers. By now London had grown to become three separate settlements: the original City, within the old Roman walls; Westminster with its palaces and abbey to the west; and slightly disreputable Southwark, just across the Thames from the City. Most of the wealthier Londoners had moved to large houses along the north bank of the river between Westminster and the City in order to escape the crowded, narrow, smelly streets.

The Tudors gave way to the Stuarts, and to turbulent times: civil war, the execution of the King, and the founding of a puritanical republic. But by 1660 the monarchy was restored, much to the relief of Londoners, who could now go to the theater, celebrate Christmas, and generally have fun, all things that were completely banned under Oliver Cromwell's regime. The town was awash with new scientific and cultural societies, and the first banks and insurance companies were founded.

Sadly, it wasn't all fun and laughter. An outbreak of plague in 1665 killed a quarter of the population, about 100,000 people; the danger of another outbreak the following year was averted mainly by a terrible fire that raged for four September days, leaving four-fifths of the City—including St. Paul's Cathedral, 87 parish churches, and more than 13,000 houses—a smoldering ruin. Out of the ashes rose a new City of London of stone and brick rather than wood, with wider streets (though to the same plan) and some striking new buildings, notably Sir Christopher Wren's magnificent St. Paul's Cathedral with its distinctive slate-gray dome.

And still London carried on growing, with the empty spaces between the City and Westminster and beyond filling up with houses as the 18th century progressed. By now, it was Britain's leading port and manufacturing center, attracting workers from the countryside and refugees from Europe escaping religious persecution, so that the population doubled in 100 years. The rich moved west, upriver, to elegant new developments such as Mayfair and St. James's, with their leafy

Key Dates

43	Roman invasion of Britain; Londinium founded soon after.
410	Romans abandon Londinium.
604	First St. Paul's Cathedral built.
1215	Signing of Magna Carta creates office of Lord Mayor of London.
1240	First Parliament sits at Westminster.
1340s	The Black Death kills a third of the population of England.
1476	First printing press set up in Westminster.
1640s	Civil War
1665	Outbreak of bubonic plague kills nearly 100,000 Londoners.
1666	Great Fire of London destroys much of the City.
1720s	First streets of Mayfair laid out.
1803	Opening of first horse-drawn railway.
1829	London's first police force established.
1863	The world's first underground railway opens.
1939	Outbreak of Second World War; by 1945, much of London had suffered from bomb damage.
1948	The London Olympics.
1960s	Swinging London becomes a music and fashion capital.
1980s	The start of the property boom; the rise of London as a world-class modern financial center.
2012	London will host the Olympics once more.

Night+Day's London Urbie

Night+Day cities are chosen because they have a vibrant nightlife scene, standard-setting and innovative restaurants, cutting-edge hotels, and enough attractions to keep one busy for six days without doing the same thing twice. In short, they are fun. They represent the quintessential *urbanista* experience. This wouldn't exist but for the creativity and talents of many people and organizations. In honor of all who have played a role in making London one of the world's coolest cities, Pulse Guides is pleased to give special recognition, and our Urbie Award, to one individual whose contribution is exemplary.

THE URBIE AWARD: David Collins

Designer David Collins has left his mark on London's dining scene in no uncertain terms, and his work graces some of the capital's most famous restaurants. His great talent lies in creating luxurious modern environments that are as memorable as the food without eclipsing it, and that's reflected in the way the restaurant critics give him as many column inches in their reviews as they give the chef's more ephemeral creations. His commissions are a roll-call of the city's most glamorous destinations: The Blue Bar at the Berkeley, perhaps his most famous design; Claridge's Bar; The Wolseley; Pétrus; Nobu Berkeley; J Sheekey; and so on. With their clever use of color and lighting to create just the right mood, these aren't just desirable places to eat and drink; they're sophisticated venues where it's a pleasure to just be, or to see and be seen. Even better, his style is constantly evolving, making each new interior a much-anticipated and always delightful surprise. Even in a city blessed with so many talented chefs, hoteliers, and designers, David Collins thoroughly deserves the London Urbie for bringing so much fun and excitement to the important business of going out.

squares and classical architecture. The shopkeepers followed, carrying exotic luxuries from around the world. London's emporia became the envy of the world, later prompting Napoleon to describe the British as "a nation of shopkeepers."

The country emerged as a superpower in the 19th century, in spite of the loss of its American colonies, with London at the center of a vast global empire. With so much cash sloshing around, science, trade, finance, and the arts thrived. The population exploded thanks to migration from the rest of the kingdom, but the new arrivals often found themselves destitute, and London was as famous for its slums as for its fine new museums, trains, and palatial houses. There were outbreaks of cholera, and in 1858 Parliament could barely function because of the smell of raw sewage from the Thames. Only a hi-tech new sewage system, still in use today, made urban life bearable again.

London continued to grow in the last century, in both size and number of inhabitants. Change was sometimes forced on the city; the German bombers of the Second World War reduced huge swathes to rubble, especially in the east, though somehow St. Paul's Cathedral survived. After the war, there was no money for fine new buildings to replace the old, so the rebuilding was done on the cheap. To add to the urban blight, the dock areas with their traditional industries were in decline thanks to changes in the world economy.

> **The country emerged as a superpower in the 19th century, in spite of the loss of its American colonies, with London at the center of a vast global empire. With so much cash sloshing around, science, trade, finance, and the arts thrived, and the population exploded thanks to migration from the rest of the kingdom.**

By the middle of the last century, London was about to enter a vibrant new phase. Even before the war, there had been a steady stream of refugees from parts of Europe, but after the war the stream of new arrivals—economic migrants from the former Empire, rather than just refugees—slowly swelled, bringing fresh ideas about everything from music to food. Throughout the 1950s the economy slowly recovered and then boomed. With growing prosperity came the rapid rise in popularity of the package holiday in the "Swinging Sixties," which brought foreign travel—to Spain, France, and Italy in particular—within the grasp of many Londoners for the first time, along with a whole new set of cultural influences.

London: What It Is

The result is the multicultural London we see today, a bustling metropolis of seven million people including around 50 ethnic-minority communities— and by community we mean more than 10,000 people—and many smaller groups, too. There are Italian coffee bars, Japanese teahouses, more Chinese restaurants than you can shake a chopstick at; there are shops selling carpets from Iran, Vietnamese silk suits, or colorful African print fabrics; you can go out at night and dance to reggae, bhangra, or salsa.

Even the look of the place is changing. The fabulous old stuff is still there, of course, but go-ahead architects are making their own mark on the skyline with curving towers of glass and steel. The docks have been given a new lease of life; the old warehouses have been converted into trendy apartments for the well-heeled workers in the ever-expanding financial district. Yes, it costs a fortune to buy one, but property costs the earth in most parts of London, helping to make it the seventh most expensive city in the world.

Not that some of London's newest residents are too worried about that. The city has become a magnet for the world's rich and famous: Russian oligarchs, Arab princes, Far Eastern billionaires all want a bit of the action. Hollywood, too, has taken London to its heart. After 30 years filming in New York, Woody Allen has switched allegiance; every movie star worth his salt has done a stint on the West End stage; and Kevin Spacey is the artistic director at the Old Vic Theatre. Make a sortie to the latest fabulous bar/gallery/restaurant—and there are plenty of those—and you've a fair chance of catching sight of Madonna, Cameron Diaz, Gwyneth Paltrow, or the like.

So London is buzzing, growing, changing, but we've hung on to the best traditions, too. This exciting old-new London has something for all of you, even the pickiest urbanista. No one's London is the same, however, so you'll have to come here to find yours. It's a big place. You might need a little help. This is it.

Welcome to fabulous London ...

THE 99 BEST of LONDON

Who needs another "Best" list? You do—if it comes with details and insider tips that make the difference between a good experience and great one. We've pinpointed the 33 categories that make London exciting, magnetic, and unforgettable, and picked the absolute three best places to go for each. With a little help from Night+Day, this dynamic metropolis is yours for the taking. Make the most of it.

Al Fresco Dining

#1–3: London's weather has become warmer over the years, and eating in parks and on pavement cafes has never been more popular. These venues offer the kind of people-watching opportunities that appeal to the voyeur in all of us.

Garden Café
Inner Circle Regent's Park, NW1, Regent's Park, 020-7935-5729 • Hip

The Draw: This natty little cafe teems with Londoners of every class, color, gender, and hairstyle, making it a prime people-watching spot.

The Scene: Garden Café serves a monthly-changing British menu in a simple, wood-paneled open-plan space that allows a lot of natural light in the summer. *Daily 10am-dusk. £ =*

Hot Tip: Come on Thursday, Friday, or Saturday at lunchtime, when there's classical and jazz piano. And order one of the indulgent ice cream sundaes.

Inn the Park
St. James's Park, SW1, Westminster, 020-7451-9999 • Hot & Cool

The Draw: Inn offers a fashionably seasonal menu in a very English setting populated by stylishly suited professionals.

The Scene: Located inside St. James's Park, bang opposite Buckingham Palace, this stylish, contemporary venue, with its wood-paneled design and turf roof, has a relaxed ambiance that is hugely popular with fashionable Londoners and visitors alike. *Mon-Fri 8-11am, noon-3pm, and 5-10pm, Sat-Sun 9-11am, noon-4pm, and 5-10pm. £ =*

Hot Tip: Try one of the excellent traditional English breakfasts, and be sure to order from the imaginative selection of breakfast beverages, which includes organic pear juice, a Virgin Mary cocktail, and Assam Tippy BOP tea.

River Café
Thames Wharf, Rainville Rd., W6, Thames Wharf, 020-7386-4200 • Hot & Cool

The Draw: Ruth Rogers and Rose Gray's Italian restaurant remains one of the most fashionable restaurants in town after more than 20 years.

The Scene: Housed inside large converted 19th-century warehouses on the Thames Wharf, the River Café has large picture windows that caress the dining room with natural light, and an outside terrace that gives lovely views of the garden and the river. Politicians, actors, writers, and TV personalities continue to throng the elegant yet informal space. *Daily 12:30-3:30pm and 7-11pm. ££ =*

Hot Tip: Call well ahead to book a table on the lovely terrace. The infamously rich chocolate nemesis is one of the most raved-about desserts in town.

Always-Hot Restaurants

#4–6: London's dining scene is notoriously fickle. One day everybody will be raving about a crème brûlée made with twice-boiled yak's milk, the next they'll be rushing to an obscure eatery showcasing cuisine of a country you didn't know existed. These restaurants, however, have transcended all those fly-by-night trends.

Hakkasan*
8 Hanway Pl., W1, Bloomsbury, 020-7907-1888 • Hot & Cool

The Draw: Chic locals flock here for the exquisite décor, a thriving scene at all hours, and a gorgeous cocktail bar. And the best dim sum in London to boot.

The Scene: A slinky staircase will lead you into a sexy subterranean world that's beautifully lit like the set of a Wong Kar-Wai movie. The handsome bar to one side, and the superglamorous dining area to the other, are always packed with a beautiful fashion, film, and music crowd. *Sun noon-5pm and 6-11pm, Mon-Fri noon-3pm and 6pm-midnight, Sat noon-5pm and 6pm-midnight.* ££ 🅱 ≡

Hot Tip: Start with cocktails amid the sexy crowd at the adjoining Ling Ling Bar.

Sketch*
9 Conduit St., W1, Mayfair, 0870-777-4488 • Hot & Cool

The Draw: Rock-star chic, killer drinks, a stupendously original décor, and celebrity clientele keep this place buzzing at all hours.

The Scene: It's a colorful, eye-popping extravaganza of food, art, and music contained in a variety of lively casual dining and drinking spaces. London's most beautiful people flock here in droves, so be sure to put your name on the list so you too can take advantage of the cocktails and Ibiza-style vibe. *The Gallery: Mon-Sat 7-11pm.* £££; *The Lecture Room: Tue-Fri noon-2:30pm and 7-10:30pm, Sat 7-10:30pm.* £££; *The Glade: noon-3pm.* £££ 🅱 ≡

Hot Tip: The much talked-about jewel-encrusted toilets are not to be missed. The Parlour transforms into an after-dark bar with edgy East London DJs.

Zuma*
5 Raphael St., SW7, Knightsbridge, 020-7584-1010 • Hot & Cool

The Draw: Arguably London's most fashionable restaurant, this sophisticated Japanese venue boasts a coolly understated Zen-inspired décor that is popular with A-listers and the fashion and media crowd.

The Scene: Diners choose from several seating options: the main dining room with an open kitchen, a sushi counter with a robata grill, a chef's table, a sake bar, and private dining rooms. *Mon-Fri noon-2pm and 6-10:45pm, Sat 12:30-3pm and 6-10:45pm, Sun 12:30-3pm and 6-10pm.* ££ 🅱 ≡

Hot Tip: Ask to be seated in the main dining room. And order the off-the-menu chocolate dessert.

Aristocratic Mansions

#7–9: You have to hand it to the nobility: They certainly knew how to build to impress. Sadly, it took an army of servants to run their palatial London homes, so when armies of servants became a thing of the past, so did the houses. Happily, a few show-stoppers survived.

Kenwood House

Hampstead Ln., NW3, Hampstead, 020-8348-1286 • Classic

The Draw: Kenwood House rewards the visitor with magnificent fine art, exquisite neoclassical interiors, and a breath of fresh air on the grounds.

The Scene: Robert Adam's graceful décor would be reason enough to make the journey to Kenwood. Within these walls, however, there's also a magnificent array of mainly 18th-century British paintings. The grounds on the fringes of Hampstead Heath are a pleasant place to linger on warmer days. *Daily Apr-Oct 11am-5pm; Nov-Mar 11am-4pm.* £-

Hot Tip: The audio tour is particularly good and contains some very intriguing details about the house.

Leighton House

12 Holland Park Rd., W14, Kensington, 020-7602-3316 • Classic

The Draw: Sumptuous interiors provide an insight into the life and times of one of the Victorian era's most celebrated artists.

The Scene: An extraordinary house for an extraordinary man. Lord Leighton's spectacular Arab Hall—a 19th-century party venue like no other—is the exotic centerpiece of his built-to-order studio-house. Other, less flamboyant rooms are lined with paintings by the owner and his Pre-Raphaelite contemporaries. *Wed-Mon 11am-5:30pm.* £-

Hot Tip: Once a month the Kensington & Chelsea Music Society (kcmusic.org.uk) holds evening recitals in the upstairs studio.

Spencer House

27 St. James's Pl., SW1, St. James's, 020-7499-8620 • Classic

The Draw: The London family home of the late Princess of Wales is restored to its 18th-century glory.

The Scene: Lady Diana never actually lived here, but when a house looks this magnificent, does it matter? The hour-long tour passes through eight rooms, each more impressive than the last, thanks to ten years of exacting restoration work. Ornate gilded stucco work, painted ceilings, columns carved like palm trees: You'll find all this and more in what was once a hub of the Georgian beau monde. *Sun 10:30am-5:45pm (last admission 4:45pm) by guided tour only.* £-

Hot Tip: Come in February to view the thousands of daffodils that add a splash of color to the views over Green Park.

Bar Interiors

#10–12: Have nothing to talk about? Bored with staring at your companion? Not to fear. You won't lack for diversions at these London hot spots that are famous for their over-the-top décor.

Kabaret's Prophecy

16-18 Beak St., W1, Soho, 020-7439-2229 • Hot & Cool

The Draw: What makes this small club so special is its walls. They are made of grids of light that change color, rhythm, and shape with the music. A live VJ controls the room's changing décor throughout the evening. It's a little like living in a Justin Timberlake video.

The Scene: On Monday nights things get ghetto fabulous with an urban party crowd, Thursdays are house and dance for older Chelsea-ites, Friday is R&B for posh kids, and Saturdays is a commercial free-for-all. The staff are trained to create over 2,000 delicious cocktails—though you may be too busy dancing to bother. Despite the doormen with attitude, Kabaret's Prophecy is a very friendly venue. *Mon-Sat 11pm-3am.* Guest list only ≡

Hot Tip: Go for one of the corner tables—you'll get a great view of the intimate dancefloor and the crazy lights.

Loungelover

1 Whitby St., E1, Hoxton, 020-7012-1234 • Hip

The Draw: When you see the flaming torches outside, you know you're in for something really over the top.The eclectic, eye-popping décor includes everything from four-foot shell lamps to antique medical illustrations to unusual stuffed animals.

The Scene: The place is seriously popular with the party crowd who like to flash their cash. Take time to peruse the very long cocktail list brimming with unusual ingredients and combinations. *Tue-Thu 6pm-midnight, Fri 6pm-1am, Sat 7pm-1am, Sun 6pm-midnight.* ≡

Hot Tip: If you have any intention of enjoying this space, be sure to book in advance. The standing area for last-minute arrivals is stifling and very tiny.

Mo Tea Room

23 Heddon St., W1, Mayfair, 020-7434-4040 • Hip

The Draw: The little sister to Momo next door is a great place to pop in for some stunning mezze, tasty cocktails, and a louche continental vibe.

The Scene: The cushioned low tables are often packed and made more crowded by hookahs, fabulous mezze, and refillable glasses of mint tea. The Arabic-fused rai music is quite loud. It's so popular it can be hard to get a seat, but it's worth the wait. *Mon-Wed noon-11pm, Thu-Sat noon-midnight.* ≡

Hot Tip: Many of the beautiful North African objects that litter the room can be bought along with your kirs.

Best

Bars with a View

#13–15: London doesn't have many tall buildings, so bars with a view of the city are sparse. The ones that do exist, however, are so beautiful that they could rival the London Eye. Binoculars are not obligatory.

The Tenth Bar

The Royal Garden Hotel, 2-24 Kensington High St., W8, Kensington, 020-7361-1910 • Classic

The Draw: The Tenth Bar is a hidden gem, and those who do know about it like to keep it firmly to themselves. The view over Kensington Palace Gardens toward the City is so lovely they don't want crowds blocking the windows.

The Scene: This quiet calm space is a place to unwind after work to live piano or drink one of 20 kinds of champagne before heading off to the Royal Albert Hall. The clientele varies from journalists from the nearby *Daily Mail* to posh locals with a taste for the life above the streets. *Mon-Fri noon-2:30pm and 5:30-11pm, Sat 5:30-11pm.*

Hot Tip: Come here as the sun goes down to catch a killer sunset.

Vertigo 42

Tower 42, 25 Old Broad St., EC2, The City, 020-7877-7842 • Classic

The Draw: The view. This champagne bar is located on the 42nd floor of Tower 42, one of the largest skyscrapers in the City, a full 600 feet above street level.

The Scene: The narrow bar curves around the building offering unsurpassable views. The only thing the suited crowd drinks here is champagne—there are 27 varieties on offer and caviar to match. This place is a special treat that will floor any date or business client. *Mon-Fri noon-3pm, 5-11:30pm.*

Hot Tip: You have to book around three weeks in advance to get a space here in the evening (though it's shorter notice if a daytime tipple appeals).

Windows at the Hilton

The Hilton Hotel, 22 Park Ln., W1, Mayfair, 020-7493-8000 • Classic

The Draw: There's one thing that hits you when you enter Windows—oh my god, the view. The top floor of Park Lane's Hilton has one of the best prospects in London. Overlooking Hyde Park and west over the city, the place comes to life at night as the capital literally sparkles.

The Scene: The décor is rather schizophrenic '70s kitsch, with mirrored walls, forgettable art, and hard leather sofa-seats. But who cares? You'll be looking out the window, not in at the well-dressed crowd slowly sipping Scotch. *Mon-Thu noon-2am, Fri noon-2:30am, Sat 5:30pm-2:30am, Sun noon-10:30pm.*

Hot Tip: Head straight to one of the four tables near the floor-to-ceiling windows, or phone to reserve one.

Celeb Haunts

#16–18: London is home to many of the world's A-listers, making it a great place for celeb-gawking, but it's infinitely more fun if you know where to go. At these celeb magnets, you're virtually guaranteed to catch sight of at least a few familiar faces.

The Ivy
1-5 West St., WC2, Covent Garden, 020-7836-4751 • Classic

The Draw: As London's most famous restaurant, The Ivy is celeb central: Every major (and minor) celebrity frequents it.

The Scene: Many of the tables are especially set aside for the celebrity fraternity, with seating position discreetly carving out their status. Done up in a classic Art Deco style, this contemporary British and continental restaurant is best loved for its exemplary English nursery classics. *Mon-Sat noon-3pm and 5:30pm-midnight, Sun noon-3:30pm and 5:30pm-midnight.* £ =

Hot Tip: Tables need to be booked several months ahead—and to avoid celeb gawkers and dine with A- rather than Z-listers, it's advisable to go on a weekday evening. Or you could take a chance and drop by at an unpopular time—say, 6pm or 9pm, when tables may be available.

Le Caprice
Arlington House, Arlington St., SW1, Mayfair, 020-7629-2239 • Classic

The Draw: Tucked away in a side street near the Royal Academy, this select restaurant, under the same ownership as The Ivy, is favored by stage and film stars, ladies who lunch, art dealers, and other diners with a dash of dosh.

The Scene: The dining room is decorated in serene Art Deco monochrome, with intimate alcoves should you want a private space from which to peek at the many visiting celebrities. *Mon-Sat noon-3pm and 5:30pm-midnight, Sun noon-4pm and 6pm-midnight.* £ –

Hot Tip: The famous faces usually come at lunchtime. Plan accordingly.

San Lorenzo
22 Beauchamp Pl., SW3, Knightsbridge, 020-7584-1074 • Hot & Cool

The Draw: This Italian restaurant has been a haunt of glitterati for more than 40 years—it was once known as Princess Diana's favorite restaurant, and nowadays attracts everyone from rising tennis stars to Madonna and hubby.

The Scene: The crowd includes eminent Knightsbridge lunching ladies and celeb watchers, and it still sports the sort of aging glam décor that harks back to the 1960s. *Mon-Sat 12:30-3pm and 7:30-11:30pm.* ££ =

Hot Tip: Be sure to come on a Friday or Saturday night when the place is sure to be at its most buzzing.

Cocktails

#19–21: Cocktail trends seem to change as quickly as skirt lengths these days. If you want to try the best of this season's muddled grapes, Prosecco, and passionfruit, place your order at one of these fine spots.

Cocoon

65 Regent St., W1, Soho, 020-7494-7600 • Hot & Cool

The Draw: The fruity cocktails here are so well executed that it is almost impossible not to drink several. The setting is lovely to boot.

The Scene: This orange-hued bar at the back of a sushi–dim sum restaurant glows with energy. The vibe is very buzzy with high-energy house music played to a chatty, clubby crowd peppered with models. Asian-fused concoctions include a delicious creamy almond martini and a variety of drinks made from passionfruit, lychees, and vodka or champagne. *Mon-Wed noon-3pm and 5:30pm-midnight, Thu-Fri noon-3pm and 5:30pm-3am, Sat 5:30pm-3am.* =

Hot Tip: The lounge bar is always busy, but Fridays are the hot night to come.

Freud

198 Shaftesbury Ave., WC2, Covent Garden, 020-7240-9933 • Hip

The Draw: If you're looking for somewhere loud and lively but hidden from the mainstream, this basement bar is it. Hidden down some metal stairs off a furniture shop, this cocktail saloon is packed with creative types and a lively post-work crowd who congregate here for well-executed classics like Long Island iced tea and trendy mojitos.

The Scene: The bar has been continuously buzzing since it opened in 1986, but its raw slate walls haven't dated. The bar is a quiet spot for a light lunch or chilled coffee during the day but gets very, very busy later, with crowds fighting for the large drinks. *Mon-Sat 11am-11pm, Sun noon-10:30pm.* =

Hot Tip: Come around 5pm to grab a table and settle in for the evening. This place gets packed the minute the office doors close.

Milk and Honey

61 Poland St., W1, Soho, 070-0065-5469 • Classic

The Draw: Perfectly concocted mixed drinks in a traditional setting.

The Scene: The dark candlelit members bar resembles a 1920s prohibition-era dive bar complete with Art Deco antique mirrors and old-fashioned jazz playing softly in the background. They also serve some lovely amuse-bouches and canapés (a shot of gazpacho anyone?) to an unpretentious media film crowd. *Nonmembers: Mon-Fri 6-11pm, Sat 7-11pm.* =

Hot Tip: The top two floors are for members only, but a limited number of intimate dark booths on the ground floor and the basement can be booked by anyone. Reserve before 5pm (though a day or two early improves your chances).

Dance Clubs

#22–24: The British like to party hard and long. The huge club culture of the 1990s may have waned a bit, but Londoners haven't calmed down when it comes to hedonism. They might not be the world's best dancers, but they aren't afraid to get sweaty 'til the early hours in these sexy spaces.

The End
18 W. Central St., WC1, Covent Garden, 020-7419-9199 • Hot & Cool

The Draw: Anyone who has come to The End since it opened over a decade ago is coming for the music. Expect a huge variety of noncommercial electronica in this large club owned by seminal DJs Mr. C and Layo.

The Scene: The crowd changes every night along with the cutting-edge music. The space is split into two rooms—a lounge space and the main room with a DJ island in the center surrounded by hardened clubbers going crazy to hard music from people like Laurent Garnier and Daft Punk. *Mon 10pm-3am, Wed 10:30pm-3am, Thu-Fri 10pm-6am, Sat 11pm-7am.* C ≡

Hot Tip: Check out Monday night's Trash, when DJ Erol Aklan plays a brilliant fusion of bootlegs and mash ups to a black eyeliner crowd or Thursday's mixed gay night Discotec for the best R&B and disco.

Fabric
77a Charterhouse St., EC1, The City, 020-7336-8898 • Hip

The Draw: The last of the super-clubs is not only still standing—it's more popular than ever. Since this behemoth opened, it has consistently hosted two perfect nights a week.

The Scene: The huge three-room industrial space linked by stairs—which are very easy to get lost in among the hordes of club kids—is mecca for a young music-centric crowd that parties hard until the morning after. *Fri 9:30pm-5am, Sat 10pm-7am.* C ≡

Hot Tip: On Fridays, Fabric Live plays edgier electro, drum and bass, and hip-hop, while Fabric is a must for highly danceable techhouse on Saturdays.

Guanabara
Parker St., WC2, Covent Garden, 020-7242-8600 • Hip

The Draw: Since this Brazilian nightclub exploded onto the scene in 2005, it has been packed. There's live Brazilian music almost every night alongside South American DJs who make even wallflowers want to show their moves.

The Scene: Among the twenty-somethings and the whole of expat South America, expect university students drawn by the sexy vibe and the caprioskas. Suits are rare. It isn't uncommon to see lines stretching around the corner as early as 8pm. *Mon-Sat 5pm-2:30am, Sun 5pm-midnight.* C ≡

Hot Tip: Try the Brazilian food—but go early to eat. Otherwise there isn't room.

Famous Chefs

#25–27: Who ever would have thought London would become one of the world's hottest dining destinations? Nowadays, it's got a whole slew of chefs making headlines and drawing fans from across the globe.

Chez Bruce (Bruce Poole)

2 Bellevue Rd., SW17, Clapham, 020-8672-0114 • Classic

> The Draw: Specializing in gimmick-free, contemporary French food served in an informal setting, Chez Bruce regularly tops lists as Londoners' favorite restaurant.

> The Scene: Filled with fashionable young locals and gastronomes, this intimate restaurant is beautifully lit, with a simple, stylish décor that's rare outside the West End. Co-owner Bruce Poole keeps a relatively low profile, and cooks in the restaurant every day. *Mon-Fri noon-2pm and 6:30-10:30pm, Sat 12:30-2:30pm and 6:30-10:30pm, Sun noon-3pm and 7-10pm. £ =*

> Hot Tip: The famous cheeseboard is a must-try.

Fifteen (Jamie Oliver)

15 Westland Pl., N1, The City, 0871-330-1515 • Hip

> The Draw: Celebrity chef Jamie Oliver's baby is one of the most coveted tables in London. The formula is quite revolutionary: Young people from disadvantaged backgrounds are trained up as professional chefs, and the profits are plowed back into the charity, Fifteen Foundation, in order to train more chefs.

> The Scene: The subterranean space, with its arty, graffiti-splattered walls, hot-pink banquettes, and retro furniture, serves a chatty menu full of funky Mediterranean food with an Italian bent. Anyone who is anyone has eaten here. *Daily noon-2:30pm and 6:30-9:30pm. ££ =*

> Hot Tip: Fifteen gets booked up months in advance—check for last-minute availability, or try the informal Trattoria on the ground floor.

St. John (Fergus Henderson)

26 St. John St., EC1, Clerkenwell, 020-7251-0848 • Classic

> The Draw: St. John's "nose to tail" eating concept, which encourages the use of every part of an animal's anatomy, has been hitting the headlines since the restaurant opened in the 1990s.

> The Scene: British chef Fergus Henderson's minimally decorated venue, containing a bar and a bread shop, is a favorite with other chefs, plus a diverse clientele that includes the cool art crowd. *Mon-Fri noon-3pm and 6-11pm, Sat 6-11pm. £ =*

> Hot Tip: The roast bone marrow and parsley salad is one of the most talked-about restaurant dishes in London.

Fine Dining

#28–30: Generally catering to an older, wealthier crowd, these fine dining establishments also tend to attract serious foodies and Michelin groupies. A jacket and tie and cocktail dress may not be a formal dress code in these elevated establishments, but they'll always guarantee excellent service.

Gordon Ramsay

68 Royal Hospital Rd., SW3, Chelsea, 020-7352-4441 • Classic

The Draw: Britain's most famous chef's eponymous French restaurant is one of the two three-Michelin star restaurants in the capital, and is regularly voted one of the top five restaurants in the world.

The Scene: The restrained, elegant interior, with its Murano glass sculptures and frosted glass panels, creates an intimate atmosphere. The well-dressed clientele ranges from reverential Michelin groupies to couples celebrating extra-special occasions. *Mon-Fri noon-2:30pm and 6:30-11pm. £££ –*

Hot Tip: Book as soon as you can, as the restaurant gets reserved months in advance. Jackets are preferred for men.

Le Gavroche

43 Upper Brook St., W1, Mayfair, 020-7408-0881 • Classic

The Draw: The first restaurant to be awarded three Michelin stars in the UK, the multiple–award-winning Le Gavroche is a legend that never fails to impress.

The Scene: The ruched curtains and banquettes in British racing green create an intimate, clubby feel that its somewhat conservative Establishment clientele clearly adores. Michel Roux Jr.'s recipes, such as Irish rock oysters and scallops poached in champagne with leeks and truffles, are fantastic. *Mon-Fri noon-2pm and 6:30-11pm, Sat 6:30-11pm. £££ =*

Hot Tip: Be sure to come early to enjoy a cocktail at the grand bar.

Tom Aikens

43 Elystan St., SW3, Chelsea, 020-7584-2003 • Classic

The Draw: The eponymous chef-proprietor cooks some of the sexiest and most thrilling food to be found in all of London.

The Scene: The quiet, Zen-like black-and-white interior is plenty chic—but it's dishes like roast piglet with pork lasagna, baby squid, and caramelized onions that have really won this place its many accolades. *Mon-Fri noon-2:30pm and 7-11pm. ££ =*

Hot Tip: The food here really is something else. Miss lunch and breakfast if you need to—and order as many items as you can for dinner. The best dishes are the ones featuring game in season.

Best

Fresh Air Experiences

#31–33: Contrary to popular opinion, it isn't always raining in London. Crisp, clear winter days and dazzling summer ones—and every dry spell in between—provide several diverting options for anyone who wants a bit of what we city dwellers like to call fresh air.

Broadgate Ice
Broadgate Circle, Eldon St., EC4, The City, 020-7505-4068 • Hot & Cool

The Draw: Show off on skates right in the financial district for a whole six months from fall to spring.

The Scene: This long-running circular outdoor rink has a loyal following of City whiz kids and their immaculately turned-out friends. During working hours, however, they can only look down enviously on the gliding few. *Late-Oct–mid-Apr, Mon-Thu noon-2:30pm and 3:30-5:30pm, Fri noon-2:30pm, 3:30-6pm, and 7-9pm, Sat-Sun 11am-1pm, 2-4pm, and 5:30-7pm. £-*

Hot Tip: Not surprisingly, the atmosphere is particularly fun on Friday evenings, when besuited young bloods twirl their stuff before (and sometimes after) a trip to the overlooking champagne bar.

Hyde Park Stables
63 Bathurst Mews, W2, Hyde Park, 020-7723-2813 • Classic

The Draw: This is the perfect opportunity to show off your riding skills and immaculate turn-out on one of the world's most prestigious bridleways.

The Scene: Rotten Row was a fashionable venue for horseback promenading way back, and it's still London's swankiest and best. Once inside the gates of Hyde Park, the big city seems miles away. *Group or private rides and lessons Mon-Fri 7:15am-5pm, Sat-Sun 9am-5pm. ££££*

Hot Tip: You'll have to rise early to catch sight of the entire Household Cavalry riding out in uniform around 10:30am, but they're worth it.

Rollerstroll
Hyde Park, W1, Hyde Park • Hot & Cool

The Draw: This upbeat Sunday afternoon skate around the streets of London comes with plenty of cool companions.

The Scene: Who says exercise can't be fun? Not the regulars at this group skating event that takes to the streets of London every Sunday afternoon. The varied circular routes generally take you past at least a few of London's most impressive landmarks, but if you're not too busy getting the lowdown on the hottest restaurant or see-and-be-seen nightspot from your yuppie fellow skaters to notice. *Sun 2pm-around 4pm.*

Hot Tip: A quick private lesson might not be a bad idea. And always wear guards and helmet: Asphalt hurts.

Gastropubs

#34–36: As old-fashioned pubs have started shutting down, the popularity of gastropubs has gone through the roof. They attract a younger, mixed crowd who love the informality, the real ales, and the unfussy comfort food.

Anchor & Hope

36 The Cut, SE1, South Bank, 020-7928-9898 • Hot & Cool

The Draw: It's known for fashionably unfashionable English dishes like duck heart on toast, or pork, bacon, and turnip stew in a quintessentially British setting.

The Scene: The venue is so popular it's hard to get a table—and due to the pub's no-booking policy, you may have to wait your turn at the bar. That's okay—it's a pub, so just chill with a pint of real ale, and see whether you can spot a stage star or two from the nearby Young and Old Vic theaters (like Kevin Spacey, who's the artistic director of the latter). *Pub: Mon 5-11pm, Tue-Sat 11am-11pm. Meals: Tue-Sat noon-2:30pm and 6-10:30pm. £- ≡*

Hot Tip: It's slightly less busy at lunchtime, but still quite fun, and snagging a table might be easier then.

Cow Dining Room*

89 Westbourne Park Rd., W2, Notting Hill, 020-7221-0021 • Hip

The Draw: A buzzing crowd of media types descends on this place to enjoy its loads of old-fashioned homely charm, bar, and leisurely Sunday roasts.

The Scene: The lively media mavens like to congregate for a drink in the pub downstairs, then head to the equally buzzy restaurant upstairs for contemporary British food. *Mon-Sat noon-midnight, Sun noon-11:30pm. £ =*

Hot Tip: To really experience it at its best, come here for a leisurely weekend lunch accompanied by pints of ale.

Gun

27 Coldharbour, Isle of Dogs, E14, Docklands, 020-7515-5222 • Hot & Cool

The Draw: Its location—perched on the increasingly chic banks of the Thames in the Docklands—its striking design, and its upscale comfort fare are all a big draw for the select crowd of media and business moguls.

The Scene: There's a bustling bar with dining room, a back bar with limited intimate seating, and a spacious terrace. British and European-style brunches and roasts on Saturday and Sunday (when there's occasional live jazz) are hugely popular. *Pub: Mon-Fri 11am-midnight, Sat 10:30am-midnight, Sun 10:30am-11pm. Meals: Mon-Thu noon-3pm and 6-10:30pm, Fri-Sat 10:30am-4:30pm, Sun 10:30am-4:30pm and 6-9:30pm. £ =*

Hot Tip: Taking a complimentary rickshaw that's available from Canary Wharf is a fantastic way to arrive at the pub in style.

Gay Bars and Clubs

#37–39: London is one of the most tolerant cities in the world, and the epicenter of all things gay is Soho. Walking up and down Old Compton Street should guarantee at least a few eager glances from the fellows at the nearby pubs and cafes. If you want to move indoors, try these popular spots.

Candy Bar

4 Carlisle St., W1, Soho, 020-7494-4041 • Hip

The Draw: This is London's top lesbian bar. If you're a gay girl, it's the place to go.

The Scene: The bar consists of two floors—a ground-floor lounge bar and a hot basement where there's sweaty action among the raucous party girls. There are DJs most nights and some must-see midweek fun, including strippers on Tuesdays and Thursdays and free karaoke on Wednesdays. Men are allowed in but only if they're gay and accompanied by gay and bi women. *Mon-Thu 5-11:30pm, Fri-Sat 5pm-2am, Sun 5-10:30pm.* C ≡

Hot Tip: Candy Bar has been accused of being a bit cliquey, but these ladies are always looking for new talent, so don't be put off.

Heaven

Villiers St., Under the Arches, WC2, Covent Garden, 020-7930-2020 • Hot & Cool

The Draw: Who wouldn't want to go to the most famous gay club in the world? Almost 30 years old, Heaven is still a big draw for a varied bunch of scenesters. Not matter what your style, you're bound to find a kindred spirit.

The Scene: There are three rooms—the ground floor, a dark and dirty second floor, and a loungey chill-out third-floor space. Music varies but most nights include some funky house, R&B, and pure pop. The vibe is so friendly even your straight friends won't feel out of place. *Mon, Wed, Fri-Sat 10:30pm-6am.* C ≡

Hot Tip: If you want something a little more exclusive, cough up the cash (£450—or ask about the Overseas membership for visitors) to become a member at the plush velvet VIP lounge.

King William IV

77 Hampstead High St., NW3, Hampstead, 020-7435-5747 • Classic

The Draw: This gay pub in Hampstead is a brilliant laid-back pickup joint without the posy Soho vibe that can intimidate or bore some. "The Willie," as it's known to friends, attracts a mixed crowd (often on their way to Hampstead Heath, which has been popular for cruising since the 19th century).

The Scene: Based in the middle of the picturesque village, the simple pub has a great outdoor space that attracts lots of boys in the summer. *Mon-Sat 11am-11pm, Sun noon-10:30pm.* – ≡

Hot Tip: Get a good seat to laugh at the unsuspecting straight tourists who stumble in on weekends.

Green Spaces

#40–42: Every city needs lungs and London is lucky in having several, so that even quite close to the center of town, it's sometimes possible to imagine you're in the country. Apart from the grandly named Royal Parks, the capital has a handful of impressive gardens and heathlands with distinguished histories.

Chelsea Physic Garden

66 Royal Hospital Rd., SW3, Chelsea, 020-7352-5646 • Classic

The Draw: This "secret garden" in fashionable Chelsea, first planted when the Stuarts were on the throne, is a lovely and easy break from the city streets.

The Scene: This fabulous botanical garden was founded more than 300 years ago, yet few people know of its existence, depriving them of the chance to marvel at England's oldest rock garden, Britain's largest outdoor fruiting olive tree, or the amazing assembly of rare and medicinal plants collected by great botanists of the past. *Apr–Oct, Wed noon-5pm, Sun noon-6pm. £-*

Hot Tip: Stump up a mere £15 to become a Friend and you can visit as often as you like during the year, even on days when the garden is closed to the public.

Hampstead Heath and Parliament Hill

NW3 and NW5, Hampstead • Classic

The Draw: Hampstead makes you feel as though you're in the country, with gorgeous views over London and lots of open space.

The Scene: You'll find hardy dog-walkers, joggers, and kite-fliers in winter, and half of London having picnics in summer, especially when there are outdoor concerts in the grounds of Kenwood House on the northern edge of the heath. From the lookout just beside Kenwood, the views over central London are splendid. Elsewhere, the tracts of woodland make for colorful vistas in late fall.

Hot Tip: It's a big place, and even with cell phones it can be impossible to track down a specific group of picnickers. Meet somewhere obvious beforehand.

Royal Botanic Gardens

Kew, Richmond, TW9, 020-8940-1171 • Classic

The Draw: This is a World Heritage Site with amazing plants.

The Scene: A garden for all seasons, Kew is known worldwide for the sheer breadth of its collections and an astonishing selection of architectural structures, too. The Pagoda is a legacy of the 18th-century fascination with all things Eastern, and the massive glasshouses are striking and weatherproof. *Apr–early-Sep, Mon-Fri 9:30am-6pm, Sat-Sun and public holidays 9:30am-7pm, early-Sep–late-Mar, 9:30am-3:45pm. £-*

Hot Tip: From April to October you can travel from Westminster to Kew by boat, a scenic and enjoyable 22 miles as the Thames flows, which takes between 55 minutes to an hour and a half depending on the tides.

Best

Hotel Bars

#43–45: Every London hotel worth its salt suddenly has a destination bar overflowing with good service, trays of nibbles, and a plethora of chic drinks. These elegant numbers, however, blow the rest out of the water.

The Blue Bar

The Berkeley, Wilton Pl., SW1, Knightsbridge, 020-7235-6000 • Classic

The Draw: The Blue Bar exudes classic decadence. This is where the super-rich come to mingle with their own. The interior—head-to-toe Regency blue and full French-style glamour—is also a big pull.

The Scene: The space only seats 55 and there's very little standing room between the blue 18th-century–style chairs and small tables. The Berkeley attracts oil barons and high-profile businessmen who want to unwind but keep their decorum. The emphasis is on discreet service and subtle people-watching. *Mon-Sat 4pm-1am, Sun 3pm-midnight.*

Hot Tip: Look sharp. This is one for well-heeled grown-ups.

Claridge's Bar

Claridge's, 55 Brook St., W1, Mayfair, 020-7629-8860 • Classic

The Draw: What really makes Claridge's so special is the service. The immaculate staff treat you like royalty. They'll always do their best to seat you in one of their two bars and have standing table service to keep you happy in the meantime.

The Scene: This delightfully classic hotel attracts a refined older clientele, though the bar is peppered with handsome twenty-somethings and Euro fashionistas. The speciality is champagne and the selection is truly staggering. *Mon-Sat noon-1am, Sun 4pm-midnight.*

Hot Tip: If you fancy something smaller and more intimate afterward, try the ruby velvet Macaudo bar, also in the hotel, next to Gordon Ramsay's restaurant. This hidden gem serves amazing signature cocktails designed in-house.

The Mandarin Bar

The Mandarin Oriental Hotel, 66 Knightsbridge, SW1, Knightsbridge, 020-7235-2000 • Classic

The Draw: It's hard to say why the Mandarin is such a perfect bar, but the warm space full of dark wood has achieved that exquisite refined yet relaxed atmosphere that is conducive to long nights.

The Scene: The space is particularly popular with transient American businesspeople. The table service is impeccable and the drinks selection both classic and modern. There's live jazz in the evenings but it just adds a mellow vibe and never intrudes on conversation. *Mon-Sat 11am-2am, Sun 11am-10:30pm.*

Hot Tip: Perch at one of the tall stools at the bar for prime people-watching.

Indian Restaurants

#46–48: Indian food is hot. Not just chili hot, you understand, but seriously fashionable. There are a dozen world-class Indian restaurants here, but these three take the experience to a whole new level.

Amaya

Halkin Arcade, Motcomb St., SW1, Knightsbridge, 020-7823-1166 • Hot & Cool

The Draw: Located inside a shopping mall and selling kebabs, this chic bar and grill is widely considered to be the best Indian restaurant in London.

The Scene: Its beautiful sandstone and rosewood interior and permanent buzz keep its sophisticated clientele—including many A-list celebrities—enthralled. There's a theatrical open kitchen, where you can see chefs cooking the famous kebabs. The restaurant and bar are elegant but manage to remain informal. *Mon-Fri 12:30-2:30pm and 6-11pm, Sat 12:30-3pm and 6-11pm, Sun 12:30-3pm and 6-10pm. ££ =*

Hot Tip: Kebabs and biryanis are the only thing to eat here—there's no point in coming here for a curry.

Rasoi Vineet Bhatia

10 Lincoln St., SW3, Chelsea, 020-7225-1881 • Classic

The Draw: Come for the postmodern Indian fare, which has been heaped with countless gushing accolades.

The Scene: The two floors in this century-old townhouse house a number of small dining rooms and private rooms. The cozy space is decorated with ornamental Ganeshas, tinkling bells from South Indian temples, colorful Indian tribal masks, and silk cushions. *Mon-Fri noon-2:30pm and 6:30-10:30pm, Sat 6:30-10:30pm. £££ –*

Hot Tip: Try the popular dessert samosas, filled with marbled chocolate.

Tamarind

20 Queen St., W1, Mayfair, 020-7629-3561 • Classic

The Draw: The healthy tandoor-based cooking served here has earned it a Michelin star.

The Scene: The cozy subterranean space, with its sleek black furniture, gold pillars, and fresh flower arrangements, buzzes with a snazzy, well-heeled crowd. Skewer-wielding kebab chefs behind glass screens provide culinary entertainment. *Mon-Fri noon-3pm and 6-11:30pm, Sat 6-11:30pm, Sun noon-2:30pm and 6-10:30pm. ££ =*

Hot Tip: The North Indian curries here are sensational.

Late-Night Haunts

#49–51: The evening is ending but you're still wired. Where do you go? Since London isn't really a 24-hour city, most people who want to push things a little further end up at members bars or illegal drink joints in Soho. If you haven't planned ahead and gotten on a guest list, try these spots to keep the party going.

Bar Italia*

22 Frith St., W1, Soho, 020-7437-4520 • Hip

The Draw: Bar Italia is more than a late-night cafe—it's an institution. This tiny Soho coffee joint is *the* place to stop in after the clubs. Don't be dismayed by its plain appearance—this is a post-drinking must if you've been partying in the area.

The Scene: At night the cafe transforms into a mecca for night owls, attracting clubbers on their way home, creative types, and posers. The interior is original 1950s retro littered with small cheap TV screens showing Italian soccer matches. *Mon-Sat 24 hours, Sun 7am-4am.*

Hot Tip: Grab one of the metal chairs outside and join the old Italian men who lounge around observing the insanity of Soho.

The Key

Kings Cross Freight Depot, N1, Kings Cross, 020-7837-1027 • Hip

The Draw: Serious partiers come for the fabulous dance floor, 24-hour drink license, and party that goes until 6am and on into Sunday.

The Scene: An edgy, hipster crowd gathers here late night after the other clubs have shut down to dance to house and disco and keep the party going until the wee hours of the morning. *Fri-Sat 10:30pm-6am, Sun 6am-1pm.*

Hot Tip: If you want to party all night long, be sure to check out cult nights Mulletover and any night James Priestley is on the decks.

Vingt Quatre*

325 Fulham Rd., SW10, Chelsea, 020-7376-7224 • Classic

The Draw: It's 4am and you're starving after a night on the tiles. This 24-hour restaurant is the holy grail at the end of a cab ride. Expect lines of eager stomachs on Fridays and Saturdays.

The Scene: The posh and young congregate at all hours at this restaurant that serves simple modern British food and great 24-hour breakfasts for early birds or early hangovers. It serves alcohol a little late (midnight), but don't expect after-hours bottles of wine. *24/7. £*

Hot Tip: The toilets are hidden behind a wall panel, just in case you can't focus when you're there.

Live-Music Venues

#52–54: If you're influential, iconic, or simply a darn good musician, chances are you'll pass through London at some point. The city is brimming with live music every night of the week, though often the venues veer toward the grotty, black-walled type. If you want something with a bit of class, try these.

Cargo
83 Rivington St., Kingsland Viaduct, EC2, Hoxton, 020-7749-7840 • Hip

The Draw: Since it opened in 2001 it's been the best place for live music and DJs in the area. If the lineup is good, lines can spread around the corner, though fun is guaranteed even with lesser-known names.

The Scene: The interior is raw and cavernous with a top-notch sound system. The main pull for the twenty-something crowd is the varied program of live music and DJs ranging from hip-hop to house. The bar food and restaurant are good for late-night munchies, and the graffiti-splattered outdoor space is great for summer sun. *Mon-Thu 6pm-1am, Fri-Sat 6pm-3am, Sun 6pm-midnight.* C ≡

Hot Tip: Check cargolondon.com so you know what kind of music to expect.

Jazz Café
5 Parkway, NW1, Camden Town, 020-7534-6955 • Hot & Cool

The Draw: It's all about the music, baby. The Jazz Café's interior is a bit '80s, but that isn't the point, as everyone is really here for the sounds. Any soul, hip-hop, and jazz icon of worth passes through these Camden doors.

The Scene: The main focus is the central stage where you will find yourself inches away from idols like Maceo Parker or Chaka Khan. The cafe is transformed into a club after the gigs on Friday and Saturday nights. The emphasis is on jazz funk dancing for an any-age, any-style crowd. *Mon-Fri 7pm-1am, Sat-Sun 7pm-2am.* C ≡

Hot Tip: If you want a perfect view rather than hot-and-heavy dancing, book a table for dinner on the upstairs balcony.

Ronnie Scott's
47 Frith St., W1, Soho, 020-7439-0747 • Classic

The Draw: It's quite simple. Ronnie Scott's is *the* jazz venue of London. When it opened its doors in 1959, it quickly established itself as the only place to hear live American musicians.

The Scene: The old-style venue has tables set around the small intimate stage. The food and drink are pretty mediocre, but you're paying for the view of the stage and the sweet music. The crowd is pretty mixed—all ages and types—unified by their love of jazz. *Mon-Sat 6pm-3am, Sun 6pm-midnight.* C =

Hot Tip: On weekends there's a salsa club upstairs, which includes a free lesson on Fridays, if you want to get lively.

Markets

#55-57: Londoners love their markets as much for the atmosphere as for the shopping. That said, the capital's better ones provide both: lots of cool locals to check out and the chance to snap up something handmade and unique.

Borough Market

Southwark St., SE1, Bankside, 020-7407-1002 • Hot & Cool

The Draw: London gourmets flock here for delicious food to graze on and a buzzy atmosphere.

The Scene: Borough's Victorian cast-iron-and-glass canopy plays host on Fridays and Saturdays to the city's most delicious food market. If it's not organic, it's free-range, homemade, and possibly French or Spanish as well, and definitely irresistible. Naturally such a cornucopia of delights brings London's foodies flocking. There's an ever-growing number of excellent grocery stores and cafes in surrounding streets. *Fri noon-6pm, Sat 9am-4pm.*

Hot Tip: If you're really serious about buying, arrive by 9:30am on Saturday, but if it's atmosphere you're after, you can afford to linger over breakfast.

Portobello Market

Portobello Rd., W11, Notting Hill, 020-7375-0441 • Hip

The Draw: People-watching, plus an eclectic range of goods from antiques to clothing by up-and-coming designers, draws a hip local crowd.

The Scene: This being Notting Hill, the vibe is distinctly hip and arty at this fantastically long street market. The antiques at the Notting Hill end are worth a browse, though prices tend to be high. Beyond that, past the food market, there are stalls of funky clothes and accessories designed by the fashion stars of tomorrow. *Sat 8am-5pm.*

Hot Tip: After visiting the market, see what's playing at the Electric Cinema at number 191, a trendy spot with armchairs and footstools in its screening room.

Spitalfields Market

Commercial St., E1, Spitalfields, 020-7247-8556 • Hip

The Draw: This charming Victorian marketplace shelters some of the most interesting young designers in London.

The Scene: Spitalfields is an example of urban regeneration at its best, and the market is its centerpiece. It's not just about the shopping, though there's everything from vintage clothing to organic food on offer, particularly on Sundays. Most people are here to browse, stop off at one of the cafes, or watch other Londoners doing the same. *Mon-Fri 10am-4pm, Sun 10am-5:30pm.*

Hot Tip: Spitalfields boasts two classical music festivals: the summer one in June, and—wonderfully Christmassy—the smaller winter one in December.

Modern Art Spaces

#58–60: If your taste in art leans toward the modern and contemporary, these are the top spots to go for a guaranteed gilt-free experience.

Hayward Gallery

Belvedere Rd, SE1, South Bank, 020-7921-0813 • Hot & Cool

The Draw: Hayward is known for thought-provoking exhibitions from the most interesting names of modern times.

The Scene: Concrete bunker from the outside, cool and clean gallery space on the inside: No wonder the Hayward remains a much-discussed venue nearly 40 years after its construction. Even those who can't bear its outward appearance have to admit that its spacious rooms provide a superb setting for a varied roster of 20th-century world greats from Georgia O'Keeffe to Dan Flavin. *Mon, Thu, Sat-Sun 10am-6pm, Tue-Wed 10am-8pm, Fri 10am-9pm. Main galleries closed between exhibitions. £-*

Hot Tip: Put away the map: The multicolored neon-light sculpture on the roof is a local landmark.

Tate Modern

Bankside, SE1, Bankside, 020-7887-8888 • Hot & Cool

The Draw: The Tate Modern displays international modern art in a starkly beautiful building, with superb views of the riverscape.

The Scene: The Tate's new home for its vast collection of modern art from around the world is an impressive and much-visited space, and thanks to an interesting and often controversial choice of temporary exhibits, it's never far from the headlines. *Sun-Thu 10am-6pm, last admission to exhibitions 5:15pm, Fri-Sat 10am-10pm, last admission to exhibitions 9:15pm. £-*

Hot Tip: The view across the river is especially striking on clear winter evenings when the silver streak of the Millennium footbridge blazes a path to the illuminated, and ethereally beautiful, St. Paul's Cathedral.

Whitechapel Art Gallery

80-82 Whitechapel High St., E1, The City, 020-7522-7888 • Hip

The Draw: This gallery is known for its consistently high-quality shows.

The Scene: It introduced artists such as Mark Rothko, Frida Kahlo, and Jackson Pollock to the UK; raised the profile of locals such as Gilbert & George and Lucien Freud, and continues to stage an ever-changing, never-dull program of temporary exhibitions of the best in modern and contemporary art. A planned expansion will double the size of the galleries, which is universally regarded as A Very Good Thing. *Tue-Wed, Fri-Sun 11am-6pm, Thu 11am-9pm. £-*

Hot Tip: Linger in the bar on Thursday nights for wine, tapas, and live music.

Oriental Restaurants

#61–63: Oriental food has seen its popularity soar in the last few years. In addition to the popular Chinese, Japanese, and Thai restaurants, Korean, Vietnamese, and Malaysian flavors are also beginning to catch on.

Eight Over Eight

392 King's Rd., SW3, Chelsea, 020-7349-9934 • Hip

The Draw: Asian cocktails and stunningly presented dishes with a Shanghai bent are served to a glossy, well-heeled young Chelsea crowd.

The Scene: The sleek look is beautifully contemporary, with red neon signage on black walls, a pretty wrought-iron screen in a floral design, lampshades shaped like inverted parasols, and a relaxed terrace, all embellished by the beautiful people perched at the bar and gossiping on sumptuous banquettes. *Mon-Fri noon-2:45pm and 6:15-10:45pm, Sat noon-4pm and 6:15-11pm, Sun 6:15-10:30pm. £* ⓑ ⚌

Hot Tip: Plan to order several dishes, as the small plates are just that.

Nobu

Metropolitan Hotel, 19 Old Park Ln., W1, Mayfair, 020-7447-4747 • Hot & Cool

The Draw: This branch of the international Japanese-Peruvian chain is one of the most celebrated restaurants in town.

The Scene: Its understated monochrome interior encompasses a bar that offers some of the most exquisite sakes available (including several containing gold leaf). Nobu is renowned for its celebrity clientele, but even without the star factor, Nobu is constantly ablaze with effervescent energy. *Mon-Thu noon-2:15pm and 6-10:15pm, Fri noon-2:15pm and 6-11pm, Sat 12:30-2:30pm and 6-11pm, Sun 12:30-2:30pm and 6-9:30pm. ££* ⚌

Hot Tip: Try the chocolate bento box dessert and book several weeks ahead.

Umu

14-16 Bruton Pl., W1, Mayfair, 020-7499-8881 • Hot & Cool

The Draw: Suffused with wealth, glamour, and elegance, this Japanese restaurant is the most expensive in London.

The Scene: Frequented by billionaire playboys and their impossibly beautiful girlfriends, the restaurant showcases highly elaborate dishes from Kyoto served on handmade pottery, and utilizes specially flown-in ingredients. A dark, hand-activated sliding-door entrance keeps the mystique intact. *Mon-Sat noon-2:30pm and 6-11pm. £££* ⚌

Hot Tip: The best time to come here is on weekday evenings, when the seriously wealthy come out to play.

Power Lunches

#64–66: "Doing lunch" is getting increasingly rare in London. But don't despair; these restaurants are filled with politicians and powerbrokers, who like to discuss mergers, takeovers, and dirty tricks in the time-honored way: over three-hour lunches and martinis.

Pétrus

The Berkeley, Wilton Pl., SW1, Knightsbridge, 020-7235-1200 • Classic

The Draw: Gordon Ramsay protégé Marcus Wareing's exquisite cooking and top designer David Collins' wine-themed interior have made this a popular spot for everybody from politicians to celebrities.

The Scene: This one-Michelin-star French restaurant became the most (in)famous restaurant in the world in 2001, thanks to six bank employees who closed a business deal here by splashing out on a £44,007 dinner—the most expensive restaurant meal at the time. It continues to attract a super-rich clientele. *Mon-Fri noon-2:30pm and 6-11pm, Sat 6-11pm.* £££ –

Hot Tip: If you've wanted to try a legendary wine, this is the place to come.

Pied à Terre

34 Charlotte St., W1, Bloomsbury, 020-7636-1178 • Classic

The Draw: Widely regarded as one of London's premier restaurants, Pied à Terre closed due to a fire, but has just risen phoenix-like from the ashes, to universal acclaim: Some people claim it's better than ever before.

The Scene: The restaurant is not much to look at, but there's plenty of buzz in both the bar and dining room. The discreet décor, the serious food, and the astonishing wine list have made this venue popular for long, lingering business lunches. *Mon-Fri 12:15-2:30pm and 6:15-10:30pm, Sat 6:15-10:30pm.* ££ =

Hot Tip: The restaurant is famous for its foie gras, and the wine list is one of the best in London.

Savoy Grill

The Savoy Hotel, The Strand, WC2, Covent Garden, 020-7592-1600 • Classic

The Draw: The Grill, an institution since the 19th century, swarms with London's movers and shakers—especially at lunchtime.

The Scene: This one-Michelin-star spot serves British food with a contemporary twist. The handsome, cozy interior vibrates at lunchtime with contented sounds from its clientele, which includes captains of industry, international businesspeople, politicians, and celebrities. *Mon-Fri noon-2:45pm and 5:45-11pm, Sat noon-4pm and 5:45-11pm, Sun noon-4pm and 7-10:30pm.* ££ =

Hot Tip: Be sure to order something from one of the famous meat, cheese, and champagne trolleys.

Pubs

#67–69: It is impossible to re-create the atmosphere of a good old-fashioned English pub. The best of these smokey, dark spaces take centuries to wear in. There are many average ones, but these gems are perfect for long conversations over longer pints of beer.

The Holly Bush

22 Holly Mount, NW3, Hampstead, 020-7435-2892 • Classic

The Draw: If every pub were as appealing as these 18th-century converted stables in a little side street in Hampstead, no one would ever go to a cocktail bar again.

The Scene: It's the epitome of coziness complete with warm wooden tables and booths, hidden rooms, open fires, and a music-free conversation-fueled vibe. While it's packed every evening with a young, relaxed, and friendly crowd, it's also lovely on a quiet afternoon. *Mon-Sat noon-11pm, Sun noon-10:30pm.*

Hot Tip: This atmospheric place is also ideal as a daytime spot for high-end British grub that includes posh beer as an ingredient.

Jerusalem Tavern

55 Briton St., EC1, The City, 020-7490-4281 • Classic

The Draw: Jerusalem has been in its current building since 1720, though the tavern has been in the area since the 14th century, attracting famous drinkers including William Hogarth and Handel. These days designers and architects rush from work to grab seats in this gem of a pub, eager to sample the real ale.

The Scene: This warren of 18th-century nooks is filled with old wooden furniture and good conversation. The Jerusalem is one of the few pubs in London to stock a huge array of classic real ales. *Mon-Fri 11am-11pm.*

Hot Tip: Expect real traditional British stuff with a twist—try the cinnamon and apple ale, summer ale, and stout with honey and fruits.

The Lansdowne

90 Gloucester Ave., NW1, Primrose Hill, 020-7483-0409 • Hot & Cool

The Draw: The original gastropub still packs a punch. It's not unusual to spot actors among the posh clientele at this far above average public house.

The Scene: The traditional Victorian space is filled with long wooden tables and roaring open fires and is music-free—though voices get so loud this isn't a place for quiet conversation. There's a great wine list, classic pints, some rich pan-European food, and arguably the best handmade pizzas in London. *Mon-Sat noon-11pm, Sun noon-10:30pm.*

Hot Tip: The space is packed Wednesday to Sunday, so go with a bit of patience.

Rainy Day Activities

#70–72: When the weather gods have decreed that the sky can be any color you want as long as it's gray, and there's more than a hint of moisture in the air, there's no cause to huddle in your hotel. Not when London offers waterproof experiences like these.

National Film Theatre

Belvedere Rd., SE1, South Bank, 020-7928-3232 • Hip

The Draw: Anything from rarities from the silent era to the best of modern indie movies—and something different every day—plays here.

The Scene: This may not be Hollywood, but London's homage to all things cinematic still offers something to even the most exacting cineaste. Recent treats have included series devoted to such diverse people as Peter Jackson, Mary Pickford, and Billy Wilder, but even if your bag is German cinema of the 1950s you could be in luck. *Daily 9am-11pm; screenings Mon-Thu from around 6pm, Fri-Sun from around 2pm.* £-

Hot Tip: No food and drink, except water, is allowed in the auditoriums, so be sure to munch that popcorn beforehand..

Tea at the Ritz

The Ritz Hotel, 150 Piccadilly, W1, Mayfair, 020-7493-8181 • Classic

The Draw: Enjoy nostalgia for a more refined age, impeccable service, and scones.

The Scene: A dressed-up crowd surrounded by Louis XVI finery sips tea from dainty bone-china cups to the accompaniment of a discreet piano player, while well-trained waiters glide among them. Some will be imagining they are Lord and Lady Somebodyorother who eats scones with cream and jam, not to mention scrumptious little cakes, every afternoon. *Daily 11:30am, 1:30, 3:30 and 5:30pm; Champagne Afternoon Tea: 7:30pm.* ££££

Hot Tip: Running shoes may be fabulous for sightseeing but will not pass muster in the Palm Court, and nor will even your most exclusive jeans.

Urban Golf

33 Great Pulteney St., W1, Soho, 020-7434-4300 • Hip

The Draw: Golf. In the center of London. And no stuffy dress codes, rules, and regulations.

The Scene: Stylish décor, cute black-clad employees, and the ultimate in computer wizardry have made this Soho basement an essential port of call for a mixed but well-dressed crowd: anyone from Lindeberg-clad twenty-somethings to seasoned pros who have better things to do than drive miles to the nearest outdoor course. *Mon-Sat 10am-11pm, Sun noon-8:30pm.* £

Hot Tip: This joint really swings, if you'll forgive the pun, from 5pm when the combination of drinking and driving proves hard to resist.

Restaurant Lounges

#73–75: Restaurants are not just about food—and an increasing number of London restaurateurs are realizing that. There's no better way to kick off an evening than with a cocktail in a swanky lounge. What's more, it's a fabulous way to meet new people.

Baltic*

74 Blackfriars Rd., SE1, South Bank, 020-7928-1111 • Hot & Cool

The Draw: This stylish restaurant and bar offers Polish and Russian dishes with a contemporary twist to a young, fashionable crowd.

The Scene: The chic décor—with its wooden trussed ceilings, exposed beams, high vaulted glass roof, and a stunningly beautiful amber wall—makes it a beautiful backdrop for the high-energy crowd that gathers here for both dinner and drinks. *Mon-Sat noon-11pm, Sun noon-10:30pm.* £- B =

Hot Tip: Blinis with assorted toppings, including osetra caviar, and flavored vodkas are the things to order here before dinner.

The Cinnamon Club*

The Old Westminster Library, Great Smith St., SW1, Westminster, 020-7222-2555 • Hot & Cool

The Draw: This elegant Indian restaurant is full of politicians and can be somewhat formal—but the basement bar attracts a younger, more relaxed crowd that loves to congregate for Asian-themed cocktails.

The Scene: The lively basement lounge bar features everything from rubber floors and leather walls to handcrafted wooden tables and projectors playing kitsch, glamorous Bollywood films. *Mon-Fri 7:30-10am, noon-2:45pm and 6-10:45pm, Sat 6-10:45pm.* ££ =

Hot Tip: Ideal for pre-dinner drinks, the bar is also a destination in its own right. And do order the Indian bar snacks—they're divine.

Pearl Bar & Restaurant*

Chancery Court Hotel, 252 High Holborn, WC1, Holborn, 020-7829-7000 • Hot & Cool

The Draw: Known for its glamorous décor, this sumptuous restaurant lounge is decorated with thousands of beautiful pearls.

The Scene: It has a gleaming tiled floor, striking lampshades decorated with long strings of real pearls, a gorgeous bar area with velvet banquettes concealed within walnut alcoves, and handmade tables decorated with mother-of-pearl. With slinky babes sipping cocktails like Pink Pearl, this gem of a place is certainly not for the twee twinset set. *Mon-Fri 11am-11pm, Sat 6-11pm.* ££ =

Hot Tip: The cocktails are great, but the wine list is one of the best in town. The bar is ideal for both pre- and post-dinner drinks.

Romantic Dining

#76-78: These romantic restaurants—with their candles, flowers, intimate alcoves, well-judged lighting, and burning incense—really know how to pull out all the stops and set the scene for a memorable evening.

The Belvedere

Holland House, off Abbotsbury Rd., W8, Holland Park, 020-7602-1238 • Classic

> The Draw: Set in beautiful Holland Park, this classy French restaurant is an ideal place to lunch with a lover.
>
> The Scene: It's popular with wealthy locals from nearby mansions, dating couples, groups of friends celebrating birthdays, and people who want to enjoy a little live jazz on weekends. *Mon-Sat noon-2:30pm and 6-10pm, Sun noon-3pm. ££* –
>
> Hot Tip: To enhance the romantic mood, walk through the park, past the streams, bridges, and waterfalls, and book an intimate alcove in the gallery.

Momo

25 Heddon St., W1, Mayfair, 020-7434-4040 • Hot & Cool

> The Draw: Popular with A-list celebrities, this sumptuously exotic Moroccan restaurant has an amazingly lively club-like vibe, excellent cocktails, and friendly black-clad staff in pop-art T-shirts.
>
> The Scene: It's a beautiful place, complete with loud music, decorated with brass lanterns, ornate windows, and jewel-encrusted antiques. The high-energy ambiance is kept vibrant by groups of young people who crowd the place nightly. This is not stuffy, old-fashioned romance, but romance at its most sexy. *Mon-Thu noon-2:15pm and 7-11:15pm, Fri noon-2:15pm and 6:30-11:45pm, Sat noon-2:15pm and 6:30-10:45pm, Sun 6:30-10:45pm. £* B ≡
>
> Hot Tip: Don't miss the opportunity to have a pre-dinner drink in the exclusive, members-only bar, which is only open to nonmembers if they're dining.

Zaika

1 Kensington High St., W8, Kensington, 020-7795-6533 • Hot & Cool

> The Draw: A seductively romantic ambiance and acclaimed contemporary Indian food makes this a popular choice for special occasions.
>
> The Scene: A small, bedouin-style bar at the entrance sells Indian-themed cocktails. The roomy but intimate dining room is done up in warm jewel colors of ruby, amethyst, emerald, and garnet. Carved ornaments, ancient antiques, and beautiful screens are judiciously scattered around, making it a popular haunt for couples. *Mon-Fri noon-2:45pm and 6:30-10:45pm, Sat 6-10:45pm, Sun noon-2:45pm and 6:30-9:45pm. ££* B =
>
> Hot Tip: Order the chocolate silk dessert—it makes for a very sexy finale.

See-and-be-Seen Spots

Best

#79–81: Sometimes staring at and posing with the glamorous people around you can be the best part of a night out, and these hot spots guarantee a regular cast of celebs and other beautiful types with whom to mingle.

Crazy Bear
26-28 Whitfield St., W1, Fitzrovia, 020-7631-0088 • Hot & Cool

The Draw: Crazy Bear's won a lot of press attention for good reason. The drinks are delectable, the staff delightful, and the whole vibe relaxed and stylish.

The Scene: The bar is downstairs from an Asian restaurant—though refreshingly the ubiquitous bamboo prints and screens aren't here. Instead there's a shining copper bar, red leather caves for intimacy, low cowhide spinning stools, and lively music to keep things upbeat. This place is full of ad execs, actors, and journalists. *Mon-Fri noon-midnight, Sat 6pm-midnight.* ≡

Hot Tip: This place is popular every night of the week—so best to reserve. There's a great whiskey list and the Bellinis are some of the best in town.

Ling Ling at Hakkasan*
Hakkasan, 8 Hanway Pl., W1, Bloomsbury, 020-7907-1888 • Hot & Cool

The Draw: With its gorgeous décor, a buzzing restaurant, fabulous drinks, and beautiful clientele, it's no wonder that Hakkasan's bar is packed seven days a week. For glamour served straight up, this is the place to be.

The Scene: The place is filled with lawyers, ad men, and City types maxing their expense accounts with clients. The bar itself is a very, very long corridor with a metal bar and stools on one side and a Japanese-style black decorative wall divider on the other. The latter is a good place to lean with Eastern-inspired drinks and stare longingly at the fabulous food being enjoyed by those dining here. *Mon-Wed noon-12:30am, Thu-Sat noon-1:30am, Sun noon-midnight.* ≡

Hot Tip: If you want something strong, go for the lemongrass martini. Or try the Jasmine FonFon, a rum, champagne, and cinnamon concoction.

Taman Gang
141 Park Ln., W1, Mayfair, 020-7518-3160 • Hot & Cool

The Draw: Enjoy superb drinks with a posh crowd in an exclusive, dimly lit, subterranean room filled with orchids and other Asian-themed touches.

The Scene: The décor is Indonesian spa meets style bar with sandstone architectural details and low intimate seating. Expect a youngish crowd in stylish party clothes, which suits the loungey house music perfectly. Signature cocktails are inventive, unusual, and often floral. *Nightly 6pm-1am.* ≡

Hot Tip: Come after 11pm for maximum buzz. And be sure to check out the toilets for a crazy combination of bronze stalagmite forms and sprays of water.

Shopping Streets

#82–84: Napoleon may have been trying to be insulting when he called the British "a nation of shopkeepers," but take one look at London's staggeringly varied and gorgeous retail outlets and you'd have to say he was right. They're everywhere, but some streets have more come-hither appeal than others.

Bond Street

Mayfair • Hot & Cool

The Draw: Designers, designers, designers. And lots of serious bling.

The Scene: The beau monde has been heading to Bond Street for those little luxuries for nearly 300 years, and it's still lined with some of the most famous names in fashion and jewelry. Prada, Versace, Cartier, Asprey, Garrard, Louis Vuitton, Bulgari, Donna Karan: the list is endless. Even the resident department store, Fenwicks—pronounced Fennicks—has a fabulous fashion section.

Hot Tip: Be sure to come Monday through Saturday. Sundays are deathly quiet, and quite a few of the shops are closed.

Brick Lane

Spitalfields

The Draw: Boutiques and coffeehouses, a youthful crowd, and more than a hint of multiculturalism are the big draws here.

The Scene: Spitalfields has been home to many communities over the years, especially Huguenots, Jews, and Bangladeshis. The newest arrivals are young creative types, attracted by the cheap (but rising) rents, hip vibe, and rich cultural diversity—not to mention the cafes and clubs—who have set up their stalls, shops, and galleries just up from curry-house row. This is definitely where to head for that stylish souvenir.

Hot Tip: The street's there all week, of course, but the best day to visit is Sunday.

Marylebone High Street

Marylebone • Hot & Cool

The Draw: Chic but individual boutiques, foodie treats, and a discreet charm make this a hugely appealing destination.

The Scene: This part of London north of Oxford Street was once better known for its private clinics, dentists, and nip-and-tuck specialists. The medicos remain, but they now share the area with an ever-growing number of fashionable clothing and houseware stores, gourmet shops, and trendy eateries. The High Street is only part of the story; the surrounding narrow roads hide some wonderful gems.

Hot Tip: Now that we know dark chocolate is actually good for us, there's no excuse for not stopping in Rococo at number 45 for delicious bars flavored with crystalized ginger, cardamom, or chili pepper.

Singles Scenes

#85–87: There's nothing like the glance across the bar, some flirty conversation, and the grope in the taxi on the way home. Part of the joy of travel is hooking up and trying the local delicacies. If that appeals—or you just want to shoot the breeze with strangers—these places are sure to provide a night of good fun.

Long Bar
The Sanderson, 50 Berners St., W1, Fitzrovia, 020-7300-1496 • Hot & Cool

The Draw: It's hard not to end up in conversation at the Long Bar. The white bar in this stylish Schrager hotel is busy every night of the week.

The Scene: Most guests dress up and lean or perch on the high stools around the long central bar, though there is a beautiful outdoor courtyard with water features and a garden, which fills up in summer. The style of the space is very clean and modernist and refreshingly bright. *Mon-Sat noon-1am, Sun noon-10:30pm.* ≡

Hot Tip: Pop in on a Thursday or Friday night to experience the scene at its best.

Pangaea
85 Piccadilly, W1, Mayfair, 020-7495-2595 • Hot & Cool

The Draw: Pure hedonism. It's the only way to describe this white-hot club for the super-rich.

The Scene: The interior is loosely African themed but pretty subtle, highlighted with spotlit African masks. The international clientele includes everyone from French soccer players to American party girls to royalty. If you've got a spare grand, get a table and a bottle of high-end spirits while the other guests dance to house music with live drums and flirt outrageously. *Wed-Thu 10pm-3am, Fri-Sat 10pm-4am.* C ≡

Hot Tip: Definitely phone ahead to get on the list or you won't have a hope in hell of getting in.

Ruby Lo
23 Orchard St., W1, Mayfair, 020-7486-3671 • Hip

The Draw: The Ruby is a popular after-work haunt splashed with red walls and redder seating and a packed dance floor, loud '80s tunes, and a young, high-energy clientele.

The Scene: As the night progresses it gets clubby, with a young crowd that puts a lot of skin on show and thirty-something men in shirts looking for fun. There's a high flirt factor as the drinks flow among the crowd dancing to disco, hip-hop, and party tunes. *Tue-Sat 5pm-2am.* C ≡

Hot Tip: It's members only, but you can get your name on the list easily via the website if you're going after 9pm on Friday and Saturday nights (ruby.uk.com).

Small Museums

#88-90: Good things come in small packages, and these gems of museums certainly support that view. They may not have the square yardage of the big boys, but what they lose in scale they more than make up for in atmosphere.

The Foundling Museum

40 Brunswick Sq., WC1, Bloomsbury, 020-7841-3600 • Classic

The Draw: This museum houses a superb and little-known collection of 18th-century paintings and has a charitable history.

The Scene: The Foundling Hospital was London's first home for abandoned children, and thanks to influential patrons soon became its most fashionable charity. All the leading artists of the late 18th century donated works, creating the first public gallery. Those superb paintings are back in the public arena again, hanging in the fabulous interiors rescued from the original and long-gone hospital. *Tue-Sat 10am-6pm, Sun and public holidays noon-6pm.* £-

Hot Tip: Make a beeline for the hi-tech armchairs in the top-floor Handel room; they have built-in speakers for your listening pleasure.

Handel House Museum

25 Brook St., W1, Mayfair, 020-7495-1685 • Classic

The Draw: This is the house where Handel composed his greatest masterpieces, looking much as it would have in his lifetime.

The Scene: The spirit of the great man haunts every paneled corner and squeaky wooden floorboard of the house where he wrote the *Messiah*, among many other famous pieces. The furniture's not original, but that hardly matters given the authenticity of the experience. *Tue-Sat 10am-6pm (to 8pm Thu), Sun noon-6pm.* £-

Hot Tip: Music still plays a large part in the life of the house, with a lively program of classical concerts in the evenings and on Sundays at lunchtime.

Sir John Soane's Museum

13 Lincoln's Inn Fields, WC2, Holborn, 020-7405-2107 • Classic

The Draw: Priceless objects are crammed into the elegant former home of a great gentleman-collector.

The Scene: Roman bronzes, Charles I's jeweled hatpin, ancient Egyptian relics, medieval stone carvings: Architect Sir John Soane's townhouse contains an idiosyncratic array of treasures. There's more art than you'd have thought possible in such a small space, thanks to some cunning false walls: Hogarth's series *The Rake's Progress* is a particular delight. *Tue-Sat 10am-5pm. Also first Tue each month, 6-9pm.* £-

Hot Tip: On the first Tuesday evening of the month, when the house stays open late, some areas are lit with candles to enchanting effect.

Spas

#91–93: What do Londoners do when they've been worn to a frazzle by all the cocktails and gallery openings and clothes shopping and fine dining? Why, they take themselves off to one of these one-of-a-kind spas for a spot of maintenance, cosseting, and downtime.

Agua Bathhouse Spa

The Sanderson, 50 Berners St., W1, Fitzrovia, 020-7300-1414 • Hot & Cool

The Draw: Agua offers sybaritic treatments for stressed-out minimalists in a dreamy white Philippe Starck setting.

The Scene: A heavenly retreat in the ultracool Sanderson, where ministering angels are on hand to buff and polish their stylish young music-or-fashion-business charges to even greater perfection. The floaty curtains that act as walls add to the otherworldly atmosphere. *Daily 9am-9pm. ££££*

Hot Tip: Try the sublimely relaxing signature Milk and Honey body treatment—your skin and your nerves will thank you.

Cowshed

119 Portland Rd., W11, Holland Park, 020-7078-1944 • Hip

The Draw: Soho House regulars come for the divine homegrown products, and a spot of "sociable grooming."

The Scene: First there was trendy private club Soho House. Then there was the country offshoot with funky spa for wicked weekends. And now Cowshed has come to town, bringing with it the offbeat products made with herbs from its country garden and the inspirational Cowgroom treatments, where two therapists at a time mean twice the effect in half the time. *Mon-Fri 8am-8pm, Sat 9am-7pm, Sun 10am-5pm. ££*

Hot Tip: It may be hip to be spontaneous, but that approach will get you nowhere here. Book ahead.

Elemis day-spa

2-3 Lancashire Ct., W1, Mayfair, 0870-410-4995 • Hot & Cool

The Draw: Elemis's rituals have an exotic slant for the ultimate in pampering.

The Scene: Mews house without, sensory wonderland within, Elemis's neat little day spa is heaven on earth. No part of the world has escaped its attention when it comes to finding the most bliss-inducing smells, sounds, and sensual therapies, a fact much appreciated by its devoted following of London-based glamour queens. Best of all, the treatments—using its own wonderful products—aren't just relaxing, they really work. *Mon-Thu 9am-9pm, Fri-Sat 9am-8pm, Sun 10am-6pm. ££££*

Hot Tip: Sexy and funny, the Rasul cleansing ritual for two involves applying healing mud all over before relaxing in a romantically lit steam room.

Sushi

#94–96: Judging from the popularity of these restaurants, it seems that sushi will never go out of fashion. Dedicated sushi fans should note that most of the sushi in London comes in classic Japanese, rather than innovative, flavors.

Matsuri

71 High Holborn, WC1, Holborn, 020-7430-1970 • Classic

The Draw: Lunchtime bento boxes and sushi hand-rolled by a top sushi chef from Japan are the greatest hits here.

The Scene: This graceful and beguiling Japanese restaurant encompasses a small bar with limited seating, a sushi counter that's popular with students from the nearby London College of Fashion, a teppanyaki room that appeals to a slightly older clientele, and a serene main dining room with slatted bamboo screens. *Mon-Sat noon-2:30pm and 6-10pm. £ –*

Hot Tip: Come at lunchtime or in the early evening when the place is buzzing.

Roka

37 Charlotte St., W1, Bloomsbury, 020-7580-6464 • Hot & Cool

The Draw: The über-trendy younger sister of Zuma, this modern Japanese restaurant specializes in healthy robatayaki cuisine that's cooked on an open charcoal grill. It also serves exquisite hand-rolled sushi.

The Scene: The centerpiece is a robata grill, surrounded by rough-hewn, chunky wooden counters. Tables are fought over during the day when the local media, fashion, and music industry folk drop by for lunch—mostly grills and sushi. The glass walls open onto the street, giving the stylish but rustic venue a casual street-party feel in the summer. *Mon-Fri noon-11:15pm, Sun 12:30-10:15pm. ££ B =*

Hot Tip: After dinner, stop in at the Shochu Lounge in the basement.

Sumosan

26 Albemarle St., W1, Mayfair, 020-7495-5999 • Hot & Cool

The Draw: This glamorous restaurant attracts a steady stream of celebs due to its vibrant atmosphere, innovative Japanese food, and cool cocktails from London's most famous mixologist, Dick Bradsell.

The Scene: The purple-and-cream interior of this über-glam contemporary Japanese restaurant and bar is like a cross between the inside of a chocolate box and a cigarette packet. Beautiful Prada-clad "it girls" rub bare shoulders with stars from the pop, film, and sports worlds. *Mon-Fri noon-3pm and 6-11:30pm, Sat 6-11:30pm. ££ B =*

Hot Tip: Salmon sashimi with strawberry jus, and tuna sushi with truffle oil, are beloved of the hedonistic party crowd—but the must-try dish is tuna and avocado tartare with sevruga caviar, quail's egg, and, yes, more truffle oil.

Trendy Tables

#97–99: Every major restaurateur wants to create a truly trendy restaurant, but few succeed. Whether it's the décor, the ambiance, the food, or the service—or a combination thereof—these places have that elusive "it" quality that keeps the fashionable crowds coming.

Bistrotheque*

23-27 Wadeson St., E2, Hoxton, 020-8983-7900 • Hip

The Draw: An in-the-know crowd from the pop, fashion, design, and music industries congregates here for fabulous French brasserie classics in a trendy industrial chic space reminiscent of New York's Meatpacking District.

The Scene: Come early for a drink in the dimly lit bar on the ground floor. Then join the hip crowd feasting upstairs in the loud, festive dining room. *Mon-Fri 6:30-10:30pm, Sat-Sun 11am-4pm and 6:30-10:30pm. £* =

Hot Tip: The cabaret room puts on a drag show on Wednesday nights, live cabaret on Saturday nights, and disco on Sunday nights. The drag show is very popular.

E & O*

14 Blenheim Crescent, W11, Notting Hill, 020-7229-5454 • Hip

The Draw: The cool, minimalist décor, bar serving Asian-themed cocktails, and small platters of pan-Asian dishes, are all enjoyed by a crowd of boho Notting Hill royalty, including Kate Moss, Stella McCartney, Gwyneth Paltrow, and Sienna Miller.

The Scene: The über-hip restaurant and bar are always packed with young Notting Hillbillies, who flock here by the limo-load. *Mon-Sat noon-3pm and 6-10:30pm, Sun 12:30-3pm and 6-10pm. £* B =

Hot Tip: Order the delicious salt chili squid, which is served in Oriental newspaper cones.

Les Trois Garçons

1 Club Row, E1, Hoxton, 020-7613-1924 • Hip

The Draw: It's renowned for its camp, kitsch interior, but the thing that keeps people coming back is the contemporary French food.

The Scene: The eccentrically eclectic décor, complete with ornate ceramic figures, stuffed animals, groovy chandeliers, and multicolored glass bottles, draws a range of chic and arty types and is also popular with City boys who want to impress their first dates. *Mon-Thu 7-10:30pm, Fri-Sat 6:45-11pm. ££* B =

Hot Tip: If the waiters are brusque and haughty, don't take it personally—it's deliberate, and meant to be part of the experience.

EXPERIENCE LONDON

Dive into the London of your choice with one of three themed itineraries: *Hot & Cool* (p.50), *Hip* (p.92), and *Classic* (p.126). Each is designed to heighten your experience by putting you in the right place at the right time—the best restaurants, nightlife, and attractions, and even the best days to go there. While the itineraries, each followed by detailed descriptions of our top choices, reflect our very top picks, the listings include a number of additional noteworthy options. So, whether you're looking to indulge in a decadent meal at one of London's top restaurants or hit the dance floor late into the night, you'll find it all right here.

Hot & Cool London

If you appreciate fabulousness, London will not disappoint. This bustling metropolis is home to many of the world's most talked-about destinations, from achingly gorgeous Oriental eateries with exquisite food to purse-luring shops that win interior design prizes. And you know which ones they are as soon as you walk in. It's the amazing décor, cunning lighting, and general all-round glamour that give them away. Then there are the people around you, long-limbed and modishly dressed—and that's just the staff. When the cocktail arrives, it's a miniature work of art and tastes divine. And the food? Well, no wonder every glossy in town is talking about it. No need to put in the legwork yourself, though. We've tracked down London's most happening spots just for your delectation.

Note: Venues in bold are described in detail in the listings that follow the itinerary. Venues followed by an asterisk (*) are those we recommend as both a restaurant and a destination bar.

Hot & Cool London:
The Perfect Plan (3 Nights and Days)

Perfect Plan Highlights

Thursday

Lunch	**Anchor & Hope, Baltic***
Afternoon	**Tate Modern**
Pre-dinner	**London Eye**
Dinner	**Hakkasan*, Ling Ling**
Nighttime	**Long Bar, Crazy Bear**
Late-Night	**Purple Bar, Mash, Movida**

Friday

Morning	**Somerset House**
Lunch	**Yauatcha, Providores**
Afternoon	**Bond Street Shopping**
Pre-dinner	**Below Zero, The Gallery at Sketch***
Dinner	**Sketch*, Maze, Benares**
Nighttime	**Light Bar, Opium**
Late-Night	**Kabaret's Prophecy**

Saturday

Morning	**Monmouth Coffee Co., Borough Market**
Lunch	**Roast, Glas**
Afternoon	**Design Museum, Oxo Tower Wharf, Elemis**
Dinner	**Amaya, Zuma***
Nighttime	**Taman Gang, Eclipse**
Late-Night	**Aka, The End**

Day After

Lunch	**Inn the Park**
Afternoon	**Rollerstroll**

Hotel: **The Sanderson**

Thursday

1pm Lunch Get your visit off to a suitably scenic start by cabbing it over to the Thames's South Bank. Settle in for a stylish lunch at über-gastropub **Anchor & Hope**—it's a meat-eater's dream. It doesn't take reservations, so if you can't cope with the lines, try nearby **Baltic*** for contemporary Eastern European fare in chic surroundings. Fill up on blinis with smoked salmon, washed down with flavored vodkas, in sophisticated company.

3pm Stroll a few blocks up to the **Tate Modern**, home to Britain's national collection of modern and contemporary art. There's more than enough in the permanent displays alone for several hours of browsing. Just don't expect to have the joint to yourself.

6pm Culturally sated, continue your tour of the South Bank with a visit to the famous **London Eye**, the city's favorite Ferris wheel, planning your arrival just in time for a restorative drink. The views on the half-hour "flight"—that's a single *slooow* rotation—are even better with a glass of champagne in hand, though for the ultimate luxury reserve a private capsule for you and your fizz.

8pm Dinner Head back to your hotel to primp for the evening ahead. Then select from one of several outstanding dining options. **Hakkasan*** is famous for outstanding contemporary Cantonese cuisine served in a stylish setting—try to allow time for an exotic drink at its see-and-be-seen **Ling Ling** bar beforehand. A short cab ride away at the other end of Oxford Street, the perennially popular Japanese-with-a-twist **Nobu** is always buzzing with a beautiful crowd. Or stay with the Asian theme at the Sanderson's stylish **Asia de Cuba**, though this time with a Latin-American slant.

10:30pm Can't get enough of that Philippe Starck vibe? Rub shoulders with the dressed-up crowd at the vibrant **Long Bar** at the Sanderson, a popular hangout for stylish media types. Or cozy up in one of the red leather caves at the slightly more low-key **Crazy Bear**, where a good-looking clientele indulges in the justifiably popular Bellinis.

Midnight Round off the evening in the chilled and oh-so-grown-up **Purple Bar** at the Sanderson. The sexy lighting, exquisite vodka cocktails, and exclusive aura—it's strictly for hotel residents and a tiny guest list—make it just the ticket for impressing your date. If you have trouble getting past the door there, don't despair. The nearby bar **Mash** serves up beer brewed on-site to a lively crowd (cocktails are available also). Or you can try your luck at the exclusive nightclub **Movida**, a Monaco-style hot spot that allows limited last-minute entry to a lucky few.

Friday

10am Begin your visit of the handsome **Somerset House** with a cafe al fresco in the courtyard. Then take the morning to view some or all of its varied collections. If you have extra time, consider a stroll across the Thames to the edgy **Hayward Gallery**.

1pm Lunch Cab it to Soho to indulge in dim sum at hotter-than-hot **Yauatcha**, with its striking yet serene pale blue and gray interior. Alternatively, head straight up to your afternoon destination to enjoy a few trendy fusion tapas at the buzzing **Providores & Tapa Room**.

3pm Hunger appeased, take a cab to Mayfair for a spot of designer shopping: Bond Street is one long parade of high-class clothing and jewelry stores. Another excellent shopping destination is the upscale Marylebone shopping district, which is lined with tempting boutiques. One exceptional nearby diversion is the Wallace Collection (see Classic Attractions, p.172). Credit cards satisfied, return to your hotel to drop your shopping bags and relax.

7pm No need to worry about warm drinks at nearby **Below Zero and the Absolut Ice Bar**; even the glasses are made from ice. The customers are equally cool, though perhaps not in the heat-retaining cloaks and mittens handed out to all. See them, and their stylish black attire, better in the clubby space downstairs. Alternatively, it's time for a killer cocktail or two at **The Gallery at Sketch***. (Be sure to book ahead for the privilege of drinking here.) This huge white space, with its eye-catching video art, is the ultimate in rock-star cool.

8:30pm Dinner Linger to dine at **Sketch***, where beautiful people migrate in droves to one of several cutting-edge dining options within. For irresistible "fine grazing," join the young and dressy at the hot spot **Maze**, where you'll be nibbling on a tantalizing mix of French-Asian dishes. Nearby **Benares** is *the* destination of choice for contemporary Indian food.

11pm It's guest-list-only time at the **Light Bar** at St. Martins Lane, yet another wildly fashionable Philippe Stark production, known for its wickedly good mojitos. If Light Bar doesn't work out, check out another nearby hot spot, the Asian-inspired **Opium**.

1am You'll need to plan ahead and get on the guest list for your next stop, whichever your choose. For later-night reveling, in-the-groove funsters make for Soho and **Kabaret's Prophecy**, with its funkadelic video walls, intimate dance floor, and select clientele of movers and shakers. Otherwise, end your evening at the decadent **Kensington Roof Gardens** with champagne and dancing.

Saturday

10am Start the day with a cab ride to Monmouth Coffee Company, right beside London's trendiest gourmet market.

11am Once the caffeine's kicked in, join the buzzy upmarket crowd—and we mean *crowd*—at **Borough Market**. Okay, so you may not be snapping up any of the organic meats, but there's no shortage of more suitable foodie souvenirs, and a wealth of grazing opportunities.

12:30pm Lunch Assuming you haven't spoiled your appetite with too many Thai tuna wraps or artisan cakes from the market, you will now be ready for a bite to eat. For classic English food, **Roast** could hardly be more convenient. Located just above the market, it offers superb views of the bustle below from its second-floor dining room. For fabulous seafood, snag one of the coveted tables at **Glas**, where fish gets a Swedish treatment.

2:30pm Work off lunch with a leisurely stroll. Follow the riverside walkway east to the **Design**

Museum, a dazzlingly white converted banana warehouse. It's not huge, but the well-thought-out displays cover everything from packaging to hats.

4pm From here, retrace your steps and keep on going along the banks of the Thames, clocking the views of the City, the Tate Modern, and the Millennium Bridge as you go. Stop for a spot of retail therapy at **Oxo Tower Wharf**. Not in the mood to shop? The superb **Elemis day-spa**, and its divine range of pampering treatments, is tucked away in a quiet alley off Bond Street.

8pm Dinner Make your way to the much-raved-about **Amaya** in Knightsbridge, which pulls in an A-list crowd hungry for its fabulous Indian cooking. Stay with the global theme at the hyper-fashionable **Zuma***, which takes Japanese cuisine to new heights of sophistication. Or pop over to Kensington to enjoy tantalizing offerings in a lush garden setting at **Babylon**.

11pm Where better to party with sleek young Londoners than **Taman Gang**? The signature cocktails in this exclusive Mayfair nightspot are inventive and delicious. Otherwise, hightail it to Chelsea and **Eclipse**, another sexy lounge bar with excellent cocktails and a mix of dressed-up locals and European princelings.

1am Still not tired? Covent Garden is home to several animated late-night options. For drinks, **Aka** is open until 5am on Saturdays. Or go for full-on glam and a good scattering of billionaires and celebrities (including the occasional prince) at **Pangaea**, though not if you aren't on the guest list.

4am To wrap up the night, head to **The End**, next door to Aka at the same address but with separate doors, where you can strut your funky stuff until dawn.

Day After
After your row of late nights, ease yourself into the day with a noonday lunch at **Inn the Park**. Linger over your meal while admiring the views of St. James's Park. Energy levels restored, consider joining the locals for **Rollerstroll**, a relaxed group skate that starts and ends in Hyde Park, and covers several scenic miles of the city's streets in between.

Hot & Cool:
The Key Neighborhoods

Bankside is a shining example of urban regeneration in a scenic riverside setting, with fantastic concert halls and theaters, power-stations-turned-modern-art-galleries, unique shopping experiences in old warehouses, and the fabulous 21st-century landmark that is the London Eye.

Fitzrovia is the hub of London's fashion and media world, with suitably stylish restaurants and bars where the décor is as fabulous as the young clientele and the global-influenced cuisine.

Knightsbridge offers upscale dining and shopping to an affluent and dressed-up international crowd of Hollywood stars, Arab princes, Russian multibillionaires, and the like.

Mayfair is an aristocratic thoroughbred that has reinvented itself with great aplomb for the 21st century. Bond Street's emporia have every modern luxury you can think of, plus restaurants to die for, and one of the city's best spas. It's a wonder anyone ever leaves.

Soho is the district that never sleeps, thanks to a buzzing nightclub scene and of-the-moment bars, not to mention some much-talked-about eateries. Even during the day, the cafes that line Old Compton Street pull in a crowd of young and young-at-heart sipping espressos and people-watching.

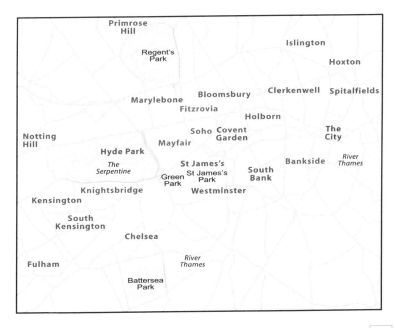

Hot & Cool London:
The Shopping Blocks

Bond Street, W1

London's ultimate upscale style mecca.

Smythson Stock up on gorgeous paper goods and leather accessories. A must. (p.90). 40 New Bond St., 020-7629-8558

Vivienne Westwood This is the ultimate British fashion designer's shop, where the 18th century meets punk. (p.171) 44 Conduit St., 020-7439-1109

Marylebone High Street, W1

A stylish corridor lined with upscale boutiques.

Cath Kidston This is the place for perfect retro British florals for kids, linens, kitchen, and even camping. (p.86) 51 Marylebone High St., 020-7935-6555

Skandium This Scandinavian design shop drips with style and will meet all your home décor needs. (p.90) 86 Marylebone High St., 020-7935-2077

Space.NK This is a branch of the best boutique apothecary and beauty shop in London. 83a Marylebone High St., 020-7486-8791

Upper Street, N1

The destination of stylish Londoners, who flock here for unusual designer labels.

Cloud Cuckoo Land Retro fans will find fabulous vintage clothes, scarves, bags, and jewelry. 6 Charlton Pl., Camden Passage, 020-7354-3141

Diverse You'll find colorful apparel for men and women. (p.87) Womenswear: 294 Upper St., 020-7350-8877; Menswear: 286 Upper St., 020-7359-0081

Sefton These high-end fashion boutiques carry European labels. Womenswear: 271 Upper St., 020-7226-9822; Menswear: 196 Upper St., 020-7226-7076

Stella Cadente Come for fanciful womenswear. 54 Cross St., 020-7359-8015

Westbourne Grove, W11

London's sexiest street for media types and jet-setters. Effortless chic a must.

Aime This fabulous French womenswear boutique and interiors shop carries hard-to-find Parisian gems. (p.85) 32 Ledbury Rd., 020-7221-7070

Emma Hope's Shoes This British women's shoemaker has a fondness for kitten heels and evening wear. 207 Westbourne Grove, 020-7313-7490

Paul Smith This shop cum converted house cum gallery carries the best of British designers. Westbourne House, 122 Kensington Park Rd., 020-7727-3553

Solane Azagury-Partridge You'll find much-in-demand fine jewelry with a very modern twist. 187 Westbourne Grove, 020-7792-0197

Hot & Cool London:
The Hotels

The Baglioni • Kensington • Trendy (68 rms)

You can't get more opulent than this Italian hotel in all of London. Once you hit the black lobby filled with black Murano glass chandeliers and gold-leaf walls, you know you're in for something exceptional. Jet-setting Italians come in droves, as do very stylish businessmen. Of the 68 rooms, 50 are suites that come with a personal butler who will pour you coffee from your in-room Illy coffee machine if you wish to take it easy. The staff will preempt your every need and the concierge services can get you anything you want in the city. Not surprisingly, the rooms are plush with a modern design approach and lots of matte gold that's pure Venetian glamour. There are also Jacuzzi baths in most of the rooms—as well as an in-house hairdresser and make-up artist if you want to get groomed before going down to the exceptionally hot private members club Avive in the hotel's basement, which is open to guests. The black-and-gold-leaf Brunello restaurant is also delightful—with fresh Italian produce flown in daily. ££ 60 Hyde Park Gate, SW7 (⊖ High Street Kensington), 020-7368-5700, baglionihotellondon.com

The Berkeley • Knightsbridge • Grand (214 rms)

The Berkeley isn't done up in froufrou frills and finery. Its bedrooms are decorated by international designers in either traditional English style (with pastels and floral prints), or contemporary design (with vibrant burgundies, deep reds, and whites). The best of these are the executive kings on the seventh and eighth floors, which have an Art Deco bed, ensuite bathrooms, walk-in showers, large office desk, and wide-screen TV. All mod cons like high-speed 24-hour internet access, UK/US modems, internet TV, DVD library, and mini-bar are available. The design element is also taken seriously in the hotel's acclaimed Pétrus restaurant and the Blue Bar (both done by top designer David Collins), and the Boxwood Café, where a crowd of elegant locals and visitors alike comes to drink and dine. Further flourishes that will appeal to fashionistas include the Japanese breakfast offered as room service, and Prêt-à-Potea afternoon tea (dainty cakes inspired by the catwalk)—and the Knightsbridge location which means Harrods and Harvey Nicks are a short walk away. There's a spa that has a stunning swimming pool with retractable roof, and a range of special treatments, including Javanese Lulur and La Stone Massage. And if you get carried away with the special doughnut menu at the Caramel Room, the hotel has thoughtfully included a hi-tech gym. £££ Wilton Pl., SW1 (⊖ Knightsbridge), 020-7235-6000, the-berkeley.co.uk

Blakes Hotel • South Kensington • Trendy (45 rms)

This trendy five-star boutique hotel, located in a quiet residential part of South Kensington, is well placed near a number of parks, museums, and Knightsbridge shops. The latter appeal to top designers from the fashion world, as well as the film stars and musicians that typically make up its clientele. Each of the rooms is individually designed by Anouska Hempel, who is also the owner—the most dramatic rooms being the director's doubles. The color scheme is bold and vibrant throughout, with fabrics and furnishings in crimsons, golds, greens, deep blues, and blacks, strikingly contrasted with white-on-white accents. No room is decorated in more than two colors, and each boasts individual design effects, such as marble, tortoiseshell, or silk and velvet. Every room has a computer and a mini-bar, and there's a full concierge service on hand to cater to your every need. The hotel claims that its WiFi has the "fastest connection in London"—which is great news for the travel-savvy crowd that it draws. Another attraction is an imaginative East-West fusion menu in the restaurant. £££ 33 Roland Gdns., SW7 (⊖ Gloucester Road), 020-7370-6701 / USA 800-926-3173, blakeshotels.com

The Charlotte Street Hotel • Fitzrovia • Timeless (52 rms)

You'd expect an upscale hotel to decorate its walls with a painting here or there, but that's not quite good enough for the Charlotte Street Hotel. This beautiful Georgian building is a classically modern ode to decadent early-20th century Bloomsbury. Its walls are filled with museum-quality artworks by Vanessa Bell, Roger Fry, Henry Lamb, and Duncan Grant. The only thing that's missing is Virginia Woolf writing frantically in the corner. Inspired by Charleston, the Sussex home of Vanessa Bell and Duncan Grant, the interior has the warmth and coziness of a real home with high-design details like painted furniture, vintage rugs, and unusual finds like fabric-covered mannequins. The rooms achieve the same effect, mixing clean lines with a low-key townhouse vibe—they manage to be warm and colorful without being fussy, and they offer all the modern amenities the business traveler could want. The modern granite-and-oak bathrooms are vast and very sleek, often with double basins, walk-in showers, and TVs. It's particularly popular with advertising and media types who fill the ever-busy lobby bar day and night. On Sunday nights the hotel has a film club in its plush leather screening rooms and shows classics like *Breakfast at Tiffany's*. The best rooms overlook Charlotte Street—the largest double is room 203 if you want extra space. ££ 15 Charlotte St., W1 (⊖ Goodge Street), 020-7806-2000 / USA 800-553-6674, firmdalehotels.com

The Halkin • Knightsbridge • Timeless (41 rms)

Tucked away in a tranquil side street near Knightsbridge, this award-garlanded five-star hotel is quite intimate in scale. Behind its Georgian-style façade, the design blends a classic style with Italian modernity, glossy marbles, and crisp linens. The spacious rooms—the deluxe rooms are the largest—are decorated in creams and beiges by an Italian designer, and feature leather-fringed taffeta curtains and marble bathrooms (some of the largest in London) with walk-in shower rooms. Amenities include secretarial services, personalized shopping itineraries, theater ticket reservations, touch-screen consoles for lighting, cell phone rental, a butler, and much more. There's an excellent concierge service—and all hotel staff are dressed in Armani. The hotel is also known for its Michelin-starred Thai restaurant Nahm, where the excellent food should be preceded by a flavored martini in the quiet bar off the lobby. £££ 5 Halkin St., SW1 (⊖ Hyde Park Corner), 020-7333-1000 / USA 888-425-5464, halkin.co.uk

K West Hotel & Spa • Kensington • Modern (220 rms)

Decorated in muted tones of whites, creams, and browns, this relatively new contemporary hotel and spa in Shepherd's Bush is accentuated with leather, suede, dark wood, stainless steel, and sandblasted glass. It's particularly popular with the music and media crowd: Following the 2006 Brit awards, Paul Weller held his afterparty here; and Franz Ferdinand and Moby (who regards this hotel as one of his favorite three places in the world) have also partied here. The rooms are furnished with handmade beds, hypoallergenic pillows, and refrigerators, and the bathrooms

HOT & COOL

have bathtubs designed by Philippe Starck. Guests can access items from communal vending machines to custom-stock their own mini-bars, and the corridors hold ice machines for drinks. Rooms measure from 260 to 350 square feet—the best being the large executive rooms equipped with sofa, desk, wide-screen TV, DVDs, hi-fis, and PlayStation. The stylish restaurant, Kanteen, offers an eclectic menu of low-fat and vegetarian options, and a cool, slick space for drinks and light meals called K Lounge has a late-night DJ and dancing. The chic, gallery-like lobby shows BBC24, and has multi-media art and sound installations. A central feature of the hotel is a spa that uses E'Spa products, and offers a range of therapeutic treatments like hot stone therapy and dry flotation tanks. ££ Richmond Way, W14 (⊖ Shepherd's Bush), 087-0027-4343, k-west.co.uk

Metropolitan London • Mayfair • Modern (150 rms)

This cool, contemporary hotel is hugely popular with guests from the music, media, and fashion industries, and its lobby is constantly abuzz with parties and launches. Fashion folks also like its trendy Nobu restaurant and lively Met Bar. The lobby area is decorated in chic creams and whites, with pear-wood paneling, suede upholstery, and glass walls that sparkle with natural light. The bedrooms are done up in pastel shades of peppermint, lilac, and cream, and strewn with antique Asian furniture. Spread over eight floors, the 53 suites, double rooms (including the popular king park rooms), and studios face Hyde Park; 97 other rooms overlook Mayfair; the king city rooms are especially popular with business clients on account of their generous desk space. Takeout breakfasts are available, and there's a fantastic concierge service. Business facilities are excellent, and guests are given private fax machines with designated numbers. There's also a well-equipped gym that offers holistic therapies. Guests staying in the coveted Penthouse Suite benefit from a chauffeur-driven limousine and a personal assistant on standby. £££ 19 Old Park Ln., W1 (⊖ Hyde Park Corner), 020-7447-1047 (reservations), metropolitan.co.uk

No. 5 Cavendish Square • Marylebone • Timeless (8 rms)

Sicilian entrepreneur Jay Maggistro wanted a change from his life as a hairdresser to royalty, so he decided to create the ultimate place for an evening out. No. 5 is a destination for pre-dinner drinks, a lavish Italian meal, cocktails, and clubbing, and has eight suites for passing out at the end of the night. The former Spanish Embassy was transformed in 2001 into this luxurious space decked in dark reds, chandeliers, and paintings by Rolling Stone Ronnie Wood. The hotel attracts international businesspeople who like a dose of decadence in their rooms, though plenty of celebrities walk through these doors. Alongside the hotel's exclusive bars, there's a private cigar bar for members and hotel guests. The real draw for many is the party downstairs, though during the week it's more popular as a base for people in town on business. Expect a lot of marble, velvet, and animal prints in the over-the-top rooms, which feature chaise longues, miles of rich fabrics, and gilt furniture. If you're feeling naughty, you could purchase something from the bath menu, including a £1,500 100% champagne bath with a bottle of Cristal, pralines, strawberries, and cream thrown in. This is also a cozy spot for Christmas extravagance when the exterior of the building is decked out like a giant gift with a huge red bow. ££ 5 Cavendish Sq., W1 (⊖ Oxford Circus), 020-7079-5000, no5ltd.com

One Aldwych • Covent Garden • Modern (105 rms)

One Aldwych is simply perfect. It has a calm, restful vibe that is a result of its modern minimalist design approach, combined with the attentive service of an old-fashioned hotel. It attracts a lot of business travelers, but the location is ideal for pleasure seekers, as it's just steps from Covent Garden. The rooms are a fusion of frosted glass, muted beiges, dark wood, clean lines, and giant beds. This is a place for grown-ups who want simplicity, good service, and ample space. Creating a soothing atmosphere is paramount, with calming drinks and chilled eye pads provided in the minibar upon your arrival. Originally a newspaper office, the building opened as a hotel in 1998 and has kept all the exterior charm of the original space. There's a 24-hour gym that attracts magazine editors from *GQ* and *Wallpaper*, as well as a beautiful swimming pool playing Mozart and Bach through underwater speakers. Rooms ending in 18 are the best as they're extra large with double windows on the corner of the building. Other highlights include the subtle green philosophy, the fabulous Lobby Bar, a destination in its own right, and two fabulous restaurants: Axis in the basement and Indigo on the mezzanine. £££ 1 Aldwych, WC2 (⊖ Covent Garden), 020-7300-1000 / USA 800-223-6800, onealdwych.co.uk

St. Martins Lane • Covent Garden • Trendy (204 rms)

St. Martins Lane was Ian Schrager's first European hotel and it opened with a big bang in 2000. It lies seconds away from Trafalgar Square, but the classic lines of the National Gallery are a complete contrast to this monument to urbane modernism. The lighting and furnishings throughout are a mix of luminescent yellow and sharp clean white. Once you're past the witty lobby filled with stools in the shape of gold teeth or small gnomes, almost every room has spectacular floor-to-ceiling walls of windows (Room 305 is extra bright). The ground-floor rooms have small gardens that open to the sky to make up for their lack of view. There are interactive light installations above every bed, so guests can change the color of the lighting depending on their mood. These blank-slate rooms are all white—with white bed, walls, furniture, and bathrooms that practically glow. The hotel attracts a lot of media types, models, and megastars like Beyoncé and Britney, though the 24-hour multilingual secretarial service on demand would certainly appeal to business types. In addition to its ever-buzzing restaurant Asia de Cuba and outstanding Light Bar, which both draw hordes of fashionable types, the basement is currently being transformed into the world's largest gym. £££ 45 St. Martin's Ln., WC2 (⊖ Leicester Square), 020-7300-5500 / USA 800-697-1791, stmartinslane.com

The Sanderson • Fitzrovia • Trendy (154 rms)

This is one of hotelier Ian Schrager and designer Philippe Starck's best collaborations. The hotel, located in a converted wallpaper factory off Oxford Street, is a perfect fusion of postmodernist humor and clean, soothing minimalism. Attracting large numbers of fashion, music, and media types (including Madonna), the Sanderson is a true destination hotel. The lobby resembles a stage set overflowing with quirky odd chairs and artworks. In contrast to the continuous buzz of the hotel's hot bars and Alain Ducasse's restaurant Spoon+, the rooms are quiet retreats. The spacious and calm white boudoirs are arranged like works of art with white drapery and two-person baths. All have romantic landscape paintings on the ceiling above the bed and a rug beneath the bed printed with a love letter written by Voltaire. Go for 606 or one of the other rooms on the sixth floor with private terraces overlooking Dean Street, which are ideal for summer sunbathing. Other draws include the stunning urban spa Agua and the hidden gift shop, which stocks Philippe Starck dumbbells, Antik Batik clothes, style magazines, and jewelry. It would be impossible to make this hotel any cooler. £££ 50 Berners St., W1 (⊖ Oxford Circus), 020-7300-1400 / USA 800-697-1791, sandersonlondon.com

The Soho Hotel • Soho • Trendy (91 rms)

It's so discreet you could easily miss it. Kit and Tim Kemp knocked out a parking lot to build this cavernous hotel, which has become a must for media types and affluent sophisticates. The pair are fond of high-design details, and the public spaces throughout reflect their eclectic style. The Drawing Room and Library chill-out spaces look like French country meets excited Orientalist. Cue pale-green floral prints with fuschia-pink highlights and a giant Botero cat sculpture. Past the paisley printed corridors, the rooms have the same vibe. Strong pink and turquoise details nestle among muted beige furniture. Those in the know grab one of the fifth-floor terrace rooms, which have balconies and stunning views. High-maintenance celebs like J-Lo, Pamela Anderson, and Naomi Campbell fight over the Terrace Suite. As a nod to Soho's role as the center of the British film world, the hotel also has a film club on Friday nights and Sunday afternoons—showing classics and pre-releases in its cow-print-lined screening rooms. The bar restaurant Refuel is a hot ticket, but Soho is really all about the location. If you were any more central, the world would revolve around you. ££ 4 Richmond Mews (off Dean St.), W1 (⊖ Tottenham Court Road), 020-7559-3000 / USA 800-553-6674, sohohotel.com

Threadneedles • The City • Modern (69 rms)

You'd never expect such a stylish hotel to exist just steps away from the Bank of England, but five minutes from the Royal Exchange lies a hidden gem. Threadneedles prides itself on being the first boutique hotel in the City. The contemporary rooms are full of warm wood furniture and classic modern lines, yet the building has retained some of its stunning original features, which date back to its earlier incarnation as a bank. The beautiful ground-floor atrium with its original stained-glass dome has an honesty bar that stays open until 1am. Considering the location, it's not surprising that Threadneedles attracts a lot of edgier and younger businesspeople with an eye for design, though it's a great place for anyone looking for a stunningly designed, soothing room. The best rooms are above the iron grates of the hotel's restaurant Bonds, as they provide more view. The rooms are quiet at night as this neighborhood really slows down after hours. That said, Bonds has a buzzing bar that provides ample diversion. Concierge perks include entry into exclusive members bars and monogram service from Thomas Pink. £££ 5 Threadneedle St., EC2 (⊖ Bank), 020-7657-8080, theetoncollection.com

The Trafalgar • Westminster • Modern (129 rms)

You couldn't get more central. This stylish boutique hotel in an Edwardian office block in Trafalgar Square attracts a lot of corporate guests midweek, but it gets lots of creative and media tourists on weekends. The interior design is clean lines in grays, browns, and leather and is surprisingly calm. There's triple glazing so you'd never hear the constant traffic outside. 303 or 203 are the best rooms as they sit just above the curved clock tower on the corner of the building and have stunning views of the square. All the rooms are repainted every three months to keep them fresh, and each has a PS2 and access to the free DVD and CD library. Sporty types use the red-walled gym with the latest techno equipment—all with integrated TV screens. The whole design is modern but retains one original feature—the board-room that was featured in films like *Dr. No* and *The Ipcress Files*. There are rotating art shows on the ground floor, a buzzing bar with live vocalists and DJs that change every night, and a stunning roof bar in summer. £££ 2 Spring Gdns., Trafalgar Sq., SW1 (⊖ Charing Cross), 020-7870-2900, trafalgar.hilton.com

Hot & Cool London:
The Restaurants

Amaya • Knightsbridge • Indian
Best Indian Restaurants One of London's most raved-about restaurants is located inside a shopping mall and sells kebabs. Owned by award-garlanded restaurateurs Namita and Camellia Panjabi, this chic, bustling bar and grill is the best Indian restaurant in London—and considered by some to be one of the best in the world. Its stylish but casual romantic sandstone-and-rosewood interior and permanent buzz has kept its sophisticated clientele—including many A-list celebrities—enthralled. The deeply fashionable kebabs are cooked using numerous elaborate techniques in a thrillingly theatrical open kitchen. Soups, salads, biryanis, and desserts make up the rest of the menu, which is designed to be shared. *Mon-Fri 12:30-2:30pm and 6-11pm, Sat 12:30-3pm and 6-11pm, Sun 12:30-3pm and 6-10pm.* ££ ⓑ≡ Halkin Arcade, Motcomb St., SW1 (⊖ Knightsbridge) 020-7823-1166, realindianfood.com

Anchor & Hope • South Bank • Gastropub
Best Gastropubs This quintessentially British gastropub opened to such raves from every London critic that it's now always packed with a young, vibrant, dressed-down crowd. In other words, it's hard to get a table—and due to the pub's no-booking policy, you may have to wait your turn at the bar. But make the most of the wait. Order a real British ale and strike up a conversation with your neighbors—it's all part of the experience. The good news is that it's slightly less busy at lunchtime, when you might find yourself tucking into fashionably unfashionable dishes like duck heart on toast, or pork, bacon, and turnip stew. If you're lucky, you'll spot a stage star or two from nearby Young and Old Vic theaters (like Kevin Spacey, who's the artistic director of the latter). *Pub: Mon 5-11pm, Tue-Sat 11am-11pm. Meals: Tue-Sat noon-2:30pm and 6-10:30pm.* £- ≡ 36 The Cut, SE1 (⊖ Southwark), 020-7928-9898

Asia de Cuba • Covent Garden • Fusion
Housed inside the stylish St. Martin's Lane Hotel, this Latin-Asian fusion restaurant boasts stunning design by iconic designer Philippe Starck. The futuristic bright white space with giant pillars is decked out with potted plants, ancient tomes, and black-and-white photos. The trendy young clientele, bespangled and besequined in their glitzy tops, doesn't eat much, so small sharing platters like lobster pot stickers with spiced rum sauce and Cuban spiced chicken with tamarind sauce are just perfect. Start your evening with fabulous cocktails at the hotel's deeply fabulous Light Bar. *Mon-Wed 6:30-11am, noon-2:30pm, and 5:30pm-midnight; Thu-Fri 6:30-11am, noon-2:30pm, and 5:30pm-12:30am; Sat 7am-2:30pm and 5:30pm-12:30am; Sun 7am-2:30pm and 5:30-10:30pm. Tea daily 3-4:30pm.* ££ ≡ St. Martins Lane Hotel, 45 St. Martin's Ln., WC2 (⊖ Leicester Square), 020-7300-5588, chinagrillmgt.com

Babylon • Kensington • Modern European
There's a cute bar at the front of this restaurant. However, the main attraction for the rich twenty- and thirty-something crowd isn't the food or the drink: It's

the setting. Stacked over two floors, this crowded bar, restaurant, and nightclub is located amid 1.5 acres of themed Spanish, Tudor, and English woodland gardens, and boasts fabulous views of London's skyline. The gardens are filled with symmetrical fountains, duck ponds, hanging wisteria, vine-covered walkways, flamingos, and Mediterranean fruit trees—whose fruit is used abundantly on the restaurant menu. To make an evening of it, stop by for a drink at the small bar at the restaurant's entrance; then after dinner, head downstairs to the ground-floor bar, which turns into a nightclub that plays everything from rap to rock 'n' roll after 8pm. *Mon-Sat noon-3pm and 7-11pm, Sun noon-3pm.* £ ≡ 99 Kensington High St., the Roof Gardens, 7th Fl., W8 (⊖ High Street Kensington), 020-7368-3993, roofgardens.com

Baltic* • South Bank • East European
Best Restaurant Lounges You think Eastern European food is all about dumplings and cabbage? Think again. This trendy restaurant and bar offers Polish and Russian dishes with a contemporary twist. Blinis with assorted toppings, including osetra caviar, and popular flavored vodkas are a huge hit with the polished young professionals that swarm the place. The chic décor is airy and bright, with its wooden trussed ceilings, exposed beams, high vaulted-glass roof—and a stunningly beautiful amber wall. *Mon-Sat noon-3pm and 6-11:15pm, Sun noon-10:30pm.* £- = B 74 Blackfriars Rd., SE1 (⊖ Southwark), 020-7928-1111, balticrestaurant.co.uk

Benares • Mayfair • Indian
Top chef Atul Kochar's restaurant is as notable for its striking design as its contemporary Indian food. There's a small bar at the front with water pools filled with colorful gerbera flowers, and furniture made from antique chests—it's not really a destination bar, but makes an ideal place for a pre-dinner drink. The restaurant at the back is lined with bright white tongue-and-groove walls, creating the effect of a Mayfair version of the holy Indian city of Benares in northern India. Evenings are popular with dating couples, wealthy Indian families, Bollywood film stars, Russian oligarchs, and celebrities—including Paris Hilton. *Mon-Fri noon-2:30pm and 5:30-10:30pm, Sat 5:30-10:30pm, Sun 6-10pm.* ££ = 12 Berkeley Sq., W1 (⊖ Green Park), 020-7629-8886, benaresrestaurant.com

Boxwood Café • Knightsbridge • American
Part of the Gordon Ramsay empire, this New York–style cafe tucked away inside the Berkeley Hotel aims to show its polished but dressed-down diners a more informal face of fine dining—if indeed there can be such a thing. Yes, you will find burgers and hot chocolate on the menu—but the burger is made from veal and foie gras, and the hot choc is Valrhona that's turned into a fondue and served with biscotti. The split-level dining and bar areas are designed by American designer Barbara Barry, and feature silver foil tea paper that's inspired by classic English gardens. Although not really a destination in its own right, the quiet bar is lovely for a drink before dinner. *Mon-Fri noon-3pm and 6-11pm, Sat-Sun noon-4pm and 6-11pm.* ££ = The Berkeley, Wilton Pl., SW1 (⊖ Knightsbridge), 020-7235-1010, gordonramsay.com

The Cinnamon Club* • Westminster • Indian
Best Restaurant Lounges Located a mere chapati-chucking distance from Westminster Abbey and the Houses of Parliament, this contemporary Indian

restaurant is housed in a building that was once the Old Westminster Library. The library theme is used judiciously throughout its vast interior: The ground-floor bar and mezzanine dining room are lined with bookshelves. The buzzy basement lounge bar features everything from rubber floors and leather walls, to handcrafted wooden tables and projectors that play Bollywood films. Even if you can't make dinner, it's worth trying the Indian and Anglo-Indian breakfast—in the company of the politicians who frequently congregate here in the mornings. Ask for a table in the ground-floor dining room. *Mon-Fri 7:30-10am, noon-2:45pm and 6-10:45pm, Sat 6-10:45pm. ££* = The Old Westminster Library, Great Smith St., SW1 (St. James's Park), 020-7222-2555, cinnamonclub.com

Deep • Fulham • Seafood

London's chattering classes have been, well, chattering away recently about dwindling fish stocks and sustainable fishing—so this Scandinavian seafood restaurant hit the headlines when it opened: It offers only environmentally friendly fish on its menu. Perched on the bank of the Thames in Chelsea, bright-ly lit and designed vaguely to look like the inside of an aquarium, it's favored by a fashionably politically correct clientele. Dishes like sautéed perch with morels, onion gnocchi, and vanilla-flavored bisque will delight and fascinate, and there's also a large but quiet bar that sells a good selection of Swedish aquavits—ideal as an aperitif. *Bar: Tue-Sat noon-11pm, Sun noon-5pm. Restaurant: Tue-Fri noon-3pm and 7-11pm, Sat 7-11pm, Sun noon-4pm. £* = The Boulevard, Imperial Wharf, SW6 (Fulham Broadway), 020-7736-3337, deeplondon.co.uk

Emporio Armani Caffe • Knightsbridge • Italian

Located inside the gorgeous Armani shop in Knightsbridge, this bright '90s-looking cafe with large windows is a popular haunt for skinny lunching ladies and European fashionistas—especially during London Fashion Week every February. Although people in fashion don't generally eat, this Italian cafe offers simple, healthy dishes like grilled squid with chorizo, sea bream with caponata, and crab and chard risotto—or you can drop by just for a cappuccino and sit on one of the cozy banquettes. The staff is refreshingly unsnooty. *Mon-Fri 10am-3:30pm, Sat 10am-4pm. £* = 191 Brompton Rd., SW3 (Knightsbridge), 020-7823-8818

Fino • Bloomsbury • Tapas

London's most stylish tapas bar has a smiling doorman at the entrance—and you don't get many of those for your pesetas. The subterranean venue has a small, buzzy cocktail bar at the entrance, and a stylish, laid-back restaurant with blond-wood interior and a backlit bar inside. The large selection of sherries always goes down well with the local media and fashion folk, and this is also one of the very few places to sell percebes—a type of shellfish that's messy, but rather sexy, to eat. *Mon-Fri noon-2:30pm and 6-10:30pm, Sat 12:30-2:30pm and 6-10:30pm. £* = 33 Charlotte St., entrance on Rathbone St., W1 (Tottenham Court Road), 020-7813-8010, finorestaurant.com

Frankie's Italian Bar & Grill • Knightsbridge • American

Frankie's serves a fairly basic but delicious menu of pizzas, meaty grills, and ice cream sundaes. So you would expect it to be a down-to-earth sort of place, right? Well, you'd be wrong—because this is one of the glitziest, most glamorous restaurants in Knightsbridge, complete with glitter balls on the ceiling and over-sized mirrors that are pure bling. It's owned by the legendary Marco Pierre White and UK's top champion jockey Frankie Dettori. Hugely popular with stylish Knightsbridge families, this place also draws a fair smattering of celebrities, particularly sports stars. *Mon-Fri noon-2:30pm and 6-11pm, Sat noon-11pm, Sun noon-10pm.* £ = 3 Yeoman's Row, SW3 (✚Knightsbridge), 020-7590-9999, frankiesitalianbarandgrill.com

Glas • South Bank • Swedish
No, it's not a printing error—it's the Swedish word for "glass." Located near London's renowned gastro-temple, the Borough Market, this contemporary Swedish restaurant with bright green frontage pulsates with friendly market-goers during Friday and Saturday lunchtimes. Scandinavian beers, frozen schnapps, and vodkas help break the ice, and the grazing platters feature a lot of fish, especially herring, on the menu. Ingredients are from the owner's popular Swedish stall at the market, called Scandelicious. This informal venue is also ideal for solo diners. *Tue-Fri noon-2:30pm and 6:30-10pm, Sat 1-10pm.* £- = 3 Park St., SE1 (✚London Bridge), 020-7357-6060, glasrestaurant.com

Gun • Docklands • Gastropub
Best Gastropubs Perched on the banks of the Thames in the Docklands, this historic pub's name comes from the cannon fired to launch the West India Import Docks in 1802. Once associated with dockers, boatmen, and smugglers, these days this strikingly designed gastropub attracts a more select crowd of media and business moguls. There's a bustling bar with dining room, a back bar with limited intimate seating, and a spacious terrace. British and European-style brunches and roasts on Saturday and Sunday (when there's occasional live jazz) are hugely popular. A complimentary rickshaw is available to ferry diners to and from Canary Wharf. *Pub: Mon-Fri 11am-midnight, Sat 10:30am-midnight, Sun 10:30am-11pm; Meals: Mon-Thu noon-3pm and 6-10:30pm, Fri-Sat 10:30am-4:30pm, Sun 10:30am-4:30pm and 6-9:30pm.* £ = 27 Coldharbour, Isle of Dogs, E14 (✚South Quay), 020-7515-5222, thegundocklands.com

Hakkasan* • Bloomsbury • Chinese
Best Always-Hot Restaurants Hard to believe, but one of London's hottest must-visit venues is a basement Chinese restaurant located in a grubby blink-and-you'll-miss-it side street. A slinky staircase leads to a sexy subterranean world that's beautifully lit like the set of a Wong Kar-Wai movie. There's the gorgeous Ling Ling bar to one side, and a super-glamorous dining area to the other encased in floor-to-ceiling ornate black screens. Lunchtimes are popular with business diners, who come for the exquisite dim sum, and evenings come alive with the fashion, film, and music crowd—including a steady stream of celebrities. With its perennially effervescent vibe, Hakkasan is without a doubt one of the buzziest restaurants in London. Be sure to come for an exotic cocktail at the bar before settling down for your meal. *Bar: Mon-Tue noon-12:30am, Wed-Sat noon-1:30am, Sun noon-midnight.* ≡ *Restaurant: Mon-Fri noon-3pm and 6pm-midnight, Sat noon-5pm and 6pm-midnight, Sun noon-5pm and 6-11pm.* ££ ⌗≡ 8 Hanway Pl., W1 (✚Tottenham Court Road), 020-7907-1888

Inn the Park • Westminster • British
Best Al Fresco Dining Fancy having cocktails with the Queen? This stylish, contemporary English cafe, with its wood-paneled design and turf roof, is located

inside St. James's Park, bang opposite Buckingham Palace. So it's possible that as you tuck into an excellent breakfast, fork through the Yorkshire rabbit, pork, and prune terrine, or sip a martini, the royal family might be watching. It's a casual place with outdoor seating that's especially popular for breakfast and lunch. On weekdays, professionals adore the fashionably seasonal, ingredient-led menu that lists all its suppliers in great detail. *Mon-Fri 8-11am, noon-3pm, and 5-10pm, Sat-Sun 9-11am, noon-4pm, and 5-10pm.* £ = St. James's Park, SW1 (⊖St. James's Park), 020-7451-9999, innthepark.com

Le Cercle • Chelsea • French
An offshoot of Club Gascon, this fashionable restaurant's USP is French tapas—that is, small sharing platters like tomato sorbet on aromatic tomato stew—and each dish is accompanied by small measures of wine to match. It's located inside a spacious, atmospheric basement, and has plenty of leather furniture in its bar, dining room, booths, and galleries—all separated by see-through curtains. The black-clad, leather-aproned staff match the sexy young clientele in terms of brooding good looks. The bar scene is vibrant with the buzz of chic diners enjoying pre-dinner glasses of wine. *Bar: Tue-Sat noon-midnight. Restaurant: Tue-Sat noon-3pm and 6-11pm. Afternoon tea: Tue-Sat 3-5:30pm.* £ B = 1 Wilbraham Pl., SW1 (⊖Sloane Square), 020-7901-9999

The Ledbury • Notting Hill • French
The wealthy bohos and celebs of Notting Hill, with their carefully dishevelled hair and artistic lifestyles sustained by Daddy's money or (as in most cases) an enviable career, have secretly longed for a fine-dining restaurant in their midst. When respected restaurateurs Philip Howard and Nigel Platts-Martin opened the Ledbury to enthusiastic reviews, they finally got it. The hushed interior—with clusters of fresh flowers adding color to an unfussy interior—and chilled ambiance belie the fireworks produced by the kitchen. Your bouche will be amused—and amazed—long after you've finished your meal. *Mon-Sat noon-2:30pm and 6:30-11pm, Sun noon-2:30pm and 6:30-10pm.* ££ = 127 Ledbury Rd., W11 (⊖Westbourne Park), 020-7792-9090, theledbury.com

Locanda Locatelli • Marylebone • Italian
Owned by handsome and charismatic chef-proprietor Giorgio Locatelli, this exquisite one-Michelin-star restaurant is undoubtedly the best Italian in town. It's located in Churchill InterContinental Hotel, but has its own separate entrance. The stylish coffee-and-caramel color scheme, curved mirrors, dim lighting, and ambient jazz have created a sort of 1970s European chic that's much appreciated by the sophisticated stockbrokers and media mavens who flock here. The sumptuous white truffle risotto, available October to January, is arguably the best in the UK. *Mon-Thu noon-3pm and 7-11pm, Fri noon-3pm and 7-11:30pm, Sat noon-3pm and 7-11pm, Sun noon-3:30pm and 7-10pm.* ££ = 8 Seymour St., W1 (⊖Marble Arch), 020-7935-9088, locandalocatelli.com

Maze • Mayfair • French / Pan-Asian
The newest baby in Gordon Ramsay's expansive empire, award-winning head chef Jason Atherton's stylish restaurant and bar offers French food cooked with pan-Asian influences. The concept is currently all the rage: Small platters of exquisitely crafted dishes are savored by a polished clientele that's generally younger and more casual than you would find in a conventional fine dining

restaurant. The lovely, hectic rosewood bar serves contemporary cocktails that are a must before dinner. Maze is, indeed, amazing. *Bar: daily noon-1am. Restaurant: daily noon-2:30pm and 6-10:30pm.* £ B≡ 10-13 Grosvenor Sq., W1 (⊖ Bond Street), 020-7107-0000, gordonramsay.com

Momo • Mayfair • Moroccan

Best Romantic Dining Owned by Mourad Mazouz of Sketch fame, this stylish Moroccan restaurant has been deeply fashionable ever since it opened several years ago. It's not because of the food, which includes perfectly lovely tagines and couscous—it's the décor and the vibe. The former includes brass lanterns, ornate windows, and jewel-encrusted antiques; and as for the latter, it's vibrant and clublike, complete with loud music, excellent cocktails, and trendily-dressed staff. Momo regularly features in the celebrity pages of magazines, as it's the A-listers' choice for celebrating birthdays. There's a stunning members-only bar in the basement—it's open to diners who are not members for pre-dinner drinks only, at the manager's discretion. *Mon-Thu noon-2:15pm and 7-11:15pm, Fri noon-2:15pm and 6:30-11:45pm, Sat noon-2:15pm and 6:30-10:45pm, Sun 6:30-10:45pm.* £ B≡ 25 Heddon St., W1 (⊖ Piccadilly Circus), 020-7434-4040, momoresto.com

Moro • Clerkenwell • Moorish

Exmouth Market is not a market, but a fashionable pedestrianized street strewn with cafes and restaurants with al fresco tables that are ideal for people-watching. It's also the location of this urbane, casual tapas bar and restaurant that serves Moorish cuisine with Spanish and North African influences. Owned by widely admired husband-and-wife team—with matching his-'n'-hers names, Sam and Sam Clark—this Mediterranean-looking venue is fragrant with cooking aromas from its charcoal grill and wood-burning oven. The all-day tapas are popular with dressed-down local office workers, especially at lunchtime. *Tapas bar: Mon-Sat 12:30-11:45pm. Restaurant: Mon-Sat 12:30-2:30pm and 7-10:30pm.* £ B≡ 34-36 Exmouth Market, EC1 (⊖ Farringdon), 020-7833-8336, moro.co.uk

Nicole's • Mayfair • British

Located in the basement of the Nicole Farhi store on Bond Street, this elegant restaurant is a favorite with ladies who shop. It's at its busiest at lunchtime, when a Farhi-clad crowd comes to eat contemporary British and continental dishes like pan-fried duck breast with peach compote and red rice and almond salad. Breakfast and afternoon tea are also available, and there's a bar if you want to chill your heels after a hard day's shopping in the neighborhood. *Bar: Mon-Fri 10am-10:45pm, Sat 10am-6pm. Meals: Mon-Sat 11:30am-5:30pm. Restaurant: Mon-Fri 10-11:30am and noon-3:30pm and 6:30-10:45pm, Sat 10-11:30am and noon-3:30pm. Tea: Mon-Sat 3-6pm.* £ B_ 158 New Bond St., W1 (⊖ Bond Street), 020-7499-8408, nicolefarhi.com

Nobu • Mayfair • Japanese (G)

Best Oriental Restaurants Famous for its black cod with miso—a dish that's launched a thousand imitations—this branch of the international Japanese-Peruvian chain inside the Metropolitan Hotel is one of the most famous restaurants in town. It's renowned for celeb-spotting—everyone from Roman Abramovich to Nicole Kidman dines here—and a few years ago it became (in)famous for "the Boris Becker broom cupboard incident," when the tennis player had a fling with a model in a broom cupboard. The small, quiet bar offers some of the most exquisite sakes in town (including several containing gold leaf). The chocolate bento box dessert is not to be missed. Book several weeks ahead. *Mon-Thu noon-2:15pm and 6-10:15pm, Fri noon-2:15pm and 6-11pm, Sat 12:30-2:30pm and 6-11pm, Sun 12:30-2:30pm and 6-9:30pm.* ££ ≡ Metropolitan Hotel, 19 Old Park Ln., W1 (⊖ Hyde Park Corner), 020-7447-4747, noburestaurants.com

Nobu Berkeley* • Mayfair • Japanese
This is a more informal branch of Nobu, but judging by the David Collins interior, the good-looking staff, and the lively buzz created by its well-dressed clientele, you wouldn't know it. What makes the restaurant informal is that it takes no bookings (unless you're in a group of more than six), so in theory you can just walk in. In practice, you'll find yourself waiting your turn, with sake or cocktails, in the large bar. This is not such a bad thing, though, as the bar is extremely lively—a celeb-studded destination in its own right. The dining room has a sushi bar and a hibachi grill, and the menu includes some newfangled wood-oven dishes that are already on their way to becoming modern classics. *Bar: Mon-Sat 6pm-2am. Restaurant: Mon-Sat 6pm-1am.* ££ ⓑ≡ 15 Berkeley St., W1 (⊖ Green Park), 020-7290-9222, noburestaurants.com

Occo* • Marylebone • Moroccan
This restaurant bills itself as modern Moroccan because its menu offers contemporary twists on traditional dishes, such as cod and prawn brochettes in cumin and ginger jus with fig and orange-blossom purée. The bar at the front offers wonderful North African–themed cocktails like fig Bellinis, and the sunken restaurant, complete with cool chandeliers and sumptuous silky cushions, is located at the back. Both the bar and the restaurant are popular meeting places for a relaxed and chatty after-work crowd. *Mon-Fri noon-3pm and 6:30-10pm, Sat-Sun 10am-4pm and 6:30-10pm.* £ ⓑ≡ 58 Crawford St., W1 (⊖ Edgeware Road), 020-7724-4991, occo.co.uk

Pearl Bar & Restaurant* • Holborn • French
Best Restaurant Lounges Part of the swish Chancery Court Hotel, but with its own separate entrance, Pearl—formerly the Pearl Assurance bank—is beautiful to behold. It has a gleaming tile floor, striking lampshades decorated with long strings of real pearls, a gorgeous bar area with velvet banquettes concealed within walnut alcoves, and handmade tables decorated with mother-of-pearl. The ingredient-led contemporary French food is delicious, and the wine list is one of the best in town. With slinky babes sipping cocktails like Pink Pearl, this gem of a place is deeply sexy, and certainly not for the twinset-and-pearls set. *Bar: Mon-Fri 11am-11pm, Sat 6-11pm. Restaurant: Mon-Fri noon-2:30pm and 7-10pm, Sat 7-10pm.* ££ ≡ Chancery Court Hotel, 252 High Holborn, WC1 (⊖ Holborn), 020-7829-7000, pearl-restaurant.com

Plateau • Docklands • French
This large, bustling Conran-owned establishment is a favorite of the media meritocracy from nearby offices. Perched on the fourth floor of the Canada Place building in Canary Wharf, it overlooks a park with pretty lawns and sculptures. There's a part-open kitchen in the center, with an informal, atmospheric bar and grill on one side, and a less hectic, formal restaurant on the other—each encir-

cled by its own terrace. The restaurant offers modern French fare like rotisserie coquelet with thyme emulsion and black truffle, and the grill serves up salads, seafood, and roast meats. The futuristic glass frontage lets in a lot of natural light—but it's the barbecues held on the terrace in summer that truly capture the taste of sunshine and draw the biggest crowds. *Bar & Grill: Mon-Sat noon-11pm, Sun noon-4pm. Restaurant: Mon-Fri noon-3pm and 6-10:30pm, Sat 6-10:30pm, Sun noon-3pm. ££* ▣= Canada Pl., Canada Sq., E14 (⊖Canary Wharf), 020-7715-7100, conran.com

The Providores & Tapa Room • Marylebone • Tapas

This fashionable fusion establishment is a venue of two halves. The casual ground-floor Tapa Room is a breakfast spot, tapas bar, and wine bar combined—with a great list of international tapas, and London's most imaginative breakfast. The upstairs Providores is a handsome, informal restaurant that's favored by the likes of Paul McCartney, Gwyneth Paltrow, and Madonna. New Zealand–born co-owner and chef Peter Gordon is credited with introducing trendy fusion flavors to London—and the changing menu here features every fashionable ingredient going, and some you never knew existed. Both spaces have a relaxing chocolate-and-cream interior—but the Tapa Room is livelier. *The Providores: Mon-Sat noon-2:45pm and 6-10:45pm, Sun noon-2:45pm and 6-10pm. ££* _ *Tapa Room: Mon-Fri 9-11:30am and noon-10:30pm, Sat 10am-3pm and 4-10:30pm, Sun 10am-3pm and 4-10pm. ££* ▯= 109 Marylebone High St., W1 (⊖Bond Street), 020-7935-6175, theprovidores.co.uk

River Café • Thames Wharf • Italian (G)

Best Al Fresco Dining Housed inside large converted 19th-century warehouses on the Thames Wharf, Ruth Rogers and Rose Gray's Italian restaurant remains one of the most fashionable restaurants in London. Set up in the '80s, it introduced the concepts of seasonal, fuss-free, ingredient-led cooking that are currently all the rage, but that went against the grain of nouvelle cuisine of the time. Large picture windows caress the dining room with natural light, and a highly coveted outside terrace gives lovely views of the garden and the river. *Daily 12:30-3:30pm and 7-11pm. ££* = Thames Wharf, Rainville Rd., W6 (⊖Hammersmith), 020-7386-4200, rivercafe.co.uk

Roast • Bankside • British

London saw this eagerly anticipated British restaurant finally open its doors at the end of 2005. It's perched atop the foodie mecca that's the Borough Market—currently one of London's premier tourist attractions—and serves classic English food (including fabulous roasts), with many of the seasonal ingredients sourced from the market itself. A great way to arrive is by taking a tube to Pimlico, then walking to the bank of the Thames; from there you can take a Tate-to-Tate boat (it's a 20-minute boat journey); then stroll through the market before heading up to the restaurant. Stop in at the small bar at the front that sells a few English wines, oysters, and bar snacks. Then head into the chic, spacious, and bustling dining room that gives a bird's-eye view of the market below. Friday and Saturday lunchtime, when the market is in full swing, is the best time to visit. Customers include contented food shoppers, as well as lawyers from nearby practices. *Mon-Fri 7am-10am and noon-3pm and 5:30-11pm, Sat 11:30am-4pm and 6-11pm. ££* ▯= The Floral Hall, Borough Market, Stoney St., SE1 (⊖London Bridge), 020-7940-1300, roast-restaurant.com

Roka • Bloomsbury • Sushi

Best Sushi The über-stylish younger sister of Zuma, this modern Japanese restaurant specializes in healthy robatayaki cuisine that's based on the use of an open charcoal grill. The centerpiece is a robata grill, surrounded by rough-hewn, chunky wooden counters piled high with beautiful displays of spanking- fresh Japanese fruits and vegetables. Tables are fought over during the day when the local media, fashion, and music industry folk drop by for lunch. The glass walls open onto the street, giving it a casual street party feel in the summer. *Bar (Shochu Lounge, basement): nightly 5pm-midnight. Meals: nightly 5:30pm-midnight.* £ B≣ *Restaurant: Mon-Fri noon-11:15pm, Sun 12:30-10:15pm.* ££ ≣ 37 Charlotte St., W1 (✆Goodge Street), 020-7580-6464, rokarestaurant.com

San Lorenzo • Knightsbridge • Italian

Best Celeb Haunts This polished but casual Italian restaurant has been famous for being a haunt of glitterati for more than 40 years, and still sports the sort of aging glam décor that harks backs to the 1960s. It was once known as Princess Diana's favorite restaurant, and nowadays attracts everyone from rising tennis stars to Madonna and hubby. The crowd includes eminent Knightsbridge lunching ladies and celeb watchers, and the food includes familiar Italian classics like taglierini with prawns and lobster. *Mon-Sat 12:30-3pm and 7:30-11:30pm.* ££ ≣ 22 Beauchamp Pl., SW3 (✆Knightsbridge), 020-7584-1074, sanlorenzo.com

Sardo • Fitzrovia • Sardinian

Sardinia is the new Tuscany—or at least, it is in London, where Sardinian food has replaced Tuscan as the fashionable, must-have regional Italian. And this small, beguiling, homely eatery is the best Sardinian restaurant in town—the sort of place where restaurant critics pay their own money to eat, and in-the-know media folk crowd in for lunch. The menu lists cocktails made from local berry liquor, Sardinian local cheeses, speciality meats, and lesser-known items like malloreddus pasta and dried mullet roe. A sunflower-yellow interior and white-washed frontage guarantee year-round sunshine. *Mon-Fri noon-3pm and 6-11pm, Sat 6-11pm.* £ ≣ 45 Grafton Way, W1 (✆Warren Street), 020-7387-2521, sardo-restaurant.com

Sketch* • Mayfair • International

Best Always-Hot Restaurants London's most extraordinary dining venue is set over two floors. Decorated in a bold, unique, visionary style, it's a colorful, eye-popping extravaganza of food, art, and music. Rock-star chic from floor to ceiling, the bright, eclectic interior is emboldened with changing art exhibitions and multimedia installations. Housed inside are a variety of dining and drinking spaces: first, the Lecture Room and Library, a one-Michelin-star fine dining restaurant with a menu from the internationally famous executive chef Pierre Gagnaire, who's adapted the dishes from his legendary, eponymous three-Michelin-star restaurant in Paris; secondly, an arty brasserie, the Gallery; and thirdly, the Glade, a newer restaurant that offers simple seasonal fare. There's also the Parlour, one of London's best tearooms, with stunning pastries; and finally, a buzzy bar called the East Bar. London's trendiest and most beautiful people swarm the place every night from opening until closing. *The Gallery: Mon-Sat 7-10:30pm.* £££ ≣ *The Lecture Room: Tue-Fri noon-2:30pm and 7-10:30pm, Sat 7-10:30pm* £££ B≣ 9 Conduit St., W1 (✆Oxford Circus), 0870-777-4488, sketch.uk.com

Spoon at Sanderson • Fitzrovia • Fusion

Internationally renowned chef Alain Ducasse introduced SpoonSum at this chic fusion restaurant inside the Sanderson—a new eating concept in which diners can mix and match ingredients to create their own dishes, which arrive on small plates as they're ready. It's been lapped up by the spangly-top-and-Versace-jeans set, who don't seem to mind if their chocolate pizza arrives before their duck foie gras burger. There's also a notable—and totally non-SpoonSum—breakfast menu that features that celeb staple, the egg-white omelette. *Mon-Sat 6:30am-2:30pm and 6-11pm, Sun 6:30am-2:30pm and 6-10pm. Tea: daily 3-5pm. ££* ⓑ= The Sanderson, 50 Berners St., W1 (⊖Oxford Circus), 020-7300-1444, spoon-restaurant.com

Sugar Hut • Fulham • Thai

Evocative of the lavish hedonism of opium dens, this sumptuous modern Thai restaurant and bar has an intimate but pulsating nightclubby ambiance. It's done up in warm jewel colors, and festooned with soft Thai and Moroccan textiles and velvet drapes. Lit with dimmed lights, candles, and lanterns, it's bedecked with antique elephants and dragons, and furnished with low-slung ornate chairs and beds with large cushions. Music- and fashion-industry people come here to see occasional live bands in the evenings. Princes William and Harry, sports stars, pop tarts, boy bands, TV presenters, and supermodels have all dropped by for Thai curries and cocktails. *Tue-Thu, Sun 7-11:30pm, Fri-Sat 7pm-midnight. £* ≡ 374 North End Rd., SW6 (⊖Fulham Broadway), 020-7386-8950, sugarhutfulham.com

Sumosan • Mayfair • Japanese

Best Sushi The purple-and-cream interior of this über-glam contemporary Japanese restaurant and bar is like a cross between the inside of a chocolate box and a cigarette packet. Beautiful Prada-clad "it girls" rub bare shoulders with stars from the pop, film, and sports worlds. Salmon sashimi with strawberry jus, and tuna sushi with truffle oil, are beloved of the hedonistic party crowd—but the must-try dish is tuna and avocado tartare with sevruga caviar, quail's egg, and, yes, more truffle oil. The decadent cocktails are from London's most famous mixologist, Dick Bradsell. *Mon-Fri noon-3pm and 6-11:30pm, Sat 6-11:30pm. ££* ⓑ= 26 Albemarle St., W1 (⊖Green Park), 020-7495-5999, sumosan.com

Tugga • Chelsea • Portuguese

Although there's no dress code, you might want to wear black or white at this informal, vivacious modern Portuguese restaurant. It's a riot of color, with a striking floral wallpaper in hot pink, red, and orange; stripy rainbow banquettes; and lime green, purple, and scarlet chairs—an antidote to ubiquitous minimalism. Glossy, skinny Chelsea babes, music producers, and local property developers love the pesticos (Portuguese tapas) made from salt cod, black pork, and pickled pig's ear. If the latter is a gastronomic adventure too far, you can always head to the lounge bar in the basement, which is popular for its cocktails. *Mon-Sat noon-11pm, Sun noon-10:30pm. £* = 312 King's Rd., SW3 (⊖South Kensington), 020-7351-0101, tugga.com

Umu • Mayfair • Japanese

Best Oriental Restaurants Suffused with wealth, glamour, and elegance, this Japanese restaurant has hit the headlines because it offers London's most expensive set meal: a multi-course kaiseki feast for £250 per person. Yes, you read that correctly. Frequented by billionaire playboys and their impossibly beautiful companions, the restaurant showcases highly elaborate specialist dishes from Kyoto served on handmade pottery, and utilizes specially flown-in ingredients—including water from Kagoshima, in which all the cooking is done. A dark, hand-activated sliding door entrance keeps the riffraff out—and the mystery and intrigue intact. *Mon-Sat noon-2:30pm and 6-11pm.* £££ = 14-16 Bruton Pl., W1 (Θ Green Park), 020-7499-8881

Wizzy • Fulham • Korean

Named after its cheerful female chef-owner—whose nickname really is Wizzy—this is London's first modern Korean restaurant. Most Korean venues in the capital tend to be homely, unassuming family-run eateries, but at this elegant venue decorated in neutral earthy tones, you'll find contemporary dishes like red-bean tiramisu presented beautifully on colorful celadon plates, in wooden boxes, stone bowls, and other striking tableware. Most diners are stylish thirty-something Westerners from nearby offices and gastronomes keen to discover this little-known but upcoming cuisine. *Daily noon-3pm and 6-11:30pm.* £ = 616 Fulham Rd., SW6 (Θ Parsons Green), 020-7736-9171

Yauatcha • Soho • Dim Sum

Owned by Alan Yau, the celebrated restaurateur behind Hakkasan, this chic Chinese eatery is a venue of two parts. The ground floor boasts a relaxed, pretty tearoom, which serves over 60 Chinese teas (including rare varieties), imaginative French-Oriental patisserie, and excellent dim sum. Tucked into the basement is a snazzy cool blue restaurant designed by Christian Liaigre, which serves all-day dim sum (some of the best in London), congee, and other Chinese dishes. Hugely popular with local media types, the restaurant regularly attracts celebrities like Donatella Versace, especially at lunchtime. The restaurant is the best place for lunch or dinner, whereas the tearoom is ideal for Asian-style afternoon tea. *Teahouse: Mon-Sat 11am-11:45pm, Sun 11am-10:30pm. £ - Restaurant: Mon-Fri noon-11:45pm, Sat 11:45am-11:45pm, Sun 11:45am-10:30pm.* ££ = 15 Broadwick St., W1 (Θ Oxford Circus), 020-7494-8888

Zaika • Kensington • Indian

Best Romantic Dining Aptly enough, the name means "good taste," and this acclaimed contemporary Indian restaurant located in a former banking hall has an elegantly romantic ambiance. There's a small, bedouin-style bar at the entrance where Indian-themed cocktails are concocted. The roomy but intimate dining room is done up in warm jewel colors of ruby, amethyst, emerald, and garnet. Carved ornaments, ancient antiques, and beautiful screens are judiciously scattered around. Snappily dressed shoppers, visitors to Kensington Park, and concertgoers from the nearby Albert Hall regularly devour the home-smoked salmon, the biryanis, and the much-imitated chocolate silk dessert. *Mon-Fri noon-2:45pm and 6:30-10:45pm, Sat 6-10:45pm, Sun noon-2:45pm and 6:30-9:45pm.* ££ B = 1 Kensington High St., W8 (Θ High Street Kensington), 020-7795-6533, zaika-restaurant.co.uk

Zetter • Clerkenwell • Italian

This contemporary restaurant inside the coolly minimalist Zetter Hotel is acclaimed for its imaginative regional Italian food cooked with seasonal ingredients. Businessmen and women drop by for cocktails at the curvy black marble bar—and mineral water sourced from its own well beneath the hotel provides a talking point. The chilled, monochrome space also offers delicious pastries for breakfast, snacks, and afternoon tea. Italian-style brunch on Saturdays and Sundays is popular with the dressed-down locals. *Mon-Fri 7am-10:30pm, noon-2:30pm and 6-11pm, Sat 7:30am-3pm and 6-11pm, Sun 7:30am-3pm and 6-10:30pm. Brunch served Sat-Sun 11am-3pm.* £ – The Zetter, 86-88 Clerkenwell Rd., EC1 (⊖ Farringdon), 020-7324-4444, thezetter.com

Zuma* • Knightsbridge • Japanese

Best Always-Hot Restaurants Arguably London's most fashionable restaurant, this sophisticated Japanese venue offers numerous seating options: the main dining room with an open kitchen, a sushi counter with a robata grill, a semiprivate chef's table, a sake bar, and private dining rooms. You would never believe that a soothing, Zen-like interior in neutral stone and wood could contain such activity and buzz. All the fashionable Japanese classics like sushi and sashimi are present and correct, but ordering the off-the-menu chocolate dessert will mark you out as a true regular. Zuma boasts an excellent sake list and the UK's first sake sommelier, both of which are popular with the A-list Hollywood stars, models, soccer players, and the fashion and media crowd that have settled into the place. *Bar: Mon-Sat noon-10:45pm, Sun noon-10:15pm. Restaurant: Mon-Fri noon-2pm and 6-10:45pm, Sat 12:30-3pm and 6-10:45pm, Sun 12:30-3pm and 6-10pm.* ££ B = 5 Raphael St., SW7 (⊖ Knightsbridge), 020-7584-1010, zumarestaurant.com

Hot & Cool London:
The Nightlife

Aka • Covent Garden • DJ Bar

The bar connected to The End club used to be a Victorian mail-sorting office, though you'd never know it from the neon-lit industrial warehouse space it is today. Aka is a loud, friendly, lively drinking joint where people go for pre-club drinks and end up sticking around to dance. The low-lit open seating around the edges and on the mezzanine above are good places to catch the changing DJs, who play everything from deep house to hip-hop. If you get hungry while enjoying any of the 300 spirits, you can order pizza in from the local Pizza Express. This place is usually more than buzzing around 9:30pm. *Tue-Thu 6pm-3am, Fri 6:30pm-5am, Sat 7pm-5am, Sun 10pm-4am.* ⃝≡ 18 W. Central St., WC1 (⊖ Tottenham Court Road), 020-7836-0110, akalondon.com

Akbar • Soho • Restaurant Bar

Indian curries are a favorite of the British, and Soho restaurant Red Fort aims to give an old classic a modern kick. The bar in the basement of this eating establishment works along the same lines. The pillow-filled red bar attracts a varied Soho crowd, including a lot of media types who come after work and on dates. There's a DJ every Thursday through Saturday, though this is a laid-back rather than high-energy dancing venue, with people focusing on their cocktails infused with dates, lemongrass, mango syrup, and ginger. If you need a place to recharge, it's the perfect quiet alcove in this buzzing part of the city. *Mon-Sat 5pm-1am.* ⌐≡ Red Fort, 77 Dean St., W1 (⊖ Tottenham Court Road), 020-7437-2525, redfort.co.uk

The Almeida • Islington • Theater

This beautiful white venue, which fuses classical architecture with minimalist lines, is one of the best theaters in the city, and plays often sell out far in advance here. This is not surprising considering the A-list Hollywood names lining up to perform here—from Kevin Spacey to Gael Garcia Bernal. The directors are equally influential, including the likes of Michael Attenborough, David Hare, and Richard Eyre. Expect high-brow productions such as Tennessee Williams, Sam Shepard, and David Mamet plays with some classic Ibsen and Shakespeare thrown in. *Mon-Sat noon-2:30pm and 5:30-11pm, Sun noon-2:30pm and 6-10pm.* ⃝≡ 30 Almeida St., N1 (⊖ Highbury & Islington), 020-7359-4404, almeida.co.uk

Baltic* • South Bank • Restaurant Bar

Best Restaurant Lounges The bar of this Russian-Polish restaurant doubles as a lively weeknight drinking spot. The white-walled venue is peppered with amber details (conceived by the owner) and features a rather mesmerizing chandelier made of strings, fiber optics, and stones. It's busiest for after-work drinks, especially on Thursday and Friday nights. Although there isn't much space, the lively crowd is here more for loud conversation and great vodka-infused drinks than DJs and dancing. At other times, the bar is an intimate place for long drinks and blinis. *Mon-Sat noon-3pm and 6-11:15pm, Sun noon-10:30pm.* ⌐≡ 74 Blackfriars Rd., SE1 (⊖ Southwark), 020-7928-1111, balticrestaurant.co.uk

HOT & COOL

Below 54 • Hoxton • Restaurant Bar
The colored-glass windows are steamed up every weekend with the hordes crowding into this popular spot. Although there's a quiet bar upstairs for day-time drinking, the downstairs bar of the stylish Asian restaurant only opens on Friday and Saturday nights. The chrome-and-silver room is filled with comfy sofas where a friendly, flirty crowd of Londoners gathers. And it manages to be cool without being intimidatingly edgy. Note that there's a strict dress-down door policy—no ties please. The music is varied but veers toward the electronic and club classics. *Fri-Sat 7:30pm-1am.* ≡ The Great Eastern Dining Room, 54-56 Great Eastern St., EC2 (⊖ Old Street), 020-7613-4545, greateasterndining.co.uk

Below Zero and the Absolut Ice Bar • Mayfair • Bar
Hot or cold? Take your pick at this two-floored space. The Absolut ice bar is as much a city attraction as a packed hit bar. The ice bar is a medium-sized room on the ground floor. Drinkers are given special silver hooded cloaks and mittens to wear before huddling in an ice-walled room, where they can enjoy strong vodka cocktails served in glasses made of ice—the whole experience is very James Bond. Downstairs, in contrast, at Below Zero, you'll find hot and warm colored rooms decorated with animal pelts and nooks filled with beds and pillows for post-snow decadence. The crowd consists largely of an older well-dressed clientele (black tailoring is de rigueur) peppered with young things nodding to the up-tempo funky house. *Sun-Wed 12:30pm-midnight, Thu-Sat 12:30pm-1am.* C= 31-33 Heddon St., W1 (⊖ Oxford Street), 020-7478-8910, belowzerolondon.com

Chinawhite • Soho • Nightclub
You may have to sell your organs to get into this celebrity pick-up joint with lightly trashy overtones. Fridays and Saturdays get very busy with dressed-up weekenders. Weeknights are a slightly classier option, but better get on the list or you'll be turned away. Wednesday members night is the best (and hardest to get into). Once you're in, expect playboys, flirting, and fun in a Balinese-Moroccan interior that has a large dance floor with live acts and a chill-out room filled with pillows. Dress to impress. *Nightly 8pm-3am.* C≡ 6 Air St., W1 (⊖ Piccadilly Circus), 020-7343-0040, chinawhite.com

The Cinnamon Club* • Westminster • Restaurant Bar
This buzzy basement lounge of this restaurant is a stylish spot for a drink. *See Hot & Cool Restaurants, p.63, for details.* = The Old Westminster Library, Great Smith St., SW1 (⊖ St. James's Park), 020-7222-2555, cinnamonclub.com

Cocoon • Soho • Restaurant Bar
Best Cocktails It's hard to get more central than this sushi–dim sum bar off Piccadilly. The orange circular bar at the back of the modernist restaurant is constantly buzzing with models, other stylish locals, and high-energy house music. The brilliantly mixed cocktails are impossibly delicious with Asian-fused flavors—expect lots of passion fruit and lychees mixed with vodka and champagne, while the almond martini is imperative. Friday nights are currently the hot night to come for pre-clubbing drinks. Be sure to book as there isn't much seating for drinkers. *Mon-Wed noon-3pm and 5:30pm-midnight, Thu-Fri noon-3pm and 5:30pm-3am, Sat 5:30pm-3am.* = 65 Regent St., W1 (⊖ Piccadilly Circus), 020-7494-7600, cocoon-restaurants.com

Crazy Bear • Fitzrovia • Bar

Best See-and-be-Seen Spots There's no obvious signage outside this amazing bar—it doesn't need it. Downstairs from a tasty Asian restaurant, Crazy Bear is one of the best bars in London. The staff is delightful and attentive, and the whole vibe is very relaxed. Hip writers, advertising types, and actors enjoy the great whiskey list and mouthwatering Bellinis in a refreshingly inventive interior. There's a shining copper bar, low cowhide seating, and intimate red-leather caves ideal for intimate conversation alongside the upbeat house music. Crazy Bear is very popular, so it's best to book in advance. *Mon-Fri noon-midnight, Sat 6pm-midnight.* ☰ 26-28 Whitfield St., W1 (⊖ Goodge Street), 020-7631-0088, crazybeargroup.co.uk

CVO Firevault • Fitzrovia • Bar

Whoever thought of this bar definitely has a creative streak. The basement of this designer fireplace shop doubles as an immensely popular lounge bar and restaurant. The comfy suede sofas create a warm setting that is perfect for intimate chats and used by all the local PRs for business meetings. Apart from having lots of open fires, naturally, the look is all soothing creams and browns. There are lovely bar snacks and fine cocktails and wine. Being here is a bit like living in the pages of *Wallpaper. Mon-Sat noon-11pm.* ☰ 36 Great Titchfield St., W1 (⊖ Oxford Circus), 020-7636-2091, cvo.co.uk

Eclipse • Chelsea • Bar

This perennially buzzing bar is nestled on one of London's most picturesque streets. The two-room lounge space attracts well-dressed Italian aristocrats, groups of groomed blondes, and pretty boys in suits on dates. The low-lit white space is filled with anthemic house music and has just the right amount of intimacy to feel sexy but not overcrowded. If you want a seat, be sure to phone and reserve a table. The fresh fruit cocktails are mouthwatering, with juicy watermelon and pineapple slices poking out of elegant martini glasses. Come around 7pm for the start of the buzz. *Mon-Fri 5:30pm-1am, Sat 2pm-1am, Sun 2pm-12:30am.* ☰ 111-113 Walton St., SW3 (⊖ South Kensington), 020-7581-0123, eclipse-ventures.com

Embassy • Mayfair • Nightclub

Embassy may be in Mayfair, but it isn't the sort of staid place you'd expect in this neighborhood. Instead, it's a noisy, boisterous weekend spot. On the ground floor, there's a small restaurant facing onto the street that attracts couples and large groups, as well as a very noisy dark-wood bar with a few tables and some standing room. Downstairs is the club, which veers strongly toward danceable commercial music à la Beyoncé. If you want a good dance and some flirting, this is a great place to settle in. Book online to get on the guest list, though that won't stop you from having to stand in line with dressed-up weekenders. *Tue-Fri noon-3pm and 6-11:30pm, Sat 6-11:30pm.* ☰ 29 Old Burlington St., W1 (⊖ Oxford Circus), 020-7851-0956, theembassygroup.co.uk

The End • Covent Garden • Nightclub

Best Dance Clubs What do you get when two superstar DJs open a club? The answer is The End, the electronic music haven owned by DJs Mr C and Layo. Over a decade old and still going strong, The End has maintained a cutting-edge music program with lots of techno, drum 'n' bass, and hard house. There's also a brilliant bootleg sound-clash night on Mondays and a super-stylish gay R&B and disco night on Thursdays. The venue is split between a chill-out room with a small dance floor and lots of sofas, and a giant main room where the DJ does his thing in an island at the center of the room. Be sure to pop to Aka next door for a pre-party drink, and don't bother showing up before midnight. *Mon 10pm-3am, Wed 10:30pm-3am, Thu, Fri 10pm-6am, Sat 11pm-7am.* C≣ 18 W. Central St., WC1 (⊖ Tottenham Court Road), 020-7419-9199, endclub.com

Freedom • Soho • Gay Bar

Soho bars have their ups and downs. Freedom was one of the hottest gay bars in Soho in the '90s but slumped. These days it's having a revival and attracts a mixed straight and gay crowd who want to sit on animal-print seats and sip great cocktails. The friendly staff pay special attention to concocting excellent drinks. There's a basement dance floor playing lots of funky house that is refreshingly friendly. If you like clubs without too many pretensions, you'll feel comfortable getting sweaty down here. *Mon-Sat 5pm-3am, Sun 5-10:30pm (cover charge after 10:30pm on weekends).* C= 66 Wardour St., W1 (⊖ Oxford Circus), 020-7734-0071

Heaven • Covent Garden • Gay Club

Best Gay Bars and Clubs If you're gay, you've almost definitely heard of Heaven. This is arguably the most famous gay club in the world and it's been running for 27 years. The giant three-floor club has a space for everyone, though usually the ground floor is mainstream and upbeat, the second floor sexier and darker, and the top floor loungey and more chilled. This club is all about meeting people and dancing your shoes to dust. Music changes each night but there's lots of pop, house, and R&B among the friendly crowd. Even if you're straight, you won't feel out of place. *Mon, Wed, Fri-Sat 10:30pm-6am.* C≣ Villiers St., Under the Arches, WC2, (⊖ Charing Cross), 020-7930-2020, heaven-london.com

Itsu • Chelsea • Restaurant Bar

Itsu gives a modern lounge twist to the classic conveyor-belt sushi restaurant. Its Chelsea branch is always lively and surprisingly unpretentious considering the location. It also has the secret bonus of an upstairs bar. Expect to find a lot of women meeting in this upstairs space—which consists of two dark cushion-filled window tables and a long line of high mini-tables for twos. The simple and clean drinks include sake and champagne cocktails—the blackberry-infused Black Beauty is particularly lovely. You can't book, but things move almost as quickly as the sushi downstairs. *Mon-Sat noon-11pm, Sun noon-10pm.* ⌐ ≣ 118 Draycott Ave., SW3 (⊖ South Kensington), 020-7590-2400, itsu.co.uk

Jazz Café • Camden • Jazz Club

Best Live-Music Venues Every big name in soul, hip-hop, and jazz you could ever think of has played this great Camden venue. One night it's De La Soul, the next it's Maceo Parker. The venue itself is not large, so there's always a pleasantly intimate atmosphere. The décor is a bit '80s, but no one cares, preferring to dive in and dance to the fabulous music. The jazz funk nights on weekends also bring their own enthusiastic multi-age crowd. If you want class rather than sweat, book a meal upstairs for a superb view of the stage from a narrow balcony. *Nightly 7pm-2am.* C≣ 5 Parkway, NW1 (⊖ Camden Town), 020-7534-6955, jazzcafe.co.uk

Kabaret's Prophecy • Soho • Nightclub

Best Bar Interiors If it's good enough for Madonna, it's good enough for anyone. This small club in Soho has the most mesmerizing walls in London. Made from grids of light, they pulse different patterns or neon color in time with the music.

It's like dancing in an MTV video. The crowd ranges from urban glam on Mondays to posh Chelsea types on Thursdays and Fridays to your usual dressed-up crowd from the suburbs on Saturdays. The cocktails are mouthwatering—leave it to the bartenders to create something you like. Be sure to call and get on the guest list in advance. *Mon-Sat 11pm-3am.* C≡ 16-18 Beak St., entrance on Upper John St., W1 (⊖Oxford Circus), 020-7439-2229, kabaretsprophecy.com

Kensington Roof Gardens • Kensington • Nightclub

Kensington Roof Gardens are exactly what they sound like—opulent gardens on the rooftop of a large building in Kensington. They even have real flamingos here among the beautiful foliage! The best part is that it also has a louche indoor club at night. You can expect to find the champagne flowing, R&B playing, and lots of dancing. It's part high glamour and part outrageous meet market. There's also a restaurant here if you want to start early. Note that you have to plan ahead if you want to come here. It's guest list only, and the dress code is stylish trendy. Boys will only be allowed in with girls or mixed groups—a more and more common requirement in clubland these days for lone wolves. Plan to come around midnight for the height of the scene. *Fri-Sat 10pm-3am.* C⎼≡ 99 Derry St., W8 (⊖High Street Kensington), 020-7937-7994, roofgardens.com

Kilo • Mayfair • Nightclub

Downstairs from the very buzzy, very stylish restaurant by the same name is a dark bar with one of the best sound systems in Mayfair. The bar attracts 30-year-olds who stumble down after a raucous dinner or an intimate date for some post-food fun. The sleek and modern décor features black seating and red graphic stools. The friendly and attentive staff serves great straight cocktails—and the Bellinis are extra peachy with fresh fruit purée. A lot of girls come here to smile at suited boys and enjoy the vocal and piano house. Strike while it's still new and hot. *Daily noon-3am.* ≡ 3-5 Mill St., W1 (⊖Oxford Circus), 020-7629-8877, kilo-mayfair.co.uk

The Lansdowne • Primrose Hill • Pub

Best Pubs The Lansdowne is the epicenter of the Primrose Hill set. Expect Oscar-nominated actors, cult celebs, music moguls, and directors to be sitting at the tables in this converted Victorian pub. The large room has a high ceiling and windows looking onto a lovely residential street. Laid-back and music-free, this venue is often packed and most likely roaring with conversation in the evenings. The rich pan-European food and handmade pizzas attract a lot of groups, though there's a great wine list and selection of drinks if you're not hungry. *Mon-Sat noon-11pm, Sun noon-10:30pm.* ≡ 90 Gloucester Ave., NW1 (⊖Chalk Farm), 020-7483-0409

Light Bar • Covent Garden • Hotel Bar

The luminescent entrance to St. Martin's Lane Hotel leads directly to the candlelit Light Bar, allowing passersby to glimpse the dramatically glistening bar from the street. As it's designed by Philippe Starck, you can expect a large dose of humor, with alcoves filled with photos of people making funny faces. The muted gray-and-purple bar with low tables is meant for hotel guests, so call ahead to get on the guest list. DJs play Latino house Thursday to Saturday to a media crowd that loves the mojitos. The Light Bar sells over 33,000 of them a year … *Mon-Sat 5:30pm-3am, Sun 5:30pm-midnight.* ⎼≡ St. Martin's Lane Hotel, 45 St. Martin's Ln., WC2 (⊖Leicester Square), 020-7300-5500, stmartinslane.com

Ling Ling at Hakkasan* • Bloomsbury • Restaurant Bar
Best See-and-be-Seen Spots People are more than happy to cram into the long narrow bar of this fabulous restaurant every night of the week. Even on a Tuesday night it's busy and bustling. Ling Ling at Hakkasan has got everything—gorgeous décor, fabulous drinks, and beautiful clientele. It often draws off-duty lawyers, ad men, and City types with dates or clients. The ultra-long metal bar has stools on one side and a Japanese-style black decorative wall divider on the other against which the chic crowd leans while sipping lemongrass martinis and a delightful rum, champagne, and cinnamon concoction called a Jasmine FonFon. *Mon-Sat 5:30pm-3am, Sun 5:30pm-midnight.* ≡ 8 Hanway Pl., W1 (⊖ Tottenham Court Road), 020-7907-1888

Lobby Bar • Covent Garden • Hotel Bar
If you're in theaterland, this is the only bar you need to know about. The pre- and post-theater crowds and a stylish local after-work gang fill up the spacious, high-ceilinged room quite early. There are very few tables and chairs, so expect to stand if they aren't available. The bar has immaculate service, an elegant array of cocktails, and lovely spiced nuts and sushi to nibble alongside your drinks. Note that late-night drinking is for hotel guests only. *Mon-Sat 9am-midnight, Sun 9am-10:30pm.* – ≡ One Aldwych, 1 Aldwych, WC2 (⊖ Covent Garden), 020-7300-1000, onealdwych.co.uk

Long Bar • Fitzrovia • Hotel Bar
Best Singles Scenes The Sanderson's lush white main bar is just what it sounds like—long. This is the best Schrager hotel in the city, and the bar is one of the most buzzing. It's very easy to end up chatting with the dressed-up guests and locals any time, but Thursday and Friday evenings are extra busy. In the summer, the outdoor courtyard that's full of trees and water features is a real pull and offers a touch of Miami-style glamour. The cocktails are fabulous—leave it to the barman to create something for you on the spot. = *Mon-Sat 11am-1am, Sun 11am-10:30pm.* The Sanderson, 50 Berners St., W1 (⊖ Oxford Circus), 020-7300-1496, sandersonlondon.com

The Lonsdale • Notting Hill • Cocktail Bar
The best cocktail bar in the area is hidden in a residential side street near Westbourne Grove, and posh Notting Hillbillies all congregate here nightly. The space is slickly designed with purple UV lighting highlighting the gray interior with a penchant for circles—there are circular tables, circles cut out on the ceiling, and circles sticking out like bubbles on the walls. The drinks are fabulous—the Polish martini, which fuses vodka, krupnik, and apple juice, is particularly notable. There's also a very long wine list defined by accessible categories like "big, bold, and spicy" or "round and elegant." *Mon-Thu 6pm-midnight, Fri-Sat 6pm-1am, Sun 6pm-11:30pm.* – ≡ 44-48 Lonsdale Rd., W11 (⊖ Westbourne Park), 020-7727-4080, thelonsdale.co.uk

Mash • Fitzrovia • Restaurant Bar
Mash gets busy in waves—first after-work fashion, marketing, and PR types, then suits and party people. The white bar has lots of curved lines highlighted by deep pink. At the back you can see the workings of the microbrewery that creates beer on-site (though there is a tasty limited selection of cocktails if you prefer). On Fridays, DJs play funk and soul, and there's an urban award–nominated R&B and

hip-hop night on Saturdays. There's table service if you're lucky to get (or reserve) one, though lots of people are happy just to stand and socialize loudly. *Mon-Sat 11am-2am.* ◾ 19-21 Great Portland St., W1 (✦ Oxford Circus), 020-7637-5555, mashbarandrestaurant.com

Match • Marylebone • Bar

Match was one of the pioneers of London cocktail culture when it opened—and was so successful that it was quickly followed up with bars in Farringdon and the City. Nowadays it's quieted down a bit and is more likely to attract office workers simply looking for post-work drinks. It's a lively, straightforward place, and very inviting. The gray metallic interior and sofas are pretty much what you'd expect, but the cocktails can still pack a punch. There are also large bowls of food that are meant to be shared—emphasizing this bar's goal to be a dynamic place for social lubrication. *Mon-Sat 11am-midnight.* ◾ 37-38 Margaret St., W1 (✦ Oxford Circus), 020-7499-3443, matchbar.com

Met Bar • Mayfair • Members Bar

This bar was notorious in the '90s as the spot where celebrities drunkenly stumbled out the door into waiting paparazzi. It's not quite as popular these days, but it still has a great cocktail list and still attracts some of the less famous celebs, which makes for some amusing name-dropping. The small, dark bar has a hotel-bar style interior with lots of deep-red leather banquettes. It's members only after 6pm, so getting in is a miracle for your average Joe—best phone first for the list (you just might get lucky). If you feel like nibbling, you can order Nobu bento boxes here from upstairs. *Daily 11am-6pm, Members 6pm-2:30am.* –≡ Metropolitan London, 18-19 Old Park Ln., W1 (✦ Hyde Park Corner), 020-7447-1000, metropolitan.co.uk

Ministry of Sound • South Bank • Nightclub

Once upon a time, Ministry was known as the best club in London. It was one of the first big monsters to arrive in the early '90s, and its emblazoned bomber jacket was everywhere. Today, it's a giant brand, record label, and industry. The club itself has an outstanding sound system and still gets very crowded. House music still dominates Saturdays, but the club is becoming more experimental with some fresh international heads like Jazzy Jeff, Grandmaster Flash, and Basement Jaxx. It's extra-popular these days with twenty-somethings and students. Be sure to get a cab here, as this place is in the middle of nowhere. *Wed 10pm-3am, Fri 10:30pm-5am, Sat 11pm-7am.* ℂ≡ 103 Gaunt St., SE1 (✦ Elephant and Castle), 0870-060-0010, ministryofsound.com

Movida • Soho • Nightclub

It's hard to believe that beneath the rather cheesy Palladium theater is Movida, a very exclusive and very buzzy club all decked out in hot pink. The music veers toward house from DJ Vittorino, who plays Flavio Briatore's Billionaire's Club. The women are every type as long as they're blonde—party girls, Sloanes, or Russian models. The men are all aristo or moneyed types in suits or designer shirts. It's a members bar, but phone to see whether you can be put on the guest list. Or turn up looking the part and try your luck, as a limited number can pay entry. It's all very Monaco. Wednesday night is the current evening du jour for giant sparklers and bottles of champagne. *Wed-Sat 10:30pm-3:30am.* ℂ≡ 8-9 Argyll St., W1 (✦ Oxford Circus), 020-7734-5776, movida-club.com

Nectar • Chelsea • Bar

A newcomer to Fulham, Nectar fits in well with the affluent British and South African crowd that goes wild in the area most nights. This spot is all about the sweet stuff—honey. It has a selection of special honey cocktails that have to be tasted, as well as vodka shots laced with spoons of Manuka honey. Excellent DJs play '80s and '90s classics alongside great house and disco, which suits the retro wallpaper. The fun and lighthearted place is ideal for energetic groups—especially after work and on weekends. There's also a buzzing terrace outside in summer. *Sun, Tue-Thu noon-midnight, Fri-Sat noon-2am.* ≡ 562 Kings Rd., SW6 (⊖ Sloane Square), 020-7326-7450, nectarbar.co.uk

Nobu Berkeley* • Mayfair • Restaurant Bar

This more informal branch of Nobu has an extremely lively, celeb-studded bar. *See Hot & Cool Restaurants, p.68, for details.* ≡ 15 Berkeley St., W1 (⊖ Green Park), 020-7290-9222, noburestaurants.com

Occo* • Marylebone • Restaurant Bar

Try a fig Bellini and mezze at the popular bar of this Moroccan restaurant. *See Hot & Cool Restaurants, p.68, for details.* = 58 Crawford St., W1 (⊖ Edgeware Road), 020-7724-4991, occo.co.uk

Opal • South Kensington • Restaurant Bar

The bar at this French-Asian fusion restaurant is a great spot for drinks and relaxation. The loungey space draws small groups who share platters of Asian food and special four- to eight-person glasses for shared cocktails. Expect some expertly prepared drinks such as a lychee champagne number called Opal Fizz or a gin and sake Niten Mojito with Shizo leaves (whatever they may be...). The space livens up after 10pm with Latin, soul, and R&B DJs. It's best to get on the list ahead of time to ensure entry. *Tue-Sat 7pm-2:30am.* – ≡ 36 Gloucester Rd., SW7 (⊖ Gloucester Road), 020-7584-9719, etranger.co.uk

Opium • Soho • Nightclub

It's no surprise that this Soho hot spot has an Asian edge—though it restricts itself to the décor with a few wooden screens and some tasty Vietnamese food. When Opium first opened, created by the same people behind Paris's infamous Buddha Bar, it was very, very hot. These days it's a little more mainstream, but at least that means people can get in. The nights vary from house on Tuesdays for City boys to slick R&B for the urban set on Thursdays, and the vibe in general is very flirtatious, lubricated by top-notch cocktails. Getting on the guest list is highly recommended. *Mon-Fri 5pm-3am, Sat 7pm-3am, Sun 8pm-3am.* ⊂ – ≡ 1a Dean St., W1 (⊖ Tottenham Court Road), 020-7287-9608, opium-bar-restaurant.com

Pacha • St. James's • Nightclub

Not content with being one of the biggest clubs in Ibiza, Pacha decided to journey to colder climes and open a venue across from Victoria Station. This indoor spot is smaller than the Spanish giant and has red drapes, warm leather seats, and a lot of style. The sounds are largely glam house for a loyal group of young clubbers and out-of-towners who like the slick look. The best night is the eclectic monthly Hed Kandi, though Defected and Kinky Malinki won't disappoint people wanting to dance the night away. *Fri 10pm-5am, Sat 10pm-6am.* ⊂ ≡ Terminus Pl., SW1 (⊖ Victoria), 020-7833-3139, pachalondon.com

Pangaea • Mayfair • Nightclub

Best Singles Scenes Mayfair is lined with bars and clubs these days, but Pangaea is definitely the best of the lot. This expensive but upbeat club is packed with a wealthy clientele. Even the younger, wilder set of British royalty likes to pop in. The luxury of a table costs at least £1,000, so be prepared. The vibe, however, is hedonistic, lighthearted, and very friendly. Expect lots of house music, European soccer players, and financiers, all enjoying a decadent night to a backdrop of African tribal drumming that complements the masks that cover the dark interior. Definitely phone ahead to get your name on the list. *Wed-Thu 10pm-3am, Fri-Sat 10pm-4am.* C ≣ 85 Piccadilly, W1 (⊖ Green Park), 020-7495-2595, pangaeauk.com

Pearl Bar & Restaurant* • Holborn • Restaurant Bar

With slinky babes sipping cocktails like Pink Pearl, this gem of a place is deeply sexy. *See Hot & Cool Restaurants, p.68, for details.* ≣ Chancery Court Hotel, 252 High Holborn, WC1 (⊖ Holborn), 020-7829-7000, pearl-restaurant.com

The Player • Soho • Cocktail Bar

The entrance to The Player is just a small door tucked away on a small street. It leads to a dark drinking den pumping out house, soul, and whatever appeals to the Soho record-shop DJs that play here. The one-room space has low seats and lower lighting, and the crowd gets dancing as the night progresses. There's no signature drink, but the bar staff are very good at helping you get what you want. Whatever people have, they tend to have a lot of it. The place gets packed with a sexy twenty- and thirty-something crowd Thursday to Sunday who can fall into drunken dancing. It's essentially a members bar with selective entry for nonmembers, so it's best to phone ahead to get on that list in case. *Mon-Wed 5:30pm-midnight, Thu-Fri 5:30pm-1am, Sat 7pm-1am.* ≣ 8 Broadwick St., W1 (⊖ Tottenham Court Road), 020-7494-9125, thplyr.com

Purple Bar • Fitzrovia • Hotel Bar

The Purple Bar is much quieter than the perennially packed Long Bar, the other bar at the Sanderson. The intimate purple-lit room is reserved for hotel residents and a small guest list, so be sure to phone in advance to get on the list. Even at its busiest, it's quite civilized as all guests are seated. Designed by Philippe Starck, this distinctly sexy spot sparkles with Venetian cut-glass mirrors and contemporary furnishings, all against a backdrop of electronica. The perfect setting for vodka cocktails and celebrity spotting, this is definitely a date space rather than crowded hub. *Nightly 6pm-3am.* C – ≣ The Sanderson, 50 Berners St., W1 (⊖ Oxford Circus), 020-7300-1496, sandersonlondon.com

Refuel • Soho • Hotel Bar

Refuel is the latest hotel bar to draw West End crowds. The seating is limited, but the vantage point from the olive-leather high chairs at the long metal bar is perfect for people-watching, so hold out for a seat. The painted graphic mural behind the bar is a bit much during the day, but looks less dazzling in the orange glow at night. This bar is always busy, but never overwhelming. Friday nights are a good bet for extra buzz. The wine list is worth a mention here—it's long, varied, and well chosen. It's no surprise that this is a favorite of the classy but laid-back clientele who gather here. *Mon-Sat 7am-11pm, Sun 8am-10:30pm.* ≣ The Soho Hotel, 4 Richmond Mews, W1 (⊖ Tottenham Court Road), 020-7559-3000, sohohotel.com

Rockwell Bourbon Bar • Westminster • Hotel Bar

Though the Rockwell is very stylish, its hotel bar attracts a surprisingly unpretentious and varied crowd of tourists, PRs, and suits—when it's not putting on parties for Beyoncé and Kevin Spacey. The monochromatic décor features low white tables and black tasseled lights. The basement bar and restaurant is darker, with black seating and a more intimate vibe. There are 120 bourbons on the menu, but for those who don't like the hard stuff, try the rose petal martini. Check the hidden bar on the roof with a spectacular view overlooking Trafalgar Square to Westminster (only open in the summer). *Mon-Sat 8am-1am, Sun 8am-10:30pm.* = The Trafalgar, 2 Spring Gdns., SW1 (⊖Charing Cross), 020-7870-2959, trafalgar.hilton.com

Shochu Lounge • Fitzrovia • Cocktail Bar

Fed up with vodka? Want something other than sake? Try Shochu, a Japanese distilled spirit at this cocktail bar devoted to it. The taste of shochu itself is something that has to be acquired, but this gray-and-wood lounge bar has a generous selection of other cocktails. Midweek, this is a date place where couples often get a little too friendly in public. Later in the week, it's more of a buzzing restaurant bar with banging house music. Bar snacks are small but tasty. Getting in can be tricky—the man at the door is rather unfriendly, so be ready to turn on the charm. Dressing sharp is a must. *Mon, Sat 5:30pm-midnight, Tue-Fri noon-midnight.* _ ≡ 37 Charlotte St., W1 (⊖Goodge Street), 020-7580-6464, shochulounge.com

Sketch* • Mayfair • Restaurant Bar

If you don't get to dine here, come for a drink at the buzzing East Bar and check out the rocker chic scene. *See Hot & Cool Restaurants, p.70, for details.* = 9 Conduit St., W1 (⊖Oxford Circus), 0870-777-4488, sketch.uk.com

Sosho • Hoxton • DJ Bar

The Sosho name plays with its off-Shoreditch location—it's "so Shoreditch," get it? This dark DJ bar with a large dance floor gets the City boys in after work. Warm leather seating and music every night make it a lively date-friendly option. Original cocktails invented by in-house bartenders include exciting options like the Fa'afafene, a combination of vodka, honey, lime, and apple juice. The refurbished lounge space downstairs, often used for private parties, is particularly worth checking out for intimate conversation. Strangely, the venue is especially popular with the underground warehouse party crowd that doesn't want to sleep on a Sunday night and does want to dance. *Mon noon-10pm, Tue noon-midnight, Wed-Thu noon-1am, Fri noon-3am, Sat 7pm-4am, Sun 9pm-4am.* C _ ≡ 2 Tabernacle St., EC2 (⊖Old Street), 020-7920-0701, sosho3am.com

Taman Gang • Mayfair • Bar

Best See-and-be-Seen Spots Nestled at the Marble Arch end of Park Lane is this exclusive and delightful subterranean bar and restaurant. It's a fantastical place to drink, with a décor consisting of Asian architectural details, carved stone walls, floating orchids, and low lighting. It attracts a stylish and festive crowd that likes the low-key loungey house music playing in the background. Expect lots of unusual cocktails with inventive ingredients and a dose of flowers thrown in. This is the perfect bar to impress a date, have fun with a mate, or just enjoy a plate. *Mon-Sat 6pm-1am.* = 141 Park Ln., W1 (⊖Marble Arch), 020-7518-3160, tamangang.com·

Umbaba • Soho • Nightclub

It is impossible not to see the African influence in Umbaba. The walls resemble adobe huts hand-painted with brown-and-white African-influenced graphics. Hookahs sit on every table, and the seats are covered with cushions. The waitresses are even dressed in sexy colonial-style shorts outfits that leave little to the imagination. It all makes a nice change of scene from the rest of the bar world—glamorous without disco lighting. This super-exclusive nightclub draws a surprisingly young crowd of very dressed-up boys and girls spending their parents' millions. The drinks are adequate (and there are £950 bottles of champagne if that appeals), but Umbaba is really all about high-energy partying with lots of music and dancing. Don't even think about not booking ahead. *Thu-Sat 10pm-3am.* C ≡ 15-21 Ganton St., W1 (⊖ Oxford Circus), 020-7734-6696, umbaba.co.uk

Woody's • Notting Hill • Bar

This converted working men's club may sit on the rather less savory outskirts of Notting Hill, but the interior is pure style. There is lots of dark purple, deep red lighting, leather seats, and a busy dance floor on two of the club's three floors. The DJs change often, and the music is funky, soulful, and fresh, with a smattering of classics. A lot of locals come here—the bar is owned by a group of West London boys—and the vibe is very friendly. Be sure to phone to get yourself on the list. *Thu 9pm-3am, Fri 8pm-3am, Sat 9pm-3am, Sun 10pm-2am.* C ⌐ ≡ 41-43 Woodfield Rd., W9 (⊖ Westbourne Park), 020-7266-3030, woodysclub.com

Zander • St. James's • Restaurant Bar

Victoria is largely a no-man's-land when it comes to good drinking holes, but Zander is a refreshing beacon in the area. At 48 meters long, the bar is the longest in the world. The minimalist but obviously spacious bar serves premium spirit cocktails to a stylish crowd after work. It also attracts a lot of clubbers on their way to the club Pacha, and DJs spin lounge music on Thursdays, soulful house on Fridays, and pre-club classics on Saturdays. *Mon-Tue 5:30-10:45pm, Wed-Sat 5:30pm-1am.* ⌐ ≡ 45 Buckingham Gate, SW1 (⊖ St.James's), 020-7379-9797, bankrestaurants.com

Zeta • Knightsbridge • Nightclub

Wander off the quiet confines of Park Lane and you'll discover some heavy action at this warm-toned, subtly Asian-themed bar. The place really comes to life on Friday and Saturday nights with a very merry crowd dancing to soulful funky house and the latest MTV-friendly R&B party tunes. (Saturdays can be harder to get in—so phone ahead to get your name on the list). Expect anyone from men in black shirts necking £400 bottles of Cristal and party girls decked out in clubwear to the occasional dressed-down international youth in T-shirt and trainers. The alcohol is here to be drunk, definitely not savored. *Mon-Tue 5pm-1am, Wed-Sat 5pm-3am.* ≡ 25 Hertford St., W1 (⊖ Knightsbridge), 020-7208-4067, zeta-bar.com

Zuma* • Knightsbridge • Sake Bar

Check out the sake bar at this über-stylish restaurant. Zuma boasts an excellent sake list and the UK's first sake sommelier. *See Hot & Cool Restaurants, p.73, for details.* ≡ 5 Raphael St., SW7 (⊖ Knightsbridge), 020-7584-1010, zumarestaurant.com

Hot & Cool London:
The Attractions

Agua Bathhouse Spa • Fitzrovia • Spa

Best Spas Stepping into the Zen-like calm of Agua is almost relaxation enough. This pure white space is divided up by ceiling-to-floor curtains instead of walls, creating a dreamlike atmosphere. Even greater levels of serenity await those who try Agua's signature treatment, inspired by ayurvedic techniques. The blissful Milk and Honey involves a soothing all-over application of warm sesame oil and honey, which is then removed with hot milk, and finished off with the lightest of body oils. Afterward, there are quiet curtained-off armchairs (with personal TV screens) for restorative napping. *Daily 9am-9pm.* ££££ The Sanderson, 50 Berners St., W1 (⊖ Oxford Circus), 020-7300-1414, sandersonlondon.com

Aime • Notting Hill • Shop

Londoners in search of Gallic style come to Aime. The two-floor shop was opened by French-Cambodian sisters Val and Vanda Heng-Vong in 1999, and has loads of Paris style with super-stylish womenswear and accessories from labels like APC, Isabel Marant, Les Prairies de Paris, and Claudie Pierlot. There are also housewares, candles, CDs, and earthy ceramics that will transform a home into the Parisian garret of your dreams. *Mon-Sat 10:30am-7pm.* 32 Ledbury Rd., W11 (⊖ Notting Hill Gate), 020-7221-7070, aimelondon.com

Borough Market • Bankside • Market

Best Markets To the coolest city-dwellers, food is no longer just food, it's a lifestyle choice. Nowhere is this more obvious than at Borough, where on Fridays and Saturdays, under a Victorian canopy, producers from all around the country sell high-end edibles to moneyed townies: everything from organic bacon and in-season game to French pâtés and Spanish sweetmeats. The incredible success of the gourmet market has transformed the whole area, with foodie stores and chic cafes popping up all around. The nightly wholesale fruit and vegetable market, which has been here since 1756, is patronized by many top chefs. *Fri noon-6pm, Sat 9am-4pm.* Southwark St., SE1 ⊖ (London Bridge), 020-7407-1002, boroughmarket.org.uk

British Airways London Eye • South Bank • Sight

The views from within this marvelous giant Ferris wheel are—weather permitting—inspirational even for those who've lived here all their life, and especially magical around sunset as the city's lights flicker on. However, you don't have to ride in it to appreciate the spare beauty of its metallic curves, which rise above the otherwise angular skyline from a multitude of different angles. Designed as a temporary structure to mark the millennium, it has rapidly become as much a symbol of London as the equally "temporary" Eiffel Tower is of Paris. *Daily 10am-8pm (June-Sept 10am-9pm).* ££ Next to County Hall, Westminster Bridge Rd., SE1 (⊖ Westminster), 0870-500-0600, ba-londoneye.com

Broadgate Ice • The City • Sports

Best Fresh Air Experiences The original, and still the one with the longest season, this outdoor skating rink in the heart of the Square Mile has been a yuppie winter playground for more than 20 years. It may not be as large or as scenic as some of London's newer outdoor rinks, but that's not as important as being able to take your spin in the company of City slickers, then recover with them in the champagne bar a mere glide away. Should your skills need a brush-up, expert tuition is available from Friday to Monday. *Late-Oct–mid-Apr only, Mon-Thu noon-2:30pm and 3:30-5:30pm, Fri noon-2:30pm, 3:30-6pm, and 7-9pm, Sat-Sun 11am-1pm, 2-4pm, and 5:30-7pm.* No credit cards. £- Broadgate Circle, Eldon St., EC4 (⊖ Liverpool Street), 020-7505-4068, broadgateice.co.uk

Cath Kidston • Marylebone • Shop
Cath Kidston has based her career on a vintage style brimming with delicate florals and sweet country-style prints. Her Marylebone flagship sells everything pastel, polka-dotted, and rose-printed you could ever want, including teapots, kids' clothing, stationery, towels, radios, wallpaper, and bed linen. She even created a floral tent—a must-buy for high-class festivalgoers. The whole vibe is very British, like a 1940s gem rather than the international blockbuster brand it has become. *Mon-Sat 10am-7pm, Sun 11am-5pm.* 51 Marylebone High St., W1 (⊖ Bond Street), 020-7935-6555, cathkidston.co.uk

Contemporary Applied Arts • Fitzrovia • Art Gallery
If their tagline "Promoting the Best of British Craft" conjures up visions of knitted tea cozies and patchwork cushions, prepare to be pleasantly surprised. CAA's gleaming white gallery—itself an award-winning design—contains a covetable selection of cutting-edge and colorful ceramics, textiles, furniture, jewelry, glass, and more. If you can't find quite the right sculptural vase or luminous glass bowl for your Manhattan loft or Santa Monica beach house, you can commission exactly what you're looking for from one of the 200 strictly vetted craftspeople on the gallery's books. *Mon-Sat 10:30am-5:30pm.* 2 Percy St., W1 (⊖ Tottenham Court Road), 020-7436-2344, caa.org.uk

Cork Street • Mayfair • Art Galleries
The phrase "Cork Street" has been synonymous with art dealing for as long as anyone can remember—unsurprising, perhaps, given its location behind the Royal Academy of Arts—and it remains the first port of call for anyone interested in buying works by 20th-century artists. Set cheek-by-jowl along "gallery row," the constantly changing window displays are tantalizing and wonderfully varied: anything from Paolozzi's etiolated sculptures to kitschy canvases by the hottest rising star of the week, and the occasional late-19th-century Impressionist masterpiece. *Various, but generally Mon-Sat 10am-6pm, Sun 10am-2pm.* Cork St., W1 (⊖ Green Park)

Dalí Universe • South Bank • Art Museum
The black-painted introductory corridors are more like those at a theme-park attraction than an art gallery, which is entirely appropriate at this permanent exhibition dedicated to one of the 20th-century's best-known showmen. There are more than 500 Dalí drawings and lithographs, pieces of furniture, and especially sculptures on display, including the Mae West sofa and lots of melting clocks. Downstairs, the Modern Masters Room has small rotating shows by other stars of the previous century. Want to take one home? There's a print room where you can buy original works by Dalí, Picasso, and Chagall, among others. *Daily 10am-6:30pm (last admission 5:30pm).* £- County Hall Gallery, Westminster Bridge Rd., SE1 (⊖ Westminster), 020-7620-2720, daliuniverse.com

Design Museum • Bankside • Museum

London's shrine to all things design looks as if it landed here direct from a chic 1930s seaside resort, an effect only heightened by the riverside location of the gleamingly white former banana warehouse. Inside, up an unprepossessing stairwell, are two floors devoted to the best of modern design, with changing displays relating to everything from packaging to graphics and from hats to chairs. Weekdays can be busy with school groups; Saturday mornings are more tranquil, though for a bit more buzz, the regular evening talks are worth checking out. *Daily 10am-5:45pm (last admission 5:15pm).* £- Shad Thames, SE1 (⊖ London Bridge), 0870-909-9009, designmuseum.org

Diverse • Islington • Shop

Diverse started off as the first high-end boutique to vamp up Upper Street, when it opened way back in 1986. It is now a mini-Islington empire with a menswear shop and even a hairdresser under the Diverse umbrella. As the name suggests, Diverse is all about individual style. This means well-chosen, unusual pieces from designers with major price tags like Missoni and Marc Jacobs, as well as gems from more reasonable Sonia Rykiel and APC. *Mon-Sat 10:30am-6:30pm, Sat 12:30-6pm.* 294 Upper St., N1 (⊖ Angel), Womenswear: 020-7350-8877; Menswear: 020-7359-8877, diverseclothing.com

Elemis day-spa • Mayfair • Spa

Best Spas Tucked away in a Mayfair mews, this compact day spa is a chic retreat in the heart of the city. Everything contributes to the atmosphere of calm, from the delicious scents wafting through the reception area to the exotic décor of the treatment rooms. But it's the treatments themselves, using Elemis's own products, that keep glamorous Londoners coming back for more. The Visible Difference Facial fully lives up to its name, the Exotic Frangipani Body Nourish Float is beyond relaxing, but for complete sensory indulgence try one of the Rituals—Balinese, Moorish, or Thai—for four-and-a-half hours of bliss for one or two. *Mon-Thu 9am-9pm, Fri-Sat 9am-8pm, Sun 10am-6pm.* ££££ 2-3 Lancashire Crescent, W1 (⊖ Bond Street), 0870-410-4995, elemis.com

Estorick Collection of Modern Italian Art • Islington • Art Museum

Appearances can be deceiving. Few passersby would guess that this Georgian house contains some of the world's finest examples of 20th-century Italian art. Brooklyn-born Eric Estorick developed a passion for Futurism during his travels in Europe after the Second World War, and spent most of the 1950s buying as much modern Italian art as he could. And here it all is: Boccioni's haunting *Modern Idol*, Carrà's enigmatic *Leaving the Theatre*, and Balla's dynamic *The Hand of the Violinist*, along with drawings by Modigliani and lesser-known names. The informal talks on Saturday afternoons (3pm) provide an insight into exhibited works. *Wed-Sat 11am-6pm, Sun noon-5pm.* £- 39a Canonbury Sq., N1 (⊖ Highbury & Islington), 020-7704-9522, estorickcollection.com

Getty Images Gallery • Fitzrovia • Art Museum

The images lining the walls of this clean-cut, industrial-chic space represent the work of many of the world's leading photographers, and cover a multitude of subjects and styles. The clientele is just as varied: everyone from photography students looking for inspiration, to interior designers looking to strike just the right classy-but-contemporary note with their finishing touches, to cool media types looking for a moody shot from the archives for their oh-so-trendy offices. The only shame is that the gallery isn't a little bit larger. *Mon-Wed, Fri 10am-6:30pm, Thu 10am-7:30pm, Sat noon-6pm.* 46 Eastcastle St., W1 (⊖ Goodge Street), 020-7291-5380, hultongetty.com

Hayward Gallery • South Bank • Art Museum

Best Modern Art Spaces The brutalist concrete edifice was controversial from the moment it was erected in 1968, and its major exhibitions of the best in contemporary art continue to be thought-provoking. Recent shows at this sizable and uncluttered space have included "Universal Experience," a refreshing look at tourism through the eyes of 50 international artists, and a retrospective of American fluorescent-light artist Dan Flavin, illuminating in both senses of the word. Fittingly, the Hayward's most distinctive external feature is in a similar vein—a multicolored neon sculpture that embellishes the roofline. *Mon, Thu, Sat, Sun 10am-6pm, Tue-Wed 10am-8pm, Fri 10am-9pm. Main galleries closed between exhibitions.* £- Belvedere Rd., SE1 (⊖ Waterloo), 020-7921-0813, hayward.org.uk

Lisson Gallery • Marylebone • Art Gallery

Since its opening in 1967, Nicholas Logsdail's Lisson Gallery has grown in both stature and size to become one of the leading names in the world of contemporary art. The enviable list of hot-and-happening international artists whose work has graced this minimal white space includes sculptors Richard Deacon and Anish Kapoor, along with Julian Opie, perhaps best known for his funky multimedia portraits. They're not afraid to take risks on up-and-coming names, however; Lisson New Space at No. 29 is reserved for bright young things. *Mon-Fri 10am-6pm, Sat 11am-5pm.* 29 & 52-54 Bell St., NW1 (⊖ Edgeware Road), 020-7724-2739, lisson.co.uk

Millennium Bridge • The City/Bankside • Sight

The newest pedestrian bridge over the Thames was opened by the Queen to great acclaim in June 2000, its glittering steel and aluminum structure creating a "blade of light" that connected venerable St. Paul's Cathedral on the north bank with the hulking Tate Modern on the south. Alas, looks aren't everything. Within three days of opening, it was forced to close again, thanks to its alarming sway, which earned it the epithet "the wobbly bridge." Fortunately, the subsequent modifications have cured the problem without taking away from the simple grace of the walkway, from which there are superb views, especially on moonlit nights. Across the River Thames between Bankside and the City (⊖ Blackfriars), arup.com/millenniumbridge

My Chocolate • Notting Hill • Activity

Chocolate brings out the best in people, so signing up for a short workshop dedicated to teaching people how to make their own is surely a heaven-sent occasion for meeting Londoners in their sunniest mood. It's not all tasting; there's a spot of educational stuff about the origins of the cocoa bean and how it's turned into the finished product. But after that it's sweet indulgence all the way, tasting the handiwork of experts or making your own to take home in a pretty ribbon-tied box. *Wed, Sat 6:30-9pm, Sun 10am-12:30pm and 2-4:30pm.* ££££ 41a Linden Gdns., Notting Hill Gate, W2 (⊖ Notting Hill Gate), 020-7792-6865, mychocolate.co.uk

Oxo Tower Wharf • South Bank • Shopping

This former meat-processing factory, with its best-known product—Oxo stock cubes—forever commemorated on its distinctive tower, is one of London's most ingenious redevelopments. The construction of an external two-story arcade and an inner galleried courtyard created 33 small but bright studio-cum-shops, which are now occupied by some of Britain's most talented young designer-makers. Imaginative and high-quality jewelry, lighting, funky clothing, furniture, and more are all on sale. But if you're not in the mood for buying, the gallery@oxo on the ground floor has rotating exhibitions of contemporary art and design. *Most shops Tue-Sun 11am-6pm.* Bargehouse St., SE1 (⊖Blackfriars), 020-7401-2255, oxotower.co.uk

Ozwald Boateng • Mayfair • Shop

Savile Row has long been a byword for classic fine tailoring for men. But snappy dressers who appreciate old-fashioned quality but want their clothes designed with a dash of witty sophistication head around the corner to London's coolest couturier. Inside the shop—all dark wood and deep red, a clever play on traditional décor—is the ready-to-wear range, impeccably cut and beautifully styled. The ultimate treat, though, is the bespoke service, where you can have a handmade suit created to fit your lifestyle and personality as well as your body. *Mon-Wed, Fri-Sat 10am-6pm, Thu 10am-7pm.* 9 Vigo St., W1 (⊖Piccadilly Circus), 020-7437-0620, ozwaldboateng.co.uk

The Photographers' Gallery • Covent Garden • Art Gallery

It may be small as galleries go, but the same cannot be said for its reputation as a leading venue for photography exhibitions. Founded in 1971, it can justifiably claim to have achieved its aim of making the newer art form more accessible through a dynamic range of exhibitions and events. Jacques-Henri Lartigue and Irving Penn had their first UK showings here, and the gallery continues to highlight the work of well-known artists as well as nurturing new talent. The bookshop is one of the largest in Europe. *Galleries & bookshop Mon-Wed, Fri-Sat 11am-6pm, Thu 11am-8pm, Sun noon-6pm. Print sales gallery closed Sun-Mon.* 5 & 8 Great Newport St., WC2 (⊖Leicester Square), 020-7831-1772, photonet.org.uk

Prescott & Mackay • Mayfair • Activity

Shoe junkies should hotfoot it to one of Prescott & Mackay's weekend courses, where they will spend two rewarding days designing and making their very own, one-of-a-kind pair. Held in premises just off Bond Street, the two-day workshops promise plenty of one-on-one attention, the chance to be creative in a thoroughly practical way, and the opportunity to mingle with some of London's high-flying women in relaxed mode. Other weekend offerings include handbags, soft or structured, if you want something that will never be seen on the arm of a Z-list celebrity. *Two or three weekends a month, 10am-6pm.* ££££ 74 Broadway Market, W1 (⊖Bond Street), 020-7923-9450, prescottandmackay.co.uk

Rollerstroll • Hyde Park • Activity

Best Fresh Air Experiences "London's second greatest free event," as the organizers modestly describe it, is a terrific way to get some exercise, see the city, and meet a young and upbeat bunch of international Londoners, everyone from City whiz kids to Euro-chic business-school graduates. This Sunday-afternoon group skate is shepherded by volunteer marshals along a pre-arranged route. Anyone who can stop on a slope is welcome, but you skate at your own risk—no suing if you have an accident. There are skate-rental shops nearby: see links on the website for details. *Sun 2-3:30pm.* Hyde Park, W1 (⊖ Hyde Park Corner), rollerstroll.com

Royal Academy of Arts • Mayfair • Art Museum

The Royal Academy's Piccadilly base was once the imposing house of the refined Lord Burlington, and it remains a cultural hot spot, thanks to the quality and scale of its rotating exhibitions. In the past, these have included Tutankhamen's treasures, art and artifacts from the Chinese Imperial Court, and Impressionist painters such as Monet. Few are aware of the Royal Academy's own collection of British art, highlights of which are displayed in the newly restored John Madejski Fine Rooms, a sight in themselves. On Friday evenings the main galleries stay open late, with live music in the lobby. *Sat-Thu 10am-6pm, Fri 10am-10pm; John Madejski Fine Rooms: Tue-Fri 1-4:30pm, Sat-Sun 10am-6pm.* JM free, exhibitions £-. Burlington House, Piccadilly, W1 (⊖ Green Park), 020-7300-8000, royalacademy.org.uk

Skandium • Marylebone • Shop

This emporium to Scandinavian design is a mecca for those who like to fill their home and kitchen with clean modernist pieces. The two floors sell Finnish glassware, Marimekko textiles, Swedish ceramics, and stunning furniture and lighting made from natural materials from birch to cork. Even those who know little about the clean, curved lines of Scando-design will find something to delight on these shelves. Practical objects never looked so beautiful. *Mon-Wed, Fri-Sat 10am-6:30pm, Thu 10am-7pm, Sun 11am-7pm.* 86 Marylebone High St., W1 (⊖ Bond Street), 020-7935-2077, skandium.com

Smythson • Mayfair • Shop

With a flourish of color and wit, this long-established stationer has reinvented itself to become one of London's coolest, classiest shops—all the more remarkable in the age of PDAs and BlackBerrys. Gwyneth Paltrow, Madonna, Harvey Keitel, Liv Tyler, and Catherine Zeta-Jones are just a few of the famous faces to discover a taste for their hot-pink leather passport covers (US ones as well as British), neat baby-blue travel wallets, iconic Fashion Diary, and simply adorned correspondence cards. Fortunately, the store also sells handbags to put them all in. *Mon-Tue, Fri 9:30am-6pm, Thu 10am-7pm, Sat 10am-6pm, Sun noon-5pm.* 40 New Bond St., W1 (⊖ Bond Street), 020-7629-8558, smythson.uk

Somerset House • Covent Garden • Sight/Art Museum

From rarely seen government offices to fabulous public space surrounded by three glorious art collections, Somerset House has been reborn in spectacular style. In summer, the central courtyard with its lively new fountains is a favorite spot for coffee al fresco or for occasional movie screenings; a fashionable ice rink occupies the space in midwinter. As for the art—aside from the variety of temporary shows—the glittering Gilbert Collection is devoted to gold and silver, the Hermitage Rooms have rotating shows from the famous St. Petersburg museum, and the Courtauld Institute boasts Impressionist and Postimpressionist works. *Daily 10am-6pm (last admission to collections 5:15pm).* £- The Strand, WC2 (⊖ Temple), 020-7845-4600, somerset-house.org.uk

Tate Modern • Bankside • Art Museum

Best Modern Art Spaces The conversion of a disused power station into a showcase for the Tate's huge collection of international modern art has been even more of a triumph than anyone could have hoped. Beyond the vast Turbine Hall—a fabulously dramatic entrance—its spacious galleries filled with important and often challenging works from the 20th and 21st centuries are permanently abuzz with art-loving visitors. Among the array of names, some stand out: Picasso and Warhol, for instance. But really, it's the sheer diversity of the pieces in the permanent and temporary exhibitions that pulls in the crowds. *Sun-Thu 10am-6pm (last admission to exhibitions 5:15pm), Fri-Sat 10am-10pm (last admission to exhibitions 9:15pm).* £- Bankside, SE1 (⊖ Southwark), 020-7887-8000, tate.org.uk

Tate to Tate • Bankside • Service/Activity

The colorful spots that adorn the nippy catamaran connecting the two Tates by water should give the game away: the designs for its decoration, inside and out, were specially commissioned from none other than Brit Art star Damien Hirst. This handy boat service, launched in 2003, also stops at the London Eye, making it not only an immensely practical tool for fitting more culture into your day, but also a stylish platform from which to admire riverside landmarks such as the Houses of Parliament and South Bank Centre. *Check online as timetables vary seasonally.* £- Between Millbank Pier and Bankside Pier, (⊖ Pimlico/ ⊖ Southwark), 020-7887-8888, tate.org.uk

2 Willow Road • Hampstead • Historic Home

Architect Ernö Goldfinger designed this Modernist house—a rare find in the UK—as his family home in 1939, and it remains as it was when the Goldfingers left it, complete with its contents. With its clean lines and imaginative use of materials, light and space, it was far ahead of its time, which may explain why it seems so fresh to modern eyes. As for those contents, Goldfinger also designed much of the furniture, including some surprisingly comfortable curvy wooden chairs. On the walls are works by Goldfinger's equally creative friends, such as Max Ernst and Marcel Duchamp. *Late-Mar–late-Oct Thu-Sat noon-5pm, Mar and Nov Sat only, noon-5pm.* 2 Willow Rd., NW3 (⊖ Hampstead), 020-7435-6166, nationaltrust.org.uk

Hip London

There's more to life than dressing to the nines, and no one does dressed-down style better than Londoners. You know what we mean: jeans that are just the right cut and color; this week's must-have sneakers, boots, or flip-flops; clothes from the market where all the edgy young designers peddle their wares. The same goes for the places where these fashion-savvy hipsters like to hang with their friends. They may not be glitzy, but it doesn't mean no one's given a thought to the décor: That "just-thrown-together" look takes work to get right. The same goes for the drinks and food: simple, unfussy, but delicious. London has lots to offer along this line. You just have to know where to look. And right here, we'll tell you everything you need to know to get started.

Note: Venues in bold are described in detail in the listings that follow the itinerary. Venues followed by an asterisk (*) are those we recommend as both a restaurant and a destination bar.

Hip London:
The Perfect Plan (3 Nights and Days)

Perfect Plan Highlights

Thursday

Pre-dinner	**Loungelover, Zigfrid**
Dinner	**Bistrotheque*, Fifteen**
Nighttime	**Bistrotheque***
Late-Night	**333, Cargo, Mother Bar**

Friday

Morning	**Fashion & Textile Museum**
Lunch	**Bermondsey Kitchen**
Afternoon	**National Film Theatre, Institute of Cont. Arts**
Pre-dinner	**ICA Bar**
Dinner	**Wapping Food, Eagle**
Nighttime	**Annex 3, Lucky Voice**
Late-Night	**Guanabara, Bar Italia*, Fabric**

Saturday

Morning	**Ottolenghi, Portobello Market**
Lunch	**Cow Dining Room***
Afternoon	**Karma Kars, Cowshed**
Pre-dinner	**Under the Westway**
Dinner	**E & O*, Electric Brasserie**
Nighttime	**Notting Hill Arts Club**
Late-Night	**The Key**

Sunday

Morning	**Brick Lane, Spitalfields Market**
Lunch	**Hoxton Apprentice**
Afternoon	**Whitechapel Art Gallery, Big Chill Bar**

Hotel: **Great Eastern Hotel**

Thursday

6pm You've arrived and the up-to-the-minute nightspots of London are right on your doorstep. So where better to start than **Loungelover**, blessed with eclectic décor, seriously fine cocktails, and a youthful party crowd? Alternatively, **Zigfrid** is the acme of hipness in already achingly hip Hoxton.

8pm Dinner Cab it to **Bistrotheque***, one of the city's trendiest restaurants set in an industrial-chic space in the edgy Hoxton area. Alternatively—if you can get in—eat funky Mediterranean food, people-spot, *and* do your bit for charity at **Fifteen**, brainchild of celebrity chef Jamie Oliver. All the young chefs are from disadvantaged backgrounds, and profits go toward training more. Kitsch rules the décor at **Les Trois Garçons**, but the media-savvy crowd lingers there for the sparklingly updated French cuisine, too.

10:30pm If you've dined at **Bistrotheque***, then you'll easily be able to stroll down the stairs to make it in time for the supremely camp cabaret at its buzzing bar, or just to sample the fresh-fruit caipirinhas in arty company.

1am Nearby **333** will keep you moving with three floors of serious dancing. Or check out what's on at **Cargo**, one of the city's premier live-music venues, for dancing.

3am Still not ready to call it a night? Head up to the **Mother Bar**, conveniently located on the top floor of 333 to wrap up the night with a pint and a flirt.

Friday

10am Set yourself up for an action-packed day with breakfast at your hotel—which, at the Great Eastern, means a proper "fry-up" or divine muesli in the relaxed, low-key brasserie Terminus.

11:30am Head over to the South Bank to check out the current show at the small—but never dull—**Fashion & Textile Museum**.

12:30pm Lunch Just down the road, the **Bermondsey Kitchen** has an easygoing vibe, where you can chill out with tapas and other Spanish-influenced dishes after a busy morning. If you've an appetite for art as well as food, **Delfina** began as a canteen for artists, but is now a vibrant lunch spot for bohemian locals.

2pm Work off lunch with a stroll along the South Bank to the **National Film Theatre**, where you can snuggle down to watch anything from rarely screened silent classics to gems of world cinema. Linger in the bar at the end, and

you'll find yourself in conversation with some dedicated cineastes. If nothing on the NFT schedules tempts, **Urban Golf** in Soho has more screens—but these ones show your perfectly placed real ball heading for a virtual hole. No need to rush off afterward for a drink; the fashionably black-clad staff can rustle up anything you want.

5pm The **Institute of Contemporary Arts** (ICA) is a famous iconoclast in the heart of royal London. This exciting venue has been at the cutting edge for years, thanks to an innovative program of screenings, talks, and performances. After checking out the works on display, settle in for a drink in artsy company at the popular **ICA Bar**, which is as much of a draw as the art itself.

8pm Dinner Cab it out to the up-and-coming Docklands area to the east to feast at **Wapping Food** on blissful modern European food in the unlikely environment of a former power station—it's well worth the journey. If you'd rather stay in town, the **Eagle** is one of the city's original gastropubs and attracts a lively young bohemian crowd. Otherwise, the nearby **Eagle Bar Diner** offers the tastes of home with a grown-up London spin if you really crave a burger and a peanut-butter martini.

10:30pm Continue the Friday night revels at **Annex 3**, a much-talked-about destination bar within shouting distance of the

Eagle Bar Diner. Come to admire the over-the-top décor, listen to disco music, and eye the gorgeous boys and girls. Another option is to flex your vocal chords in select company at **Lucky Voice**, a short walk away in Soho. Several A-listers have been seen sipping cocktails and warbling with friends in the private booths of this stylish karaoke club.

Midnight It's time to check out the Brazilian festivities at **Guanabara**, where the infectious music will have you strutting your stuff in no time.

2am Take a breather at **Bar Italia***; this cult coffeehouse is open 24 hours a day, making it a magnet for night owls of all varieties.

3am If you can't bear for the night to end, cab it to **Fabric**, where nonstop music can keep you grooving until dawn.

Saturday

10am Go west for a full day in boho-chic Notting Hill, kicking off with breakfast at **Ottolenghi**, a glorious little cafe-cum-deli with fabulous pastries and a suitably designer-dressed-down clientele.

11am When you've finished your coffee and browsed the bulging Saturday papers, **Portobello Market** beckons. It's one of the largest and most fashionable markets in London, with everything from fine antiques to quirky clothing from up-and-coming designers, though it's as much a case of see-and-be-seen as shop-'til-you-drop.

1:30pm Lunch Join a relaxed crowd of Notting Hillbillies—as the hip young locals are nicknamed—at the **Cow Dining Room***, a deservedly popular gastropub with a fine line in modern European cooking. Another option is **Food @ The Muse**, where you can feast on Asian-inspired dishes surrounded by contemporary art (it doubles as a gallery).

3pm Time to give your feet a treat. Give **Karma Kars** a call, and it'll whisk you off in one of its opulently kitsch vintage Ambassador cars from India for a memorable customized tour: avant-garde art, quirky attractions, whatever you want.

5pm Book in your paws for a pampering pedicure at **Cowshed**, the urban offshoot of the original spa at achingly trendy Babington House in Somerset.

7pm As evening falls, join the West London creatives on the guest list at **Under the Westway**. This hard-to-find airy space surrounded by studios is the best place around for a drink and a quick game of pool. In the mood for something a bit more colorful? Tiki triumphs at **Trailer Happiness**, which means vintage cocktails served up with a large dose of good-humored kitsch and a superb range of rums.

HIP

8:30pm Dinner Sample exquisite pan-Asian food at **E & O***, where the décor is as stylish as the model-designer-actor customers. For heartier fare, the **Electric Brasserie** serves classic dishes from around Europe to a starry and animated crowd of diners. Up the road, **Notting Hill Brasserie** is a more restful experience, with live jazz and blues to soothe the soul (and a great line in seafood).

10:30pm Move on to the **Notting Hill Arts Club**, where a varied rota of DJs and live bands keep the music going to the early hours.

1am Cab it to **The Key**, where a thriving and colorful disco scene and 24-hour drinks license can keep you going until dawn and well beyond.

Sunday

10am Grab breakfast to go at the **Brick Lane Beigel Bake**, whose smoked-salmon-and-cream-cheese confections are a London legend (though you might want to give the hot drinks a miss).

11am Refueled, cruise the boutiques along Brick Lane, where you can pick up quirky jewelry, clothes, and housewares, as well as enjoying a caffeine hit at one of the chilled cafes. From here, it's the shortest of strolls to **Spitalfields Market** for more retail splurging on one-off designs, but this time under cover.

1pm Lunch If all that shopping, or the sheer weight of people, has tired you out, then **Hoxton Apprentice** will refresh your spirits with a combination of good Mediterranean-style food and good deeds (chefs from disadvantaged backgrounds). Alternatively, **Canteen** is the new star on the block, winning rave reviews for its straightforward British cooking—pies, copious breakfasts, and flavorsome stews—and unfussy appearance.

3pm Have a cultural epiphany at the **Whitechapel Art Gallery**, just beyond Brick Lane. It's been a groundbreaker for more than a century, and its rotating exhibitions of international modern art are still something to cheer about.

5pm Afterward, mooch back around for lazy afternoon drinks at the **Big Chill Bar**. As relaxed as its name suggests, this super-hip bar is the perfect place to wrap up your weekend in style—listen to music, sip a last pint or two, and chat up the friendly crowd of fellow hipsters.

Hip London:
The Key Neighborhoods

Hoxton, on the northern fringes of the financial district, teems with artists and other creative types attracted by the (relatively) low rents. At its heart is Hoxton Square, home to groovy cafes, avant-garde galleries, and laid-back eateries.

Notting Hill appeals to boho Londoners and international celebrities of the dressed-down persuasion: Think Sienna Miller, Kate Moss, and so on. This is largely thanks to its heady mix of quirky boutiques, cool-and-casual bars and cafes, and excellent-but-relaxed restaurants. Jeans, of the right label of course, are de rigueur. Portobello Road is the venue for a varied and unmissable weekend market.

Spitalfields lies in the shadow of the Square Mile's gleaming skyscrapers, but with its streets of early Georgian houses could hardly be more different. At its heart is the old Victorian market, which draws huge crowds at weekends, and the multicultural delights of Brick Lane, home to curry houses and funky boutiques.

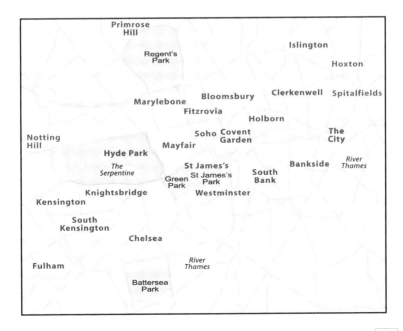

Hip London:
The Shopping Blocks

Cheshire Street, E2

The cream of East London shops clusters together on this strip off Brick Lane.

Beyond Retro This giant vintage clothing emporium at the far end of Cheshire Street is a tribute to dressing up. 110-112 Cheshire St., 020-7613-3636

Labour and Wait This temple of 1940s-style retro living sells enamel kitchenware, gardening goodies, and stripey sweaters. 18 Cheshire St., 020-7729-6253

Mimi Come for the edgy but very wearable leather handbags and purses. 40 Cheshire St., 020-7729-6699

Shelf This delightful gift shop carries European artworks, ceramics, and unusual creative ephemera. 40 Cheshire St., 020-7739-9444

Newburgh Street, W1

This cobbled lane is where Soho creatives go for fashionable inspiration.

Beyond the Valley This mini DIY concept store sells artwork and designs from London art graduates. 2 Newburgh St., 020-7437-7338

Bond International This laid-back men's shop is filled with street styles from Stussy, Alife, and Silas. 17 Newburgh St., 020-7437-0079

Cinch This design shop carries rare vintage Levis, art, and unusual Adidas. 5 Newburgh St., 020-7287-4941

The Dispensary This edgy women's boutique has lots of rare little labels, including the highly desirable Mine. 8 Newburgh St., 020-7287-8145

Jess James This shop carries jewelry and designs from 60 contemporary and precious jewelers. 3 Newburgh St., 020-7437-0199

Seven Dials, WC2

Seven streets converge on this roundabout in the back streets of Covent Garden.

Coco de Mer This is the shop for lingerie and erotica for women and men of discerning taste. (p.121) 23 Monmouth St., 020-7836-8882, coco-de-mer.co.uk

Koh Samui Stock up on sexy womenswear like Balenciaga and a few jewels as well. 65-67 Monmouth St., 020-7240-4280

Magma This always-packed bookshop specializes in design, art, photography, and magazines. (p.123) 8 Earlham St., 020-7240-8498

Poste Mistress This women's shoe shop carries everything from Converse to Westwood boots. 61-63 Monmouth St., 020-7379-4040

Stussy This is the UK flagship of the iconic streetwear label. Best for the boys. 19 Earlham St., 020-7836-9418, stussystore.co.uk

Hip London:
The Hotels

The Great Eastern Hotel • The City • Trendy (267 rms)

The location alone makes this one of the hippest hotels in the city. A stone's throw from edgy and happening Hoxton, the Great Eastern attracts trendsetters, big-name celebrities who want to avoid attention (Kate Moss, Jennifer Aniston), and businesspeople who like to walk to work. The original hotel was built by the same architects who built the Houses of Parliament, but when Terence Conran reopened the GE in 2000, he added modern touches, including minimalist rooms with a clean masculine edge. This is high luxury that walks the perfect line between sexy boutique design and modernist minimalism. The large rooms are beautifully laid out, and the hotel is always filled with changing contemporary art exhibitions and installations. There are also four restaurants, one of the trendiest members bars in the city (not always open to guests), and an original Victorian Masonic lodge. Be sure to ask for a room facing out on the fifth and sixth floors, which have giant round porthole windows overlooking the City. There are whimsical amenities for guests, including a brilliant video library with cult films; a magazine shop in the lobby with an impressive selection of international style magazines like *i-D* and *Wallpaper*; and a CD library that is so hip even a DJ would be impressed. The in-house guest relations teams are also happy to help you with anything you need—from restaurant reservations to theater tickets to booking your flight home. £££ Liverpool St., EC2 (⊖ Liverpool Street), 020-7618-5000, great-eastern-hotel.co.uk

Guesthouse West • Notting Hill • Modern (20 rms)

Originally built as a family home, this small boutique hotel is a relative newcomer. An antithesis of big, overpriced hotel chains, it offers a modern take on the old-fashioned British bed and breakfast. Guesthouse has ties with neighborhood businesses, and the idea is to live in a simple but comfortable space and blend in with the locals. A no-frills breakfast of pastries, toast, and cereal is included in the cost. The small rooms have clean lines, warm colors, unfussy black-and-white linen, en-suite bathrooms, soft white towels, and Molton Brown toiletries. The most attractive is Room 3, which has a skylight that can be opened, as well as a four-poster bed. There's also a small bar and lounge area for guests that leads to a terrace and gardens. Services include tailor-made personal shopping trips, in-room massage and beauty treatments, personal training sessions, and a guided tour of London with a personal Bentley driver. £ 163-165 Westbourne Grove, W11 (⊖ Notting Hill Gate), 020-7792-9800, guesthousewest.com

The Main House • Notting Hill • Modern (7 rms)

Russian princesses, Japanese pop stars, LA film producers, French novelists—and the odd business traveler—have all stayed at this award-winning venue that's the first of a new breed of guesthouses. A narrow white Victorian townhouse belies the spaciousness within. Each of the four rooms and three suites is appended with a balcony. The first and second floors are best, with one suite per floor, while the top floor has two single rooms, a sitting room, and a shared shower. They're uncluttered, simply decorated in creams and whites, and furnished with large, comfy beds, antiques, and quirky artifacts from Portobello Road. The hotel is not state-of-the-art: there's internet, for instance, but no broadband. Organic continental or English breakfast is available—and special rates have been negotiated at nearby Tom's Delicatessen as well as Lambton Place health club. Other services include shoe repairs, bicycle rental, and chauffeur pick-up. There's no bar or restaurant, but drinks are available upon request. Portobello Market, boho designer shops, art galleries, restaurants, bars, clubs, theaters, parks, and museums are all nearby. £ 6 Colville Rd., W11 (⊖ Notting Hill Gate), 020-7221-9691, themainhouse.co.uk

Miller's Residence • Notting Hill • Timeless (8 rms)

Miller's Residence is not really a hotel so much as a decadent home with beautiful rooms for rent. This is for visitors looking for something truly unusual. Hidden behind a subtle red door is an Aladdin's cave. The overwhelming interior is a veritable den of antiques—every wall space is covered, every surface displays something—from 17th-century porcelain to 18th-century sedan chairs to Dutch 16th-century paintings. Owner Martin Miller is best known for his iconic series of *Antique Price Guides* and his own rather delicious gin. The eight rooms are each named after Romantic poets and are filled with paintings and antiques, and enhanced by mood lighting. The Byron Room, with its warm yellow Regency furniture and four-poster bed, is especially attractive. Most often the rooms are occupied by regulars—often actors, artists, musicians, and writers—who like the laid-back vibe. Guests are given their own key to the front door and allowed to help themselves to the free bar. There's no room service but there's a nice continental breakfast in the morning. This is definitely the place for those looking for the antithesis of an impersonal, sterile hotel experience. £ 111a Westbourne Grove, W2 (⊖ Notting Hill Gate), 020-7243-1024, millersuk.com

myhotel Chelsea • Chelsea • Modern (45 rms)

Located in a peaceful residential street in the very exclusive Brompton Cross area of Chelsea near trendy shops and restaurants, this fashionable hotel has the feel of a contemporary country house. It's designed according to the principles of feng shui and Eastern philosophy, with crystals and buddhas in many of its rooms. There's a large, quiet, and very purple cocktail bar where guests can relax on designer chairs and order from a new menu of Asian-style bento boxes. The hotel's goal is to offer an individually tailored stay, so before arrival, visitors are sent a preference form on which they can indicate their choice of music, scent, and so on. The rooms are quietly glamorous, decorated in soft pinks with specially designed furniture. The sexiest ones are the ruby and scarlet rooms. Exotic teas and coffees are available, along with complimentary newspaper, magazines, and Aveda toiletries. There's a jinja spa, a free gym, and a fantastic conservatory with library where books, CDs, and DVDs can be borrowed. Sightseeing tours and nights out can be arranged by the hotel. ££ 35 Ixworth Pl., SW3 (⊖ South Kensington), 020-7225-7500, myhotels.co.uk

The Portobello Hotel • Notting Hill • Timeless (24 rms)

These days the word "townhouse" is bandied about willy-nilly when it comes to London's hotels—but this neoclassical Victorian mansion terrace is London's first townhouse boutique hotel, located in a quiet street near Portobello Market, cool shops, and restaurants. The Portobello's design is stunning, eccentric, quirky—and definitely sexy. The drawing room has scarlet drapes and potted palms, and the bedrooms are done up in eclectic style with four-poster beds and deep luxuriant baths. All rooms, particularly superior rooms, are special—but "the round bedroom" is more special than others on account of its round bed and Victorian bathroom. The hotel is co-owned by the romantic Julie's restaurant, where you can get a 10 percent discount as a guest. Complimentary evening membership at the renowned private members club, the Cobden Club, is also available, and the nearby Lambton Place health club offers swimming pool, sauna, steam room, gym, and hairdressing. Other facilities include a 24-hour bar and restaurant (open only to hotel guests), cell phone rental, and courier service. Little wonder the hotel is popular with actors, models, musicians, writers, poets, and fashionistas—Kate Moss, Gwyneth Paltrow, U2, and Kylie, to name but a few. £ 22 Stanley Gdns., W11 (⊖ Notting Hill Gate), 020-7727-2777,   portobello-hotel.co.uk

The Zetter • Clerkenwell • Modern (59 rms)

Zetter's décor is quite unique, reflecting the area's reputation as the place to be for designers and architects who like quirky details. The design blends clean curved lines with unusual retro furniture, vintage wallpaper displayed as art, secondhand books, and highlights in bright orange. The medium-sized rooms have a minimalist modern edge, spiced up with retro details. The best rooms are undoubtedly on the top floor, with each of the seven studios there boasting private terraces with stunning views of the city's rooftops. Although the area is quiet, it is an ideal midpoint between the West End and East London. The hotel's bright modern Italian restaurant does a great breakfast (and lunch and dinner). Memorable features include vending machines for emergency champagne or toothpaste on each floor—in addition to room service of course. There's also a great interactive TV service, which includes an on-screen guide to the local area and internet access. £ 86-88 Clerkenwell Rd., EC1 (⊖ Farringdon), 020-7324-4444, thezetter.com

Hip London:
The Restaurants

Bar Italia* • Soho • Cafe

Serving pizza and panini around the clock, this is an ideal place for people-watching in the heart of Soho. *See Hip Nightlife, p.111, for details.* £- ≡ 22 Frith St., W1 (◉ Leicester Square), 020-7437-4520

Bermondsey Kitchen • Bankside • British

This relaxed contemporary British and continental eatery has an easygoing vibe, and is popular with arty, fashionable locals for its weekend brunches, which include options like eggs Florentine. The open kitchen is surrounded by a lively bar, which overlooks a casually laid-out dining area. The bar serves a good selection of cocktails and wines by the glass, and the restaurant menu specializes in tapas and Spanish-inflected hot dishes. *Mon-Fri noon-3pm and 6:30-10:30pm, Sat 6:30-10:30pm. Brunch: Sat-Sun 9:30am-3:30pm.* £ ≡ 194 Bermondsey St., SE1 (◉ London Bridge), 020-7407-5719, bermondseykitchen.co.uk

Bistrotheque* • Hoxton • French

Best Trendy Tables Plonked seemingly in the middle of nowhere—with an unmarked door, natch—this trendy East End venue wouldn't look out of place in New York's Meatpacking District. Look for the monastery-style wooden benches outside—which are perfect for Sunday brunch. Inside, there's a dimly lit bar on the ground floor, with a cabaret room next door that offers a drag show on Wednesday nights, live cabaret on Saturdays, and disco on Sundays. The lively restaurant above is done up in industrial warehouse chic, with seating areas on either side of an open kitchen. The classic French brasserie menu is a huge hit with people from the pop, fashion, design, and music industries. *Bar: Mon-Sat 5:30pm-midnight, Sun 5:30-10:30pm. Restaurant: Mon-Fri 6:30-10:30pm, Sat-Sun 11am-4pm and 6:30-10:30pm.* £ ≡ 23-27 Wadeson St., E2 (◉ Bethnal Green), 020-8983-7900, bistrotheque.com

Brick Lane Beigel Bake • Spitalfields • Bagels

This historic bagel bakery is a London institution: Open 24 hours a day year-round, it's frequented by local artists and designers during the day, and a snaking line of clubbers, students, cab drivers, and off-duty chefs at night. With some of the best bagels with classic fillings in town, plus rye breads and cheesecakes baked on the premises, it's a perfect place to grab breakfast on the go. *24/7.* £- ≡ 159 Brick Ln., E1 (◉ Liverpool Street), 020-7729-0616

Café Corfu • Camden Town • Greek

There's a permanent party at this effervescent restaurant, which specializes in modern regional Greek cooking that's both imaginative and prettily presented. Weekends come alive with belly dancers, a resident DJ, and English and Greek pop music on Friday and Saturday nights; live bouzouki bands play on Sunday evenings. Nothing as tacky as plate smashing takes place here, but shot drinking contests are de rigueur—with an all-Greek wine list and a wide selection of ouzo fueling the proceedings. Although the Café is popular with local office groups, it's also frequented by Greek celebrities like George Michael and Stelios

Hadji-Ioannou (millionaire owner of the trendy EasyJet group). *Tue-Thu, Sun noon-10:30pm, Fri noon-11:30pm, Sat 5-11:30pm.* £ ≡ 7 Pratt St., NW1 (✆ Camden Town), 020-7267-8088, cafecorfu.com

Canteen • The City • British

This no-frills eatery, with large picture windows and chunky wooden tables, has got the critics in a tizzy. Why? Because it offers beautifully executed traditional English food—the sort that Ma or Grandma used to cook—without fuss and pretension. It's like English Wagamama, if you will. Even menu descriptions are down-to-earth, like "soup, bread, and butter" and "macaroni cheese"—no jus, foams, or truffle oil here, which is exactly its appeal. It's located in the fashionable Spitalfields Market, and regularly attracts a steady stream of market shoppers, students, and a few City suits every day. *Mon-Fri 11am-11pm, Sat-Sun 9am-11pm.* £ = Unit 2, Crispin Pl., E1 (✆ Liverpool Street), 0845-686-1122, canteen.co.uk

Champor-Champor • Bankside • Malaysian

The name is Malaysian for mix and match, and the term applies to both food and décor at this lively, eccentric, contemporary Malaysian eatery. The small space is filled with bohemian locals, who love the Asian-themed cocktails and quirky Asian beers (including ones from Mongolia and Tasmania) at its bar. The restaurant's stylishly wacky interior is filled with soft fabrics in clashing rainbow colors, tribal artifacts, Buddha statues, kitsch puppets, antique wooden chests, and flickering candles and oil lamps. With zany concoctions on its menu like water buffalo with truffle oil mash, and smoked banana ice cream, Champor-Champor will linger long in your memory—and on your palate. *Mon-Sat 6:15-10:15pm. Lunch Mon-Sat by appointment only.* £ = 62-64 Weston St., SE1 (✆ London Bridge), 020-7403-4600, champor-champor.com

Clarke's • Kensington • International (G)

One of the few top female chefs in the UK, Sally Clarke owns this cozy eponymous restaurant that specializes in supplier-led cooking, inspired by the food markets that have recently become fashionable in London. Her mentor was Alice Waters of Chez Panisse in Berkeley—and it shows. The daily-changing menu showcases seasonal produce from specialist suppliers. Lunchtimes are abuzz with ladies who lunch and their willowy daughters. Clarke's breads, baked on-site and sold in its shop at the front, are legendary—so the lunching ladies had better not be on some faddy, wheat-free, Atkins diet. *Mon 12:30-2pm, Tue-Fri 12:30-2pm and 7-10pm, Sat 11am-2pm and 7-10pm.* £ – 124 Kensington Church St., W8 (✆ Notting Hill Gate), 020-7221-9225, sallyclarke.com

Club Gascon • The City • French (G)

This stylish modern French restaurant has a beautiful carved-wood entrance, leading to an atmospheric, intimate, dimly lit interior. Foie gras is a specialty—it's served hot or cold with a wide variety of playful flavor combinations like powdered popcorn and rose sangria jelly. Savory ices in flavors like mustard and suckling pig, and the all-French wine list, are also a hit with a dressed-up art and fashion crowd. *Mon-Thu noon-2pm and 7-10pm, Fri noon-2pm and 7-10:30pm, Sat 7-10:30pm.* £ = 57 West Smithfield, EC1 (✆ Farringdon), 020-7796-0600

Cow Dining Room* • Notting Hill • Gastropub

Best Gastropubs Located on a tiny stretch of a road that's teeming with good places to eat and drink, the first-floor dining room of this popular gastropub has long seduced its media clientele, who come for the leisurely Sunday roasts. It's a minuscule place with loads of homely old-fashioned charm—but the fresh, seasonal menu littered with seafood and pasta dishes boasts contemporary European dishes like goat cheese and broad bean pasta, and sea trout with fennel. The vibe is unruffled, so it's ideal for a lingering lunch accompanied by pints of ale. The vaguely Irish-themed pub downstairs is hectic, often frequented by local celebrities, and a popular destination in its own right. *Bar: Mon-Sat noon-11pm, Sun noon-10:30pm. Meals served Mon-Sat noon-3:30pm and 6-10:30pm, Sun noon-3:30pm and 6-10pm. Restaurant: Mon-Sat noon-midnight, Sun noon-11:30pm.* £ = 89 Westbourne Park Rd., W2 (⊖ Westbourne Park), 020-7221-0021

Delfina • Bankside • Fusion

Located inside an art gallery and exhibition space, this spacious restaurant started life as a canteen for resident artists, but is now a destination restaurant and cafe with curved white walls, contemporary art, and cool peppermint-and-blue furniture. It's only open at lunchtime—except on Friday evenings, when it serves dinner as well. These Friday evening dinners have proved to be such a hit that you'll need to book in advance. The changing menu offers a fusion of Asian and Mediterranean flavors, with Australian fish like barramundi a particular speciality. A mixed crowd of suited and booted businesspeople and local artists lends vibrancy to the place. *Mon-Thu noon-3pm, Fri noon-3pm and 7-10pm.* £ = 50 Bermondsey St., SE1 (⊖ London Bridge), 020-7357-0244, delfina.org.uk

E & O* • Notting Hill • Pan-Asian

Best Trendy Tables Popular with the boho Notting Hill royalty, including Kate Moss, Stella McCartney, Gwyneth Paltrow, and Sienna Miller, this über-hip restaurant and bar attracts young Notting Hillbillies by the limo-load. It bears all the hallmarks of a typical venue from popular Australian-born restaurateur Will Ricker, who also owns other similar ventures in London: cool, minimalist décor; stylish, muted color scheme; a small bar serving Asian-themed cocktails; and small platters of pan-Asian dishes like dim sum, soups, salads, tempura, curries, sushi, sashimi, and roasts. Salt chili squid served in cute Oriental newspaper cones is a modern classic that's been imitated by many restaurants, party caterers, and supermarkets all over the UK. Weekday evenings are quieter, but you're more likely to see local celebrities then; weekends are more vibrant with groups of fashionably attired friends catching up over attractive small plates. *Bar: Mon-Sat noon-11pm, Sun noon-10:30pm. Restaurant: Mon-Sat noon-3pm and 6-10:30pm, Sun 12:30-3pm and 6-10pm.* £ B = 14 Blenheim Crescent, W11 (⊖ Ladbroke Grove), 020-7229-5454, eando.nu

Eagle • Clerkenwell • Gastropub

Widely regarded as London's first gastropub, Eagle pulsates with the lively vibe created by its hip, lefty, young clientele, many of whom work in the nearby *Guardian* offices. The cozy space throbs with a sort of fashionably rough-and-ready atmosphere and loud music. Simple British and Mediterranean fare is freshly cooked in full view of the diners, and includes the likes of pork chops with salsa verde. There's a great variety of wines, ales, and continental white beer available to wash it all down. *Pub: Mon-Sat noon-11pm, Sun noon-5pm.*

Meals: Mon-Fri 12:30-3pm and 6:30-10:30pm, Sat 12:30-3:30pm and 6:30-10:30pm, Sun 12:30-3:30pm. £ ≡ 159 Farringdon Rd., EC1 (❸Farringdon), 020-7837-1353

Eagle Bar Diner • Bloomsbury • American

Part diner, part bar, this New York–style eatery is excellent as a diner at breakfast and lunch, and as a cocktail bar in the evening. Set on a split level, one side has cozy green booths and Formica tables, where young men and women from nearby offices come for classic American breakfasts, salads, sandwiches, burgers, hot dogs, brownies, cheesecakes, shakes, and malts. In the evening, the stylish but informal bar is filled with pretty people enjoying bespoke cocktails, hot alcoholic beverages, and bourbons. *Mon-Wed noon-11pm, Thu-Fri noon-midnight, Sat 10am-midnight, Sun 11am-6pm.* £ ≡ 3-5 Rathbone Pl., W1 (❸Tottenham Court Road), 020-7637-1418, eaglebardiner.com

Eight Over Eight • Chelsea • Chinese

Best Oriental Restaurants Another restaurant in Will Ricker's mini-empire, this pan-Asian restaurant and bar's name is based on a Chinese proverb that means "lucky forever." The sleek look is beautifully contemporary, with red neon signage on black walls, pretty wrought-iron screens in floral designs, lampshades shaped like inverted parasols, and a relaxed terrace. The glossy, well-heeled young Chelsea crowd congregates every evening for Asian cocktails and stunningly presented Asian dishes with a Shanghai bent, such as duck, watermelon, and cashew salad. *Mon-Fri noon-2:45pm and 6:15-10:45pm, Sat noon-4pm and 6:15-11pm, Sun 6:15-10:30pm.* £ ₿ = 392 King's Rd., SW3 (❸Sloane Square), 020-7349-9934, eightovereight.nu

Electric Brasserie* • Notting Hill • British

Swish restaurateur Nick Jones owns this brasserie, the cinema next door, and several private members clubs around the UK. The brasserie is Notting Hill Central— a local hangout for young people in Alice Temperley tea dresses and floaty skirts designed by Matthew Williamson. There's a loud, bustling bar at the front with communal tables and benches, and a quieter, more intimate restaurant at the back that serves classic cafe and brasserie fare from Britain and the Continent. Open all day from breakfast through dinner, the brasserie offers a taste of the rich, flavorful, and low-fat life in this perennially fashionable neighborhood. *Mon-Sat 8am-midnight, Sun 8am-11pm. Meals: Mon-Sat 8am-5pm and 6-11pm, Sun 8am-5pm and 6-10pm.* £ ≡ 191 Portobello Rd., W11 (❸Ladbroke Grove), 020-7908-9696, the-electric.co.uk

Fifteen • The City • Italian

Best Famous Chefs Celebrity chef Jamie Oliver's baby (that's rapidly gaining international siblings) is one of the most desirable tables in London. You know the formula: Young people from disadvantaged backgrounds are trained up as professional chefs, and the profits are plowed back into the charity, Fifteen Foundation, that owns the place in order to train more chefs. The subterranean space, with its arty, graffiti-splattered walls, hot-pink banquettes, and retro furniture, serves a chatty menu full of funky Mediterranean food with an Italian bent. Anyone who is anyone has eaten here: As a result, it gets booked up months in advance—check for last-minute availability, or try the informal Trattoria on the ground floor. *Trattoria: Mon-Sat 7:30am-11am, noon-3:30pm,* *and 6-10pm, Sun 9-11am, noon-3:30pm, and 5:30-9:30pm. £ ≡ Restaurant: Daily noon-2:30pm and 6:30-9:30pm. ££* ≡ 15 Westland Pl., N1 (⊖ Old Street), 0871-330-1515, fifteenrestaurant.com

Food @ the Muse • Notting Hill • Fusion

Located inside a small, elongated art gallery, this chilled eatery sells fusion food that's a marriage of Asian and Mediterranean flavors—the idea is to showcase "rot chart," the Thai concept of blending hot, sour, sweet, and salty flavors that are meant to balance perfectly in dishes like roasted prawn and watermelon salad. White tables are crammed together in a white space (if you are on your own you may have to share with fashionable and arty Notting Hillbillies), and the gallery at the back exhibits changing art displays. Be sure to come for breakfast or lunch when it's most buzzing. *Mon 6-11pm, Tue-Thu 11am-11pm, Fri-Sat 10am-11pm, Sun 10am-6pm. £* – 269 Portobello Rd., W11 (⊖ Ladbroke Grove), 020-7792-1111, themuseat269.com/foodatthemuse.php

1492 • Fulham • Latin American

Named after the year in which Columbus allegedly "discovered" America, this frantic restaurant is as outgoing as its Latin identity: The sunset-colored walls are enlivened with bright Latin art, and the young Latin American and British clientele throbs to Latin soundtrack, live guitar, and salsa dancing. To experience it at its peak, come for the live Latin jazz Wednesday through Friday nights, and all day Sunday. This is no tacky theme restaurant, however: The menu features authentic and unusual beef dishes, plus a great selection of coffees and cocktails. *Mon-Fri 6pm-midnight, Sat-Sun 12:30pm-midnight. £* ≡ 404 North End Rd., SW6 (⊖ Fulham Broadway), 020-7381-3810, 1492restaurant.com

Garden Café • Regent's Park • British

Best Al Fresco Dining Teeming with Londoners of every class, color, gender, and hairstyle, this natty little cafe from the 1970s has recently been refurbished and relaunched at Inner Circle in Regent's Park—near the Rose Gardens and the famous Open Air Theatre. The monthly-changing British menu offers breakfast, lunch, afternoon tea, and dinner—with everything from soups and ploughman's lunch, to ice cream sundaes and wines on offer. The simple, wood-paneled open-plan design allows a lot of natural light in the summer. It's especially popular Thursday through Saturday at lunch when there's classical and jazz piano. *Daily 10am-dusk. £* – Inner Circle Regent's Park, NW1 (⊖ Regent's Park), 020-7935-5729, thegardencafe.co.uk

Hoxton Apprentice • Hoxton • Mediterranean

Culinary social enterprises are the unlikely hot new trend of the 21st century, and the Apprentice is another establishment in the Jamie Oliver mold (disadvantaged young people are trained as chefs, and profits are plowed back into the charity—in this case, Training for Life). Far from being a soup kitchen, however, the spacious historic building (formerly a primary school) has an original interior spruced up with contemporary touches. Large windows ensure that the dark-wood interior is bathed in natural light, and a terrace opens out onto the fashionable Hoxton Square. Trendy young locals like to gather for cocktails at the bar, and to share classic, seasonal Mediterranean-style dishes. *Bar: Tue-Sun noon-11pm. Restaurant: Tue-Sun noon-4pm and 7-10:30pm. £-* ≡ 16 Hoxton Sq., N1 (⊖ Old Street), 020-7749-2828, hoxtonapprentice.com

Inc Bar & Restaurant* • Greenwich • British

Located in historic Greenwich, this bar and restaurant was designed by flamboyant and popular British TV designer Lawrence Llewelyn-Bowen. Its fashionably
louche look, inspired by the "slum and splendor" of the Georgian era, is a huge
hit with the area's hip twenty-somethings, especially on Friday and Saturday
nights, and there are many different spaces in which to relax and enjoy a cocktail or two. There's a divan with a tasteful, old-style pornographic wallpaper; a
small bar complete with swirly carpet and comfy furniture; a large bar with carriage clocks, chandeliers, and plasma screens showing cult films; and a dining
area that serves contemporary British and continental food. Even the toilets are
wonderful—based on the concepts of Heaven (for the ladies) and Hell (sorry,
guys). *Bar: Mon-Thu, Sun 6pm-midnight, Fri-Sat 6pm-1am. Tapas: daily
6-10pm. Restaurant: daily 6-10pm.* £ ◙ = 7 College Approach, SE10 (● Cutty
Sark DLR), 020-8858-6721

La Fromagerie • Marylebone • Mediterranean

Cheese is cool—quite literally, at this fashionable cheese shop and delicatessen,
where it's stored in an on-site temperature-controlled storage room. There's a rustic lunchtime-only cafe that sells cheesy Mediterranean lunch fare like salads,
soups, and cheese-and-bread platters to local ladies. The occasional cheese and
wine dinners in the evenings, designed to showcase specific seasonal cheeses
like Vacherin du Mont d'Or, attract a younger, hipper crowd. To find out about the
evening events, phone the restaurant to inquire, or pick up a leaflet in the shop
during the day. *Mon 10:30am-7:30pm, Tue-Fri 8am-7:30pm, Sat 9am-7pm,
Sun 10am-6pm.* £ = 2-4 Moxon St., W1 (● Baker Street), 020-7935-0341,
lafromagerie.co.uk

Les Trois Garçons • Hoxton • French

Best Trendy Tables You've gotta love a restaurant that offers torchon of foie gras
with banana lollipop, walnut crust, coriander jus, and sherry vinegar.
Contemporary French food is offered with a witty, international interpretation at
this informal, eccentrically eclectic restaurant that's renowned for its camp,
kitsch interior. Such upscale eccentricity is what the team behind this restaurant
(which also owns Le Cercle, Loungelover bar, and Annex 3) is renowned for—and
it's increasingly popular with a young, fun-loving crowd. Ornate ceramic figures,
stuffed animals, groovy chandeliers, and multicolored glass bottles compete for
attention with diners from the art, fashion, music, and media industries. *Mon-
Thu 7-10:30pm, Fri-Sat 6:45-11pm.* ££ ◙ = 1 Club Row, E1 (● Shoreditch),
020-7613-1924, lestroisgarcons.com

Little Earth Café • Primrose Hill • Raw Food

Raw food has gained a foothold in New York and California—but in London it
hasn't quite taken off. However, this tiny vegetarian cafe inside the trendy
Triyoga Centre (popular with Primrose Hill yummy mummies and celebrities like
Gwyneth Paltrow) opened in a blaze of publicity as London's first raw food cafe.
The menu comprises uncooked dishes (like raw sushi) that are designed to taste
like the real thing, plus a few cooked ones (like tagines with couscous) for those
of us who are not quite so virtuous. *Mon-Fri 10am-8pm, Sat 10am-6pm, Sun
11am-5pm.* £- _ 6 Erskine Rd., NW3 (● Chalk Farm), 020-7449-0700

Maison Bertaux • Soho • French

This French cafe is a Soho landmark: It serves sumptuous pastries, cakes, tarts, and pies hot from the oven. Students, actors, local workers, and ladies of leisure come here for breakfast on rickety furniture, or a solo cup of coffee with a newspaper. Filled with eccentric ornaments, the place boasts service that's ditzy, but charming in an old-fashioned way. *Daily 8:30am-11pm.* £- ☰ 28 Greek St., W1 (☻ Tottenham Court Road), 020-7437-6007

Medcalf • Clerkenwell • British

Housed inside a former butcher's shop, this informal British restaurant has a chunky wooden bar on one side, and casually set tables on the other. The place used to be popular mainly with trendy Exmouth Market locals, but as its reputation has grown, more young people from far and wide have started flocking here, making it a real destination restaurant. The daily-changing menu lists seasonal, often organic, produce, and simply prepared dishes include grilled pork chop with apple mash and smoked black pudding. On Friday nights, the relaxed vibe gives way to a distinctly lively one, when DJs and live musicians crank out soul, raga, disco, and funky flavas. *Mon-Thu, Sat noon-11pm, Fri noon-12:30am, Sun noon-5pm. Meals served Mon-Thu noon-3pm and 6-10pm, Fri noon-3pm, Sat noon-4pm and 6-10pm, Sun noon-4pm.* £ ☰ 40 Exmouth Market, EC1 (☻ Farringdon), 020-7833-3533, medcalfbar.co.uk

Notting Hill Brasserie • Notting Hill • French

This brasserie has a classy, understated décor, a neutral color scheme, and small armchairs to slink into at every table. Little wonder it attracts well-heeled locals who like to linger over the great wines and the marvelous food, which is standard European-style brasserie fare. Seafood is a strong point on the menu here, and the oysters, scallops, and mussels prepared without fuss won't disappoint. There are jazz and blues musicians every evening, when the place literally swings. Leisurely Sunday lunches are also popular. *Mon-Sat noon-3pm and 7-11pm, Sun noon-3pm.* £ ☰ 92 Kensington Park Rd., W11 (☻ Notting Hill Gate), 020-7229-4481

Ottolenghi • Notting Hill • Cafe

Gorgeous cakes, muffins, macaroons, and tarts are artfully piled up in the windows of this achingly hip eatery; and Technicolor salads, snacks, soups, and artisanal breads are beautifully displayed inside. This small cafe looks like a cross between an art gallery and a designer boutique, with bright white walls and extravagant fresh flower arrangements. It's an ideal place to drop by and get takeout, but there's also a table for communal dining, where you'll see budding writers, poets, artists, and filmmakers enjoying a coffee and a snack while perusing their novels and newspapers. *Mon-Fri 8am-8pm, Sat 8am-7pm, Sun 8:30am-6pm.* £- ▯▬ 63 Ledbury Rd., W11 (☻ Notting Hill Gate), 020-7727-1121, ottolenghi.co.uk

Pâtisserie Valerie • Soho • Cafe

Swarming with trendy art students, media moguls, writers, celebrities, and film stars, this long-established cafe is a Soho institution. Its 1950s décor is renowned for its Toulouse-Lautrec cartoons and vintage film posters. With luscious offerings of gâteaux, tarts, and omelettes—served in the cafe on the first floor—breakfast and afternoon tea are the best times to visit. Nab a table outside in fine weather, and you're guaranteed to be entertained by the colorful characters who have made Old Compton Street their spiritual home. *Mon-Tue 7:30am-8:30pm, Wed-Fri 7:30am-9pm, Sat 8am-9pm, Sun 9:30am-7pm.* £- = 44 Old Compton St., W1 (⊖ Leicester Square), 020-7437-3466, patisserie-valerie.co.uk

Princess • Hoxton • Gastropub

This Australian-owned gastropub is located in ever-fashionable Shoreditch, renowned for its trendy bars and hip eateries. It boasts two dining areas: the informal pub on the ground floor, which has a short menu, and is better for drinking (try the excellent real ales or international wines); and a more formal dining room on the first floor. The restaurant is done up in Art Deco style, with funky floral wallpaper and a striking mirror above the fireplace. Both spaces are popular with the area's hipsters, who love the menu's strident continental and international flavors, showcased via dishes like springbok sausages with pancetta gravy and mash. *Bar: Mon-Fri noon-11:30pm, Sat 5:30-11pm, Sun noon-5:30pm. Restaurant: Mon-Fri 12:30-3pm and 6:30-10:30pm, Sat 6:30-10:30pm.* £ ⓑ = 76 Paul St., EC2 (⊖ Old Street), 020-7729-9270

The Real Greek • Hoxton • Greek

Situated in voguish Hoxton, this ground-breaking Greek restaurant—by London standards, not Greece's, obviously—is lauded for selling authentic, regional modern Greek food. Young Hoxtonians, who can tell their cool from stone-cold, continue to swarm the place. There are superior mezze, souvlaki, and small plates on the menu, which also includes an all-Greek wine list. The vibrant blue-and-brushed-metal interior lends a contemporary touch. *Mon-Sat noon-3pm and 5:30-10:30pm.* £ = 15 Hoxton Market, N1 (⊖ Old Street), 020-7739-8212, therealgreek.co.uk

Smiths of Smithfield • Clerkenwell • European

Sprawled over four floors, celebrity chef John Torode's buzzy, spacious venue is located in the heart of Smithfield Market, London's only meat market. It's done up in New York–style industrial warehouse chic, with brick, concrete, wood, steel, cast iron, glass, and leather accents lending texture. There's something for everyone: breakfast and brunch in the lively brasserie on the ground floor; a stylish, busy cocktail bar on the first floor; an informal second-floor eatery, and a dressy, formal restaurant on the rooftop that's popular for Sunday brunch. The crowd throughout is young and casual. *Bar/cafe (ground floor): Mon-Fri 7am-5pm, Sat 10am-5pm, Sun 9:30am-5pm. £- = Cocktail bar (first floor): Mon-Wed 5:30-10:30pm, Thu-Sat 5:30pm-1am. £ ≡ Dining room (second floor): Mon-Fri noon-3pm and 6-11pm, Sat 6-10:45pm. ££ = Top floor restaurant (third floor): Mon-Fri noon-3pm and 6:30-10:45pm, Sat 6:30-10:45pm, Sun noon-3:45pm and 6:30-10:30pm.* ££ = 67-77 Charterhouse St., EC1 (⊖ Farringdon), 020-7251-7950, smithsofsmithfield.co.uk

Story Deli • Spitalfields • Deli

Run by a designer who owns a fashion boutique nearby and contributes to Italian *Vogue*, this small, stylish eatery is thronged by the art and fashion crowd. It's done up in industrial warehouse chic, with exposed brickwork and a mezzanine kitchen. There's a chunky wooden communal table, around which rough-hewn chairs are casually arranged, and all the food is served in cardboard boxes. There's a good breakfast menu, tempting cakes, hot pastas, and snacks—but it's

HIP

the pizzas that are exceptional. Thin, crispy, and with a bubbly topping, they're some of the best this side of Naples. *Daily 8am-7pm.* £- ☐⊟ 91 Brick Ln., E1 (⊖ Liverpool Street), 020-7247-3137

Tapas Brindisa • Bankside • Tapas

Brindisa is a leading importer of top-quality Spanish foods in the UK, with a deli that sells all its products to an enthralled foodie clientele. This tapas bar is its recent offshoot: It showcases many of its premium products on the menu, and attracts a casual, food-loving clientele that's too young to indulge in any kind of fancy fine dining. The red-and-cream walls are lined with shelves laden with Brindisi products. Come early to enjoy a drink in the separate bar area before settling in for dinner. *Mon-Thu 11am-11pm, Fri-Sat 9am-11pm.* £- ⊟ 18-20 Southwark St., SE1 (⊖ London Bridge), 020-7357-8880

Tom's Delicatessen • Notting Hill • British

One of the best-known places to eat breakfast and lunch around Notting Hill, this small cafe and deli is owned by Tom Conran (son of Sir Tel), and is always teeming with local celebrities, writers, artists, filmmakers, students, and young mothers. There's an enticing display of confectionery from around the world at the entrance, and a delightful deli in the basement. The cafe area is decorated with Pop Art posters of iconic British food items like HP sauce. The cafe is exceptionally busy at breakfast and lunch, but there are a few tables in the small garden and terrace at the back, where seating is easier to come by. *Mon-Sat 8am-6pm, Sun 9am-5pm.* £- ⊟ 226 Westbourne Grove, W11 (⊖ Notting Hill Gate), 020-7221-8818

Wapping Food • Docklands • British

Housed inside a converted hydraulic power station, this dramatic-looking restaurant, bar, and exhibition space is one of London's most extraordinary dining destinations. The vast, bustling, industrial space has a number of interconnecting rooms, the best ones being on the mezzanine floor. The modern British and continental menu offers dishes like char-grilled pigeon with caramelized turnips; plus there's an all-Australian wine list and a good selection of cocktails. In summer, the restaurant screens classic movies outside (in fine weather) or inside (in case of inclement weather). Little wonder the place is popular with artists, filmmakers, movie lovers, and other creative types. *Mon-Fri noon-3:30pm and 6:30-11pm, Sat 10am-4pm and 7-11pm, Sun 10am-4pm.* £ ⊟ Wapping Hydraulic Power Station, Wapping Wall, E1 (⊖ Wapping), 020-7680-2080

Hip London:
The Nightlife

Ain't Nothin But The Blues Bar • Soho • Blues Bar

Ain't Nothin But started in 1993, but you'd expect it to date back to another era. The décor and vibe are reminiscent of an old American blues dive, with neon signs, guitars hanging on the walls, and a touch of New Orleans. This is the place to catch live blues every night of the week, often from American musicians as well as British hopefuls. Sunday and Monday are jam nights, in case you're in town with some talent. The rest of us come to see the professionals do their thing and enjoy a bottle of expensive beer. *Mon-Wed 6pm-1am, Thu 6pm-2am, Fri noon-3am, Sat 2pm-3am, Sun 3pm-midnight.* ℂ ≡ 20 Kingly St., W1 (⊖ Oxford Circus), 020-7287-0514, aintnothinbut.co.uk

Annex 3 • Marylebone • Restaurant Bar

If Austin Powers and Elton John decided to create a bar, it would look like Annex 3. The first West End bar-restaurant in the Les Trois Garçons portfolio has the kitschiest design this side of Vegas. After being open only a week, it was attracting all the stylish Top Shop–clad PR and marketing girls that populate the area. The room is half destination spot, half restaurant, but the focus is on the décor. People come to this hyper-camp spot to pose, talk over the Brazilian disco music, and stare at the gold lamé seating, giant vintage seats in the shape of high heels, and glitter graphic wall panels. *Mon-Sat noon-midnight.* ∟ ≡ 6 Little Portland St., W1 (⊖ Oxford Circus), 020-7631-0700, loungelover.co.uk

Bar Italia* • Soho • Cafe

Best Late-Night Haunts Open 24 hours a day, six days a week (and until 4am on Sundays), this 60-year-old Italian cafe is a Soho institution that's popular with clubbers, people working night shifts, and fabulously attired young gay men. The retro-style interior boasts chrome and Formica, red leather barstools, and a famous Rocky Marciano poster. Drop by for a late-night coffee, or grab a table outside if you can (they're always in demand) and tuck into pizza or panini. An ideal place for people-watching in the heart of Soho. *Mon-Sat 24 hours, Sun 7am-4am.* ∟ 22 Frith St., W1 (⊖ Leicester Square), 020-7437-4520, baritaliasoho.co.uk

Bar Kick • Hoxton • Bar

In this bar, table football or baby foot isn't just a game. It's a way of life. Groups of twos or fours play rounds of fantasy soccer at some 15 foosball tables scattered on two floors, and the bar even runs a very thorough tournament. This very European pursuit is always fun and best accompanied by bottles of imported beer—though Bar Kick also serves some great exotic spirits and unpretentious international bar snacks. The crowd is young, dressed down, and laid-back—after all, they come here to play. *Mon-Wed noon-11pm, Thu-Sat noon-midnight, Sun noon-10:30pm.* ≡ 127 Shoreditch High St., E1 (⊖ Old Street), 020-7739-8700, barkick.co.uk

Big Chill Bar • Hoxton • DJ Bar

The Big Chill is the new Glastonbury. Profits from the laid-back summer festival were pumped into creating one of the slickest bars off Brick Lane. Although popular every night, it is also considered far and wide to be one of the best places for Sunday late-afternoon drinking and people-watching. (There's also board games if you fancy a play.) The interior is simple and well designed—though in summer those in the know grab one of the rough wooden tables outside with slabs of unfinished tree trunks to sit on. Go to hang out with twenty-somethings while having super-long drinks and pints to a great selection of cutting-edge soul and breakbeat music. *Mon-Sat noon-midnight, Sun noon-11:30pm.* ≡ Dray Walk, off Brick Ln., E1 (Liverpool Street), 020-7392-9180, bigchill.net

Bistrotheque* • Hoxton • Bar

After dinner, don't miss cabaret and fabulous cocktails at the ground-floor bar. *See Hip Restaurants, p.102, for details.* − ≡ 23-27 Wadeson St., E2 (⊖ Bethnal Green), 020-8983-7900, bistrotheque.com

Candy Bar • Soho • Lesbian Bar

Best Gay Bars and Clubs Roll on up, ladies, this is the bar for you. The Candy Bar has been the lesbian mecca in London for ten years now. There's a lounge bar on the ground floor, but the hot party girls all head for the raucous basement where strippers, karaoke, and other events are the big draw throughout the week. The London scene is a little cliquey, but once you crack it expect lots of fun. Men are only allowed in if they're gay and accompanied by gay and bi women, so no worries about any unwanted attention here. *Mon-Thu 5-11:30pm, Fri-Sat 5pm-2am, Sun 5-10:30pm.* C ≡ 4 Carlisle St., W1 (⊖ Tottenham Court Road), 020-7494-4041, thecandybar.co.uk

Cargo • Hoxton • Nightclub

Best Live-Music Venues Hoxton's best live-music venue is also one of its most popular clubs. Cargo is in a large raw space with a top-notch sound system. The programming is varied—from Afro-reggae to hip-hop to jazz house, but always guarantees a good night. The crowd is largely twenty-somethings who want to dance or catch specific acts, though post-work drifters from local media industries stumble by for large bottles of imported beer. There's also a great graffiti-filled outdoor space in the summer and a restaurant that serves burgers and bites. *Mon-Thu 6pm-1am, Fri-Sat 6pm-3am, Sun 6pm-midnight.* C ≡ 83 Rivington St., Kingsland Viaduct, EC2 (⊖ Old Street), 020-7749-7840, cargolondon.com

Comedy Store • Soho • Comedy Club

There's nothing quite like the dry, surreal humor of British alternative comedy. For decades the place to see big names and Perrier award-winners has been London's Comedy Store. From stand-up to improvisation, this venue catering to a crowd aged 18 to 80 has hosted familiar British names like Lee Evans, Ben Elton, Keith Allen, Jo Brand, and Eddie Izzard. Cultural differences aside, these are seriously funny people. Be warned—the later the set, the ruder the jokes. *Hours vary.* C ≡ 1 Oxendon St., SW1 (⊖ Leicester Square), 020-7344-0234, thecomedystore.co.uk

Cow Dining Room* • Notting Hill • Gastropub

The vaguely Irish-themed pub below this popular restaurant is hectic, often frequented by local celebrities, and a popular destination in its own right. *See Hip Restaurants, p.104, for details.* ≡ 89 Westbourne Park Rd., W2 (⊖ Westbourne Park), 020-7221-0021

Donmar Warehouse • Covent Garden • Theater

Looking for some cutting-edge theater? This basement theater in Covent Garden was once the vat room for a Victorian brewery and a banana-ripening depot in the 1920s before it was converted into a theater in 1961. The Royal Shakespeare Company made the theater its home in the late 1970s, but for several decades now, it has put on some spectacular independent productions (it's here that Nicole Kidman stripped off in *The Blue Room*). Sam (*American Beauty*) Mendes was director here for years before Hollywood beckoned. The plays change regularly, but this is high-caliber stuff that is guaranteed to entertain. *Hours vary.* C = 41 Earlham St., WC2 (◒ Covent Garden), 020-7240-4882, donmarwarehouse.com

Dragon Bar • Hoxton • Bar

There's no sign outside the Dragon Bar, only a bronze step with metal skulls embedded in it. The two-floor bar has exposed brick walls, worn leather sofas, and a bathroom demolished by graffiti in pure New York–punk style. There's a street art gallery with changing free shows upstairs. DJs play hip-hop and electro most nights to the edgy crowd of designers and journalists. Sadly, the building has recently been sold from behind the bar's back, so its days are limited. Catch it while you can and wear your Nikes. *Mon noon-11pm, Tue-Wed noon-midnight, Thu noon-1am, Fri-Sat noon-2am, Sun noon-11pm.* = 5 Leonard St., EC2 (◒ Old Street), 020-7490-7110

Duke of Cambridge • Islington • Gastropub

When this gastropub first opened, the word "organic" was barely a blip on the radar. Now the original organic gastropub has proved it was far ahead of its time. Everything—from the delicious food to the beers, wines, and spirits—is organic here. The main triangular room has a Victorian décor with found chairs and tables, often with ecclesiastical overtones, and there are smaller tables at the back. Expect well-off Islington local types rather than anything hippie-ish. Be ready for crowds on weekends. *Mon-Sat noon-11pm, Sun noon-10:30pm.* = 30 St. Peter's St., N1 (◒ Angel), 020-7359-3066, singhboulton.co.uk

E & O* • Notting Hill • Restaurant Bar

This über-popular Asian restaurant has a buzzing bar that you don't have to reserve for. *See Hip Restaurants, p.104, for details.* = 14 Blenheim Crescent, W11 (◒ Ladbroke Grove), 020-7229-5454, eando.nu

Egg • Kings Cross • Nightclub

Unlike most of the gritty hedonistic house clubs in the wilds of Kings Cross, Egg prides itself on its sexy Ibizan-style décor. The three floors of warehouse space are filled with red-leather furnishings and loft-living details. The focus on this very late-night venue is on house, techno, and electro for a club-literate gang that likes to dress up and party the night away. This is the kind of place that invents new strains of electronic music—anyone want to try electro tech, dirty house, or polysexual disco? One for the night owls. *Fri 10pm-5am, Sat 10pm-6am.* C≡ 200 York Way, N7 (◒ Kings Cross), 020-7609-8364, egglondon.net

Electric Brasserie* • Notting Hill • Restaurant Bar

The perennially packed bar isn't large, though it's a pleasant place to come for drinks (or an afternoon coffee) solo. The members bar upstairs is the truly exclusive option—but unless you're Kevin Spacey, don't even bother trying to get in. *See Hip Restaurants, p.105, for details.* – ≡ 191 Portobello Rd., W11 (⊖ Ladbroke Grove), 020-7908-9696, the-electric.co.uk

The Endurance • Soho • Gastropub

There are pubs for every type in Soho—Victorian ones, ones for market traders, ones for the film world, ones for tourists—but the most stylish is this gastro conversion in the middle of Berwick Street market. This is where all the record shops and edgier film and fashion creatives congregate. The pub is arranged around a large central bar in a single room with dark wood-paneled walls and black banquettes. It also serves hearty food to accompany the pints of Belgian beer. Expect funk and alternative music to liven things up. *Mon-Sat noon-11pm, Sun 12:30-10:30pm.* ⌐ ≡ 90 Berwick St., W1 (⊖ Oxford Circus), 020-7437-2944

Fabric • The City • Nightclub

Best Dance Clubs While most of the UK's notorious 1990s super-clubs died, Fabric lives on—largely because of the venue's top-notch lineups. Rather than stay open all week, the cavernous metal maze of a venue sticks to the weekends with edgier electro, drum and bass, and hip-hop on Fridays and tech-house on Saturdays. The ever-changing party crowd attracts students and twenty-somethings who want to keep going until the sun comes up. Be sure to arrange a meeting point—getting lost in Fabric is easily done, especially as the night gets messy ... *Fri 9:30pm-5am, Sat 10pm-7am.* ⓒ ≡ 77a Charterhouse St., EC1 (⊖ Farringdon), 020-7336-8898, fabriclondon.com

Freud • Covent Garden • Cocktail Bar

Best Cocktails Bohemia flocks to Freud when it's thirsty. The loud and lively bar is super central in Covent Garden but is easily overlooked—look for the metal stairs leading into the basement of a housewares store. The venue is basic, with slate walls and a raw edge that is surprisingly contemporary for a place that opened in 1986. Once you find it, expect to line up at the bar alongside creatives and students for the brilliant large and lethal cocktails. Go early to get a table—even the steps at the back get filled with drinkers early on. *Mon-Sat 11am-11pm, Sun noon-10:30pm.* ≡ 198 Shaftesbury Ave., WC2 (⊖ Covent Garden), 020-7240-9933, freudliving.co.uk

G-A-Y Bar • Soho • Gay Bar

A relative newcomer to Old Compton, the G-A-Y bar was a spin off of the packed weekender G-A-Y, which stills happens at the Astoria. The big club night is a homage to all things camp and pop, with PAs from icons including Kylie, Donna Summer, and even Madonna, and this upbeat, extra-bright bar attracts the same kind of fans with the flush of youth still in their cheeks. There's a wall of pop videos, which may not be quite the same as seeing a diva in real life, but it's enough to keep this crowd happy. *Daily noon-3am.* ≡ 30 Old Compton St., W1 (⊖ Leicester Square), 020-7494-2756, g-a-y.co.uk

Ghetto • Soho • Gay Bar

When the electroclash scene burst out a few years back, Ghetto was its epicenter. The gay bar behind the Astoria still reigns supreme for very edgy scenesters who like to play hard to dirty music while wearing outrageous clothes. The music in this alleyway basement ranges from rock and hip-hop on Mondays to bubblegum pop on Tuesdays to funky house. Nag nag nag on Wednesday is hugely popular, and worth a try whether you're straight or gay—full-on '80s-influenced fashion is de rigueur. This is definitely one of the edgiest clubs in Soho. *Sun-Thu 10:30pm-3am, Fri 10:30pm-4am, Sat 10:30pm-5am.* C ≡ Falconberg Ct., behind the Astoria, W1 (⊖ Tottenham Court Road), 020-7287-3726, ghetto-london.co.uk

Grill Room at the Café Royale • Soho • Nightclub

Who wouldn't want to hang out in the over-the-top gilt glamour of the Grill Room? Oscar Wilde and Bosie used to meet for dalliances here among the red velvet and painted murals. Now it's a restaurant for the earlier part of the evening, but at 11pm, it turns into one of the edgiest clubs in town. On Tuesday nights is Rakehell's Revels, a retro night where you have to dress up in 1930s style and swing. Thursday attracts punk-rock royalty à la Kelly Osbourne. This is classicism with a naughty side. *Mon-Fri noon-3pm and 6-11pm, Sat 6-11pm; Club: Tue, Thu 11pm-3am.* = 68 Regent St., W1 (⊖ Oxford Circus), 020-7439-1865

Guanabara • Covent Garden • Nightclub

Best Dance Clubs Shake your hips and arrive early if you want a chance to get into the best Brazilian nightclub in London. The venue exploded in 2005 and has lines around the block every night from 8pm on. The crowd is really mixed—excited girls in party tops, dressed-down men in Diesel and denim, students, office types after work, and of course every South American clubber who passes through the city. There's live Brazilian music almost every night and South American DJs who make it impossible not to move. The superb berry caprioskas, mojitos, and bottles of Brazilian beer are a huge draw in and of themselves. *Mon-Sat 5pm-2:30am, Sun 5pm-midnight.* C ≡ Parker St. (corner of Drury Ln.), WC2 (⊖ Holborn), 020-7242-8600, guanabara.co.uk

Harlem • Notting Hill • Restaurant Bar

Like the name suggests, Harlem is a restaurant bar that is a friendly nod at New York City's finest. The space is owned by Arthur Baker, an eccentric hip-hop producer who's also the man behind the Elbow Rooms pool hall chain (one of which is across the road). The two-floor venue is quite small, with a restaurant upstairs serving burgers in a dark, wooden, masculine environment. Downstairs at the club, DJs spin hip-hop, soul, and party tunes. The whole place is very West London—stylish, in the know, and low-key. *Mon-Sat 10:30am-2am, Sun 10:30am-midnight.* — ≡ 78 Westbourne Grove, W2 (⊖ Westbourne Park), 020-7985-0900, harlemsoulfood.com

Herbal • Hoxton • Nightclub

Herbal was the first large DJ bar club to arrive on the very edgy Kingsland Road, and it's still one of the best. Here, a cool, dressed-down crowd—sneakers are almost obligatory—comes for post-pub drinks and dancing. Expect a lot of drum 'n' bass, hip-hop, soul, and breakbeats on two floors. Harder music is on the ground floor but it's the second-floor space that really captures the spontaneous party vibe. This is the place to hear iconic DJs like Jazzie B from Soul to Soul, and jungle innovator Grooverider, in a small, fun space. *Tue-Thu, Sun 9pm-2am, Fri-Sat 9pm-3am.* C ≡ 10-14 Kingsland Rd., E2 (⊖ Old Street), 020-7613-4462, herbaluk.com

ICA Bar • St. James's • Bar

An interest in contemporary culture isn't obligatory at the ICA, but it helps. The Institute of Contemporary Arts (ICA) is a white-walled Georgian building off the regal Mall. It's a members bar—though anyone can buy a night's entry for a tiny sum. The bar area itself is quite small and changes depending on what cultural events or DJs are playing that night. The crowd ranges from music-industry trendspotters to eccentric art students who drink beer and show up for Brazilian breakbeat, underground UK hip-hop, one-off guitar bands, and performance art. *Mon noon-11pm, Tue-Sat noon-1am, Sun noon-10:30pm.* C_≡ Institute of Contemporary Arts, The Mall, SW1 (⊖Charing Cross), 020-7930-3647, ica.org.uk

Inc Bar & Restaurant* • Greenwich • Restaurant Bar
Enjoy a cocktail in one of several bars adjoining this restaurant. *See Hip Restaurants, p.107, for details.* ≡ 7 College Approach, SE10 (⊖Cutty Sark DLR), 020-8858-6721

The Key • Kings Cross • Nightclub
Best Late-Night Haunts If you've ever dreamed of disco, you simply must head out to dance on the illuminated honeycomb dance floor at Key. There's a real touch of glamour to this club, decorated with flowers, chandeliers, and lots of warm tones. The music is heavy with deep house, hard disco, and techno from people like Bugz in the Attic, James Priestly, Laurent Garnier, and François K. It also has a 24-hour drink license, so expect a bad hangover. Every Sunday morning from 6am, the club hosts house party Formulate for people who don't want to sleep. Ever. *Fri-Sat 10:30pm-6am, Sun 6am-1pm.* C≡ Kings Cross Freight Depot, N1 (⊖Kings Cross), 020-7837-1027, thekeylondon.com

Lab • Soho • Cocktail Bar
This small bar on buzzing Old Compton Street is a little past its prime in the interior stakes, but it still holds its own when it comes to cocktails. The cocktail list is so big it is almost a novel. Expect groups of post-work friends as well as people propping up the bar to stare at the mixologists as they shake and pour. It's the kind of place people stumble to in their everyday clothes, so don't worry too much about the scene. There are DJs every night of the week, but the place is a bit too narrow to allow for much dancing. But no one minds when you've got drinks like this. *Mon-Sat 4pm-midnight, Sun 4-10:30pm.* ≡ 12 Old Compton St., W1 (⊖Leicester Square), 020-7437-7820, lab-townhouse.com

The Lock Tavern • Camden • Pub
The hip and hungover head here on Sundays to drown their sorrows after a heavy night with a pint of beer and a square pie. The pub was bought up by DJ Jon Carter, who transformed it into something that straddles DJ bar, club, and pub. He kept it old-fashioned and very relaxed but added a fat dose of music and edge. It's a mecca for band babes, older skaters, and anyone with leanings toward street style. The upstairs terrace is the best spot, with large wooden benches and tables that are ideal for starting conversations with strangers. It's always crowded and always fun. *Mon-Sat noon-11pm, Sun noon-10:30pm.* ≡ 35 Chalk Farm Rd., NW1 (⊖Chalk Farm), 020-7482-7163, lock-tavern.co.uk

Loungelover • Hoxton • Cocktail Bar
Best Bar Interiors The interior of this bar is so over-the-top that you cannot help but enjoy it. Forget Zen—Loungelover is filled with medical posters, taxidermy animals, and thousands of other odd antique objects. The cocktail list is so long it's like reading a book, and not surprisingly, there are a lot of off-the-wall options and odd liquors. Be sure to book ahead, as this spot owned by Les Trois Garçons is excep-

tionally popular and has next to no standing room. It's perfect for a hot date. *Tue-Thu 6pm-midnight, Fri 6pm-1am, Sat 7pm-1am, Sun 6pm-midnight.* ≡ 1 Whitby St., E1 (⊖ Liverpool Street), 020-7012-1234, loungelover.co.uk

Lucky Voice • Soho • Karaoke Bar

Book in advance for one of the surprise hits of modern London. Everyone's gone crazy for karaoke, and this stylish basement spot in Soho is the venue of choice. Minimalist private black boxes can be rented by the hour. In fact, the whole venue is painted slick black. This space is all about hanging out with your friends and making a fool of yourself by singing an encyclopedic selected list of songs from an easy-to-use touch screen. Asian nibbles and fusion cocktails are brought to the rooms by waiters when you feel the need to refuel. *Mon-Sat 6pm-1am.* _ ≡ 52 Poland St., W1 (⊖ Oxford Circus), 020-7439-3660, luckyvoice.co.uk

Market Place • Fitzrovia • DJ Bar

This relaxed place near Oxford Circus is just the right side of upmarket. It is lined with planks of light wood scorched with text as signage that give it a hip design vibe. Hordes from all the nearby media and advertising companies spill outside onto the street most weekdays after work (especially in summer). Sneakers and jeans mingle with work wear, but the crowd is definitely laid-back. There are DJs throughout the week, and you'll find a menu of filling, loosely Spanish-themed food and burgers. All in all, this is an accessible venue with a great central location. *Mon-Wed noon-midnight, Thu-Sat noon-1am, Sun noon-10:30pm.* = 11-13 Market Pl., W1 (⊖ Oxford Circus), 020-7079-2020, marketplace-london.com

The Medicine Bar • Hoxton • DJ Bar

Medicine Bar is the sibling to a funky Islington pub with a predilection for funk and soul. The Hoxton branch is a little slicker, with nightly changing DJs and a clubbier atmosphere. The décor is pretty nondescript—expect the usual warm-toned lights, stools along the bar, and some dance-floor space for the wiggling crowds. Hot names like Norman Jay and Metalheadz have played everything from house to hip-hop here. There's also an upstairs bar with quirkier music that's open on busy nights. These days, it's so popular it's become a Hoxton staple. *Mon-Wed 5-11pm, Thu, Sat 5pm-2am, Fri 4pm-2am.* = 89 Great Eastern St., EC2 (⊖ Old Street), 020-7739-5173, medicinebar.net

Mo Tea Room • Mayfair • Restaurant Bar

Best Bar Interiors Mo crosses the line between bar and tearoom. The stunning little venue is located next door to the big restaurant Momo. Little Mo in contrast feels more like a Moroccan fashion den in Paris and attracts a very international crowd, which all packs in on the cushions around low tables in a narrow space. Expect to be cramped, but it's worth it for the fabulous kirs, great mint tea, and mezzes. There are peach-flavored hookahs if the reclining or the rai music get you in the mood. This is definitely one to go to in small numbers if you want to stand a chance of getting a table. It's generally packed from 6:30pm to midnight every night. *Mon-Wed noon-11pm, Thu-Sat noon-midnight.* = 23 Heddon St., W1 (⊖ Piccadilly Circus), 020-7434-4040, momoresto.com/momo.html

Neighbourhood • Notting Hill • Nightclub

This club under the Westway off Portobello Road has smartened up décor-wise since its former incarnation as Subterrania. Suits won't fit in here among the music-industry talent spotters and sexy Notting Hill youths. The slick room is spiced up with a dose of purple neon and the main dance floor has a balcony overlooking it, from which you can watch the clubbily dressed dancers shaking it. Expect lots of soulful and funky house as well as some good live sets from bands before they've broken. Check the website to make sure the club is open, as private parties sometimes take over. *Thu-Sat 8pm-2am, Sun 5pm-midnight.* ⓒ≣ 12 Acklam Rd., W10 (⊖ Ladbroke Grove), 020-7524-7979, neighbourhoodclub.net

93 Feet East • Hoxton • Nightclub

Weekends are the best time to come down to this large three-room venue on Brick Lane. It may not have the most high-tech sound system, but it does put on a good night for an edgy, scruffy crowd. With label showcases from Twisted Nerve and Wall of Sound, as well as MTV parties, you're assured of varied but consistently cutting-edge music. The stylish white downstairs bar is always packed while the larger upstairs bar and dance floor is more kitsch. The outdoor terrace and occasional summer barbecues are a real bonus (call ahead to find out when these are). *Mon-Thu 5-11pm, Fri 5pm-1am, Sat noon-1am, Sun noon-10:30pm.* ⓒ≣ 150 Brick Ln., E1 (⊖ Liverpool Street), 020-7247-3293, 93feeteast.co.uk

Notting Hill Arts Club • Notting Hill • Nightclub

The crowd at the Notting Hill Arts Club varies as much as the music. Nights at this basement bar vary from the punk and indie crowd for Alan McGee's Wednesday night Death Disco, and urban heads for hip-hop and soca on Thursdays, to soulboys at long-running friendly funk night on Fridays. Often live bands will spice up the evening. The décor is plain and forgettable, but features some interesting changing graphic exhibitions. NHAC is a great place to extend the party late into the night and enjoy some good music. Note the dress code— no suits and no team colors. *Mon-Wed 6pm-1am, Thu-Fri 6pm-2am, Sat 4pm-2am, Sun 4pm-1am.* ⓒ≣ 21 Notting Hill Gate, W11 (⊖ Notting Hill Gate), 020-7460-4459, nottinghillartsclub.com

The Perseverance • Bloomsbury • Gastropub

London is full of back streets that you stumble across like hidden gems. The design-filled Lamb's Conduit Street is one of those secret places. Despite its hidden location, you'll have to persevere to get a table at this lively gastropub. But it's worth it, as this is without a doubt the loveliest bar remotely near Russell Square. Once inside, you'll find a dark walled space filled with animal heads that attracts the local design types and artists—authentically British with a modern twist. Alongside the ales, there are great Spanish tapas and mezze and a romantic dining room upstairs for intimate couples. *Mon-Sat 4-11pm, Sun 4-10:30pm.* ≣ 63 Lamb's Conduit St., WC1 (⊖ Russell Square), 020-7405-8278

Plastic People • Hoxton • Nightclub

Small. Miniature. Tiny. These are the only words to describe Hoxton's most cramped bijou club. The basement space consists of a bar with a few tables and a small room filled with people dancing the night away to loud sounds. This is the heart of cutting-edge breakbeat music. Coop, on the last Sunday of each month, is the night to come if that strikes your fancy. Other nights focus on everything from hip-hop and drum 'n' bass, to deep house, bringing in a varied, slightly older set of music fans who like dancing more than drinking. *Thu 10pm-2am, Fri-Sat 10pm-3:30am, Sun 7:30pm-midnight.* ⓒ≣ 147-149 Curtain Rd., EC2 (⊖ Old Street), 020-7739-6471, plasticpeople.co.uk

Ruby Lo • Marylebone • DJ Bar

Best Singles Scenes There aren't too many clubs around the Selfridges end of Oxford Street, but that isn't the only reason this after-work haunt is popular. This red basement room is full of a young crowd dancing the night away to '80s hip-hop and classic disco. There's lots of flirting going on here among the young clubbers and older loosened-tie brigade—pepped up by the fruity cocktails brimming with berries. You can get your name on the list easily via the website—which is a must on Friday and Saturday nights. *Tue-Sat 5pm-2am.* C ≡ 23 Orchard St., W1 (⊖ Marble Arch), 020-7486-3671, ruby.uk.com

Salvador and Amanda • Covent Garden • Bar

This tapas bar aims for real Spanish authenticity—with a dash of urban London. There are DJs most nights playing classics alongside Balearic beats, though don't be surprised if you catch live sets and cabaret in between. The emphasis is equally on the sangria and bottles of Spanish beer for this lively crowd of Mediterranean internationals and London twenty-somethings. The paella, tapas, and tortillas are all good for grazing over some conversation and flirting. Reservations aren't necessary but are recommended. *Mon, Wed-Thu 5pm-2am, Tue 5pm-1am, Fri-Sat 9pm-3am.* = 8 Great Newport St., WC2 (⊖ Leicester Square), 020-7240-1551, salvadorandamanda.com

The Social • Fitzrovia • DJ Bar

Upstairs you'll discover a low-key burger bar with four booths for groups of friends. Downstairs is where the media types go for cutting-edge music. The space is quite cramped and resembles a Londoner's idea of a New York dive. It consists of a narrow white long rectangle with limited seating and a small backroom bar. The bottle-beer drinkers don't seem to mind, as they are really here for the hedonism and to look at the streetwise beautiful people in crisp clothes. DJs play anything from reggae and Ibiza classics to edgy garage rock and hip-hop karaoke almost every night of the week. *Mon-Fri noon-midnight, Sat 1pm-midnight.* ≡ 5 Little Portland St., W1 (⊖ Oxford Circus), 020-7434-0620, thesocial.com

333 and Mother Bar • Hoxton • Nightclub

Gritty and rough around the edges, 333 Old Street is nevertheless one of the largest clubs in the area. A young crowd congregates here for the three floors of dirty breaks and beats. Everyone who hangs out in the area has stumbled to the Mother Bar on the top floor at some point after the pubs close for a beer. The Mother Bar is a serious meet market, but that's just what makes it so fun. Dress seriously down, be prepared to line up at the side door, and dance like you just don't care. *Mon-Wed 8pm-3am, Thu 8pm-4am, Fri-Sat 8pm-5am.* C ≡ 333 Old St., EC1 (⊖ Old Street), 020-7739-5949, 333mother.com

Trailer Happiness • Notting Hill • Cocktail Bar

You can't get more kitsch than this tiki basement den. Here a chilled-out Australian–West London crowd drinks vintage cocktails that recall the heady days of the original Trader Vic's in 1930s California. If you're there as a couple, order the dramatic and rather ridiculous Volcano bowl—a two-person bowl of icy cocktails, consumed through straws while its rum burns with blue flames. Regulars also buy tiki-shaped shot glasses, which sit on a special shelf waiting to be filled from the huge selection of West Indian rums. Though quieter midweek, it picks up on weekends, and is perfect for some spirited tongue-in-cheek fun. *Tue-Fri 5-11pm, Sat 6-11pm, Sun 6-10:30pm.* ▭ ≡ 177 Portobello Rd., W11 (⊖ Notting Hill Gate), 020-7727-2700, trailerhappiness.com

Turnmills • The City • Nightclub

Turnmills has been going for years and was once home to some seminal nights, including the infamous gay club Trade and the edgy Heavenly Social. Today the décor is a little dated and worn by decades of hard-core clubbers, but no one notices since it still hosts lots of big-name DJs—Danny Rampling, CJ Mackintosh, and Xpress 2 all still play here. In general, house music reigns supreme; the regular event The Gallery is one of the big crowd-pullers. *Wed 8pm-1am, Thu 9pm-3am, Fri 10:30pm-7:30am, Sat-Sun 10pm-6am.* ⓒ ≡ 63B Clerkenwell Rd., EC1 (⊖ Farringdon), 020-7250-3409, turnmills.co.uk

Under the Westway • Notting Hill • Bar

The bar under the Westway is almost as big as its namesake (the freeway that crosses the city from central to west London). This is a truly cavernous space with a ceiling at least two stories high. It essentially serves as the meeting space for those who work in the trendy offices and studios that fill the building—meaning it's full of West London creatives who wear their low-key designer trainers and jeans just right. There are brown-leather banquettes, pool tables, plus great gastropub style food and DJs. Getting in is potluck—often you can just walk in, but if you can, phone in advance and get on the guest list. *Mon-Sat 8:30am-1am, Sun 5pm-midnight.* ▭ ≡ 242 Acklam Rd., W10 (⊖ Ladbroke Grove), 020-7575-3123, barworks.com

The Westbourne • Notting Hill • Gastropub

Notting Hill has more chilled-out gastropubs than any area in London, and the Westbourne is the top of the crop. The upmarket pub has a French-bistro style interior, with worn roundback cafe chairs and framed graphic posters and original art. Any day of the week the venue attracts twenty- and thirty-somethings with a posh-meets-street edge—fashion girls, men in shirts and baggy jeans worn skate-style. The whole place gives off a low-key vibe, though it's packed day and night on weekends. Alongside the standard drinking fare and simple food, the Westbourne does a mean Bloody Mary with fresh horseradish for extra kick. *Mon 5-11pm, Tue-Fri 11am-11pm, Sat noon-11pm, Sun noon-10:30pm.* ▭ ≡ 101 Westbourne Park Villas, W2 (⊖ Westbourne Park), 020-7221-1332

Zigfrid • Hoxton • DJ Bar

Zigfrid is a relative newcomer to the Hoxton Square bar scene but has quickly established itself as one of the most popular. The space has a lively vibe and a lovely outdoor section looking onto the square, which is always packed during the summer months. Drinks are large and not especially fancy. DJs crank up the noise factor, even though no one ever quite breaks into full-on dancing. Instead this is a place for chatting with the opposite sex and lounging in concrete-meets-drawing-room seats. A club recently opened in the bar's basement and is still testing the waters. However, if you're drunk enough, it's a very easy stumble from upstairs. *Mon-Sat noon-midnight, Sun noon-11:30pm.* ≡ 11 Hoxton Sq., N1 (⊖ Old Street), 020-7613-3105, zigfrid.com

Hip London:
The Attractions

The Circus Space • Hoxton • Activity

See London from an unexpected angle with one of the Circus Space's short courses. In the huge rooms of an old electricity-generating station in trendy Hoxton, participants have the chance to spend a novel morning or afternoon in the company of an infinitely varied bunch of Londoners trying out trapezes (flying and static), juggling, and acrobatic balancing, or perhaps cracking whips, throwing knives, and lassoing stallions as an introduction to Western skills. Elect for a full day of circus training and you can add stilt-walking and tight-wire walking to your repertoire of talents. *Half-days twice monthly, Sat 10:30am-2pm or 2:30-6pm; whole days once a month 10:45am-5:15pm.* ££££ Coronet St., N1 (⊖ Old Street), 020-7613-4141, thecircuspace.co.uk

Coco de Mer • Covent Garden • Shop

If you think sex shops are seedy, then you're in for a lovely surprise. This decadent homage to erotica is beautifully decorated like a Victorian boudoir. Inside it sells erotic literature and art books, handmade exclusive lingerie, silk pillows, and playthings that have more in common with Prada than Soho. All the glamorous girls who work here are very helpful with recommendations, though the shop is also ideal for browsing for a rather unusual gift or two. *Mon, Tue, Wed, Fri 11am-7pm, Thu 11am-8pm, Sat 11am-7pm, Sun noon-6pm.* 23 Monmouth St., WC2 (⊖ Covent Garden), 020-7836-8882, coco-de-mer.co.uk

Columbia Road Flower Market • Spitalfields • Market

On Sunday mornings, this narrow street turns into one of London's most happening spots, thanks to the colorful flower market. The name is slightly misleading, as it also sells a huge range of rare plants, shrubs, and trees, making this nirvana for the green-thumbed urbanite. However, even those without gardens flock here for the fabulous range of blooms from around the globe, before retreating to one of the nearby cafes for a full English breakfast or a smoked-salmon bagel and a stack of Sunday newspapers. *Sun 8am-2pm.* Columbia Rd., E2 (⊖ Shoreditch), columbia-flower-market.freewebspace.com

Cowshed • Holland Park • Spa and Salon

Best Spas To the joy of fans of the original Cowshed at achingly hip Babington House in rural Somerset, the recently opened London branch is just as fun. The rustic chic of the original gets a more urban spin here, but fortunately the signature Cowgroom treatments—two therapists, not one, for maximum effect in minimum time—are all here. Trust-fund babes in skinny jeans come to watch DVDs of *Desperate Housewives* while their hands and feet are groomed to perfection, then stock up on Cowshed's quirky, natural products with tongue-in-cheek names such Frisky Cow Invigorating Foam. *Mon-Fri 8am-8pm, Sat 9am-7pm, Sun 10am-5pm.* ££ 119 Portland Rd., W11 (⊖ Holland Park), 020-7078-1944, cowshedclarendoncross.com

HIP

Fashion & Textile Museum • Bankside • Museum

London's first museum dedicated to contemporary clothing and textiles is the brainchild of designer Zandra Rhodes, whose legendary love of color is reflected in the bright hues of the exterior. Inside the former warehouse, the color comes from the displays, a small but consistently interesting series of shows—about three or four major ones a year—covering every aspect of the topic, from influential magazines such as *i-D* to a retrospective of the clothing and styles of the 1970s. There are occasional fashion-inspired workshops and short courses. *Tue, Thu-Sat 10am-4pm, Wed 10am-8:30pm. £-* 83 Bermondsey St., SE1 (⊖ London Bridge), 020-7403-0222, ftmlondon.org

Feliks Topolski's *Memoir of the Century* • South Bank • Art Museum

Art crops up in some unlikely venues. Take the late Feliks Topolski's extraordinary 600-foot-long panoramic painting, a personal visual diary of the events and people of the 20th century, which is tucked away in three arches under Hungerford Bridge, steps from the Royal Festival Hall. There's fascination and color in every corner of the huge hardboard panels: scribbled images of the end of the Raj, China under Mao, and the horror of Belsen, or of punks and City gents and society beauties. Yet few Londoners even know this quirky jewel exists. *Mon-Sat 5-8pm. £-* Hungerford Bridge Arches, Concert Hall Approach, SE1 (⊖ Waterloo), felikstopolski.com/memoir.htm

Haunch of Venison • Mayfair • Art Gallery

Tucked away in a tiny Mayfair courtyard, Haunch is nevertheless firmly on the map when it comes to the hippest openings in town. Big-name contemporary artists such as Dan Flavin and Wim Wenders make up the backbone of its stable, but the stars of the future aren't overlooked. All this, and a glorious setting in a cleverly adapted Georgian townhouse where Lord Nelson once lived, has attracted a starry set of customers, including Jude Law, Cindy Crawford, and Salma Hayek. *Mon-Wed, Fri 10am-6pm, Thu 10am-7pm, Sat 10am-5pm.* 6 Haunch of Venison Yard, W1 (⊖ Bond Street), 020-7495-5050, haunchofvenison.com

Institute of Contemporary Arts • St. James's • Art Museum

The location may be traditional, but otherwise the ICA is as up-to-the-minute as it gets in the art world. Behind that classical Nash exterior, there's an innovative mix of film screenings, new media exhibitions, thought-provoking talks, and performance art that keeps switched-on locals flocking. It also presents the UK's richest annual art prize, Beck's Futures, with the shortlisted works on view at the gallery from March to May. That said, many of the regulars come not for the global cinema but for the atmospheric bar. *Mon noon-10:30pm, Tue-Sat noon-1am, Sun noon-11pm. Gallery and digital studio: daily noon-7:30pm. £-* The Mall, SW1 (⊖ Charing Cross), 020-7930-3647, ica.org.uk

Jerwood Space • Bankside • Art Museum

The Jerwood Foundation has been associated with sponsorship of the arts for several decades, and this contemporary space fashioned from a Victorian school is one of its newest ventures, providing rehearsal studios for both new and established theater and dance groups. The attached gallery has small but fascinating rotating exhibitions throughout the year, including the winners of the Jerwood's prestigious annual prizes for painting, drawing, and sculpture. Once you've admired their handiwork, there's more to see in the bright, clean-cut cafe and the courtyard. *Daily 10am-6pm.* £- 171 Union St., SE1 (⊖Southwark), 020-7654-0171, jerwoodspace.co.uk

Karma Kars • Various • Tour
Customized tours don't get much more fabulous than this. Karma Kars' small fleet of vintage Ambassador cars from India have been done up in exuberant style, with every inch of the incense-scented interior decked out with lavish fabrics, beads, crystals, and wonderful kitsch touches like flashing Ganeshas. While sticking firmly to the philosophy that the journey is more important than the destination, Tobias and his laid-back crew of drivers will make to measure any tour you want: radical art galleries, retail therapy, or the coolest bars. ££££ 020-8964-0700, karmakabs.com

Magma • Covent Garden • Shop
It's easy to miss this tiny shop on the edge of Covent Garden, but it's worth the effort to find it. The bookshop is always packed with creatives and designers fighting to get their hands on the latest tomes and magazines. If a visual book is new and hot, it's here. The books are arranged by topics such as photography, graphic design, illustration, graffiti, architecture, and fashion. Comics, toys, DVDs, and T-shirts also fill up these already crowded shelves. *Mon-Sat 10am-7pm, Sun 1-7pm.* 8 Earlham St., WC2 (⊖Covent Garden), 020-7240-8498, magmabooks.com

National Film Theatre • South Bank • Film Center
Best Rainy Day Activities For the sheer variety of movies screened here, the National Film Theatre is hard to beat. Among the thousand or so films shown every year, you might catch anything from rare gems from the silent age to archive TV shows or cult hits from any era, as well as indie flicks from around the globe. All this is backed up by an excellent range of talks, workshops, and courses, though if that sounds too energetic you can always just hang out in the bar surrounded by sharp media students and fellow cineastes. *Daily 9am-11pm; screenings Mon-Thu from around 6pm, Fri-Sun from around 2pm.* £- Belvedere Rd., SE1 (⊖Waterloo), 020-7928-3232, bfi.org.uk

Portobello Market • Notting Hill • Market
Best Markets One of the largest markets in London, Portobello is as much a place to see and be seen as to shop, thanks to its resident film stars (but not Hugh Grant) and other media types. That said, the end nearest fashionable Notting Hill has superb, if overpriced, antiques; indeed, it's supposedly the largest antiques market in the world. And beyond the traditional fruit-and-vegetable stalls that follow are the rich offerings of local young designers: individual costume jewelry, way-out clothing, cool accessories. There's nothing quite like it. *Sat 8am-5pm.* Portobello Rd., W10/W11 (⊖Notting Hill Gate), 020-7375-0441, portobelloroad.co.uk

Riflemaker • Soho • Art Gallery
Success was pretty much assured when collector Charles Saatchi bought the first show in its entirety, and this small contemporary gallery has gone from strength to strength in the short time since. From its quirky headquarters behind a Georgian shop front—Soho's oldest commercial building, once occupied by a

rifle-maker, hence the name—it exhibits work by established international names, but also by homegrown new artists, which assures a steady stream of visitors from among the local media folk as well as serious art buyers. *Mon-Fri 10am-6pm, Sat 11am-6pm.* 79 Beak St., W1 (⊖ Oxford Circus), 020-7439-0000, riflemaker.org

Serpentine Gallery • Hyde Park • Art Museum

Don't be fooled by the classical exterior. Within the walls of this former tea kiosk in Kensington Gardens, dating from a relatively recent 1934, lies a consistently exciting and forward-looking art gallery. Since its foundation in 1970, it has gained a reputation for showcasing only the best in modern and contemporary art, with exhibitors ranging from Man Ray and Andy Warhol to Damien Hirst and Henri Basquiat. With up to five shows each year to provide novelty, and an architectural commission each summer, it's no surprise this rates as one of London's most popular public galleries. *Daily 10am-6pm (but check for short closures between exhibitions).* Kensington Gdns., W2 (⊖ Knightsbridge), 020-7402-6075, serpentinegallery.org

Spitalfields Market • Spitalfields • Market

Best Markets In the shadow of the financial district's glass towers, this lively market has everything from vintage clothing and offbeat jewelry to organic bread and 20 different types of olives. By far the busiest day—and the one with the widest variety of one-of-a-kind offerings—is Sunday, when the whole central hall of the Victorian market is crammed with stalls. There's also an intriguing range of shops around the perimeter of the main space, should the pressure of people in the middle get too much. *Mon-Fri 10am-4pm, Sun 10am-5:30pm.* Commercial St., E1 (⊖ Liverpool Street), 020-7247-8556, spitalfields.org

Triyoga • Primrose Hill • Sports

For those who can't get through the week without saluting the sun, this long-established and highly regarded yoga center has a huge range of classes for all levels and at nearly every hour of the day. This serene place also offers small-group or individual Pilates sessions, alternative treatments such as cranial sacral therapy and zero balancing, plus almost every kind of massage you can think of. The lounge is a relaxing place to recover afterward, with a raw-food cafe for guilt-free grazing. *Mon-Fri 6am-9:30pm, Sat 8am-8pm, Sun 9am-9pm.* £-6 Erskine Rd., NW3 (⊖ Chalk Farm), 020-7483-3344, triyoga.co.uk

Urban Golf • Soho • Sports

Best Rainy Day Activities Frustrated metropolitan golfers of all ages flock to this ingenious basement golf center, which unites the thrill of computer games with this normally sedate and, in England at least, clubby game. The six hi-tech simulators let you "play" a round on some of the world's best courses, without having to don the plus-fours and Argyll checks, while the good-looking staff keep you supplied with drinks. Nothing, however, beats the bizarre thrill of watching your ball roll across the real floor and drop into a virtual hole. Equally impressive hi-tech lessons are also available. *Mon-Sat 10am-11pm, Sun noon-8:30pm.* £ 33 Great Pulteney St., W1 (⊖ Oxford Circus), 020-7434-4300, urbangolf.co.uk

Vertical Chill • Covent Garden • Sports

Cardiovascular machines, pah! For a proper, nerve-tingling workout, Vertical Chill is the real deal. This two-story indoor ice-climbing wall in the heart of the city offers thrills aplenty to both experienced climbers with all their own gear for whom the concave ice face presents a decent challenge, and to adrenaline-junkie novices who can take their first "steps" under the expert guidance of the enthusiastic instructors. It's a rare bit of outdoor-indoor fun for anyone who wasn't put off by *Touching the Void*. *Tue 12:30-6:30pm, Wed and Fri 10:30am-6:30pm, Thu 10:30am-5:30pm and 6-7pm, Sat 10am-6pm, Sun noon-5pm.* ££ Tower House, 3-11 Southampton St., WC2 (↔Covent Garden), 020-7395-1010, ellis-brigham.com

White Cube • Hoxton • Art Gallery

While it's not quite true to say that Brit Art wouldn't have happened without Jay Jopling's influential gallery, White Cube is widely regarded as its commercial hub, and not without reason. This sharp, bright space—which does indeed look like a white cube—has hosted shows by Damien Hirst, Tracey Emin, Gavin Turk, Jake and Dinos Chapman, and a host of other young British artists. However, there are also international stars such as Chuck Close and Raoul de Keyser on its books, so there's always something surprising to see. *Tue-Sat 10am-6pm.* 48 Hoxton Sq., N1 (↔Old Street), 020-7930-5373, whitecube.com

Whitechapel Art Gallery • The City • Art Gallery

Best Modern Art Spaces A groundbreaker from the start, the Whitechapel remains one of the country's most influential galleries more than 100 years later. Over the years, it has carved out a reputation for temporary exhibitions of the best international modern art. Picasso's iconic *Guernica* was given its only UK showing here in 1939, and such luminaries as Jackson Pollock, Mark Rothko, and David Hockney had their first British shows within these walls. An ambitious project to double the size of the gallery is under way, which is excellent news for artists and art lovers alike. *Wed, Fri-Sun 11am-6pm, Thu 11am-9pm.* £- 80-82 Whitechapel High St., E1 (↔Aldgate East), 020-7522-7888, whitechapel.org

Classic London

The city acquired its name from the Romans, whose "Londinium" thrived for nearly 400 years on the north bank of the River Thames. So, not surprisingly, there's a huge amount of history to appreciate and enjoy, from aristocratic mansions to ancient cathedrals, and from royal palaces to shops in business since well before the Declaration of Independence. Enduring pleasures come in many forms, however. Of course you're going to visit the **British Museum** and the **National Gallery**, but shouldn't you also eat in style at **Le Gavroche**, and take the air in **Hyde Park**? And no visit would be complete without divine cocktails at **Claridge's**, a nostalgic ride on a traditional red **Routemaster** bus, or a late-night shot of espresso at the much-loved **Bar Italia** ... This is your guide to the capital's classic good times.

Note: Venues in bold are described in detail in the listings that follow the itinerary. Venues followed by an asterisk (*) are those we recommend as both a restaurant and a destination bar.

Classic London:
The Perfect Plan (3 Nights and Days)

Perfect Plan Highlights

Thursday
Morning	St. Paul's Cathedral
Lunch	The Ivy, Savoy Grill
Afternoon	National Gallery
Pre-dinner	Albannach
Dinner	Le Gavroche, Pétrus
Nighttime	Claridge's Bar
Late-Night	Ronnie Scott's

Friday
Morning	The Wolseley, The British Museum
Lunch	Matsuri
Afternoon	Sir John Soane's Museum, Lincoln's Inn, London Silver Vaults
Pre-dinner	Jerusalem Tavern
Dinner	St. John, China Tang
Nighttime	Mandarin Bar, The Blue Bar
Late-Night	Vingt Quatre*

Saturday
Morning	The Rib Room, V & A Museum
Lunch	Bluebird Dining Rooms
Afternoon	Hyde Park, The Spa at the Dorchester
Pre-dinner	Tea at the Ritz, Rivoli Bar
Dinner	Gordon Ramsay
Nighttime	Dover Street Jazz Bar
Late-Night	Floridita

Morning After
Morning	Spencer House, Kenwood House

Hotel: **The Connaught**

Thursday

10:30am After settling into your antique-strewn room, get your trip off to a suitably impressive start with a visit to the the iconic **St. Paul's Cathedral** (consider taking one of the Supertours at 11am), easily reached by hopping on the tube at Bond Street.

1pm Lunch Stroll along Fleet Street— the thoroughfare that was the longtime headquarters of the British press, but today is lined with law-related businesses— and the Strand in the direction of Trafalgar Square. Not far from the square are two classic luncheon spots. **The Ivy** is a favorite of celebrities, as famed for its clientele as for its skillfully rendered nursery-food classics. There's more people-watching at the **Savoy Grill**, which has been a magnet for the rich and powerful for over a hundred years, though the impeccable British cooking is reason enough to book.

3pm After lunch, it's just a short stroll to the fabulous **National Gallery** in Trafalgar Square. Fine-art fanciers can hardly fail to find something to please them among the 2,300 paintings of the permanent collection; there are key works from all the important

CLASSIC

Western European movements from the mid-13th century to 1900. Superb temporary exhibitions mean that there's never a dull moment.

6pm Recover from cultural overload with a wee dram at **Albannach**, a mere totter away across the square. The Scottish theme is mercifully subtle—no screaming tartan here—but there is a stupendous choice of whiskeys. Try not to spoil your appetite for dinner, though, by overdoing it on the smoked-salmon bar snacks.

8pm Dinner A stone's throw from the hotel is Mayfair's much-lauded **Le Gavroche**, with its classical French cuisine, served with panache in a clubby formal dining room. In Knightsbridge, **Pétrus**'s wine-themed décor is the perfect backdrop for an imaginative selection of accomplished French-inspired dishes. For fishier tastes, **J Sheekey** conjures up delectable seafood in the heart of theaterland.

11pm It's been a hard day. You so need pampering, and nobody does it better than **Claridge's Bar**. The attentive service strikes just the right note with the Mayfair clientele, as do the masterful cocktails and refined, but not stuffy, atmosphere. Or take in the twinkling after-dark views from **Windows at the Hilton**, the hotel's top-floor bar with tremendous views over Hyde Park. Or round the night off at jazz club **Ronnie Scott's**, where

all the greats have played. The drinks may be average, but it's the live performances you and your fellow music lovers are here for. The main act generally starts at midnight on Thursdays.

Friday

9:30am Start the day in the grand-cafe elegance of **The Wolseley** on Piccadilly. Indulge in a marrochino, an inspired blend of espresso and dark chocolate with steamed milk.

11am Take the tube from Green Park to Holborn and follow signs to **The British Museum**. There's everything here from parts of the Parthenon to Egyptian sarcophagi, along with the impressive Great Court, a mixture of classical architecture and modern design that is one of London's most-admired public spaces.

1pm Lunch After covering so much ground, both culturally and physically, you deserve a restful lunch. Head east and you'll find **Matsuri**, where you can fortify yourself with top-notch sushi. If you're after something more substantial, linger in the calm dining room over your choice of bento box and a cup of sake. In the opposite direction in Bloomsbury, the intimate **Pied à Terre** offers sophisticated modern French cuisine of exceptional quality.

3pm The afternoon holds a trio of delights. The first is **Sir John**

Soane's Museum, a pocket-sized gem crammed with an eclectic array of classical sculpture, archaeological finds, and art.

4pm Just across the way is historic **Lincoln's Inn**, whose graceful buildings have been home and workplace to London's attorneys for hundreds of years. A short walk away is one of the city's secret places, the **London Silver Vaults**, a subterranean mall with gleaming displays of antique and modern silverware.

6pm Clear your head with a walk along Holborn and through the diamond district of Hatton Garden to the **Jerusalem Tavern**. This tiny slice of history is the place for olde-worlde atmosphere and superb beers-with-a-twist: warming winter ale, fruit beer, or honey porter. The current building dates from the early 18th century.

8pm Dinner You're barely a stone's throw from carnivores' delight **St. John**, whose unfussy décor and robust and flavorful dishes have made it the talk of the town. For something lighter, hop in a cab to glossy **China Tang** at the Dorchester, which looks as if it has strayed here from 1930s Shanghai. Also a ride away, in Knightsbridge, is **Zafferano**, where well-heeled locals chow down on exquisite Italian cooking in artfully rustic surroundings.

11pm Round off the evening in Knightsbridge at the discreetly

theatrical **Mandarin Bar**, in the Mandarin Oriental Hotel, where the refined atmosphere and impeccable table service make it hard to leave. For more wow factor, but with an equally serene ambiance, join the super-rich at the aptly named **The Blue Bar** at the Berkeley for thoroughly civilized cocktails. Or wallow in tradition with a vintage champagne cognac at the **Library at the Lanesborough**, which could have been plucked wholesale from some grand country house.

1am Tuck into some British comfort food with other hungry hedonists at the late-night mecca **Vingt Quatre*** in Chelsea.

Saturday

9:30am A short cab ride away in Knightsbridge, **The Rib Room & Oyster Bar** is a haven of calm and comfort where you can fortify yourself with superbly executed traditional breakfast fare.

11am A short stroll away is London's temple to the applied arts, the **Victoria & Albert Museum**, with its cornucopia of delights: Italian silver, British furniture, historic high fashion, Islamic artifacts, and a great deal more. For a restorative mid-visit coffee, eschew the main cafe for the fabulously ornate Gamble Room.

1pm Lunch Join the lunching ladies in their favorite spots in Chelsea, a brief cab ride away. Top of the list is the highly acclaimed **Bluebird Dining Rooms**, which also attracts the gourmets with its emphasis on fresh seasonal ingredients. For a change of scene, **Daphne's** offers the option of lingering over Italian fare in a Mediterranean garden setting.

3pm Take advantage of a sunny afternoon with a gentle ride in **Hyde Park** along one of the world's classiest bridleways. If equestrianism isn't your thing, the park also offers **boating on the Serpentine**, a romantic lake with rowboats for rent. If the weather's bad, **The Spa at the Dorchester** is a perfect alternative.

5:30pm It's time for the quintessentially English experience of **Tea at the Ritz**. It's all so wonderfully Edwardian, from the dainty cucumber sandwiches to the tinkling piano music and the rococo decor. (Book well in advance.)

7pm After primping at your hotel, get the evening under way with a fabulous pre-dinner cocktail at the reassuringly formal **Rivoli Bar** at the Ritz, especially perfect if you're headed to dinner at Claridge's. Another option is **The Tenth Bar** at Kensington Royal Garden Hotel, a hidden gem with superb views over Kensington Gardens.

8:30pm Dinner Don your best bib-and-tucker for classically inspired cuisine in Art Deco splendor at **Gordon Ramsay at Claridge's**;

you're sure to be surrounded by slender A-listers and other upscale locals. In Knightsbridge, the Michelin-favored **Capital** serves up modern European dishes to millionaires, ladies that dine as well as lunch, and appreciative foodies. Or enjoy a taste of the Orient at long-running **Mr. Chow**, a thoroughly glamorous venue.

11pm Wrap up the evening at the **Dover Street Restaurant & Jazz Bar**, for sultry live music or a whirl on the dance floor.

1am For those eager to end the night with a bang, join the stylish crowd for live Cuban music—and fabulous rum drinks—at sparkling Cuba-themed **Floridita**.

Morning After

10am After breakfast at your hotel, go on a tour of one of London's few remaining aristocratic townhouses. The magnificent **Spencer House** in Mayfair opens its doors to visitors most Sundays. History lesson over, department store **Fortnum & Mason** beckons, with its irresistible selection of foodie souvenirs. An alternative to these, especially on a sunny day, is to take a cab to **Kenwood House** in Hampstead, where you can admire the art and interiors before taking in the views and fresh air on **Hampstead Heath.**

Classic London:
The Key Neighborhoods

Chelsea is the traditional home of the Sloane Ranger, a phrase coined in the 1980s for the well-bred sons and daughters of the nation's gentlefolk. Nowadays, they share the area with high-flying international financiers and their impeccably groomed spouses. Naturally, that means a plethora of retail opportunities, grooming emporia, and expensive restaurants.

Kensington, all stucco villas and Victorian museums, is delightfully quiet and leafy, and thoroughly respectable. Even the Diana worshippers who come to pay homage at her former home, Kensington Palace, can't spoil the prosperous aura.

Knightsbridge may be famed for its shops, but the savviest visitors avoid the touristy swarms at Harrods and savor its culinary delights instead. A clutch of luxury hotels shelters stylish bars that could have come from another century.

Mayfair has been home to the rich and titled for nearly 300 years, and it's still as posh as ever. It has some of London's most elegant historic hotels, high-quality shops oozing tradition, and a wealth of dependably wonderful restaurants and drinking dens.

St. James's is the heart of gentlemanly London, with its exclusive private clubs, traditional shirtmakers, cigar shops, and the like, though these days even nice girls come here for drinks and dinner.

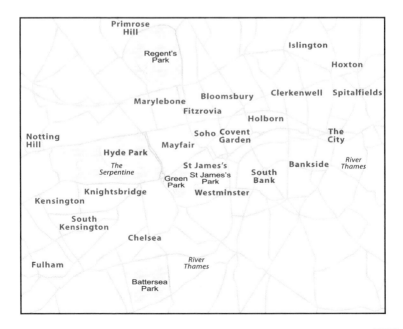

Classic London:
The Shopping Blocks

Bond Street, W1

One of the big names on the Monopoly board, Bond Street has been the main thoroughfare for big-name designers' flagships for over a century.

Asprey The ultimate British store since 1781, Asprey sells everything from housewares to cufflinks to china. (p.163) 167 New Bond St., 020-7493-6767

Burberry This classic British fashion label has a penchant for trench coats and the infamous beige plaid. 21-23 New Bond St., 020-7839-5222

Burlington Arcade This stunning Georgian arcade has small shops selling cashmere, antiques, and gifts. Burlington Arcade, off Piccadilly, burlington-arcade.co.uk

Brompton Cross, SW3

Brompton Cross is what those in the know call the junction of Draycott Avenue, Fulham Road, and Brompton Road. Fur and sunglasses are optional.

Chanel This giant branch of the fashion giant sells a range of ready-to-wear handbags, shoes, and sunglasses. 278-280 Brompton Rd., 020-7581-8620

Conran Shop This has been the biggest name in classic modernist home designs since the 1960s. The Conran Shop Chelsea, Michelin House, 81 Fulham Rd., 020-7589-7401

Ginka Textile designer Neisha Crosland's boutique carries Art Deco–style prints for home, stationery, and fashion. 137 Fulham Rd., 020-7589-4866

Joseph This is Joseph's flagship store of own-label classic womenswear and international labels with giant price tags. 315 Brompton Rd., 020-7225-3335

Jermyn Street, SW1

Filled with small classic boutiques and specialist shops, this road parallel to Piccadilly feels more like 1906 than 2006.

Berry Bros & Rudd Britain's oldest wine and spirit merchant is a living museum to drinking. (p.163) 3 St. James's St., 020-7396-9600

Church's Shoes Come here for classic leather footwear and the best brogues in Britain. 108-110 Jermyn St., 020-7930-8210

Fortnum & Mason Brilliantly British store has been purveying fabulous foodstuffs for 300 years. (p.164) 181 Piccadilly, 020-7734-8040

J Floris You'll find handcrafted and stunningly packaged fragrances and soaps at this shop that's been open since 1730. 89 Jermyn St., 0845-702-3239

Thomas Pink This is the ultimate luxury shirtmaker. 85 Jermyn St., 020-7498-3882

Classic London:
The Hotels

Brown's Hotel • Mayfair • Modern (117 rms)

This classic 170-year-old, five-star hotel just off Bond Street is steeped in history: It was the inspiration for the Agatha Christie thriller *At Bertram's Hotel*, it's where Rudyard Kipling wrote *The Jungle Book*; Franklin and Eleanor Roosevelt spent their honeymoon here, and it was where Alexander Graham Bell made the world's first phone call. Although it's full of old money, don't expect it to be stuffy. Recently bought by Sir Rocco Forte, the hotel, which has been completely redesigned by his sister, the renowned designer Olga Polizzi, has just reopened its doors. The refurbishment alone cost more than £20 million—and it shows, in its refined English interior of gilt mirrors, antique furniture, mosaic floors, and a dramatic color scheme. The rooms range in size from approximately 375 to 1,000 square feet—the best being the deluxe rooms as they are spacious and have a separate seating area. All rooms are decorated in a contemporary classic style in a soft color scheme that's as relaxed and comfortable as being in somebody's home. There's a Bill Amberg–designed bar with leather accents, and an elegant English restaurant called The Grill. Also worth noting are three treatment rooms, a spa, and a gym. The concierge service is notably good. And the Brown's famous tearoom has made a comeback with plenty of modern flourishes. £££ 33 Albemarle St., W1 (⊖ Green Park), 020-7493-6020, brownshotel.com

The Cadogan • Knightsbridge • Timeless (50 rms)

This genteel, award-winning Edwardian hotel (which is not officially rated, but considers itself to be five-star) is most famous for having had Oscar Wilde as a guest—he was arrested in Room 118 in 1895 (an incident subsequently enshrined in John Betjeman's poem "The Arrest of Oscar Wilde at the Cadogan Hotel"). These days Room 118 has pale blue and chocolate walls and silk curtains—surely Oscar would have approved. Despite its age, the hotel is bright and not fusty, and is divided up in two sections: traditional Edwardian and contemporary English—if you're looking for something with old-fashioned English decor, it's worth booking the Edwardian deluxes. The hotel feels like a large modern townhouse, with its old-world-meets-21st-century-style of crystal chandeliers, over-sized lampshades, marble fireplaces, Louis XV-style chairs, and a scarlet glass bar. The rooms measure between 185 and 400 square feet, and have mini-bars, bathrobes, slippers, safes, WiFi—and that quintessentially English touch, umbrellas. There's a medium-sized cocktail bar for hotel guests that doubles up for afternoon teas—which has just relaunched its much-loved, gin-based signature cocktail, the Cadogan Cooler. There's also a restaurant, a gym, private gardens, tennis courts—and a designer dog bed for pampered pooches. Located between Knightsbridge and Sloane Square, the hotel is within easy reach of Harrods, Harvey Nicks, Buckingham Palace, parks, museums, and boutiques. ££ 75 Sloane St., SW1 (⊖ Sloane Square), 020-7235-7141, cadogan.com

CLASSIC

Claridge's • Mayfair • Grand (263 rms)

Cary Grant once said that when he died he didn't want to go to heaven—he wanted to go to Claridge's. One visit to this stunning beacon of old-school British glamour and you'll understand why. The space is a fusion of Edwardian gilt classicism and stunning original Art Deco design. A pianist even plays Gershwin in the lobby most nights. Everyone from the Queen to Audrey Hepburn has graced these halls at some point, and the hotel is just as popular today with an international clientele. Each of the rooms and suites is completely individual, decorated with original Art Deco or gilt Edwardian antiques. It's all about what you prefer—1920s jazz age, bright light, pure silence, floral, gilt, deep reds. Claridge's has such good service they'll even bring your favorite chair in from home if you wish. The hotel is really for decadent tourists who want pure clean classicism without modern soullessness. Many of the rooms are as big as apartments, with adjoining changing rooms and marble bathrooms. It's remarkable that the place manages to create such a haven of luxury without being stifling. The Gordon Ramsay restaurant is one of the best in the city, the two fabulous destination bars draw a chic clientele, and the lovely lobby space is open for tea and lunch. £££ 55 Brook St., W1 (⊖ Bond Street), 020-7629-8860 / USA 800-637-2869, claridges.co.uk

The Connaught • Mayfair • Grand (92 rms)

This five-star hotel is housed inside a modern country house, and is handily close to a range of attractions, from Bond Street, the West End stores, and antique shops to theaters, museums, restaurants, and parks. It's most famous for celebrity chef Angela Hartnett's restaurants, Menu and The Grill Room. There's also Connaught Bar, the American Bar (which has a gentlemen's club feel, and is best for cigars and brandy after dinner), as well as a place for afternoon tea—all are teeming with hotel guests and diners, but not really destination spaces. A modern gym boasts a range of massages, beauty treatments, yoga, and a personal trainer. The intimate—some would say smallish—rooms are decorated by famous designer Nina Campbell in traditional English countryhouse style in rich blues, pale yellows, reds, and creams, with roaring fires and antique furnishings. The best rooms are the four or five deluxe doubles that overlook the villagey Carlos Place, with views of the church, church green, and square. The UK/US modem points, high-speed internet access, TV with internet, hi-fi, mini-bar, and personal fax and telephone numbers are sure to please both business and leisure clientele. And to further indulge every guests' whims, there's also butler service on each floor. £££ Carlos Pl., W1 (⊖ Green Park), 020-7499-7070 / USA 800-637-2869, theconnaughthotellondon.com

The Dorchester • Mayfair • Grand (248 rms)

As one of London's grandest hotels—a favorite with the likes of Michael Jackson, Julia Roberts, and the obligatory paparazzi—this is one off the most decadent five-star venues in London. Four of the hotel's suites are perched on the roof gardens, and have their own private staircases and huge open-air balconies overlooking either Hyde Park or the hotel's own landscaped gardens. No expense has been spared in the Art Deco–style furnishings, which reflect the building's 1930s origins. Rooms are sumptuously decorated with antiques and paintings from the hotel's own collection, and bathrooms have Italian marble baths that are said to be the deepest in London. The best rooms are the spacious executive deluxe doubles—some of which overlook the park—with four-poster beds, walk-in wardrobes, and a desk. Beauty and therapeutic treatments here are legendary, and include spa, steam and sauna rooms, Jacuzzi, hairdresser, and treatments for ailments from jet lag to stress. Other facilities include a medical center, e-butler services, and a desk for booking theater tickets. There are several eating and drinking options, but the small Promenade bar is closed for refurbishment until June; your best bet is the newly opened China Tang restaurant, which has a separate bar crowded, increasingly, with beautiful people. ££££ Park Ln., W1 (✆ Hyde Park Corner), 020-7629-8888, thedorchester.com

Dukes Hotel • St. James's • Grand (89 rms)

Located near Green Park, St. James's Park, and myriad other attractions, this privately owned hotel is set in a tiny street with a cobbled courtyard, walled garden, and gas lamps. The interior has been recently renovated in an elegant and classic, yet fuss-free, style. The lobby areas have cream walls and furniture and fringed velvet drapes, and the rooms and suites are furnished with tasteful artifacts. There are two other reasons why discerning American visitors love this place: The single and double rooms, measuring between 160 and 700 square feet, are larger than those you'd find in most English hotels, and the destination bar is renowned for doing the best martinis in town. The most spacious rooms are the luxury doubles that have en-suite marble bathrooms and overlook the park or the courtyard. All mod cons, like two-line telephones with data port and voicemail, satellite TV, room safes, and mini-bar, are present and correct. There's also a health club that offers spa, and beauty treatments and a gym. £££ St. James's Place, SW1 (✆ Green Park), 020-7491-4840, dukeshotel.co.uk

The Gore Hotel • South Kensington • Grand (49 rms)

The Gore has an entirely Victorian aesthetic. The entrance hall is like walking into an E.M. Forster novel, with portraits of Queen Vic covering the walls from floor to ceiling among the 19th-century fittings. This grand old hotel with 49 rooms over five floors is very traditional in spirit, but now has a modern, somewhat less cluttered look after a recent £2.5 million refurbishment. The dramatically decorated rooms brim with original details and rich fabrics and colors, including mahogany four-poster beds, soaring ceilings, and acres of plush red velvet drapes. Room 305 is particularly lovely with lots of light. The Tudor Room is a complete reinvention of an Elizabethan bedroom complete with stained glass, a huge fireplace, and secret wall panels leading to a whispering gallery. This place attracts tourists with taste rather than business types. It is perfectly located, within walking distance of the Royal Albert Hall, the Natural History Museum, and Harrods. The lovely bistro, 190 Queen's Gate, is sunny and bright during the day and intimate and candlelit at night. The private Bar 190 is often filled with diplomats and open to all guests. ££ 190 Queen's Gate, SW7 (✆ South Kensington), 020-7584-6601, gorehotel.co.uk

Hazlitt's • Soho • Timeless (23 rms)

If you're of a literary persuasion, this hotel is pure catnip. Hazlitt's has been a lodging house since the 18th century and has attracted some illustrious names, including William Hazlitt, Charles Lamb, and Jonathan Swift, who wrote some small book called *Gulliver's Travels*. The space consists of three Georgian townhouses knocked together to become one of the most stunning and unusual hotels in London. The whole listed building structure is crooked and tilted (though obviously safe). There are antiques throughout, in addition to four-poster beds,

CLASSIC

original fireplaces, dark walls, shutters, and paneled walls. The room colors veer from muted grays and greens to deep browns. This kind of style hasn't been in fashion since 1750—which is why it can never go out of fashion. But fear not, there are plenty of modern touches. The bathrooms have been modernized with the occasional vintage freestanding bath and brass fittings. You can check emails for free on the TVs. A lot of authors stay here and donate books for a special cupboard that guests can peruse (including Harry Potter first editions). It's an acquired taste—real authenticity rather than manicured antiques—and won't appeal to everyone. The rooms can be small and often odd sizes, but that is part of the hotel's charm. For those who want to step back in time, there are few better places to do so than Hazlitt's. ££ 6 Frith St., Soho Sq., W1 (⊖ Oxford Circus), 020-7434-1771, hazlittshotel.com

The Lanesborough • Knightsbridge • Grand (95 rms)

The ornate Regency décor and 18th- and 19th-century-style handcrafted furniture of this lavish five-star hotel belies its 21st-century heartbeat: There's a computer with free internet access in every room and in-room video games. The rooms and suites have marble bathrooms fringed with princess-style curtains, inlaid parquet floors, silk wallpapers, antiques, and paintings. The spacious rooms on the first and second floor are the best as they have high ceilings, desk, and separate seating area, and overlook the park. Other facilities include spa, steam room, gym, a translation service aimed at business travelers, and a 24-hour butler service. The hotel's lobby areas are decked out in creams, maroons and blues, and have marble floors, soft velvet drapes, and flamboyant fresh flower arrangements. The small Library Bar with a gentleman's club feel is very famous for its rare Cuban cigars and vintage cognacs (some dating back to 1800). The Conservatory restaurant, complete with potted palms and bling-y chandeliers, is where renowned executive chef Paul Gayler works his magic. Situated just across from Hyde Park, the Lanesborough is close to the designer boutiques and shops of Knightsbridge and West End theaters. £££ Hyde Park Corner, SW1 (⊖ Hyde Park Corner), 020-7259-5599, lanesborough.com

The Milestone Hotel and Apartments • Kensington • Timeless (57 rms)

Located near the Royal Albert Hall, Knightsbridge, and the West End, this popular, award-winning hotel has historical and royal associations, and overlooks Kensington Palace. Ornately and romantically decorated with lots of fresh flowers, open fireplaces, and soft, floral drapes, the venue is simply sumptuous. Leisure travelers will love the superior twin rooms that give views of either the palace gardens or the hotel's own courtyard and conservatory. They're more spacious than the other rooms, equipped with a small seating area, desk space, elegant bathrooms, and, occasionally, themed décor (like safari or military). For business travelers, for whom this hotel is ideal, the most appropriate are the business-ready rooms with extra workspace, two private phone lines, high-speed internet access, and availability of local business cards. There's also 24-hour room service (or 24-hour butler service in the suites, with canapés delivered every evening). The concierge is excellent at advising on the local area. There's one quiet bar for guests, and four restaurants ranging from formal to casual. A special effort has been made for women travelers, such as specially allocated rooms, female service staff, and extra lighting. Even pets have their own beds and their own menus. ££ 1 Kensington Court, W8 (⊖ High Street Kensington), 020-7917-1000, milestonehotel.com

Number Eleven Cadogan Gardens • Chelsea • Timeless (60 rms)

Pretty and feminine, this privately owned, family-run boutique hotel reeks of understated Englishness. It's set in a townhouse amid beautiful gardens on Lord Chelsea's estate, between Buckingham Palace and Harrods. The lobby areas are papered with William Morris wallpaper, portrait and landscape paintings, Victorian busts, large vases, and a grandfather clock. The dining room has ancient blue-and-white china—but offers a thoroughly modern breakfast. There's no bar as such, but drinks can be ordered from waiters in the classical drawing room. The bedrooms and suites are decorated in period furnishings with Colefax & Fowler fabrics, white Egyptian cotton bedlinen, and marble bathrooms with deep bathtubs and Molton Brown toiletries. The grand double rooms are the most spacious, and have a separate sitting area. Once Victorian celebrities used to stay here; nowadays they'd be baffled by such amenities as gym, sauna, WiFi, and broadband. ££ 11 Cadogan Gdns., SW3 (⊖ Sloane Square), 020-7730-7000, number-eleven.co.uk

The Pelham Hotel • South Kensington • Timeless (52 rms)

Housed inside a lavish Georgian townhouse in South Kensington, this four-star hotel is handily close to museums and Hyde Park. The interior is done up in a modern classic style without frills or fuss. The two drawing rooms have fireplaces, oil paintings, antiques and fresh flowers. Fifty bedrooms and two suites, measuring around 130 square feet, are decorated in gentle pastel colors and bold fabrics reminiscent of an English country house. The granite, mahogany, and marble bathrooms come with large tubs and American-standard showers. The best room is Room 101 on the first floor—which has a balcony, high ceiling, and separate seating area. All mod cons are supplied, and there's a small gym, a well-stocked honor bar on the ground floor, and three restaurants. The Kemps bar is festooned with bright artwork from well-known British designers, and is popular with hotel guests and shoppers from the Knightsbridge stores and designer boutiques of Brompton Cross. It serves breakfast and afternoon tea during the day, and is romantically candlelit at night. The concierge service is on the ball, as befits a hotel that's favored with well-traveled Europeans. ££ 15 Cromwell Pl., SW7 (⊖ South Kensington), 020-7589-8288, pelhamhotel.co.uk

The Ritz Hotel • Mayfair • Grand (133 rms)

This legendary, internationally renowned five-star hotel is synonymous with extravagant splendor and sumptuousness. The décor is as classical as it comes, with patterned carpets, ruched drapes, and Louis XVI–style fabrics characteristic of a French country house. All the rooms and suites are painted in the Ritz's signature color scheme of peaches, pinks, yellows, and blues, and furnished with rich fabrics and restored antique furniture inlaid with 24-carat gold leaf. The deluxe rooms are the most desirable as they overlook Green Park. There are high levels of personal service, with two staff to each guest, plus 24-hour porters who provide an excellent concierge service. There's a small Art Deco cocktail bar, a majestic restaurant, and the famous Palm Court where taking tea is something of an institution. There's also a doctor on call, a gym, and a salon for hairdressing and beauty treatments. The hotel sells its own jewelry, and has a gaming club located in its former ballroom. £££ 150 Piccadilly, W1 (⊖ Green Park), 020-7493-8181 / USA 877-748-9536, theritzlondon.com

The Rookery • Clerkenwell • Timeless (33 rms)

The owners of this boutique hotel kept the 18th-century façade, knocked out the rest, and rebuilt the interior in the style of a century ago. The warm Victorian-style interior with real fires, olive leather seats, and a restful conservatory exudes coziness. The hotel itself is a warren with plenty of quirky details like trompe l'oeil painted murals of servant girls along the halls and no elevators. One of the best and most distinctive rooms uses former ecclesiastical church architecture to create a toilet that looks more like a papal throne. The dark-wood Victorian furniture in the bedrooms sits well with the clean modern bathrooms. Most of them are a healthy size with lots of functional Victorian storage. The Rookery prides itself on its history—this is the area on which Dickens based *Oliver Twist* after all. Each of the rooms is named after a servant, shop owner, or Victorian prostitute who once lived in the building in its earlier incarnation as as a butcher shop, bakery, and pharmacy. The area is perfect for people working in the City, though the discreet and quiet space has also been attracting wild musicians like Liam Gallagher and notorious couple Kate Moss and Pete Doherty. Be sure to visit the hotel's suite, the Rook's Nest, a fabulously camp space with a rococo bed, a vintage Victorian bath in the bedroom, and a view of the rooftops, including St. Paul's Cathedral. ££ Cowcross St., EC1 (⊖ Farringdon), 020-7336-0931, rookeryhotel.com

The Savoy • Covent Garden • Timeless (263 rms)

This classic five-star hotel is located on banks of the River Thames, close to Trafalgar Square and the theaters, opera house, and shopping of Covent Garden. It's very elegant, with Art Deco flourishes and all mod cons. The riverview suites—including deluxe double room and deluxe junior suites—offering prime views of the Thames are the best. They're furnished with feather pillows and feather duvets, with Penhaligons toiletries in the bathrooms. There's a business center to cater for businesspeople, who make up most of the clientele. There are several bars, such as the popular celeb-studded destination bar, the American Bar, tea areas, and restaurants on site—the best known being the Savoy Grill. There's also a health club and day spa with rooftop pool. The high-quality concierge team is justly renowned. £££ The Strand, WC2 (⊖ Charing Cross), 020-7836-4343 / USA 800-637-2869, fairmont.com/savoy

22 Jermyn Street • St. James's • Timeless (18 rms)

At 22 Jermyn Street, the staff prides itself on its ability to get you anything. This intimate boutique hotel is all about the concierge service, as there's little real public space here apart from the entrance hall. The interiors of the rooms—all done in chintz, plaid, and florals—are very restrained and traditional. They are spacious, though, with a cozier, more personal design than a modern boutique hotel. None of the rooms have views, as the building is lodged in a narrow 17th-century street, but they still manage to feel bright and comfortable. Not that you'll be spending much time in them since it's set in a perfect location for exploring London. It sits on the same street as Fortnum & Mason, Floris perfumers, and men's tailors in the heart of Piccadilly. The hotel is happy to arrange an itinerary for you. If you do choose to stay in, there's 24-hour room service, a DVD library (served with popcorn), and anything else you might need. Breakfast is always served in bed. Most guests are American, though it attracts a Japanese clientele as well. Ask for a top-floor room to enjoy a bit more quiet. ££ 22 Jermyn St., SW1 (⊖ Piccadilly Circus), 020-7734-2353, 22jermyn.com

Classic London:
The Restaurants

The Admiralty • Covent Garden • French
One of the most beautiful venues in central London, the Admiralty is located inside Somerset House in an 18th-century building that also houses art collections and exhibitions. There's a stunning fountain at the front of the building, and from late November to late January the front courtyard is turned into a magical winter wonderland featuring a beautiful ice rink. The intimate, laid-back restaurant with classically feminine décor offers a gorgeous chocolate fondant on its modern French menu, which is popular with an urbane, arty clientele. *Mon-Sat noon-2:45pm, 6-10:45pm, Sun noon-2:30pm. ££ =* Somerset House, The Strand, WC2 (Temple), 020-7845-4646, somerset-house.org.uk

Alastair Little • Soho • British
Although chef Alastair Little is no longer involved, this intimate contemporary British and continental restaurant continues to be popular with Soho's media set and has been pretty much continuously since the 1980s. The place has an understated elegance, with plain décor composed of little more than a corner bookcase and paintings. The food, too, is simple: Try dishes like smoked eel with potato cakes, or trout with samphire and shrimp and cucumber butter sauce. Service is superb, and the restaurant attracts discerning, well-groomed thirty- and forty-somethings from near and far. *Mon-Fri noon-3pm and 6-11:30pm, Sat 6-11:30pm. ££ _* 49 Frith St., W1 (Leicester Square), 020-7734-5183

Allium • Pimlico • French
This tranquil gourmet restaurant and bar is a place of pilgrimage for chef Anton Edelmann's fans—an older, formal crowd—who travel great lengths to sample his classic French meat cookery. Precisely cooked dishes include pan-fried frogs' legs with endive salad and garlic croûte, and roast partridge with creamed cabbage and wild mushroom tortellini. The Art Deco interior has the hushed reverence of a blue, gray, and silver color scheme that makes the place look a little like the inside of a cruise liner—but thankfully it all works. *Tue-Fri noon-3pm and 6-10pm, Sat 6-10:30pm, and Sun noon-2:30pm. ££ _* Dolphin Sq., Chichester St., SW1 (Pimlico), 020-7798-6888, allium.co.uk

Angela Hartnett • Mayfair • Italian
Strangely enough, London doesn't have many top women chefs: Gordon Ramsay's protégé Angela Hartnett is one of the very few. At her one-Michelin-star restaurant, the menu offers dishes inspired by her Italian heritage, like ham minestrone with mushroom tortellini, and duck breast with balsamic onions. The interior boasts an ornate gilded ceiling with chandeliers, thick patterned carpet, and comfy chairs—all in traditional dark wood, maroons, and creams. A refined thirty-something crowd congregates here on weekends in great numbers to "do lunch." Stop in at the hotel's American Bar for a drink beforehand. *Mon-Fri 7-10:30am, noon-2:45pm, and 5:45-11pm, Sat 7-11am, noon-2:45pm, and 5:45-11pm, Sun 7-11am, noon-2:45pm, and 6-10:30pm. ££ =* The Connaught, 16 Carlos Pl., W1 (Bond Street), 020-7592-1222, gordonramsay.com

Aubergine • Chelsea • French (G)

This upscale, formal restaurant is done up in a signature aubergine color scheme, which lends it an intimate and moody feel. It's probably best known as the venue in which top chef Gordon Ramsay cut his teeth. Contemporary French classics like duck with prunes and Madeira jus, and blanquette de veau, are a hit with a moneyed and manicured Chelsea crowd. The place is particularly lively on Saturday nights—ask for a table in the center if you want to catch the buzz. *Mon-Fri noon-2:15pm and 7-11pm, Sat 7-11pm.* ££ = 11 Park Walk, SW10 (⊖Gloucester Road), 020-7352-3449, atozrestaurants.com

Automat • Mayfair • American

When Automat opened in Mayfair, some of the smart locals thought that, with such a name, it must be a laundromat. Of course, it isn't. In fact, it's an upmarket American diner—an oxymoron, perhaps—but with its luxuriant green leather banquettes and an interior fashioned like a superior railway carriage, who's to argue? Certainly not the financiers, celebrities, and media babes who crowd the place nightly for retro-style dishes like mac 'n' cheese, crab cakes with guacamole, and iceberg lettuce salad with ranch dressing. This is a great place to drop by after visiting the shops and art galleries of nearby Bond Street. *Mon-Fri noon-1am, Sat 11am-4pm and 6-11pm, Sun 11am-4pm.* ££ = 33 Dover St., W1 (⊖Bond Street), 020-7499-3033, automat-london.com

The Avenue • St. James's • British

Popular with art dealers, royal courtiers, ladies who lunch, and other upscale clientele, this tasteful, lively restaurant boasts one of the longest bars in London, and is a great place to people-watch. The gently lit bar area with curved wall and easy chairs gives way to a bright, spacious restaurant with a cream-and-white interior enlivened with vivid abstract paintings. The changing menu offers fuss-free seasonal British and continental fare, such as cream of celeriac soup with spiced apples and walnuts, and roast bream with artichokes, red pepper confit, and thyme. *Bar: Mon-Fri noon-11pm, Sat 6-11pm, Sun noon-10pm. Restaurant: Mon-Thu noon-3pm and 5:45pm-midnight, Fri noon-3pm and 5:45pm-12:30am, Sat 5:45pm-12:30am.* £ = 7-9 St. James's St., SW1 (⊖Green Park), 020-7321-2111, egami.co.uk

The Belvedere • Holland Park • French

Best Romantic Dining Sprawled inside the magnificent Holland Park, this contemporary French restaurant was once the summer ballroom of a 17th-century Jacobean mansion. Set over two floors, the spacious interior has a bar, two dining rooms, and a gallery with alcoves—all of which give excellent views of the park, and of the beautiful mansions owned by the wealthy local clientele. Recently redecorated by top designer David Collins, it's filled with twinkly lights, velvet drapes, pretty wallpaper, and mirrors. To make the most of the natural light, it's best to visit at lunchtime, especially during weekends when there is occasional live jazz. The ground-floor dining room is the liveliest place to sit, and the gallery the most intimate—making it a restaurant, indeed, to suit all moods. *Mon-Sat noon-2:30pm and 6-11pm, Sun noon-3:30pm.* ££ = Holland House, off Abbotsbury Rd., W8 (⊖Holland Park), 020-7602-1238, whitestarline.org.uk

Bentley's Oyster Bar & Grill* • St. James's • Seafood
The old Bentley's restaurant has been given a makeover, and recently opened to glowing reviews; it's now owned by the chatty and charismatic Irish chef Richard Corrigan of Lindsay House. The ground floor houses a ritzy cocktail and champagne bar, and a separate oyster bar that's fast establishing itself as *the* place to eat oysters in London: Both are ideal for solo diners. Upstairs is a restaurant with an elegant cream and electric blue interior, where you can enjoy everything from fish pie to baby squid stuffed with chorizo and organic feta. The oyster bar, however, is the best place to sit and strike up a conversation with the regulars. Mayfair's captains of industry and the pinstripe army have taken Bentley's to heart. *Oyster Bar: daily noon-11pm.* £ = *Restaurant: daily noon-2:30pm and 5:30-10:30pm.* ££ – 11-13 Swallow St., W1 (⊖ Piccadilly Circus), 020-7734-4756, bentleysoysterbarandgrill.co.uk

Bevis Marks Restaurant • The City • Kosher
Jewish restaurants in the capital tend to be rooted in the past, but this polished contemporary eatery, licensed by the Sephardi Kashrut Authority, proves that it's possible to be kosher and stylish. The venue is attached to the attractive 18th-century Bevis Marks Synagogue, and has a sloping glass roof and a contemporary décor that appeals to the stockbrokers and deal makers that make up its City clientele. The wine list is kosher with a few Israeli bottles, and the menu offers a mixture of traditional Jewish and international dishes, ranging from wild mushroom and barley soup to Caribbean pepperpot. *Mon-Thu 5:30-9pm, Fri noon-3pm.* £ – Bevis Marks, EC3 (⊖ Liverpool Street), 020-7283-2220, bevismarkstherestaurant.com

Bibendum • Chelsea • French
Owned by the quintessentially British restaurateur Sir Terence Conran, this modish Art Deco restaurant is housed inside a building once owned by the Michelin Tyre Company in Chelsea. Walk past the fresh fish counter and coffee bar at the front to catch the buzz of the informal Oyster Bar on the ground floor; it's usually teeming with born-again Sloanes. Caviar and seafood platters are perfect for their post-Atkins diet, but for more serious grub they head to the more genteel restaurant on the first floor to tuck into French fare like rosé veal, escargot, and frogs' legs. The restaurant, which is the best place to eat in the building, boasts one of London's most celebrated wine lists. *Mon-Fri noon-2:30pm and 6:30-11pm, Sat 12:30-3pm and 7-11:30pm, Sun 12:30-3pm and 7-10:30pm.* ££ = 81 Fulham Rd., SW3 (⊖ South Kensington), 020-7581-5817, bibendum.co.uk

Blue Elephant • Fulham • Thai
This vast and buzzing restaurant is stunningly decorated with abundant greenery, waterfalls, lotus ponds, bamboo bridges, traditional antiques, and bentwood furniture. The elaborately carved gilded bar at the front serves exotic cocktails like the tamarind martini. The dining room serves the royal cuisine of Bangkok, and regional food festivals throughout August are a highlight. Moneyed locals, large groups, and couples on first dates dressed to impress love this place. Service from traditionally attired staff is smooth as Thai silk. *Mon-Thu noon-2:30pm and 7pm-midnight, Fri noon-2:30pm and 6:30pm-midnight, Sat 6:30pm-midnight, Sun noon-3pm and 7-10:30pm.* £ ≡ 3-6 Fulham Broadway, SW6 (⊖ Fulham Broadway), 020-7385-6595, blueelephant.com

Bluebird Dining Rooms • Chelsea • British

Restaurateur Terence Conran's son Tom is at the helm of this heavily acclaimed modern British restaurant in Chelsea, which evokes the old-fashioned glamour of the 1920s and '30s. Located on the first floor, the dining room and bar are done up in a handsome, masculine style—all browns, creams, wood panels, and framed prints. Head chef Mark Broadbent's menu espouses state-of-the-art culinary concepts of seasonality and provenance of ingredients. Gourmands and Chelsea babes alike have taken his potted meats, coastal British cheeses, and rarely seen British ingredients to heart. *Mon-Sat noon-3:30pm and 6-11pm, Sun noon-3:30pm and 7-11pm.* ££ ⎖ 350 King's Rd., entrance in Beaufort St., SW3 (⊖ Sloane Square), 020-7559-1129, conran.com

Bonds* • The City • European

Housed in a stylish boutique hotel, this venue bustles and bristles with City bankers and power brokers in the evenings. Church candles add drama to an elegant cream-and-brown décor. The crowded bar offers wittily named cocktails like "Lost in the Boot," and the restaurant's European menu keeps the fun factor high with an eyebrow-raising bubblegum ice cream with space dust on its menu. Dishes are listed by the main ingredient as is currently fashionable—so the abruptly named "Crab" is, in fact, tian of fresh Cornish crab with pink grapefruit jelly and pistachio bavarois. *Mon-Fri 6:30-10:30am, noon-2:30pm and 6-10pm, Sat-Sun 7-10:30am.* ££ ⎓ Threadneedles, 5 Threadneedle St., EC2 (⊖ Bank), 020-7657-8088, bonds-restaurant.com

Cambio de Tercio • South Kensington • Spanish

Vibrant reds, yellows, and pinks; colorful Picasso prints; and motifs of bulls and bullfighters in this award-winning Spanish restaurant have brought a touch of Mediterranean sunshine to fashionable South Kensington. The young crowd that flocks here is also blessed with sexy Mediterranean looks and sunshine smiles. Foie gras mousse with rum and jelly is highly recommended, along with other prettily presented tapas. Lovers of everybody's favorite holiday wine, Rioja, are also in for a treat—the regional Spanish wine list offers an exclusive selection of vintage Rioja from 1964 to 1985. *Mon-Fri 12:30-2:30pm and 7-11:30pm, Sat 12:30-3pm and 7-11:30pm, Sun 12:30-3pm and 7-11pm.* £ ⎓ 163 Old Brompton Rd., SW5 (⊖ Gloucester Road), 020-7244-8970, cambiodetercio.co.uk

The Capital • Knightsbridge • French (G)

Ensconced inside the high-class Capital Hotel, chef Eric Chavot's two-Michelin-star French restaurant is a leading culinary destination. The rugged, masculine bar—all nickel, granite, and leather—is inspired by Harry's Bar in Venice, and offers a premium selection of champagnes, spirits, and cigars. The upscale restaurant is done up in soft creams and blues, and offers the likes of crab lasagna with langoustine cappuccino. You're likely to rub (padded) shoulders with ladies who shop with nannies and maids in tow; self-made millionaires and the foodie fraternity make up the rest of the clientele. *Bar: daily noon-11pm. Restaurant: Mon-Sat 7-10:30am, noon-2:30pm and 7-11pm, Sun 7:30-10:30am, noon-2:30pm and 7-10:30pm.* ££ ⎖ Capital Hotel, 22-24 Basil St., SW3 (⊖ Knightsbridge), 020-7589-5171, capitalhotel.co.uk

Chez Bruce • Clapham • Modern British (G)

Best Famous Chefs Filled with fashionable young locals and gastronomes, this intimate neighborhood restaurant is owned by Bruce Poole and Nigel Platts-Martin, two of the leading names on London's dining scene. It regularly tops "best restaurant" lists in customer surveys. The main appeal is the contemporary food that's gimmick-free and firmly rooted in classical style. Another attractive feature is the informality of the place: Unlike many other fine dining establishments, it's not starchy. Beautifully lit, and with a simple décor, the place also offers a must-try cheeseboard. *Mon-Fri noon-2pm and 6:30-10:30pm, Sat 12:30-2:30pm and 6:30-10:30pm, Sun noon-3pm and 7-10pm.* £ = 2 Bellevue Rd., SW17 (⊖ Balham), 020-8672-0114, chezbruce.co.uk

China Tang • Mayfair • Chinese

Tucked into the basement of the sumptuous Dorchester Hotel, this glamorous new Chinese restaurant—filled with antiques, birdcages, and classic paintings—is done up in the style of 1930s Shanghai. The bar and dining room throbs in the evenings with hotel guests, celebrities (in many cases, this amounts to the same thing), and wealthy Mayfair businessmen with their beautiful companions. All the Cantonese classics are present, such as Peking duck, which is properly served in three courses—and there's even a whole roast suckling pig on the menu. *Bar: daily 11am-1am. Restaurant: Mon-Fri 11am-3:30pm and 5:30pm-11:30pm, Sat-Sun noon-4pm and 5:30-11:30pm.* £££ = The Dorchester, 53 Park Ln., W1 (⊖ Hyde Park Corner), 020-7629-9988, thedorchester.com

Cipriani • Mayfair • Italian

This high-class Mayfair Italian is a branch of the legendary Harry's Bar in Venice, so two things are to be recommended straightaway: the Bellinis and the carpaccio—modern classics that were invented at Harry's Bar decades ago. There's a lively bar where you might have to wait (even if you've booked) and a classy dining room that's always teeming with celebrities like Robbie Williams, Naomi Campbell, and Prince Charles. The high-octane, champagne-fueled energy and the vibe created by the presence of the famous and infamous good-time clientele are like nowhere else in London. *Daily noon-3pm and 6pm-midnight.* ££ ≡ 23-25 Davies St., W1 (⊖ Bond Street), 020-7399-0500, cipriani.com

Daphne's • Chelsea • Italian

Popular with wealthy Chelsea matrons, this modern Italian restaurant has a swish entrance that opens up to a rustic interior—all brick walls, tile flooring, and a Mediterranean garden that grows olive and citrus trees. Both wine and food are regional Italian—the latter includes braised venison shank with white polenta and red cherries on its specials menu. The place is part of a group of restaurants that are owned by the company behind the legendary Ivy, so it's never short on buzz. *Mon-Fri noon-3pm and 5:30-11:30pm, Sat noon-3:30pm and 5:30-11:30pm, Sun 12:30-4pm and 5:30-10:30pm.* ££ = 112 Draycott Ave., SW3 (⊖ South Kensington), 020-7589-4257, daphnes-restaurant.co.uk

1880 • South Kensington • French

There's lots of bling inside the restful, romantic restaurant of this lavish hotel that was built in 1880. It attracts an older crowd, mainly groups of friends who are out to enjoy special occasions. The marble-and-gold interior may not be to everybody's taste—but the menu is a hit with foodies who gravitate in great numbers toward head chef Andrew Turner's numerous grazing menus. And with dishes like French pigeon and confit leg pithiviers with creamed savoy cabbage, who can blame them? The bread basket—like the interior—is one of the most extravagant in London. *Mon-Sat 6-10pm.* £££ – The Bentley Hotel, Harrington Gdns., SW7 (⊖ Gloucester Road), 020-7244-5555, thebentley-hotel.com

Elena's L'Étoile • Fitzrovia • French

Named after its legendary 80-something maitre d' Elena Salvoni, this small bistro is a Soho institution. Ms. Salvoni started working here as a waitress decades ago, was then promoted to maitre d', the restaurant's name was changed to include her name—and the rest, as they say, is history. She still turns up to work every day, and stories abound on the London dining scene of her skills as a hostess—she has a knack for combining firmness with diplomacy to deal with many a difficult situation. The fuss-free French food here is popular with businesspeople, and stars of the TV and film industries—particularly at lunchtime. *Mon-Fri noon-2:30pm and 6-10:30pm, Sat 6:30-10:30pm.* £ – 30 Charlotte St., W1 (⊖ Goodge Street), 020-7636-7189

Galvin Bistrot de Luxe • Marylebone • French

Owned by chef brothers Chris and Jeff Galvin, this upscale French bistro recently opened its doors on Baker Street to enthusiastic reviews, and it won't take detective work to see why. It's distinctly cozy and inviting, with its traditional bistro furniture, glossy leather banquettes, and dark wood paneling. Local businessmen, lawyers, and ad executives come here for power lunches—which include elaborate renditions of French comfort food such as wood pigeon pithiviers with glazed chestnuts. *Mon-Sat noon-2:30pm and 6:30-11pm, Sun noon-3pm and 6:30-10:30pm.* £ = 66 Baker St., W1 (⊖ Baker Street), 020-7935-4007, galvinbistrotdeluxe.co.uk

Gordon Ramsay • Chelsea • French (G)

Best Fine Dining Britain's most famous chef's eponymous French restaurant is one of the two three-Michelin-star restaurants in the capital, and is regularly voted as one of the top five restaurants in the world—in other words, it might be an idea to give it a go. The only catch: It's booked up months in advance, and is closed on weekends. The restrained interior, with its Murano glass sculptures and frosted glass panels, is small and intimate. The beautifully dressed clientele ranges from reverential Michelin groupies to couples celebrating extraspecial occasions. *Mon-Fri noon-2:30pm and 6:30-11pm.* £££ – 68 Royal Hospital Rd., SW3 (⊖ Sloane Square), 020-7352-4441, gordonramsay.com

Gordon Ramsay at Claridge's • Mayfair • Modern European (G)

Cocooned amid the understated glamour of Claridge's Hotel, this is the second restaurant to bear the name of one of London's star chefs. This one-Michelin-star venue is more accessible than Ramsay's original (although you'll still need to book in advance), and is a favorite with the hotel's A-list celebrity guests and a voluptuous-wallet-carrying, dressed-up crowd. The notable feature here is the chef's table, which overlooks the kitchen and seats a small number of diners—the experience is quite a contrast to the unruffled calm of the main restaurant. Try a Bellini in the Claridge's Bar beforehand. *Mon-Fri noon-2:45pm and 5:45-11pm, Sat noon-3pm and 5:45-11pm, Sun noon-3pm and 6-10:30pm.* ££ = Claridge's, 55 Brook St., W1 (⊖ Bond Street), 020-7499-0099, gordonramsay.com

Green's • St. James's • British

A traditional British restaurant, Green's is renowned for game in season, and a daily-changing selection of crustacea served at its marble-topped oyster bar—an excellent spot for solo diners. The restaurant appeals very much to the British Establishment's conservative sensibilities. Hence the intimate gentlemen's club feel created by mahogany panels and leather banquettes attracts senior figures from the world of politics and business. The regional, seasonal menu in the dining room serves classics ranging from potted shrimps to Oxford Burnt Cream. Cheeses are from Britain's oldest cheesemongers, Paxton & Whitfield. *Sept-Apr: Mon-Sat 11:30am-3pm and 6-11pm, Sun noon-3pm and 6-9pm. May-Aug: Mon-Sat 11:30am-3pm and 6-11pm. £££* ▬ 36 Duke St., SW1 (⊖Green Park), 020-7930-4566, greens.org.uk

The Greenhouse • Mayfair • French

An abundance of greenery outside this contemporary restaurant makes it a pleasant spot to try the chef's signature dish of espresso foie gras while reclining on chunky wooden furniture. The interior is more luxurious, with silver champagne ice buckets dotted around wooden floors, red-and-cream leather banquettes, velvet drapes, and walls painted in shimmering fairy-tale colors. The menu changes eight times a year, and the cheeses are supplied by artisanal French cheesemakers—a fact that's not lost on the sophisticated food-savvy clientele. *Mon-Fri noon-2:30pm and 6:45-11pm, Sat 6:45-11pm. £* = 27A Hay's Mews, W1 (⊖Green Park), 020-7499-3331, greenhouserestaurant.co.uk

The Ivy • Covent Garden • British

Best Celeb Haunts As London's most famous restaurant, The Ivy is celeb central: Every major (and minor) celebrity frequents it, and many of the tables are especially set aside for the celebrity fraternity, with seating position discreetly carving out their status. Done up in a classic Art Deco style, this contemporary British and continental restaurant is best-loved for its fuss-free but exemplary English nursery classics like shepherd's pie and sticky toffee pudding. Tables need to be booked several months ahead, though—and to avoid celeb-gawkers and dine with A- rather than Z-listers, it's advisable to go on a weekday evening. Or you could take a chance and drop by at an unpopular time, say, 6pm or 10pm, when tables may be available on the off-chance: This is not difficult to achieve as there are plenty of theaters nearby to keep you occupied. There's a small bar at the entrance that's ideal for a pre-dinner drink. *Mon-Sat noon-3pm and 5:30pm-midnight, Sun noon-3:30pm and 5:30pm-midnight. £* = 1-5 West St., WC2 (⊖Leicester Square), 020-7836-4751, the-ivy.co.uk

J Sheekey • Covent Garden • British

The understated elegance of this stunningly popular seafood restaurant belies the fireworks that the kitchen is capable of: Everything from jellied eels (a working-class East London classic that's a must-try), to the legendary fish pie, to lobster and oysters, is beautifully executed. The venue is popular for business lunches, when the pinstripe army discussing mergers and takeovers rubs shoulders with actors and producers from nearby West End theaters. The décor is elegantly minimalist, and service is refreshingly unsnooty and professional. *Mon-Sat noon-3pm and 5:30pm-midnight, Sun noon-3:30pm and 6pm-midnight. £* = 28-32 St. Martin's Court, WC2 (⊖Leicester Square), 020-7240-2565, j-sheekey.co.uk

Kai Mayfair • Mayfair • Chinese (G)

This sumptuous restaurant sells London's most expensive soup: It's poetically described as "Buddha Jumps Over the Wall" and contains exclusive ingredients like abalone and premium-quality shark's fin. The cost? A snip at £108. That's small change for the beautiful squillionaires that include Arab princes and international playboys, who make up most of its Mayfair clientele. Glamour oozes from every pore—from the stripy chaise longue at the bar, to the semiprecious stones that adorn the silverware. If bling is your thing, this is the kind of place to conjure up a fantasy romance. *Mon-Fri noon-2:30pm and 6:30-11pm, Sat 12:30-3pm and 6:30-11pm, Sun 12:30-3pm and 6:30-10:30pm.* £££ ≡ 65 South Audley St., W1 (⊖ Bond Street), 020-7493-8988, kaimayfair.com

Kaya • Mayfair • Korean

Korean food is heralded as the next big thing—although by the time you read this, it's likely that the cuisine of a little-known military regime near Iceland is what everybody will be getting hot and bothered about; such things happen in London. Most Korean eateries in the capital tend to be cheap and cheerful—but this stylish, formal Mayfair joint is elegantly lit by paper lanterns, and diners are served by traditionally attired staff. Dishes like jellyfish with seafood in mustard sauce are popular with an elevated Mayfair clientele. *Mon-Sat noon-3pm and 6-10pm.* £ ≡ 42 Albemarle St., W1 (⊖ Green Park), 020-7499-0622

Ladurée • Knightsbridge • Tearoom

Located inside Harrods, this upmarket tea shop is a branch of the famous chain based in Paris. It's sumptuously done up and boasts three dining areas, all gloriously camp and over-the-top in terms of their look—ornate statues of semi-naked men, gilded mirrors, and the like. Ladies who lunch love to munch on the legendary macaroons and nibble on the gorgeous selection of cakes, pastries, and teas served in bone china. If you yearn to feel like you're in Paris for an afternoon, this place will do the trick. *Mon-Sat 9am-9pm, Sun noon-6pm.* £ ≡ Harrods, 87-135 Brompton Rd., Door 1B (Hans Rd. entrance), SW1 (⊖ Knightsbridge), 020-3155-0111, laduree.com

Le Caprice • Mayfair • British

Best Celeb Haunts Tucked away in a side street near the Royal Academy, this select restaurant is favored by ladies who lunch, art dealers, and other diners with a dash of dosh. The dining room is decorated in serene Art Deco monochrome, with intimate alcoves should you want a private space from which to peek at the many visiting celebrities. Classic continental and British fare includes such signature dishes as eggs benedict, and salmon fishcake with buttered spinach and sorrel sauce. *Mon-Sat noon-3pm and 5:30pm-midnight, Sun noon-5pm and 6-11pm.* £ – Arlington House, Arlington St., SW1 (⊖ Green Park), 020-7629-2239, le-caprice.co.uk

L'Escargot • Soho • French

Serving elaborately executed French dishes in bright, contemporary surroundings, this cozy restaurant is owned by Marco Pierre-White, who, before hanging up his apron, was said to cook food so legendary that gourmets still get misty-eyed talking about it, and whisper in hushed tones about "the best chef Britain has ever known." These days it attracts a dapper media clientele from nearby offices, who love the Picasso prints on the walls as much as the Goosnargh duckling and Blenheim Estate lamb on the menu. The ground-floor dining room is livelier, whereas the Picasso Room has a more private, exclusive feel. *Restaurant (ground floor): Mon-Fri noon-2:15pm and 6-11:30pm, Sat 6-11:30pm. £ = Picasso Room (first floor): Tue-Fri noon-2:15pm and 7-11pm, Sat 7-11pm. ££ –* 48 Greek St., W1 (◒ Leicester Square), 020-7437-2679, whitestarline.org.uk

Le Gavroche • Mayfair • French (G)
Best Fine Dining The first restaurant to be awarded three Michelin stars in the UK, the multi–award-winning Le Gavroche in the West End is a legend that is still somehow intimate enough to make you feel like you're being pampered in a wealthy relative's sitting room. The ruched curtains and banquettes in British racing green create an intimate, clubby feel that its somewhat conservative Establishment clientele clearly adores. Michel Roux Jr.'s recipes, such as Irish rock oysters and scallops poached in champagne with leeks and truffles, has enthralled many a gastro-traveler, and the bar is a grand place to cool your (Wellington) boots. *Mon-Fri noon-2pm and 6:30-11pm, Sat 6:30-11pm. £££ =* 43 Upper Brook St., W1 (◒ Marble Arch), 020-7408-0881, le-gavroche.co.uk

Le Pont de la Tour • Bankside • French
In the late 1990s, the Conran-owned Pont hit headlines when Tony Blair brought Bill Clinton here on his first official visit to the UK; these days it's hitting the headlines for altogether different reasons. This spacious waterfront venue has continued to attract a steady stream of powerful international figures, who love the fruits de mer at the lively Bar & Grill, and unhurried Sunday lunches in the restaurant. Sunshine brings a pleasant dilemma: whether to eat on the lovely outside terrace overlooking the river—or pack a picnic of gourmet charcuterie from the attached Foodstore. *Bar & Grill: daily noon-3pm and 6-11pm. £ ≡ Restaurant: Mon-Fri noon-3pm and 6-11:30pm, Sat 6-11:30pm, Sun noon-3pm and 6-11pm. £ =* Butlers Wharf Building, 36D Shad Thames, SE1 (◒ London Bridge), 020-7403-8403, conran.com

Lindsay House • Soho • Irish
Set over four floors, this one-Michelin-star restaurant is located within a 1740s townhouse, and you'll need to ring the doorbell to gain entry. The charismatic, award-winning celebrity chef Richard Corrigan's modern Irish cooking has attracted a mixture of discerning foodies and well-groomed romantic couples, who like the hushed intimacy of the numerous small dining rooms and private rooms (the best tables are in the main dining room on the ground floor). With its flickering candles, fresh flowers, gilt-edged crockery, and fireplace, it will make you feel like you're visiting an elegant friend's house for a dinner party. *Mon-Fri noon-2:30pm and 6-11pm, Sat 6-11pm. £ –* 21 Romilly St., W1 (◒ Leicester Square), 020-7439-0450, lindsayhouse.co.uk

Luciano • Mayfair • Italian
Owned by Marco Pierre-White—London's first three-Michelin-star chef and a legendary figure on London's dining scene—this contemporary Italian opened to gushing reviews, especially from male reviewers who love the gentlemen's club feel. The spacious dining room is decorated with Art Deco flourishes and has 1930s paintings, plenty of leather accents, and dramatic lighting. There are two bars, one with an attractive Art Deco piano. An ideal place for a business lunch,

Luciano's truffle dishes (in truffle season) are not to be missed. *Bar: Mon-Sat noon-11pm. Restaurant: Mon-Sat noon-2:30pm and 6-11pm. £* ⊜ 72-73 St. James's St., SW1 (⊖ Green Park), 020-7408-1440, lucianorestaurant.co.uk

Matsuri • Holborn • Sushi

Best Sushi This graceful and beguiling Japanese restaurant encompasses a small bar with limited seating, a sushi counter that's popular with students from the nearby London College of Fashion, a teppanyaki room that appeals to older fans of this fashionable cuisine, and a serene main dining room with slatted bamboo screens—the latter is the best place to sit if you want to catch the buzz, but all the rooms have distinctly different crowds. Lunchtime bento boxes and sushi hand-rolled by a top sushi chef from Japan are the greatest hits, and there's a wonderful selection of sake that's popular with local businesspeople. *Mon-Sat noon-2:30pm and 6-10pm. £* ⊟ 71 High Holborn, WC1 (⊖ Holborn), 020-7430-1970, matsuri-restaurant.com

Mirabelle • Mayfair • French

Famous since the 1950s when it attracted royalty and Hollywood celebs, this glamorous Mayfair restaurant and bar continues to appeal to the rich and the famous—as well as oenophiles who can't help but enthuse about the 50 different vintages of Chateau D'Yquem on its wine list. The menu is largely French—with a touch of British. The best time to visit is for Sunday lunch, when the restaurant is abuzz with the contented hum of well-heeled diners tucking into English breakfast dishes and classic French and British roasts. *Mon-Fri noon-2:30pm and 6-11:30pm, Sat noon-3pm and 6-11:30pm, Sun noon-3pm and 6-10:30pm. ££* ⊜ 56 Curzon St., W1 (⊖ Green Park), 020-7499-4636, whitestarline.org.uk

Mr. Chow • Knightsbridge • Chinese

The look of this trendsetting Chinese restaurant is as important as its food: little wonder, as the owner, Michael Chow, is not only a restaurateur, but also a designer, actor, artist, collector, and jet-setting businessman, who has set up branches on other continents. The glamorous entrance gives way to a bar bedecked with fresh flower arrangements, and the thriving restaurant interior is filled with expensive Asian artifacts—and with expense-account diners and their beautiful, bejeweled girlfriends. *Daily 12:30-3pm and 7pm-midnight. ££* ⊜ 151 Knightsbridge, SW1 (⊖ Knightsbridge), 020-7589-7347, mrchow.com

Morgan M • Islington • French

Chocoholics will adore the acclaimed dark chocolate moelleux, which can be ordered with the chocolate of your choice at French chef Morgan Meunier's signature restaurant in the cool area of Islington. Other elaborately prepared and presented seasonal dishes also entice trendy North Londoners and fans of fine dining; and there's a gourmet vegetarian menu that's worth a special journey. The intimate dining room with its cream walls, oak floors, green armchairs, and huge opaque glass windows has an ambiance that's soothing but never overly reverential. *Tue and Sat 7-10:30pm, Wed-Fri noon-2:30pm and 7-10:30pm, Sun noon-2:30pm. ££* ⊜ 489 Liverpool Rd., N7 (⊖ Highbury & Islington), 020-7609-3560, morganm.com

Nahm • Knightsbridge • Thai

Located inside the subdued Halkin Hotel, UK's only Michelin-starred Thai restaurant has a separate bar at the front that's teeming with young businessmen and their carefully manicured girlfriends enjoying lychee martinis. The cozy restaurant attracts a slightly older crowd, who are reverential about multiple–award-winning consultant chef David Thompson's modern interpretation of the royal Thai cuisine of Bangkok. The austere maroon-and-gold décor creates an aura of understated elegance, so that the attention is firmly focused on the food—which some consider to be the best of its kind in the world. *Mon-Fri noon-2:30pm and 7-11pm, Sat 7-11pm, Sun 7-10pm.* ££ _ The Halkin, 5 Halkin St., SW1 (⊖ Hyde Park Corner), 020-7333-1234, halkin.co.uk

Nipa • Marylebone • Thai

Reputed to serve the best Thai green chicken curry in London, Nipa is the Thai community's choice for special-occasion dining. This comfortable restaurant, bejeweled with Thai antiques, handcrafted ornaments, and carved wooden furniture, is a favorite with visiting Thai dignitaries such as the Thai royal family, politicians, and pop stars. Prettily presented dishes decorated with carved fruit and vegetables add a dash of fire and spice to the otherwise composed and collected teak-paneled environs. The small, quiet bar offers Asian-themed cocktails and Thai wines. *Bar: Mon-Sat 11am-11pm, Sun 11am-10:30pm. Restaurant: Mon-Fri noon-2pm and 6:30-10:30pm, Sat 6:30-10:30pm.* £ _ Royal Lancaster Hotel, Lancaster Terrace, W2 (⊖ Lancaster Gate), 020-7551-6039, niparestaurant.co.uk

1 Lombard Street* • The City • British

Housed inside a converted bank, this stylish, roomy venue boasts a bar and brasserie and a one-Michelin-star restaurant whose look is inspired by Titian's neo-classical *Rape of Europa* painting. The serene brasserie serves up classic English breakfast fare such as grilled kippers; and the bar comes alive in the early evening, when there's occasional live music and City suits drop by for cocktails with names like Wall Street. The restaurant serves British and continental fare, so you'll find both sauerkraut and Guinness ice cream on the menu. *Bar: Mon-Fri 11am-11pm. Brasserie: Mon-Fri 7:30-11am and 11:30am-10:30pm.* ££ = *Restaurant: Mon-Fri noon-3pm and 6-10pm.* £ = 1 Lombard St., EC3 (⊖ Bank), 020-7929-6611, 1lombardstreet.com

Origin • Covent Garden • British

Located inside a multimedia center in Covent Garden, this contemporary British and continental restaurant attracts an arty crowd, especially actors working in nearby theaters. The place has been refurbished and relaunched, and now displays an elegant, attractive, and well-lit look. The acclaimed chef offers a mixture of three-course meals and small sharing platters, such as foie gras, lobster, and pork belly. The restaurant has an informal but stylish, clubby look, and the cool lounge bar does great cocktails. Don't miss the sumptuous chocolate soufflé. *Bar: Mon-Fri noon-midnight, Sat 5pm-midnight. Restaurant: Mon-Fri noon-2:30pm and 6-10:30pm, Sat 5-11pm.* ££ Ⓑ = The Hospital, 24 Endell St., WC2 (⊖ Covent Garden), 020-7170-9200, origin-restaurant.com

Palm Court • Mayfair • Tearoom

Tea at the Ritz is an institution—a throwback to the days when Oscar Wilde ruled the world (or at least English literature), and sitting down to dainty finger sandwiches, bulbous scones dolloped with clotted cream, and a cup of Earl Grey could solve all the world's problems. At the genteel but lavish Palm Court, with its marble columns and extravagant chandeliers, it's possible to experience that Oscar Wilde moment—but be warned: There are five seatings a day, so you won't

CLASSIC

be able to linger, and you'll have to book at least six weeks in advance. *Tea served daily (reserved sittings) 11:30am, 1:30, 3:30, 5:50, and 7:30pm. ££££* ⊟ The Ritz, 150 Piccadilly, W1 (⊖ Green Park), 020-7493-8181, theritzlondon.com

Pasha • Kensington • Moroccan

With its deeply romantic ambiance, it's little wonder that this Moroccan restaurant is the place where gorgeous young men and women come to fall in love. The scene is set from the moment you enter the carved doors lit with flickering candles. More candles—and brass lanterns and oil lamps—scatter shadows and light onto cozy souk-like alcoves and hidden tables. Low-slung seating with cushions, a marble fountain strewn with rose petals, and the spicy aroma of incense help nudge things along in the right direction. The cocktail lounge offers flavored sheesha pipes that are an ideal way to end—or start—the evening. *Mon-Sat noon-3pm and 6-11pm, Sun 6:30-10pm. £* ⊟ 1 Gloucester Rd., SW7 (⊖ Gloucester Road), 020-7589-7969, pasha-restaurant.co.uk

Patara • Soho • Thai

This exquisite restaurant is the latest addition to an upmarket chain—which has three other branches in some of the most salubrious parts of London. The centerpiece is a gold-leaf lacquered teak palace—definitely the best place to sit—and other design features include traditional royal pavilions, sculpted sandstone walls, and luxurious scarlet seating. The modern Thai menu is popular at lunchtime with the young men and women from the advertising and design industries who work nearby; in the evenings the restaurant comes alive with the buzz of dating couples. *Mon-Sat noon-3pm and 6:30-10:30pm, Sun 6:30-10:30pm. £* ⊟ 15 Greek St., W1 (⊖ Tottenham Court Road), 020-7437-1071

Pétrus • Knightsbridge • French (G)

Best Power Lunches Before moving into The Berkeley, Gordon Ramsay protégé Marcus Wareing's one-Michelin-star French restaurant was located at another address nearby—and in 2001 became the most (in)famous restaurant in the world. Why? Because six bank employees closed a business deal here by splashing out on a headline-grabbing £44,007 dinner that included several bottles of Chateau Pétrus—the most expensive restaurant meal at the time. The current clientele may wear less bling, but it's certainly super-rich. Designer-god David Collins's vinous décor of lush purples, designer wine racks and other wine motifs, and the celebrated wine list complement each other. A tour of the kitchen is offered to all diners. *Mon-Fri noon-2:30pm and 6-11pm, Sat 6-11pm. £££* ⊟ The Berkeley, Wilton Pl., SW1 (⊖ Knightsbridge), 020-7235-1200, gordonramsay.com

Pied à Terre • Bloomsbury • French (G)

Best Power Lunches Widely regarded as one of London's premier restaurants, Pied à Terre closed due to a fire, but has risen, phoenix-like, from the ashes, to universal acclaim: Some people reckon the food and the ambiance are better than ever before. The contemporary French food draws hedonistic foodies from miles away. The restaurant is famous for its foie gras, and there's also an exquisite gourmet vegetarian menu, and one of the best wine lists in London. Located in a townhouse, the restaurant is not much of a looker—it's rather plain—but there's a lovely bar upstairs, and plenty of buzz in both the bar and the dining room. *Mon-Fri 12:15-2:30pm and 6:15-10:30pm, Sat 6:15-10:30pm. ££* ⊟ 34 Charlotte St., W1 (⊖ Goodge Street), 020-7636-1178, pied-a-terre.co.uk

Quaglino's • St. James's • European

Suffused with old-fashioned starry glamour, the opening of this Terence Conran restaurant was a momentous occasion in the early 1990s. It's located on the site of the old Quaglino's—London's most famous society restaurant in the first half of the 20th century. You enter by descending a sweeping staircase—although the "it girls," celebrities, and the fashion, music, and media crowd are usually too busy quaffing champagne to greet you with applause as they would have done in yesteryears. Fashionable retro touches include Art Deco ashtrays, cigarette girls, live jazz every night, and baked Alaska on its retro-chic brasserie menu. *Bar: Mon-Thu 11:30am-1am, Fri-Sat 11:30am-2am, Sun noon-11pm. Restaurant: Mon-Thu noon-3pm and 5:30pm-midnight, Fri-Sat noon-3pm and 5:30pm-1am, Sun noon-3pm and 5:30-11pm. Afternoon tea: daily 3-5:30pm.* £ B = 16 Bury St., SW1 (⊖ Green Park), 020-7930-6767, quaglinos.co.uk

Racine • Knightsbridge • French

Styled like an elegant, old-fashioned Parisian restaurant—all heavy curtains, dark leather banquettes, smoked mirrors, and dimmed lighting—top chef Henry Harris's acclaimed restaurant is a mecca for gastronomes. The eminent and immaculately clad ladies and gents of Knightsbridge can be seen giving their GI diets a wide berth, in favor of rich food like foie gras, cassoulet, and sweet-breads. Service is slickly professional and friendly. *Mon-Fri noon-3pm and 6-10:30pm, Sat noon-3:30pm and 6-10:30pm, Sun noon-3:30pm and 6-10pm.* £ = 239 Brompton Rd., SW3 (⊖ South Kensington), 020-7584-4477

Rasoi Vineet Bhatia • Chelsea • Indian

Best Indian Restaurants Translating as "Vineet Bhatia's Kitchen," this cutting-edge restaurant owned by the eponymous Indian chef has been heaped with gushing accolades, including a new Michelin star. It's located inside a century-old town-house: Entry is by ringing the doorbell, and the two floors house a number of small dining rooms and private rooms—of which the ground floor dining rooms are the buzziest. The cozy space is decorated with ornamental Ganeshas, tinkling bells from South Indian temples, Indian tribal masks, and silk cushions. Keen followers of the chef and eminent Chelsea locals come here to enjoy dishes like ginger and chili lobster dusted with cocoa, and samosas filled with marbled chocolate. *Mon-Fri noon-2:30pm and 6:30-10:30pm, Sat 6:30-10:30pm.* £££ – 10 Lincoln St., SW3 (⊖ Sloane Square), 020-7225-1881, vineetbhatia.com

Rhodes Twenty-Four • The City • British

Pulsating with company directors and stockbrokers, popular TV chef Gary Rhodes's British restaurant is a favorite for power lunches. Located on the 24th floor (that's high by London standards), it affords excellent views of east London, especially such landmarks as Sir Norman Foster's "Gherkin" tower. Contemporary British classics like roast chicken with sage are superb—but it's English nursery puddings (like bread and butter pud) that are the star of the show. There's also a champagne and oyster bar, Vertigo 42, on the 42nd floor (that's *very* high by London standards). Due to tight security, you'll have to book in advance for both the bar and the restaurant, and obtain a pass at the door. *Mon-Fri noon-2:30pm and 6-9pm.* £ = Tower 42, 25 Old Broad St., 24th Fl., EC2 (⊖ Bank), 020-7877-7703, rhodes24.co.uk

The Rib Room & Oyster Bar • Knightsbridge • British

Good English breakfast, fresh seafood at the popular Oyster Bar, and traditional British dishes with a slight American touch are the draw at this refined restaurant on the ground floor of the Carlton Tower Hotel. The bustling gentlemen's club interior is a hit with successful businesspeople and their spouses, and groups of friends celebrating special occasions; and a pianist in the evenings heightens the feeling of refinement. Must-try dishes include Loch Fyne salmon, Aberdeen Angus rib of beef, and Yorkshire pudding. The best time to come is for Sunday lunch, when the restaurant is a haven for carnivores. *Mon-Sat 12:30-2:45pm and 7-10:45pm, Sun 12:30-2:45pm and 7-10:15pm.* ££ = The Carlton Tower, Cadogan Pl., SW1 (⊖ Knightsbridge), 020-7858-7053, carltontower.com

Roussillon • Chelsea • French (G)

Despite having earned itself a Michelin star, this sleek, elegant French restaurant is regularly described by those in the know as "a hidden gem." Popular with politicians and well-groomed Establishment figures, it's a tranquil place with a minimalist monochrome interior. French chef-proprietor Alex Gauthier is renowned for his vegetable cuisine—so the gourmet vegetarian menu is particularly memorable. Roussillon also offers one of the best desserts in town: a spicy soufflé of duck eggs with gingerbread soldiers and maple infusion. *Mon-Fri noon-2:30pm and 6:30-11pm, Sat 6:30-11pm.* ££ ⌐ 16 St. Barnabas St., SW1 (⊖ Sloane Square), 020-7730-5550, roussillon.co.uk

Royal China Queensway • Kensington • Dim Sum

Dim sum is enormously, almost unfathomably, popular in London right now—and the Cantonese Royal China chain (with a few branches in the capital, and one in Singapore) offers some of the best and most authentic in the UK. This West London branch attracts sophisticated Chinese families as well as slim-hipped babes who worship at the altar of this newfangled culinary religion. The chic black interior, with its mirrored ceiling, glossy columns, lacquered surfaces, and beautiful Chinese screens, positively throbs on weekends at lunchtime. Dim sum is not served on trolleys, however: A battalion of waiters brings the dishes on large, beautiful platters when they're ready. *Mon-Thu noon-11pm, Fri-Sat noon-11:30pm, Sun 11am-10pm. Dim sum: Mon-Sat noon-5pm, Sun 11am-5pm.* £- ≡ 13 Queensway, W2 (⊖ Queensway), 020-7221-2535, royalchinagroup.co.uk

Rules • Covent Garden • British

One of the oldest restaurants in London, this traditional British venue has been doing a roaring trade since the 18th century—so it can't be too bad then. Certainly the hunting and shooting set, and actors who tread the boards in nearby theaters, don't think so. Filled with antique clocks and political cartoons, the place is particularly busy for Sunday lunch. The menu showcases game from the restaurant's own estate in the Pennines, as well as rarely seen meats such as Belted Galloway beef, Tamworth suckling pig, blackgame, ptarmigan, pochard, and widgeon. An ideal spot to indulge your Madonna-style lady-of-the-manor fantasy. *Mon-Sat noon-11:30pm, Sun noon-10:30pm.* £ ≡ 35 Maiden Ln., WC2 (⊖ Covent Garden), 020-7836-5314, rules.co.uk

St. John • Clerkenwell • British

Best Famous Chefs British chef Fergus Henderson's low-key, minimally decorated venue, containing a bar and a bread shop, is one of the most famous restaurants in the world. Its "nose to tail" eating concept, which encourages the use of every part of an animal's anatomy, has been an unexpected hit with international restaurant critics, bad boy chefs like Anthony Bourdain, an older clientele that remembers the taste of smoked sprats, and an alternative art crowd that's been discovering the delights of veal tongue. The roast bone marrow and parsley salad is one of the most talked-about restaurant dishes around. *Bar: Mon-Fri 11am-11pm, Sat 6-11pm. Restaurant: Mon-Fri noon-3pm and 6-11pm, Sat 6-11pm.* £ = 26 St. John St., EC1 (✪ Farringdon), 020-7251-0848, stjohnrestaurant.com

Savoy Grill • Covent Garden • British
Best Power Lunches Swarming with celebrities, politicians, royalty, and London's movers and shakers—especially at lunchtime—the Grill has been an institution since the 19th century. This one-Michelin-star establishment ensconced within the Savoy Hotel is part of the Gordon Ramsay empire. Ramsay protégé Marcus Wareing, an acclaimed chef in his own right, cooks classic British food with a contemporary twist. The handsome, cozy interior boasts a gold-effect ceiling, leather and suede banquettes, and a black, chestnut, and caramel color scheme. *Mon-Fri noon-2:45pm and 5:45-11pm, Sat noon-4pm and 5:45-11pm, Sun noon-10pm.* ££ = The Savoy Hotel, The Strand, WC2 (✪ Charing Cross), 020-7592-1600, savoy-group.com

Shanghai Blues • Covent Garden • Chinese
Steamed salmon dumplings with gold flakes, dim sum filled with abalone, sea cucumber, and shark's fin, and rare teas like thousand-day flower tea are some of the delights at this sumptuous restaurant that specializes in dim sum and the seafood of Shanghai. Housed in a historic building that was once St. Giles library, this spacious restaurant and bar with mezzanine floor is styled in the fashion of 17th- and 21st-century Shanghai. There are hand-painted silk awnings, Chinese antique altar tables, and chairs painted with calligraphy. A swanky crowd throngs the place, especially when there's live blues and dancing on some weekends. To catch the action, book a table on the ground floor. *Daily noon-11:30pm.* £ = 193-197 High Holborn, WC1 (✪ Holborn), 020-7404-1668, shanghaiblues.co.uk

The Square • Mayfair • French
Some would argue that the best dining experiences are to be had at venues that have two Michelin stars—because instead of getting complacent, they will pull out all the stops to gain their third one. Revered restaurateurs Philip Howard and Nigel Platts-Martin's roomy restaurant certainly aims to impress. The contemporary French menu is notable for its desserts and cheeseboard. The earth-toned interior festooned with abstract art is a hit with a rarefied, elevated crowd, who like to pop in after visiting nearby designer shops and art galleries. *Mon-Fri noon-3pm and 6:30-10:45pm, Sat 6:30-10:45pm, Sun 6:30-10pm.* ££ – 6-10 Bruton St., W1 (✪ Bond Street), 020-7495-7100, squarerestaurant.com

Tamarind • Mayfair • Indian
Best Indian Restaurants The past few years have seen unexpected things come into fashion—such as knitting, karaoke, and kebabs. This acclaimed one-Michelin-star Indian restaurant specializes in the latter (and thankfully not the first two), with its healthy tandoor-based cooking that borrows from the Mughlai tradition of northwest India. The cozy subterranean space, with its sleek black furniture, gold pillars, and fresh flower arrangements, is popular with a snazzy, well-heeled

crowd that appreciates chef Alfred Prasad's light touch and careful spicing. *Mon-Fri noon-2:45pm and 6-11:30pm, Sat 6-11:30pm, Sun noon-2:45pm and 6:30-10:30pm.* ££ ≡ 20 Queen St., W1 (⊖ Green Park), 020-7629-3561, tamarindrestaurant.com

Tom Aikens • Chelsea • French
Best Fine Dining The eponymous chef-proprietor is one of London's top chefs, and at his elegant but casual one-Michelin-star baby he cooks some of the most sexy and thrilling food to be found in London. The quiet, Zen-like black-and-white interior doesn't fool the rarefied, lustrous older clientele—who knows that dishes like roast piglet with pork lasagna, baby squid, and caramelized onions are like an orgasm on a plate. *Mon-Fri noon-2:30pm and 6:45-11pm.* ££ ≡ 43 Elystan St., SW3 (⊖ South Kensington), 020-7584-2003, tomaikens.co.uk

Vingt Quatre* • Chelsea • Late-Night Restaurant
Best Late-Night Haunts This 24-hour eatery is the Holy Grail for anyone needing a late-night bite. *See Classic Nightlife, p.162, for details.* £ ≡ 325 Fulham Rd., SW10 (⊖ Gloucester Road), 020-7376-7224

Wiltons • St. James's • British
Established in the first half of the 18th century, this classic family-owned restaurant is as British as the royal family, cricket, and the stiff upper lip. Indeed, it's popular with aristocracy, businesspeople, politicians, and eminent sporting figures. It's renowned for fish (at its Oyster & Seafood Bar) and game in season. Fussily and elaborately presented dishes—including seasonal specialties like gull's eggs—are served in an English country house setting that incorporates a British racing green and mustard color scheme, framed sporting pictures, and intimate alcoves. *Mon-Fri noon-2:30pm and 6-10:15pm.* ££ ≡ 55 Jermyn St., SW1 (⊖ Green Park), 020-7629-9955, wiltons.co.uk

The Wolseley • St. James's • Cafe
An homage to the grand cafes of central Europe, this continental brasserie is housed inside a beautiful historic building. It's owned by Chris Corbin and Jeremy King (two enigmatic personalities on the London restaurant scene) and designed by top designer David Collins. It has vaulted ceilings, beautiful chandeliers, a striking monochrome tiled floor, and intimate booths and alcoves. The coveted seats are the ones in the inner ring in the center. The classic brasserie menu, which is excellent for breakfast, lunch, and afternoon tea, is a hit with A-list celebrities and the well-heeled customers that swarm the place at all hours. *Mon-Fri 7am-midnight, Sat 9am-midnight, Sun 9am-11pm.* £ ≡ 160 Piccadilly, W1 (⊖ Green Park), 020-7499-6996, thewolseley.com

Zafferano • Knightsbridge • Italian (G)
This one-Michelin-star Italian restaurant draws a typically high-class Knightsbridge crowd, who love its rustic interior and relaxed ambiance. The clipped, manicured plants at the entrance give little clue to the fact that there's an informal, comfortable venue inside—all stripy banquettes, Venetian blinds, potted plants, large mirrors, and burnished hues. The menu offers house-made pasta, truffles in season, and traditional desserts. There's also a thriving bar. *Mon-Fri noon-2:30pm and 7-11pm, Sat 12:30-3pm and 7-11pm, Sun 12:30-3pm and 7-10:30pm.* £ ≡ 15 Lowndes St., SW1 (⊖ Knightsbridge), 020-7235-5800, zafferanorestaurant.com

Classic London:
The Nightlife

Albannach • Westminster • Restaurant Bar

Although Trafalgar Square is the epicenter of tourism, Albannach manages to attract a local London crowd. The theme of the bar is Scottish, though décor-wise it's subtle rather than tartan. The ground-floor whiskey bar attracts an older crowd, while the basement playing soul, house, and hip-hop is clubbier. The drinks are top notch, and there is a stupendous selection of over 200 whiskeys. The friendly staff dressed in black shirts and kilts are very professional. Try the superlative Scottish bar snacks—including some of the best smoked salmon in London—and come after work around 7pm to experience it at its most buzzing. *Mon-Sat noon-1am.* – ≡ 66 Trafalgar Sq., WC2 (⊖ Charing Cross), 020-7930-0066, albannach.co.uk

The American Bar • Covent Garden • Hotel Bar

The American Bar opened in the 1890s but really came into its own in the 1920s with star barman Harry Craddock, who singlehandedly popularized the dry martini. The drinks are simple and classic. The dress code is smart casual rather than overly formal, ideal for the tourist clientele. This is a place for grown-ups to have easy conversation and sleepy nightcaps in a classically Deco space. If you want to impress, grab one of the quiet tables at the back that overlook the Thames and enjoy the American pianist who sings jazz tunes every night. *Mon-Sat noon-1am, Sun noon-10:30pm.* – The Savoy Hotel, The Strand, WC2 (⊖ Charing Cross), 020-7836-4343, savoy-group.com

Bentley's Oyster Bar & Grill* • St. James's • Restaurant Bar

This restaurant has separate ritzy cocktail and champagne bar. *See Classic Restaurants, p.141, for details.* – 11-13 Swallow St., W1 (⊖ Piccadilly Circus), 020-7734-4756, bentleysoysterbarandgrill.co.uk

The Blue Bar • Knightsbridge • Hotel Bar

Best Hotel Bars There's no standing at this decadent Regency-style bar in Knightsbridge. There's nothing gimmicky about the entirely blue space, which has garnered serious attention for its old-school glamour. This is where oil barons, refined business types, and the super-rich come to mingle over nuts and long drinks. The discreet and professional staff caters to an elegantly dressed and often international crowd. The space seats only 55 but don't expect many empty seats—it's best to book in advance if you want to be sure of your chance to experience this very grown-up place. *Mon-Sat 4pm-1am, Sun 3pm-midnight.* – The Berkeley, Wilton Pl., SW1 (⊖ Knightsbridge), 020-7235-6000, the-berkeley.co.uk

Bonds* • The City • Hotel Bar

Situated in the dome of a converted Georgian bank, this hotel bar has high ceilings and a mosaic floor. The drinking brokers who lean against the bar are a little more upmarket than most of the Essex boys in the City. Hence cocktails and champagne are preferred over beer. It is extra busy when the work doors close and empties out as the night progresses. The restaurant, which serves classy modern French food, is a good choice for a quiet date. *Daily noon-11pm.* = The Threadneedles Hotel, 5 Threadneedle St., EC2 (⊖ Bank), 020-7657-8088, bonds-restaurant.com

Café de Paris • Soho • Nightclub
Café de Paris celebrated its 80th birthday with a bang—in this case burlesque stripper Dita von Teese getting wet in a giant champagne glass. Over the years the gold-and-gilt circular venue has attracted everyone from Frank Sinatra to Kelis. It holds a lot of private parties, but on Friday and Saturday nights large groups of twenty-somethings come to shake their thang to R&B and commercial dance music. Alternatively you may prefer the monthly Kitsch Lounge Riot, an homage to all things retro. This is definitely the place if you're looking for a scene that's lively and loud. *Showcase: Fri 6:30-9:30pm. Restaurant: Sat 6-8pm. Nightclub: Fri-Sat 10pm-4am.* ℂ≣ 4 Coventry St., W1 (⊖ Piccadilly Circus), 020-7734-7700, cafedeparis.com

Cellar Gascon • The City • Restaurant Bar
Comptoir Gascon is more than just the hottest restaurant in Smithfields. The attached destination wine bar is filled with warm leather, low lights, and some seriously tasty bottles of southern French wine. As it is owned by the same people who are behind Loungelover and Annex 3, expect some quirky details like flowerpot ashtrays and random Gascony-inspired objects. The romantic low-lit bar gets packed early with a varied crowd of lawyers and businesspeople who migrate up from their offices a short distance away. *Daily noon-10pm.* ≣ 59 West Smithfield, EC1 (⊖ Farringdon), 020-7796-0600

Claridge's Bar • Mayfair • Hotel Bar
Best Hotel Bars It's simply too decadent, darling. Claridge's Bar is the ultimate in high class and immaculate service. The Art Deco hotel's two stunning bars are always filled with refined thirty-somethings and Euro-fashionistas. Champagne and champagne cocktails are the main draw here, though it being Claridge's, the bartenders can get you anything you could possibly want. The main bar is buzzing and busy, though even those who are standing get waiter service. If you want something different, be sure to get yourself into the intimate ruby-red Macaudo bar, which has only four small tables, delicious cocktails, and quite possibly the best bar snacks on earth. Although busy most evenings, it's generally most popular around 8pm. *Mon-Sat noon-1am, Sun 4pm-midnight.* ⌐≣ Claridge's, 55 Brook St., W1 (⊖ Bond Street), 020-7629-8860, claridges.co.uk

Counting House • The City • Pub
The domed interior of the old banking hall at the back of the Royal Exchange is so beautiful that it's hard to believe people are allowed to drink here. There's even part of a Roman basilica in the walls. It used to be the headquarters of NatWest bank, but for the past few years it's been a pub, and a very popular one at that. It's a very busy place for local (largely male) banking types who like to talk loudly and drink beer, and you can almost certainly count on there being a crowd of them at the bar. It can get rather cliquey in here, but the setting is so gorgeous that it's worth popping in for at least a quick pint. *Mon-Fri 11am-11pm.* ≣ 50 Cornhill, EC3 (⊖ Bank), 020-7283-7123

Dover Street Restaurant & Jazz Bar • Mayfair • Jazz Club
It's amusing that somewhere so posh can have so many people clamoring to get in on weekends, but you'll find crowds lining up for the nightly live jazz, blues, and Latin music. An in-house DJ also plays until 3am if you get itchy feet. The patrons at the venue's three bars are suited and elegant, and like to make the most

of the jovial, rather flirtatious, atmosphere. Reservations are highly recommend-ed. *Mon-Thu 5:30pm-3am, Fri-Sat 7pm-3am.* = 8-10 Dover St., W1 (⊖ Green Park), 020-7491-7509, doverst.co.uk

Dukes Bar • St. James's • Hotel Bar

The Dukes Hotel is Mecca for martinis. This exceptionally traditional destina-tion is a quiet bolt-hole that attracts an older crowd who like to slow-sip the high-quality drinks. Maestro barman Tony Micelotta takes great care of his beau-tifully dressed clientele and his drinks, so you're sure to feel very well looked after. If martinis aren't your thing, the champagnes are a lovely choice, as are the rare vintage cognacs. You can even try a bottle from 1815 as a reminder of the Napoleonic War. Be sure to dress to fit in. *Daily noon-midnight.* − Dukes Hotel, St. James's Pl., SW1 (⊖ Green Park), 020-7491-4840, dukeshotel.co.uk

The Engineer • Primrose Hill • Gastropub

If you're wondering where all the celebrities who want to keep a low profile go in Primrose Hill, look no further. The Engineer is a bright Victorian pub and restau-rant built by the infamous engineer Brunel. The bar itself is a small L-shaped space that seats no more than 30, and is generally filled with media, fashion, and film types. The big, sunny beer garden at the back is the place to grab pitchers of simple cocktails in summer, while the cozy quiet indoor bar is a relaxed and civilized destination for mulled wine when it's cold. *Mon-Fri 9am-midnight, Sat-Sun noon-4:30pm and 7-11pm.* − ≡ 65 Gloucester Ave., NW1 (⊖ Chalk Farm), 020-7722-0950, the-engineer.com

Floridita • Soho • Restaurant Bar

Terence Conran's Floridita is a fabulous ode to 1950s Cuba. The venue is black and red, with a very modern take on retro with lots of dramatic lighting and graphic posters. Live Cuban bands play every night, which inspires dancing as the evening progresses. Drinkers line up at the bar or grab some of the limited non-dining tables, but consider having a bite to eat here, as the food is deli-cious. The fabulous daiquiris are the real draw, though a stunning array of pre-mium rums and rum cocktails beckons, including a brilliant basil reworking of a mojito called a Basilique. *Mon-Wed 5:30pm-2am, Thu-Sat 5:30pm-3am.* = 100 Wardour St., W1 (⊖ Oxford Circus), 020-7314-4000, floriditalondon.com

French House • Soho • Pub

The French Resistance used to meet here during World War II—and you can't blame them. This vintage pub still has the vibe of an intimate Gallic dive. The sepia walls are covered in vintage theatrical photographs. London's literati, actors, and fascinating oddballs occupy the three little tables at the back and stools along the window every night of the week. Despite the name, French House is the epitome of British eccentricity. The bar staff will happily speak their mind, they serve halves, not pints, of beer, and cell phones are strictly not allowed. *Mon-Sat noon-11pm, Sun noon-10:30pm.* = 49 Dean St., W1 (⊖ Leicester Square), 020-7437-2799

The George Inn • Bankside • Pub

You're taking a step back in time when you enter the George Inn. This 18th-century coaching inn near the river has somehow managed to survive for cen-turies. Charles Dickens used to hang out in the coffee room here (it was men-tioned in *Little Dorrit*), and today it's a National Trust monument. Everyone from students to an older clientele loves the old-fashioned interconnected buildings with their old beams and low ceilings. There are great outdoor picnic tables in summer where locals come to sit and enjoy a good pint off the beaten track. *Mon-Sat 11am-11pm, Sun noon-10:30pm.* ‒≡ The George Inn Yard, 77 Borough High St., SE1 (⊖London Bridge), 020-7407-2056, pubs.com/george1.htm

Gordon's Wine Bar • Westminster • Wine Bar

This wine bar has been going strong since 1890 and is filled with old tables lit by candlelight. To add to the history, the building was home to Samuel Pepys in the 1680s and Rudyard Kipling lived upstairs in the 1890s. Old regulars and suited connoisseurs fill the bar fast after work, drawn to the music-free ambiance. Try the brilliant broad list of wines by the glass or bottle or go for the superb madeira, sherry, and ports served by schooner, beaker, or bottle straight from the barrel. *Mon-Sat 11am-11pm, Sun noon-10pm.* ‒≡ 47 Villiers St., WC2 (⊖Embankment), 020-7930-1408, gordonswinebar.com

The Holly Bush • Hampstead • Pub

Best Pubs Don't tell everyone about The Holly Bush. This amazing 18th-century pub is so delightful that you won't want to share it with the masses. It's already a hot spot rammed with Hampstead intellectuals, young couples, and lots of jovial groups. The ultra-cozy venue has open fires, wooden tables and benches, and lots of little snugs. The dining room upstairs has larger tables. There's no music, but the vibe is buzzing and friendly—unless you're lucky enough to arrive before the weekend hordes. There's also a great posh pub menu with pies and classic British dishes (all of which include a drop of beer). *Mon-Sat noon-11pm, Sun noon-10:30pm.* ≡ 22 Holly Mount, NW3 (⊖Hampstead), 020-7435-2892

Hush • Mayfair • Restaurant Bar

Looking for something romantic? You can't beat this restaurant bar located in a small Mayfair courtyard. The venue attracts the posh and well dressed, including celebrities who want to be left alone. The outside tables are packed outside in the summer months, but it's more intimate indoors the rest of the year. There's a long wine list and great Taittinger Champagne cocktails that include fresh apricot and cantaloupe, and pear Bellinis. The bar also has a second atmospheric wine boutique called La Cave around the corner that specializes in rare, fine wine. *Mon-Sat noon-12:30am.* ‒≡ 8 Lancashire Ct., Brook St., W1 (⊖Bond Street), 020-7659-1500, strictlyhush.com

The Jamaica Wine House • The City • Pub

In a capital filled with so much history, it's an impressive thing to be the city's oldest pub. The Jamaica Wine House got its name from the fact that it was the meeting place for sugar and slave traders in the early 18th century, though there was a coffeehouse on the site before the Great Fire of London in 1666. This smoky, atmospheric spot in the heart of the City now attracts boisterous pint-drinking City boys. The Jampot, as it is also known, is a friendly old-fashioned place to grab a hearty sandwich and dose of history. *Mon-Fri 11am-11pm.* ≡ St. Michael's Alley, Cornhill, EC3 (⊖Bank), 020-7929-6972, massivepub.com

Jerusalem Tavern • The City • Pub

Best Pubs If you want to find old London, this is the place. This hidden gem of a pub has been here since 1720, with drinkers like Hogarth and Handel propping up the bar. Only open on weekdays, the pub is now the haven of local Clerkenwell designers and architects. Drinks-wise, the pub stocks real ales from St. Peter's Brewery in Norfolk, so expect some beer connoisseurs. If you've never tried ale, this nooky wooden pub is a great start—with lots of choices, including seasonal beers, stout with honey and fruits, and even apple ale. Be sure to get here before the workday is over if you want a table. *Mon-Fri 11am-11pm.* – 55 Briton St., EC1 (⊖Farringdon), 020-7490-4281, stpetersbrewery.co.uk

King William IV • Hampstead • Pub

Best Gay Bars and Clubs Only in London could you have a 17th-century gay pub. This laid-back pickup joint in the heart of Hampstead Village is perfectly located for those who want to visit the Heath (which has been a popular cruising stop for two centuries). The Willie draws a mixed crowd and is much calmer and quieter that its Soho brethren. There's also a small but pleasant outdoor space in the back to enjoy in summer, simple pub fare to eat, and lots of boys to chat up. *Mon-Sat 11am-11pm, Sun noon-10:30pm.* – ≣ 77 Hampstead High St., NW3 (⊖Hampstead), 020-7435-5747, kw4.co.uk

Library at the Lanesborough • Knightsbridge • Hotel Bar

Inside this impressive Georgian building that overlooks Hyde Park Corner is one of the loveliest traditional bars in the city. Decorated in the style of a book room from a British stately home, it is lined with dark wood paneling and worn hardback books and makes a cozy setting for the intimate tables. There is a long list of pre- and post-dinner cocktails, champagnes, and an impressive wall of vintage champagne cognacs dating back to 1865. The drinks are served in heavy cut-crystal glasses, which makes them taste even better. *Mon-Sat 11am-1am, Sun noon-10:30pm.* – Lanesborough Hotel, Hyde Park Corner, SW1 (⊖Hyde Park Corner), 020-7259-5599, lanesborough.com

The Mandarin Bar • Knightsbridge • Hotel Bar

Best Hotel Bars Knightsbridge's Mandarin Oriental is big with American business types passing through town—perhaps the brown-leather seats, dark-wood accents, and warm atmosphere remind them of New York. It's the kind of place you want to while away the hours over long glasses of scotch. The long cocktail list manages to be both modern and classic—you'll need a few to wash down the bowls of wasabi peas and sweet nuts that are impossible not to devour. Conversation flows easy here, and isn't hampered a bit by the live jazz which plays in the background in the evenings. *Mon-Sat 11am-2am, Sun 11am-10:30pm.* = Mandarin Oriental, 66 Knightsbridge, SW1 (⊖Knightsbridge), 020-7235-2000, mandarinoriental.com

Milk and Honey • Soho • Members Bar

Best Cocktails Milk and Honey is a real find—a members bar that takes bookings for a limited number of nonmembers each night. The venue resembles a 1920s dive bar, and is filled with low lighting and lots of Art Deco antiques. They even play old-fashioned jazz while drinkers sit in black banquettes. As it's in Soho, the venue's big with media and film types who come for the killer vintage cocktails and some lovely amuse-bouches and canapés. Be sure to book a table a day or two in advance as space is limited. *Nonmembers: Mon-Fri 6-11pm, Sat 7-11pm.* = 61 Poland St., W1 (⊖Oxford Circus), 070-0065-5469, mlkhny.com

No. 5 Cavendish Square • Marylebone • Bar

This private club draws a buzzing celebrity-fused crowd to its staid setting. Non-members are allowed into the main ground-floor bar and a busy basement club, but you'd better get your name on the list ahead of time. The main red velvet bar attracts a lot of TV and music-industry trendsetters, alongside very well-heeled suits and blondes. The more extravagant go for the £400 champagne cocktail, which includes the gift of a free handmade champagne flute. The rest enjoy strong cocktails and some good soul and house music. *Ground Floor Bar: Mon-Sat 11am-1am, Sun 6pm-1am. Club: Thu-Sat 10pm-1am.* ▬ ≡ 5 Cavendish Sq., W1 (⊖ Oxford Circus), 020-7079-5000, no5ltd.com

1 Lombard Street* • The City • Restaurant Bar

This bar is part of a restaurant and draws brokers and bankers who want to sip champagne while sharing plates of Asian nibbles or tapas. *See Classic Restaurants, p.149, for details.* ▬ ≡ 1 Lombard St., EC3 (⊖ Bank), 020-7929-6611, 1lombardstreet.com

Oscar • Fitzrovia • Hotel Bar

If it's a weekday, you can guarantee that the bar at the Charlotte Street Hotel is going to be busy. One of the choice meeting places for the nearby advertising and media agencies, Oscar is often packed around lunchtime and especially after work. Weekends are variable. The bar's style is classic English meets bright Bloomsbury-colored stripes. A bright wall mural inspired by artist Roger Fry lines one wall. The bartenders' focus in this upbeat space is on fresh cocktails using seasonal ingredients and seriously top-notch spirits. *Mon-Sat 11am-11pm, Sun 11am-8pm.* ▬ ≡ Charlotte Street Hotel, 15-17 Charlotte St., W1 (⊖ Tottenham Court Road), 020-7806-2000, charlottestreethotel.com

Pizza on the Park • Knightsbridge • Restaurant Bar

No one comes to this pizzeria at Hyde Park Corner for the food. It's really an experiential destination where you go to catch great jazz with friends. Every night in the basement room, there are acts like Barefoot doing burlesque cover versions of house anthems or Frank Sinatra tribute bands. There are two sets every night, and the guests quiet down and the waiters stop serving when the music's on. The décor isn't anything special, but the vibe is lovely and great for groups of friends. Definitely reserve. *Daily noon-midnight.* C≡ 11 Knightsbridge, SW1 (⊖ Hyde Park Corner), 020-7235-5273, pizzaonthepark.co.uk

The Rivoli Bar • St. James's • Hotel Bar

You can't get more Art Deco than the Rivoli Bar, whose frosted glass windows face onto Piccadilly: Muted chandeliers emit an amber glow from shell-shaped alcoves in the ceiling. The walls are dark marble highlighted with Deco reliefs of stylized nudes. The hotel attracts an older international business clientele, so best dress the part and stick on a tie. The formal staff serve some of the most expensive cocktails in London. Note that the bar closes promptly—no chance of entry after 11pm. *Mon-Sat noon-11pm, Sun noon-10:30pm.* ▬ The Ritz Hotel, 150 Piccadilly W1 (⊖ Green Park), 020-7493-8181, theritzlondon.com

Ronnie Scott's • Soho • Jazz Club

Best Live-Music Venues If you like jazz, you already know about Ronnie Scott's. The venue has been hot since 1959, attracting everyone from Miles Davis to Donald Byrd through its doors. It still gets big names—Roy Ayers' regular annual slot is unmissable. The venue has a classic jazz style—lots of small tables facing an intimate stage. There's a full menu, but don't expect anything too exciting. The brilliant music program is distracting enough for the enthusiastic crowd of music fans. There's also Friday night salsa upstairs (complete with an hour-long lesson) if you want to shake things up. *Sun 6pm-midnight, Mon-Sat 6pm-3am.* C = 47 Frith St., W1 (⊖ Tottenham Court Road), 020-7439-0747, ronniescotts.co.uk

The Royal Opera House • Covent Garden • Theater

This is a world-class venue right up there with Milan's La Scala. The theater began after the success of John Gay's infamous Beggar's Opera in 1732 and has continued to grow ever since. There is no diva over the past two centuries who hasn't played or danced here—from Maria Callas to Margot Fonteyn. Now home to the Royal Opera and the Royal Ballet, it always offers superlative performances. The newly refurbished building also has a beautiful and serene cafe overlooking Covent Garden's piazza and a lovely sparkling bar that's open between performances. *Check performance times for hours.* C Royal Opera House, Bow St., WC2 (⊖ Covent Garden), 020-7304-4000, royaloperahouse.org

The Tenth Bar • Kensington • Hotel Bar

Best Bars with a View The Tenth Bar at Kensington Royal Garden Hotel is a beautiful spot that is surprisingly undiscovered so far. The big pull is the view over Kensington Palace Gardens and the relaxed, calming vibe among the walnut-leather seats. The local *Daily Mail* editors congregate here for after-work drinks, and concertgoers come for a decadent pre–Royal Albert Hall glass of champagne. Be sure to come as the sun goes down to enjoy the full sunset experience. *Mon-Fri noon-2:30pm and 5:30-11pm, Sat 5:30-11pm.* – The Royal Garden Hotel, 2-24 Kensington High St., W8 (⊖ High Street Kensington), 020-7361-1910, royalgardenhotel.co.uk

Trader Vic's • Mayfair • Restaurant Bar

Who knew that something so kitsch could find a home on Park Lane? This basement bar is a 1950s haunt that still echoes with the sounds of tiki and swaying raffia. The over-the-top décor features canoes hanging from the bamboo ceiling alongside stuffed fish. Despite the whimsical furnishings, the space attracts an older, suited crowd (adulterous couples appear to be de rigueur). On late nights there are unusual live-music acts—a one-man band playing retro music on a keyboard, for example. A good place for quiet conversation, intimacy, strong tropical drinks, and a certain dated form of whimsy. *Mon-Thu 5pm-1am, Fri-Sat 5pm-3am, Sun 5-10:30pm.* – The London Hilton, 22 Park Ln., W1 (⊖ Hyde Park Corner), 020-7208-4113, tradervics.com

The Troubadour • Chelsea • Bar

Wistful for the coffee shops of the 1960s? The Troubadour was one of the original folk venues, once drawing the likes of Bob Dylan and Joni Mitchell. Filled with myriad antique tools and objects, this combination pub, cafe, and live-music venue attracts laid-back intellectuals, upscale locals, and older paper-reading men who come for the simple food and beer and to see weekly comedy and singer songwriters perform by candlelight. *Daily 9am-midnight.* – ≡ 263-267 Old Brompton Rd., SW5 (⊖ West Brompton), 020-7370-1434, troubadour.co.uk

Vertigo 42 • The City • Champagne Bar

Best Bars with a View Vertigo 42 is so impressive that you need to book a table three weeks ahead, but if you want to sip one of the 27 varieties of bubbly alongside some caviar 600 feet above street level, it's worth the wait. This champagne bar is on the 42nd floor of one of the City's tallest skyscrapers. The bar curves around the building and all seats face the view—echoed in mirrors along the wall. Businesspeople gather here, alongside dates and people impressing the in-laws. Everyone dresses up, but don't worry about cutting-edge fashion. If you can't get in at night, try for a more easily reserved lunch spot. *Mon-Fri noon-3pm, 5-11:30pm.* ⊟ Tower 42, 25 Old Broad St., EC2 (⊖ Bank), 020-7877-7842, vertigo42.co.uk

Vingt Quatre* • Chelsea • Late-Night Restaurant

Serving simple modern British food and great 24-hour breakfasts for early birds and early hangovers, this 24-hour eatery is the Holy Grail at the end of a taxi ride for anyone who wants a late-night bite. It serves alcohol a little late (midnight) but not at all hours yet (though new licensing laws may change that). The crowd is young and posh—who else would come here for 5am breakfast? Expect to line up with other hungry hedonists on Fridays and Saturdays. *24/7.* ☰ 325 Fulham Rd., SW10 (⊖ Gloucester Road), 020-7376-7224

Windows at the Hilton • Mayfair • Hotel Bar

Best Bars with a View Starry, starry night. A seat near the windows of this bar guarantees a lovely view of the stars. The top floor of Park Lane's Hilton overlooks Hyde Park and beyond over the city. It's a must in the evening when the neon sparkle of the city turns on. The décor (which is due for refurbishment) is '70s kitsch with mirrored walls and hard leather sofa-seats. But who cares? You'll be looking out the window and sipping Scotch while musicians play cabaret tunes. Phone to reserve a window table ahead of time. *Mon-Thu noon-2am, Fri noon-2:30am, Sat 5:30pm-2:30am, Sun noon-10:30pm.* ⊟ The London Hilton, 22 Park Ln., W1 (⊖ Hyde Park Corner), 020-7493-8000, hilton.co.uk

Windsor Castle • Kensington • Pub

The Windsor Castle exudes authenticity. It's filled with Kensington locals, others in the know, and precious few tourists. The pub dates back to 1835, when it was the haunt of farmers bringing their cows to market at Hyde Park. It still has a touch of country air with its open fires and cozy wooden tables. This is a good place for a traditional Sunday roast and a pint of Guinness or some fresh oysters and Pimms. The spacious beer garden at the back is packed during the summer months. *Mon-Sat noon-11pm, Sun noon-10:30pm.* ⊟☰ 114 Campden Hill Rd., W8 (⊖ Notting Hill Gate), 020-7243-9551, windsor-castle-pub.co.uk

Ye Olde Mitre • The City • Pub

Take a map because you're bound to get lost. Ye Olde Mitre is so hidden that even hardened Londoners have trouble finding it. But it's worth the trouble, as this eccentric old pub is brimming with period details, including low ceilings, dark wood, and real ales. It was founded in 1546, though the current version dates back to 1772. This hidden jewel is populated by lawyers and drinkers with a penchant for atmosphere and no music. Early birds get the four-person snug, Ye Closet, for real intimacy. The toilets are outside, but hey, this is real old-fashioned Britain we're talking about. *Mon-Fri 11am-11pm.* ⊟ 1 Ely Ct., Ely Pl. (off 8 Hatton Gdns.), EC1, (⊖ Chancery Lane), 020-7405-4751

Classic London: The Attractions

Asprey • Mayfair • Shop

Founded in 1781, Asprey is famous for its silverware, watches, leather goods, jewelry, and every other luxury tidbit imaginable. Its style is traditional with a timeless edge. The original store on Bond Street is fabulous, selling everything from ties and cashmere to first editions and hunting gear. An icon of truly British glamour, Asprey is where the landed aristocracy and royalty go for gifts. The Norman Foster–redesigned interior, with its inventive architecture, is worth the trip. *Mon-Sat 10am-6pm.* 167 New Bond St., W1 (⊖ Green Park), 020-7493-6767, asprey.com

Benjamin Franklin House • Westminster • Historic Home

As the only surviving residence of the great American statesman, inventor, and all-around brainbox, this painstakingly restored early Georgian townhouse is not to be missed. Franklin lived here for almost 16 years from 1757 to 1775, and that time is vividly brought to life with an imaginative mixture of live performance and 21st-century technical wizardry. Of dusty artifacts there are none, apart from a pair of bifocal spectacles and a few other inventions in the basement waiting room; instead there's a costumed guide whose lines interweave seamlessly with those in the projected films. *Wed-Sun 10am-5pm.* £- 36 Craven St., WC2 (⊖ Charing Cross), 020-7930-6601, benjaminfranklinhouse.org

Berry Bros & Rudd • St. James's • Shop

Britain's oldest wine and spirit merchant has been trading from these premises for more than 300 years, and there's history in every crooked wooden panel and wonderfully sloping floorboard. The main part of the shop feels almost like a museum, with pride of place given to an enormous set of scales on which Georgian swells used to get weighed. Side rooms contain an impeccable selection of fine wines, and a superb range of malt whiskeys and cognacs. As for the service, it's as flawless as you'd expect in such a long-established business, even if you're only buying a bottle of armagnac and not a case of Château Lafitte. *Mon-Fri 10am-6pm, Sat 10am-4pm.* 3 St. James's St., SW1 (⊖ Green Park), 020-7396-9600, bbr.com

The British Museum • Bloomsbury • Art Museum

One of the world's major museums, its vast collection encompasses everything from Egyptian mummies to Easter Island statues. However, the latest draw is not the incredible array of cultural artifacts, but an empty space. Not just any old empty space, of course. The Great Court is one of the triumphs among various millennium projects, with Sir Norman Foster's glass mosaic of a roof helping to transform a dusty bookstore for the British Library (now in new headquarters) into a spectacular focal point, with the graceful Victorian Reading Room at its very core. *Galleries: Sat-Wed 10am-5:30pm, Thu-Fri 10am-8:30pm. Great Court: Sun-Wed 9am-6pm, Thu-Sat 9am-11pm.* £- Great Russell St., WC1 (⊖ Russell Square), 020-7323-8299, thebritishmuseum.ac.uk

Chelsea Physic Garden • Chelsea • Garden

Best Green Spaces History and botany combine in this secluded garden, founded in 1673 by the Worshipful Society of Apothecaries as a center for studying rare and medicinal plants, a role it fulfills to this day. Among the pleasingly laid-out curiosities is the oldest rock garden in England still open the public, created in 1773 from a mixture of Icelandic lava, stones from the Tower of London, chalk, and flint; a cluster of glasshouses with specimens from around the world; and the largest outdoor fruiting olive tree in Britain, which thrives in the garden's relatively warm and dry microclimate. *Apr–Oct Wed noon-5pm, Sun noon-6pm.* £- 66 Royal Hospital Rd., SW3 (⊖ Sloane Square), 020-7352-5646, chelseaphysicgarden.co.uk

Clarence House • St. James's • Historic Home

More like a much-loved country house than a palace, Clarence House was the London home of the Queen Mother for nearly 50 years. Her grandson the Prince of Wales lives here now, hence the summer-only opening times, in relatively plainly decorated rooms filled with books, antiques, and paintings from the collection of the late Queen Mother, principally by 20th-century British painters such as John Piper, Graham Sutherland, WS Sickert, and Augustus John, along with art from Prince Charles's own collection. *Admission by guided tour; all tickets are timed and must be pre-booked.* Stableyard Rd., SW1 (⊖ Green Park), 020-7766-7303, royal.gov.uk

Dennis Severs' House • Spitalfields • Historic Home

To call this restored 18th-century silk-weavers' house a museum doesn't do it justice. It's more like a candlelit work of art, a three-dimensional masterpiece by the late Californian artist Dennis Severs, who used to live in this captivating time warp. Thanks to occasional tours, visitors can still walk here, quietly, absorbing the atmosphere, smells, sights, and sounds of the past. The attention to detail is phenomenal: In the kitchen, warmed by a real fire, there's a recipe book open on the table, with a half-eaten cake beside it, and from the first-floor parlor, the rattle of passing coaches is plainly audible. *Mon evening, times vary by season; 1st and 3rd Sun of the month 2-5pm, and the following Mon noon-2pm.* £- 18 Folgate St., E1 (⊖ Liverpool Street), 020-7247-4013, dennissevershouse.co.uk

Fortnum & Mason • St. James's • Shop

There's something deeply reassuring about a shop that has been purveying fabulous foodstuffs to the gentry for nearly 300 years. Fortnum's, as regulars call it, has outlasted dynasties, empires, and fashions without letting standards slip. Not for nothing is the cornucopian food hall permanently abuzz with shoppers stocking up on everything from decorative tins of Earl Grey to pots of Gentleman's Relish, or ordering a well-filled wicker hamper for picnics or presents. Some products can be ordered online from the United States, but where's the fun in that? *Mon-Sat 10am-6:30pm, Sun noon-6pm.* 181 Piccadilly, W1 (⊖ Green Park), 020-7734-8040, fortnumandmason.com

The Foundling Museum • Bloomsbury • Art Museum

Best Small Museums Touching, informative, and inspiring, the Foundling Museum is widely regarded as one of London's best new attractions. The long-gone Foundling Hospital it celebrates was established in 1745 by wealthy shipwright Thomas Coram to help destitute children. It soon became a fashionable cause; famous artists donated paintings and Handel gave benefit concerts. The ground-floor gallery deals movingly with the story of the hospital itself, while upstairs is the art, much in three grand reception rooms rescued when the home was demolished in 1926. At the top is a display of Handel memorabilia, but the real draw is four armchairs with built-in speakers for sampling the maestro's work in comfort. *Tue-Sat 10am-6pm, Sun and public holidays noon-6pm. £-* 40 Brunswick Sq., WC1 (⊖ Russell Square), 020-7841-3600, foundlingmuseum.org.uk

Hampstead Heath and Parliament Hill • Hampstead • Park

Best Green Spaces With its rolling hills and extensive wooded sections, Hampstead Heath is definitely more country park than town garden, despite being just four miles north of the center, an effect only enhanced by the near-complete absence of signposts. On winter days, the joggers, kite-fliers, and dog-walkers have the place to themselves, but in summer it's a different story, with lavish picnics at every turn. On clear days, there's a fabulous view down over central London from the north of the heath, close to Kenwood Nursery. After hours, the West Heath, between Jack Straw's Castle and Golders Hill Park, is a popular gay cruising area, as it was in the 19th century. NW3 and NW5 (⊖ Hampstead), cityoflondon.gov.uk

Handel House Museum • Mayfair • Museum

Best Small Museums One of London's newer museums, the house where George Frideric Handel lived for 36 years is still filled with his music. On the first floor are the wonderfully atmospheric paneled and soberly painted rooms, complete with squeaky wooden floorboards, where he wrote and rehearsed his most famous compositions, including the *Messiah*. Above is Handel's bedchamber and dressing room, hung with portraits of his contemporaries. The museum also incorporates the next-door building, briefly home to Jimi Hendrix, where there are displays of Handel's papers and manuscripts, and a corner where you can listen to CDs of the maestro's masterpieces. *Tue-Wed, Fri-Sat 10am-6pm, Thu 10am-8pm, Sun noon-6pm. £-* 25 Brook St., W1 (⊖ Bond Street), 020-7495-1685, handelhouse.org

Hyde Park Stables • Hyde Park • Activity

Best Fresh Air Experiences Saddle up, English-style, to ride along Britain's most upmarket bridleway, which runs for three-quarters of a mile through the leafy environs of Hyde Park. Rotten Row and the adjoining Ladies' Ride have provided high-society Londoners with somewhere to show off their skills on horse-back—not to mention their riding attire—for several centuries, and there's still a good chance of finding a celebrity face beneath those unflattering safety helmets. If not, there's always the Household Cavalry, which rides out en masse between 7am and 8am most days, and in smaller groups later in the morning. *Group or private rides and lessons Mon-Fri 7:15am-5pm, Sat-Sun 9am-5pm. Upper weight limit for riders 175 lbs. ££££* 63 Bathurst Mews, W2 (⊖ Marble Arch), 020-7723-2813, hydeparkstables.com

Imperial War Museum • South Bank • Museum

Despite the mighty array of modern military hardware on display, the overwhelming message is really, "War, what is it good for?" The First World War gallery includes an all-too-realistic mock-up of a muddy front-line trench, the Second World War section has the unnerving Blitz Experience, and the personal mementos in the Holocaust Exhibition are deeply touching. Dig deeper in the recent Crimes

CLASSIC

Against Humanity gallery, which offers insight into why genocide isn't a thing of the past. The audio tour has some fascinating first-hand accounts from those who lived through 20th-century conflicts. *Daily 10am-6pm.* £- Lambeth Rd., SE1 (⊖Lambeth North), 020-7416-5320, iwm.org.uk

Kensington Palace • Kensington • Historic Home

Kings, queens, and lesser royalty have lived here since Christopher Wren converted it from a simple country retreat in the village of Kensington into something more appropriately regal. Not too regal, though; the State Apartments here are more homely than in other royal palaces, and it's just about possible to imagine real people—albeit staggeringly rich ones—living in these elegant rooms. You can also see how they dressed, thanks to a regularly refreshed display of articles of clothing worn by princes, courtiers, and debutantes, and the late Princess of Wales, whose home this was. The two-hour audio guide is exhaustive. *Mar-Oct daily 10am-6pm (last admission 5pm), Nov-Feb daily 10am-5pm (last admission 4pm).* £ Kensington Gdns., W8 (⊖High Street Kensington), 0870-751-5170, hrp.org.uk

Kenwood House • Hampstead • Historic Home

Best Aristocratic Mansions Neoclassical Kenwood House makes an impact for two reasons—three, if you count the Elysian setting high up on the edge of Hampstead Heath. The first is its outstanding Robert Adam interiors, in particular the barrel-vaulted library with its delicate stucco work, gilded classical friezes, and painted panels, designed to impress upon guests the marvelous taste of its noble owner Lord Mansfield. Second is the magnificent art collection donated by a later owner, with British names such as Gainsborough, Reynolds, and Romney, though there's also Vermeer's *The Guitar Player* and a highly regarded Rembrandt self-portrait. *Apr-Oct daily 11am-5pm, Nov-Mar 11am-4pm.* £- Hampstead Ln., NW3 (⊖Hampstead), 020-8348-1286, english-heritage.org.uk

Leighton House • Kensington • Historic Home

Best Aristocratic Mansions Frederick Leighton was one of the leading figures of the late Victorian art scene, and his studio-house is a supreme example of the flamboyant and colorful tastes of the time. Its centerpiece is the Arab Hall, an opulent affair lined with antique blue-and-green-patterned Islamic tiles and embellished with golden mosaics, with a small fountain splashing in the middle. Other rooms are hung with paintings by Leighton and contemporaries such as Burne-Jones and Millais, and there's a small collection of Leighton's drawings and travel sketchbooks. His grand first-floor studio, lined with more paintings and color sketches, was—and is—used for musical evenings. *Wed-Mon 11am-5:30pm.* £- 12 Holland Park Rd., W14 (⊖High Street Kensington), 020-7602-3316, rbkc.gov.uk/leightonhousemuseum

Liberty • Soho • Shop

Almost from its opening in 1875, Arthur Liberty's department store was the height of fashion, thanks to its stock of exotic goods and silks from the Near and Far East. Another feather in its cap was, and remains, its championing of home-grown design talent. What this means for modern shoppers is finding Arts and Crafts furniture cheek-by-jowl with fabulous Oriental rugs and funky lighting. There's also a small beauty hall stocking only the most desirable labels of the moment, plus fashion for men and women. That distinctive half-timbered exterior, however, is strictly 1920s Tudor Revival and not the real thing. *Mon-Wed 10am-7pm, Thu 10am-8pm, Fri-Sat 10am-7pm, Sun noon-6pm.* 214 Regent St., W1 (⊖ Oxford Circus), 020-7734-1234, liberty.co.uk

Lincoln's Inn • Holborn • Sight

Charles Dickens used it as a setting for *Bleak House*, and he would recognize it still, as it looks much the same as it has for hundreds of years. It's the most imposing of the four Inns of Court, whose ancient chambers are occupied by attorneys—barristers in England—though only a minority now actually live as well as work on the premises. Few of the buildings are normally open to the public, apart from the atmospheric Jacobean chapel. However, it's a pleasure just to wander through the spacious and surprisingly tranquil grounds admiring the outside of the fine Old Hall (1485) or the lovely New Square (1693). *Mon-Fri 7:30am-7pm; Chapel: 12:15-2:30pm.* £- WC2 (⊖ Holborn), 020-7405-1393, lincolnsinn.org.uk

London Silver Vaults • Holborn • Shopping

You need to be seriously in the know to locate this hidden treasure trove, as it's in the basement of an unremarkable office building. On the other side of its reassuringly thick vault door, however, is an underground arcade like no other, with row after row of silver dealers. It's the largest collection of antique fine silver in the world, apparently, and the alluring displays gleam with everything from Jacobean spoons to Victorian candlesticks. It's a total visual treat even if you have no plans to buy, though you may find it hard to resist. *Mon-Fri 9am-5:30pm, Sat 9am-1pm.* 53-64 Chancery Ln., WC2 (⊖ Chancery Lane), thesilvervaults.com

London Walks • Various • Tour

Obsessed by the Beatles? Have a passion for Sherlock Holmes? Can't hear enough about Charles Dickens? London Walks' huge range of themed strolls with expert guides allow even the most fanatical to satisfy their need for the minute and entertaining details about their chosen subject. Those with darker tastes may prefer to walk in the bloodstained steps of Jack the Ripper, be chilled by tall tales of ghouls and ghosts, or learn about the everyday horrors endured by Londoners during the Blitz of 1940. *Daily, start times vary, about two hours.* £- 020-7624-3978, recorded information 020-7624-9255, walks.com

Moss Bros • Covent Garden • Service

Traveling light has its attractions, but not when it comes to having precisely the right apparel for that formal dance, wedding, or social occasion. That's where clothes rental specialist Moss Bros, who's been doing this for more than 150 years, comes in. The main outlet in Covent Garden has everything for the gentleman about town: frock coats, morning coats, black tie (tuxedo), white tie and tails, tailcoats, and striped trousers for Royal Ascot, and even full Highland rig for those whose knees are up to it. *Mon-Wed, Fri, Sat 9am-5:30pm, Thu 9am-6:30pm, Sun noon-6pm.* ££££ 27-28 King St., WC2 (⊖ Covent Garden), 020-7632-9700, mossbros.co.uk

Museum of London • The City • Museum

Don't be put off by the slightly grim building, which from the outside resembles a dull, dumpy chimney in the middle of a roundabout. Once across the walkway, there's not just greenery but an educational and enjoyable museum devoted to the lengthy history of Britain's capital city. The fabulous new Medieval Gallery brings to life this turbulent time with everything from pointy shoes to displays about mass graves for Black Death victims. Elsewhere, there are Victorian shop fronts and Georgian room sets, Roman artifacts and Elizabeth jewelry, as well as the Lord Mayor's gloriously carved and gilded coach. *Mon-Sat 10am-5:50pm, Sun noon-5:50pm.* £- 150 London Wall, EC2 (⊖ Barbican), 0870-444-3852, museumoflondon.org.uk

National Gallery • Westminster • Art Museum

The statistics speak volumes: 102,332 square feet of gallery space, 2,300 paintings, and 650 years of Western European art history. From humble beginnings in 1824, the National Gallery has become a world-class institution, with a permanent collection that spans the period from about 1250 to 1900. The highlights are numerous: masterpieces such as Leonardo da Vinci's *The Virgin of the Rocks*, Vermeer's *Young Woman Standing at a Virginal*, and Van Gogh's *Sunflowers* (one of four versions). There are some excellent temporary exhibitions, too. The expertly led regular tours give a helpful oversight, complemented by a range of talks. *Daily 10am-6pm (Wed to 9pm). Tours: daily 11:30am and 2:30pm, Wed 6 and 6:30pm, Sat 12:30 and 3:30pm.* £- Trafalgar Sq., WC2 (⊖ Charing Cross), 020-7747-2885, nationalgallery.org.uk

National Portrait Gallery • Westminster • Art Museum

It's not only the great and the good of yesteryear whose painted faces gaze out at the viewer. The National Portrait Gallery, founded around 150 years ago to celebrate famous Britons, also houses paintings and photographs of more modern characters: the perpetually Rolling Stone Sir Mick Jagger, actor Sir Laurence Olivier, and filmmaker Derek Jarman among them. That said, the Tudor, 17th-century, and 18th-century rooms are endlessly fascinating, even if the names aren't always familiar. Every Friday evening, musicians perform in different parts of the buildings. *Sat-Wed 10am-6pm, Thu-Fri 10am-9pm. Last admission to paying exhibitions 45 mins before closing.* £- 2 St. Martin's Pl., WC2 (⊖ Charing Cross), 020-7306-0055, npg.org.uk

Percival David Foundation of Chinese Art • Bloomsbury • Museum

The finest collection of Chinese porcelain outside China is tucked away in an unremarkable 19th-century townhouse belonging to the University of London, which means few people find their way here. Don't let the dull exterior or drab stairways put you off, however. There are around 1,700 exceptionally fine items of Chinese ceramics on display, some more than a thousand years old. The first-floor gallery is all simple elegance, with delicate shades and shapes. After the restraint below, the second floor is a riot of pattern and color, from the much-imitated blue-and-white designs to ginger pots in vivid green. *Mon-Fri 10:30am-5pm.* £- 53 Gordon Sq., WC1 (⊖ Euston Square), 020-7387-3909, pdfmuseum.org.uk

The Queen's Gallery • St. James's • Art Museum

All that glitters probably *is* gold at this opulent little showcase for some of the most precious items from the Royal Collection. It was created 40 years ago from the bomb-damaged remains of Buckingham Palace's private chapel, though the recently restored décor is strictly old-school—think stucco ceilings, mahogany doors, and rich, dark colors on the walls. Within, a traditionally minded clientele marvels at the sparkling displays of fine art, diamond jewelry, ornate gold and silverware, gilded furniture, and other finery sampled from various royal residences, before plundering the gift shop for postcards of the family and other suitably regal souvenirs. *Daily 10am-5:30pm (last admission 4:30pm) except Jul 25-Sep 24, 9:30am-5pm (last admission 4pm).* £- Buckingham Gate, SW1 (⊖ Victoria), 020-7766-7301, royal.gov.uk

Royal Botanic Gardens • Richmond • Garden

Best Green Spaces Established in the mid-18th century, Kew is one of the world's most renowned gardens, a World Heritage Site with an outstanding collection of plants from around the world. And it's not just the flora that is remarkable; this riverside strip of land one mile by a third of a mile also contains 40 listed follies, bridges, and greenhouses, some nearly 250 years old. Highlights include the steamy Palm House, particularly tempting in winter, and the eye-catching Pagoda, along with the striking new glass Alpine House. Carpets of crocuses in late February, blossoms and bluebells in May, roses in summer, colorful foliage in fall, and Christmas roses in winter provide year-round interest. *Apr–early-Sep, Mon-Fri 9:30am-6pm, Sat-Sun and public holidays 9:30am-7pm, early-Sep–late-Mar, 9:30am-3:45pm.* £- Kew, Richmond, TW9 (⊖ Kew Gardens), 020-8940-1171, rbgkew.org.uk

St. Martin-in-the-Fields • Westminster • Sight

The meadows may be long gone, but happily James Gibbs's 1726 church remains, and it's as graceful as ever. Technically the parish church for Buckingham Palace, it has strong royal connections; George I was a churchwarden, and one of the gorgeous old box pews is reserved for the royal family. It's best known for classical music, however. Handel used to perform here, and there are frequent lunchtime and evening concerts. The Vergers lead fascinating guided tours of the church, crypt, and vaults most Thursdays at 11:30am. *Mon-Fri 8am-6pm, Sat 9am-6pm, Sun 8am-7pm. Restricted access during services.* £- Trafalgar Sq., WC2 (⊖ Charing Cross), 020-7766-1100, tour tickets 020-7839-8362, smitf.org

St. Paul's Cathedral • The City • Sight

The huge slate-gray dome of St. Paul's is one of London's most distinctive, and most loved, features. But Sir Christopher Wren's masterpiece, built to replace the medieval cathedral destroyed in the Great Fire of 1666, is even more magnificent inside. Thanks to an ongoing restoration program, the stonework almost glows, and the gold Byzantine-style mosaics that Queen Victoria had installed because she thought the interior "dingy" positively sparkle. There are audio guides, but even better are the Supertours, guided explorations lasting nearly two hours. *Mon-Sat 8:30am-4pm (last admission). Supertours: 11, 11:30am, 1:30 and 2pm.* £- Ludgate Hill, EC4 (⊖ St. Paul's), 020-7236-4128, stpauls.co.uk

Serpentine Boating Lake • Hyde Park • Activity

For those who agree wholeheartedly with Ratty in *The Wind in the Willows* that "there is nothing—absolutely nothing—half so much worth doing as simply messing about in boats," a quick session with the oars on the Serpentine should be high on the agenda. The setting in the middle of Hyde Park is positively sylvan, though not private; you're likely to have an audience, so be sure your rowing skills are up to the job. *Mar-Oct daily 10am; closing time 5-8:30pm depending on light and weather. Feb weekends, weather permitting.* £- The Boat House, Serpentine Rd., W2 (⊖ Knightsbridge), 020-7262-1330, royalparks.gov.uk

Shakespeare's Globe • Bankside • Sight/Museum

The first Globe was destroyed by fire, its replacement demolished by the Puritans, but Sam Wanamaker's latter-day reconstruction close to the site of the original looks set to be an important London landmark for many years. From May to September, performances take place in authentic Shakespearean conditions: with the "groundlings" standing in the circular yard in front of the stage, and the wealthier clientele sitting in the sheltered galleries around the outside. Guided tours are available all year, however, and there's also a permanent exhibition about Elizabethan London and the Bard himself. *Exhibition (including guided tour), daily, May-Sep 9am-5pm, Oct-Apr 10am-5pm. £-* 21 New Globe Walk, SE1 (⊖ Southwark), 020-7902-1500, box office 020-7401-9919, shakespeares-globe.org

Sir John Soane's Museum • Holborn • Museum/Historic Home

Best Small Museums The restrained façade conceals a jewelbox of an interior, filled with an eclectic but unimpeachable selection of antique sculpture and carving, plaster casts, King Charles I's hatpin, archaeological treasures, and fine art amassed by Sir John Soane, one of England's greatest architects. The Picture Room is a particular delight, with false walls that open to reveal further layers of paintings, including a series by the 18th-century artist Hogarth. In the basement, lit from above, is the sarcophagus of Seti I, one of the finest Egyptian pieces outside Egypt. *Tue-Sat 10am-5pm. Also first Tue each month, 6-9pm. £-* 13 Lincoln's Inn Fields, WC2 (⊖ Holborn), 020-7405-2107, soane.org

The Spa at the Dorchester • Mayfair • Spa

Tucked away in the basement, the Dorchester's Art Deco spa—the décor, not the treatments—is frequented by well-heeled Mayfair locals as well as hotel guests. Its signature Renew Rose Anti-Age Facial is unbelievably soothing, and the Eve Lom Facial also has a loyal fan base. For jetlag, however, nothing quite beats the Jet Shower Body Treatment, a restorative combo of exfoliation, cold-water spray, and moisturizing. Hair care is provided by Charles Worthington, and there's a traditional barber shop where the gentlemen can be shaved and manicured. *Mon-Sat 8am-9pm, Sun 9am-9pm. ££££* Park Ln., W1 (⊖ Hyde Park Corner), 020-7495-7335, thedorchester.com

Spencer House • St. James's • Historic Home

Best Aristocratic Mansions The eight state rooms on show give a real sense of how impressive this neoclassical mansion must have been in its 18th-century heyday. It's one of the few great aristocratic townhouses to have survived the 20th century, though the Spencer family—as in Lady Diana—hasn't actually lived here since the '20s. That it looks so magnificent is the result of a painstaking ten-year restoration project by the current tenants, Rothschild Investment Trust. The Palm Room with its glittering columns is Palladianism at its finest, while the Painted Room's exquisite murals are a fine insight into 18th-century taste. *Sun 10:30am-5:45pm (last admission 4:45pm) by guided tour only. Closed Jan and Aug. £-* 27 St. James's Pl., SW1 (⊖ Green Park), 020-7499-8620, spencerhouse.co.uk

Tate Britain • Pimlico • Art Museum

Once the one-and-only Tate, the original gallery on Millbank has benefited enormously from recent redevelopment. With the creation of Tate Modern downriver, it has reverted to what it was intended to be, a showcase for the national collection of British art from 1500 to the present. And it's a pretty impressive one, with examples of works by well-known 18th-century artists such as Hogarth, Reynolds, and Gainsborough; the Pre-Raphaelites; and 20th-century luminaries such as Francis Bacon and Henry Moore. But it's the Turners, something like 300 of them, that are the stars of the show. The restaurant, by the way, often wins awards for its wine list. *Daily 10am-5:50pm. Special exhibitions: 10am-5:40pm (last admission 5pm).* £- Millbank, SW1 (⊖ Pimlico), 020-7887-8888, tate.org.uk

Tea at the Ritz • Mayfair • Activity

Best Rainy Day Activities The tinkling sounds of a piano or harp, the dainty pots of Darjeeling First Flush or Ritz Royal English, the tiered china cake stands carefully arranged with cucumber sandwiches, scones, and irresistible cakes: It's as if the Edwardian era had never ended. A leisurely afternoon tea in the rococo Palm Court at The Ritz is one of those events that still captures the imagination even in these more go-getting times. However, it's not for the spontaneous as, in spite of five daily sittings—"afternoon" being a flexible measurement of time here—you are still advised to book at least six weeks in advance. *Daily 11:30am, and 1:30, 3:30 and 5:30pm; Champagne Afternoon Tea: 7:30pm.* ££££ The Ritz Hotel, 150 Piccadilly, W1 (⊖ Green Park), 020-7493-8181, theritzlondon.com

Tower of London • The City • Sight

Judging by the lines—truly appalling on summer afternoons—the main event at this World Heritage Site is the sparkling exhibition of the Crown Jewels. There is, indeed, plenty to gawk at, including the fabulous Koh-i-Noor diamond, all 105.6 carats of it, firmly attached to the late Queen Mother's crown, and a scepter with a 530-carat glint. However, the surrounding towers merit exploration, as there are medieval and Elizabethan room sets, elaborately carved graffiti by former prisoners, and a particularly gruesome display of instruments of torture. The oldest and largest structure, the 900-year-plus White Tower, is filled with antique armor and weaponry. *Mar–Oct Sun-Mon 10am-6pm, Tue-Sat 9am-6pm; Nov–Feb Sun-Mon 10am-5pm, Tue-Sat 9am-5pm.* £ Tower Hill, EC3 (⊖ Tower Hill), 0870-756-6060, hrp.org.uk

Victoria & Albert Museum • South Kensington • Museum

Home to a huge variety of decorative and applied arts, the V&A—as Londoners refer to it—is one of those rare places you can dip into again and again and always find something new and remarkable. The 19th-century life-size plaster copies of famous monuments such as Trajan's Column are enthralling, and in better condition than the originals; the fine furniture in the British Galleries is eminently covetable; and the fashion department is wonderfully entertaining. On Wednesday evenings, expert speakers give talks on all aspects of art, design, and history; tickets must be bought in advance. *Daily 10am-5:45pm (Wed and last Fri of month until 10pm).* £- Cromwell Rd., SW7 (⊖ South Kensington), 020-7942-2000, vam.ac.uk

Vivienne Westwood • Mayfair • Shop

Westwood may have begun as the grand dame of punk, but over the decades, her innovative designs have become the epitome of classic individual chic. Although her cuts are modern, much of her inspiration is historic, often with a dose of 18th-century rococo fantasy or 1950s sex appeal. This flagship on Conduit Street is a wood-paneled dream with three floors showcasing all her clothing and accessories for men and women. If nothing else, pick up some of the diamante skull jewelry. 44 Conduit St., W1 (⊖Oxford Circus), 020-7439-1109, viviennewestwood.co.uk

Wallace Collection • Marylebone • Art Museum

Surely ranking as one of the most generous presents ever, this breathtaking collection and the capacious Georgian townhouse that contains it were bequeathed to the nation in 1897 by one Lady Wallace, hence the name. Beyond the imposing front entrance is an almost overwhelming array of fine art and objects, including some of the finest 18th-century French paintings, Sèvres porcelain, and furniture outside Paris, and world-famous works such as Frans Hals' *Laughing Cavalier*. Sensory overload is a real possibility, but the glass-roofed cafe—popular with cultured ladies and actor types—makes a good recovery spot. *Daily 10am-5pm.* £- Hertford House, Manchester Sq., W1 (⊖Bond Street), 020-7563-9500, wallacecollection.org

Westminster Abbey • Westminster • Sight

Generations of British monarchs have been crowned and buried here ever since Edward the Confessor built the first place of worship on this spot in 1066. Only a few scraps of the original church remain, though the founder's tomb was recently rediscovered under the magnificent later cathedral, which dates from between the 13th and 18th centuries. Inside this World Heritage Site, there's plenty to hold the attention: Poets' Corner with the graves of famous writers; the fabulous octagonal Chapter House, with fan tracery, stained glass, and medieval tiled floor; the meditative cloisters; and the tranquil College Garden. *Mon-Tue, Thu-Fri 9:30am-3:45pm, Wed 9:30am-6pm, Sat 9:30am-1:45pm. College Garden: Apr–Sep Tue-Thu 10am-6pm, Oct–Mar Tue-Thu 10am-4pm. Chapter House: daily 10:30am-4pm. Cloisters: daily 8am-6pm.* £- 20 Dean's Yard, SW1 (⊖Westminster), 020-7222-5152, westminster-abbey.org

PRIME TIME LONDON

Everything in life is timing (with a dash of serendipity thrown in). Would you want to arrive in Pamplona the day *after* the Running of the Bulls? Not if you have a choice, and you relish being a part of life's peak experiences. With our month-by-month calendar of events, there's no excuse to miss out on any of London's greatest moments. From the classic to the quirky, the sophisticated to the outrageous, all the events that are worth your time are right here.

Prime Time Basics

Eating and Drinking

London is fairly flexible when it comes to mealtimes; restaurants are generally open for lunch between noon and 3pm, and for dinner from 6 to 11pm, with the busiest time from 8pm onwards. For pre-dinner drinks, count on starting around 7pm, though popular after-work places can be busy from 5:30pm onwards. Any bar worth its salt will be completely packed by 10pm, though there's no point going to nightclubs before midnight (unless that's the only way you'll get in). Thanks to recent changes in the law, pubs and bars can stay open later than 11pm, and many in London do, though that still means last orders at 2am at the latest.

Weather and Tourism

Londoners may complain about the weather, but it's really just a safe way of kicking off a conversation with people you don't know well. In reality, it's a pretty benign "temperate maritime" setup, if you want to get technical: mild, damp winters and gentle summers. It doesn't even rain that much; in fact, the past few years have been a drought. The only real problem is the unpredictability, which is a good reason for traveling in the shoulder seasons, along with the fact that you'll encounter fewer tourists outside the summer school holidays. You may save money on your hotel, too, as there are more deals then.

Jan-Feb: There are more gray days than sunny ones, and more chance of rain than snow. Restaurants and bars can be quiet.

Mar-May: Spring brings a mixed bag of glorious sunny

Seasonal Changes

Month	Fahrenheit		Celsius		Hotel
	High	Low	High	Low	Rates
Jan	44	33	07	00	L
Feb	45	33	07	01	L
Mar	50	35	10	02	L
Apr	55	38	13	03	S
May	61	43	16	06	S
June	67	49	20	09	H
July	71	52	22	11	H
Aug	70	52	21	11	H
Sept	66	48	19	09	S
Oct	59	44	15	06	S
Nov	50	37	10	03	L
Dec	50	34	08	01	L

H-High Season S-Shoulder L-Low

days and showers, though May can be one of the loveliest months of the year. During the Easter school break there are lots of families in the streets and museums.

June-Aug: Summer is as unreliable as the rest of the seasons. Average highs are in the 60s and low 70s, but temperatures can head much higher. Indeed, it's often been said that the best outfit for a British summer would be swimwear with a sweater and raincoat. The chances of meeting a native Londoner diminish radically, as they've gone on holiday to escape the hordes of tourists.

Sept-Oct: Often the most comfortable time to visit, fall ("autumn" in the UK) brings a final flourish of fine weather without the fierce heat that can blight August explorations.

Nov-Dec: Winter sets in with a vengeance, bringing cold, damp days, though the run-up to Christmas brings a sparkle to the streets and stores. Given London's meteorological unpredictability, the layered look is the best one to adopt when it comes to clothing. Just because the day starts dull and drizzly doesn't mean it won't be sunny by noon, and, alas, vice versa.

National Holidays

New Year's Day	January 1
Valentine's Day	February 14
Mothering Sunday	Fourth Sunday of Lent
Good Friday	First Friday after full moon that follows March 28
Easter Monday	First Monday after Good Friday
May Day	First Monday in May
Spring Bank Holiday	Last Monday in May
Father's Sunday	Third Sunday in June
August Bank Holiday	Last Monday in August
Halloween	October 31
Bonfire Night	November 5
Christmas Day	December 25
Boxing Day	December 26
New Year's Eve	December 31

Listings in blue are major celebrations but not official holidays.

PRIME TIME

The Best Events Calendar

January
- Chinese New Year Celebrations
- London Art Fair
- New Year's Day Parade

February
- London Fashion Week

March
- Oxford and Cambridge Boat Race

April

May
- Chelsea Flower Show

June
- Glastonbury Festival
- Holland Park Opera
- London Garden Squares
- Meltdown
- Royal Acad. Summer Ex.
- Royal Ascot
- Trooping the Colour
- Vodafone Derby Festival
- Wimbledon

July
- BBC Sir Henry Wood Promenade Concerts
- Pride London

August
- Edinburgh Fringe Festival
- Notting Hill Carnival

September
- Brick Lane Festival
- Chelsea Antiques Fair
- London Design Festival
- London Open House
- Mayor's Thames Festival

October
- Frieze Art Fair
- London Film Festival

November
- Bonfire Night
- London to Brighton Vintage Car Run
- Lord Mayor's Show

December
- Hogmanay

The **Night+Day**'s Top Events are in blue.
High Season from June to August is represented by blue background.

The Best Events

January

Chinese New Year Celebrations

Around Chinatown, W1, Leicester Sq. and Trafalgar Sq., WC2, and Charing Cross Rd., 020-7851-6686, chinatownchinese.co.uk

The Lowdown: Already lively Chinatown fairly fizzes with a multicultural crowd during the New Year's celebrations, and every year events spill just a bit further into neighboring districts. Highlights include a parade of stunningly costumed performers, the traditional Dragon Dance in Trafalgar Square, and open-air performances of everything from Chinese opera to martial arts, with fireworks to round off the afternoon in style. Local restaurants also join in with stalls in the street and special menus, which ensures they're packed until well after the end of the official events.

When and How Much: *Sunday following the Chinese New Year, which falls between late January and early February, 11am-5:30pm.* Free.

London Art Fair

Business Design Centre, 52 Upper St., N1, 020-7288-6456, londonartfair.co.uk

The Lowdown: A rigorously vetted 100 leading galleries take part in this prestigious annual showcase for modern and contemporary British art, where serious collectors rub shoulders with artists and the merely arty. It's noted for the quality and variety of the work on display, so if you hanker for a Henry Moore or a Damien Hirst, this is definitely the place to look.

When and How Much: *From Wednesday to Sunday of the penultimate week of January.* £

New Year's Day Parade

From Parliament Sq., SW1, to Piccadilly, W1, 020-8566-8586, londonparade.co.uk

The Lowdown: Marching bands, dance troupes, decorated floats, acrobats, and huge character balloons: London's massive New Year's Day Parade has them all and more, with participants from all over the world, including the US. It's perhaps not the most sophisticated entertainment you'll ever witness, but it's a fun way to mark the end of the holiday season—and raises money for charity in the process. For the best views, book tickets in advance for the grandstand seating in Piccadilly and Whitehall.

When and How Much: *January 1, which is a public holiday in the UK, from noon to around 3pm.* Free; grandstand tickets £

PRIME TIME

February

London Fashion Week

Natural History Museum, South Kensington, SW3, 020-7636-7788,
londonfashionweek.co.uk

The Lowdown: Twice-yearly Fashion Week is a glittering showcase for London's
eclectic mix of modistes, who hope to woo the buyers and famous front-row
guests into diving into their pocketbooks. As it's essentially a trade show, you
can't just turn up and strut in on your Manolos. Invitations to the individual shows
are at the discretion of the designer concerned, who will be listed on the website.

When and How Much: *One week (Monday through Saturday) in mid-February and
one week in mid-September.* Free

March

Oxford and Cambridge Boat Race

Thames, from Putney to Mortlake, 01225-383483, theboatrace.org

The Lowdown: Eight strapping lads from the country's two oldest and grandest
universities slug it out over four and a quarter miles of the River Thames, as they
have over 150 times since 1829. Cambridge, in dark blue, currently leads 78-
72 (one year was a dead heat), but the "Light Blues"—that's Oxford—have
recently been on a winning streak. Not interested in rowing? Neither are many
of the spectators, but that doesn't stop them from packing the riverside pubs
along the route.

When and How Much: *Saturday in the last three weeks in March or the first week
in April, depending on the tides and the academic calendar.* Free

May

Chelsea Flower Show

Royal Hospital Chelsea, SW3, 020-7649-1885, booking line 0870-906-3781,
rhs.org.uk

The Lowdown: The British love gardening, and nowhere is this clearer than at this
long-running annual gathering of the green-thumbed, with its inspiring show
gardens and displays from international growers and designers. Wistful
Londoners with tiny patios mingle with wealthy ladies up from the country and
a plethora of celebrity gardeners.

When and How Much: *Tuesday through Saturday of the last full week in May; the
first two days are reserved for members of the Royal Horticultural Society.* £-£££

June

Glastonbury Festival

Worthy Farm, Pilton, Shepton Mallet, Somerset, tickets 0870-165-2005, overseas booking 011-44-1159-934163, glastonburyfestivals.co.uk

The Lowdown: The world's largest open-air music festival—in a bucolic setting 125 miles southwest of London—gets more boho-chic each year, with a starry lineup not just on the many stages but in the audience, too. Camping is de rigueur; for comfort, book into Camp Kerala, a private tented village on the edge of the festival grounds.

When and How Much: *Friday through Sunday of the last full weekend in June.* ££££

Holland Park Opera

Holland Park, Kensington High St., W8, 020-7602-7856, box office 0845-230-9769, operahollandpark.com

The Lowdown: There can be few experiences that say summer more than listening to music in the open air with birdsong for background. In the ultra-classy environs of Holland Park, it's opera on the playlist and the birds are peacocks, but the repertoire is reassuringly broad, offering excellent but obscure works along with the classics. Be sure to reserve a picnic when you buy your tickets, and enjoy it, rain or shine, under the theater's protective canopy.

When and How Much: *From early June to early August.* ££-£££

London Garden Squares Weekend

Various venues across London, opensquares.org

The Lowdown: London is a surprisingly green city, but those enticing gardens in the middle of many of its squares are usually off-limits to nonresidents. For one weekend a year, however, many throw open their gates to the public. Fine weather brings out the horticulturists and the just plain curious of all ages in droves, especially to the better-known places or those with limited opening hours. The full list of participating gardens can be found on the website.

When and How Much: *The second full weekend in June.* £-

Meltdown

South Bank Centre, Belvedere Rd., SE1, box office 0870-380-0400, rfh.org.uk

The Lowdown: You can expect plenty of happy surprises from this festival of contemporary culture thanks to its policy of having a different guest curator every year. In the past, the hand at the helm has included such luminaries as David Bowie and Patti Smith, each bringing his or her own particular slant on life and the arts to bear on an always-excellent but unpredictable mix of rock, visual arts, theater, modern dance, and literary events.

When and How Much: *Around three weeks in June.* £-£££

PRIME TIME

Royal Academy Summer Exhibition

Burlington House, Piccadilly, W1, 020-7300-8000,
recorded information 020-7300-5760/1, royalacademy.org.uk

The Lowdown: A regular on the art-world calendar for more than 200 years, the Summer Exhibition is the world's largest open contemporary art competition, covering mainly painting and sculpture, all by living artists. The private view on the opening night is a hot ticket. As for the art itself, there have been complaints that there's a world of difference between amateur and amateurish.

When and How Much: *Early June to mid-August. £*

Royal Ascot

Ascot Racecourse, Ascot, Berkshire, tickets 0870-727-1234, royalascot.co.uk

The Lowdown: By far the most social of the summer race meetings, this five-day extravaganza is as much about fine clothes and millenary as horses. Queen Anne started it all in 1711, and nearly 300 years later the Royal Family still attend Royal Ascot daily, arriving in horse-drawn open carriages. You have to be a regular or be recommended by one to lay your hands on a badge for the exclusive Royal Enclosure, where the most dressed-up racegoers saunter. No luck this year? Fortunately, the newly renovated facilities include plenty of elegant eateries where you can console yourself with good food and champagne, or you could be wildly extravagant and hire a private box.

When and How Much: *Tue-Sat of third week in June. £££-££££*

Trooping the Colour

Horse Guards Parade, Whitehall, SW1, booking line 020-7414-2479, royal.gov.uk

The Lowdown: Dating back to at least the 18th century, this colorful spectacle sees Her Majesty travel by carriage from Buckingham Palace to Horse Guards Parade in Whitehall to inspect her troops—more than 1,400 soldiers in their full regimental regalia with their "colors" or flags, and ten marching bands. To see the whole ceremony, book tickets early in the year for the grandstand seating on the parade ground. Otherwise, get to the Mall in plenty of time to watch the troops escort the Queen back to Buckingham Palace.

When and How Much: *The second or third Saturday in June, depending on the monarch's other commitments.* Free; parade ground tickets £

Vodafone Derby Festival

Epson Downs Racecourse, Surrey, 01372-470047, epsomderby.co.uk

The Lowdown: The Derby itself, run on the Saturday, is the most important race of the flat season. Friday is Ladies' Day, a glamorous occasion with female race goers in their most stylish outfits. Watch it all from one of the grandstands; the Queen's Stand has the best seats, a restaurant, and several champagne bars. Keep your eyes peeled for royalty—the Queen usually attends if she can.

When and How Much: *First Friday and Saturday in June. £-£££*

Wimbledon Lawn Tennis Championships

P.O. Box 98, Church Rd., Wimbledon, SW19, 020-8971-2473,
recorded information 020-8946-2244, wimbledon.org

The Lowdown: There's something timelessly magical about the only Grand Slam played on grass, both for the players and the spectators. It's not just a major sporting event, but a social one as well. Centre Court and Court No. 1 are the ones to be seen in; the most coveted seats are in Centre Court's royal box, for which you'll need seriously good contacts.

When and How Much: *Fourteen days, starting exactly six weeks before the first Monday in August, which translates into late June to early July. £-££££*

July

BBC Sir Henry Wood Promenade Concerts

Royal Albert Hall, Kensington Gore, SW7, information 020-7765-5575,
box office 020-7589-8212, bbc.co.uk/proms

The Lowdown: Started in the late 19th century with the aim of introducing classical music to as many people as possible, the Proms, for short, are still much appreciated by music fans. Around 70 concerts offer something for all. The Last Night of the Proms is a must-see riot of raucous, good-natured patriotism.

When and How Much: *Eight weeks, from a Friday in mid-July to a Saturday in mid-September. £-££££*

Pride London

Parade from Oxford Street to Victoria Embankment, stage in Leicester Sq., WC2,
020-7494-2225, pridelondon.org

The Lowdown: London's sizable gay and lesbian community comes out to play in outrageous style for this good-humored parade through the center of London, a relaxed mix of floats, dancing groups, drag queens, and bands. Parade completed, the party continues with a rally and cabaret in two of the city's main squares. A recent innovation is the festival preceding it, which now occupies the two weeks leading up to the march.

When and How Much: *The first Saturday in July.* Free

August

Edinburgh Fringe Festival

Various venues in Edinburgh, 0131-226-0026, edfringe.com

The Lowdown: No, it's not in London—but it might as well be, as the entire arts community (in the widest sense of the word "arts") heads up there for a few heady summer weeks. The Fringe is only one of several more-or-less simultaneous Edinburgh festivals covering everything from books to opera, but is by far

PRIME TIME

the most diverse. Among nearly two thousand acts, comedy and theater domi-
nate, but Fringe is proof there are many types of both, as the handy printed
Daily Guides show. Book ahead if there's something in particular you want to
see, especially if it's a weekend show, but leave some time free for this year's
unexpected gem that's causing a buzz or for your own spontaneous discoveries.

When and How Much: *First Sunday to the last Monday in August. £-££*

Notting Hill Carnival

Notting Hill, W11, 0870-059-1111, lnhc.org.uk

The Lowdown: Started by homesick immigrants from Trinidad in the 1950s,
Carnival is now Europe's biggest street party, attracting a staggering two million
revelers over the three days. Saturday is the steel band competition and Sunday
the Kids Carnival, with the main event—hundreds of floats, thumping music,
and amazing costumes—on Monday drawing the largest crowds to this very fashionable part of London.

When and How Much: *Three days, Saturday to the last Monday in August.* Free

September

Brick Lane Festival

Brick Lane, Hanbury St. and Allen Gdns., E1, 020-7655-0906, visitbricklane.com

The Lowdown: This happening street party in the heart of trendy Spitalfields is a
shining example of the area's cross-cultural vibe. On the music and dance stage,
performers include stars from the UK's vibrant Asian music scene, banjo bands,
and Bangladeshi folk singers. Elsewhere, there's plenty more, including stalls
selling curries, rickshaw rides, stilt walkers, and free historical walking tours.

When and How Much: *Second Sunday in September.* Free

Chelsea Antiques Fair

Chelsea Town Hall, King's Rd., SW3, 01825-744074, penman-fairs.co.uk

The Lowdown: Chelsea Town Hall plays host once a year to this highly respected
gathering of around 35 carefully vetted antique and fine art dealers. Serious collectors and dabblers alike are drawn in droves by the sheer quality of the mainly
smaller antique goods on offer, whether it's Chinese porcelain, English silver, or
Oriental rugs. Prices start at under US$200, rising to around US$50,000.

When and How Much: *Ten days from a Friday in mid-September.* £-

London Design Festival

Various venues, 020-7014-5313, londondesignfestival.com

The Lowdown: It may be early days yet, but this has already become a leading
showcase for London's diverse design talents. The city is, after all, home to thousands of people working in a variety of creative fields—advertising, set design,
furniture, and applied arts such as ceramics and glassware, to name only a few.

When and How Much: *September 15-30.* Free-££

London Open House Weekend
Various venues, 09001-600-061, londonopenhouse.org

The Lowdown: The capital's biggest architectural happening gives everyone the chance to poke their nose into more than a hundred buildings not normally open to the public. The varied selection, which changes every year, includes everything from particularly interesting private houses to ultramodern offices such as Lloyds of London. It's a good idea to download the guide from the website in advance, as reservations are required for some of the properties. Talks and walks by architects, architectural historians, and engineers complete the weekend's schedule.

When and How Much: *Third full weekend in September.* Free

Mayor's Thames Festival
Between Westminster and Tower Bridges, 020-7928-8998, thamesfestival.org

The Lowdown: Sunday evening sees the highlight of this festival to celebrate the city's famous river: the lively Night Carnival procession, with the lantern-carrying participants dressed to dazzle, followed by a spectacular fireworks display. It's the culmination of two days of watery activities such as boat trips and naval displays, plus music, bazaars, and a full program for the children.

When and How Much: *Third full weekend in September, noon-10pm each day; Night Carnival, Sunday 7:30-9:30pm.* Free

October

Frieze Art Fair
Regent's Park, W1, 020-7833-7270, friezeartfair.com

The Lowdown: Inaugurated the same year as the London Design Festival (see September), this contemporary art show has had a similar meteoric rise to preeminence in its field. In a specially commissioned temporary structure in Regent's Park, 150 leading international galleries wow the stylish public, not to mention a slew of famous faces. Supporting events include Friezes Music, Talks and Projects, specially commissioned works by emerging artists.

When and How Much: *Four days, from the second or third Friday in October to the following Monday.* £

London Film Festival
Various venues, 020-7928-3232, lff.org.uk

The Lowdown: Its movie industry may not match the scale of Hollywood or Bollywood, but London's tribute to all things celluloid nevertheless offers the moviegoer plenty to savor. Cinemas all over town screen some 300 features and shorts from around the world, everything from the cream of new indie flicks from the US to gripping world cinema discoveries. If just looking at movies isn't enough, there's also a small but select program of talks by industry names.

When and How Much: *Two weeks, from a Wednesday in mid-October to early November.* Free-££

PRIME TIME

November

Bonfire Night

Various venues, see local listings for details

The Lowdown: The UK's pyrotechnic extravaganza has its roots deep in the past. Believe it or not, it commemorates the foiling of a plot to blow up the king and Houses of Parliament over 400 years ago. The chief conspirator, Guy Fawkes, is still sometimes burned in effigy, but mostly it's an excuse for a big blaze and fireworks. The best displays are held on the weekends either side of Bonfire Night itself.

When and How Much: *November 5.* Free

London to Brighton Vintage Car Run

Hyde Park via Westminster Bridge to Brighton, 01327-856-024, lbvcr.org

The Lowdown: There's something wonderfully romantic about vintage cars, and this longstanding—and just a tad eccentric—event boasts more than 500 glorious specimens, all manufactured before 1905. Early risers can watch the staggered start in Hyde Park or catch the slowly passing motors later along the 60-mile route.

When and How Much: *First Sunday in November.* Free

Lord Mayor's Show

Between Mansion House and the Royal Courts of Justice; fireworks between Waterloo and Blackfriars bridges, 020-7332-1456, lordmayorsshow.org

The Lowdown: Even in a city so rich in history, not much can claim such deep roots as this ancient piece of pomp. Its origins date to 1215, when King John allowed the citizens to elect their own mayor, as long as the new dignitary paid him a visit to swear allegiance to the Crown. From simple beginnings grew this entertaining pageant, with floats, marching bands, and the new mayor in his glittering state coach. See it all from Mansion House or St. Paul's, but get there early as it gets very crowded; or watch the return trip from Queen Victoria Street or Embankment. The day ends with fabulous fireworks, launched from a barge in the Thames; try the South Bank between Waterloo and Blackfriars bridges for maximum impact.

When and How Much: *Second Saturday in November, parade 10:55am-2:30pm, fireworks 5-5:30pm.* Free

December

Hogmanay

Edinburgh, 0131-529-3914, edinburghshogmanay.org

The Lowdown: Scotland in general, and Edinburgh in particular, celebrates the New Year with far more enthusiasm than London, and for longer. Technically Hogmanay is just New Year's Eve, but Edinburgh has four days of festivities— torchlight processions, fireworks, music, Scottish dancing—to mark the event.

When and How Much: *Four days from December 29 to January 1.* Free-££££

HIT the GROUND RUNNING

In this section, you'll find all the indispensable details to help you enhance your trip—from tips on what to wear and how to get around to planning resources that will help your vacation come off without a hitch. You'll also find suggestions for making business trips a pleasure, as well as some fun, surprising facts that will help you impress the locals.

City Essentials

Getting to London: By Air

London is served by five international airports. The majority of long-haul flights land at Heathrow and Gatwick, though one airline from the US uses Stansted. Otherwise, Stansted, Luton, and London City airports mainly handle flights to domestic and European destinations.

London Heathrow Airport (LHR)
0870-000-0123, heathrowairport.com

London Heathrow is located 20 miles west of central London, off junction 4 of the M4.

LHR is the world's busiest international airport, handling some 68 million passengers a year from all parts of the globe, reflecting London's status as a city of world importance. Currently this major hub has four terminals, but a dazzling and hi-tech new Terminal Five, due to be finished in 2008, will raise capacity by a further 30 million.

There's little chance of travelers going hungry here, with a

Flying Times to London

Nonstop From	Airport Code	Time (hr.)
Amsterdam	AMS	1
Atlanta	ATL	8
Chicago	ORD	8
Frankfurt	FRA	1½
Los Angeles	LAX	10½
Miami	MIA	8½
New York	JFK	7
Paris	CDG	1
San Francisco	SFO	10
Toronto	YTO	7
Washington, D.C.	IAD	7½

myriad of options. If all you want is a good Italian-strength coffee, there's Est-Presso in Terminal One, and Costa Coffee and Caffè Nero in Terminals One, Two, and Four. Grab a gourmet sandwich with your caffeine hit at Pret à Manger in Terminals One and Four; it's not one of Britain's best-loved chains for nothing. For something more substantial, there's global cuisine at LHR's offshoot of Giraffe in Terminal One, French brasserie fare at the local Chez Gérard in Terminal Three, and delicious Italian food at Est Est Est in Terminals One and Two. Feast on platters of superb smoked salmon at the Caviar House Seafood Bar; there's one in each of the terminals. As for drinks, you can sup on Guinness at O'Neill's in Terminal Three or real ales at the retro pub the Tin Goose in Terminal One.

Major Airlines Serving LHR & LGW International Airports

Airlines	Website	Phone Number	LHR	LGW
Aer Lingus	aerlingus.com	0845-0844-444	1	
Air Canada	aircanada.com	020-8751-1331	3	
Air China	airchina.com	020-7744-0800	3	
Air France	airfrance.com	020-8750-4043	2	N
Air India	airindia.com	020-7495-7950	3	
Air New Zealand	airnewzealand.com	0800-028-4149	3	
Alitalia	alitalia.com	0870-544-8259	2	
All Nippon	fly-ana.com	0870-837-8866	3	
American Airlines	aa.com	0845-778-9789	3	N
British Airways	britishairways.com	0870-5511-155	1, 4	N
Cathay Pacific	cathaypacific.com	020-8897-9335	3	
Continental Airlines	continental.com	0845-607-6760		S
Delta Airlines	delta.com	0845-600-0950		N
Iberia	iberia.com	0870-609-0500	2	
Japan Airlines	jal.co.jp/en	0870-837-8866	3	
KLM	klm.com	0870-507-4074	4	
Kuwait Airways	kuwait-airways.com	020-7412-0007	3	
Lufthansa	lufthansa.com	0870-837-7747	2	
Malaysia Airlines	malaysiaairlines.com	0870-607-9090	3	
Northwest Airlines	nwa.com	0870-507-4074		S
SAS	scandinavian.net	020-8990-7159	3	S
Singapore Airlines	singaporeair.com	0870-414-6666	3	
Swiss	swiss.com	0845-601-0956	2	
Thai Airways Internat.	thaiairways.com	0870-606-4911	3	
United Airlines	united.com	800-864-8331	3	
US Airways	usair.com	0845-600-3300		S
Virgin Atlantic	virgin-atlantic.com	01293-5562-345	3	S

Low-Cost Airlines

EasyJet (Gatwick, Luton, Stansted)	easyjet.com		S
Ryanair (Gatwick, Luton, Stansted)	ryanair.com		S

HIT THE GROUND

If you're a fan of airport art, you've come to the wrong place. If you're a fan of shopping, however, you've just landed in tax-free heaven. As well as high-street names selling books, perfume, sunglasses, electronic gadgetry, and the like, there's a wealth of designer outlets, particularly in Terminals Three and Four. Here you can browse the latest gear and baubles at Chanel, Dior, Bulgari, and Cartier, and snap up heavenly travel accessories and stationery at true-Brit celebrity-favorite Smythson. Terminal Three also has Emporio Armani, Paul Smith, and Versace; a variety of fabulous offerings from Liberty; scented treats at Jo Malone; and stylish cosmetics at Mac. There's an equally impressive range at Terminal Four: admire the scarves at Hermès, sexy underwear at Agent Provocateur, and high-quality offerings at the British Museum Company. Traditionally minded shoppers in Terminal Two can get outfitted at Barbour and stock up on edible treats at Fortnum & Mason, while Terminal One offers the chance to browse the surfer gear at Fat Face or get your nails done at Manicure Express. As for those British icons Harrods, wine merchants Berry Bros & Rudd, and Burberry, there's no escape: You'll find one in each of the terminals (and toy store Hamley's in all but One).

Business travelers will appreciate the availability of high-speed WiFi internet access throughout the airport provided by BT Openzone and T-Mobile. T-Mobile's laptop stations mean no worries about flat batteries. The Heathrow Business Centre, between Terminals One and Two, before security, has 20 meeting rooms, and a full range of facilities. All terminals have lounges for first- and business-class passengers; or you can pre-book tickets for the Servisair lounges through the airport website.

Into Town By Taxi: There are usually black cabs lined up outside the terminals. Journeys are metered; expect to pay about £50 to central London from Heathrow; average journey time is about an hour.

Into Town By Train: The Heathrow Express takes 20 minutes from LHR to Paddington station, in west London; from there, you'll find transport links to all areas (0845-600-1515; heathrowexpress.co.uk).

Into Town By Underground: Heathrow (two stops; one for Terminal Four, one for Terminals One to Three) is on the London Underground (the Tube) system, with the journey to the center of town taking about 50 minutes; tickets cost £4.

London Gatwick (LGW)

0870-000-2468, gatwickairport.com

Gatwick may play second fiddle to LHR, but it's still the world's sixth-busiest international airport. Around 80 airlines operate out of LGW's two terminals, taking 30 million people a year to over 200 destinations. The buildings themselves may not win architectural plaudits, but they do a great job of accommodating the voyaging public in comfort, and the nippy little monorail that connects the North and South Terminals is a joy to use.

Both terminals are well equipped for travelers when it comes to the little matter of food and drink, though the choice isn't quite as impressive as at LHR. However, you'll still be able to indulge at the Caviar House Seafood Bar; there's a branch in each terminal. The North Terminal offers tasty Japanese snacks at Yo! Sushi, delicious simple French food at Chez Gérard, and more fishy fare at the Seafood Bar. Lighter offerings are provided by Pip (juices and smoothies) and EAT (soups and sandwiches). The South Terminal has tasty Italian cooking at Est Est Est, and the Metro Café for coffee and pastries; before security you'll also find a branch of long-running chain Pizza Express, and great coffees at Costa and Caffè Nero.

Shopping is definitely the other top activity at LGW. Don't expect the glitzy designer names here, though; most of the outlets will appeal more to a younger, dressed-down crowd in a holiday mood. The South Terminal offers laid-back garb from Fat Face, cool beachwear at Beachparty, and with-it high-street fashion from FCUK and Ted Baker.

Rental Cars: We don't recommend it, but if you insist, these reputable companies have outlets at both airports:

Agency	Website	(USA) 800 Number	Local Number
Alamo	alamo.com	800-412-5266	0870-400-4580
Avis	avis.com	800-331-1212	0870-606-0100
Europcar	europcar.com	877-940-6900	0845-758-5375
Hertz	hertz.com	800-654-3001	0870-599-6699
National	nationalcar.com	800-227-3876	0870-556-5656

Limos:
- Blueback — blueback.com — 0870-771-1711
- Mayfair Corporation — mayfaircorp.co.uk — 020-8255-0522

HIT THE GROUND

Over at the North Terminal, the range includes surfer label Quiksilver, top name Burberry, and perennially desirable Lacoste. There's a branch of Harrods in both. If you're all shopped out, head to the Clarins Studio in the South Terminal where you can get a fake tan or indulge in one of several other pampering beauty treatments.

Businesspeople on the go can stay connected with high-speed WiFi internet access throughout the airport, and plug-in work stations in many locations. The United Business Centre in the South Terminal has 17 fully equipped meeting rooms for hire. Gatwick Airport has a suite of modern meeting rooms available for rent in the airport complex on weekdays, 8am-6pm. There are lounges for first- and business-class ticket holders; others can pre-book space in the Aviace lounge for a small fee on the airport website.

Into Town By Taxi: As LGW is 28 miles south of central London, traveling by road can be a time-consuming and expensive business. Licensed private car services are provided by the airport's official concession, Checker Cars (01293-567-700; checkercars.com). A journey to central London takes a little over an hour and costs around £85 (plus £5 congestion charge if your destination is within the charging zone).

Into Town By Train: The speediest way to reach the center of London is the Gatwick Express (0845-850-1530; gatwickexpress.com), a nonstop service from the South Terminal to Victoria Station, which takes around 30 minutes. Tickets can be purchased on board; £25 roundtrip.

London Stansted (STN)
0870-000-0303, stanstedairport.com

This is London's third international gateway and one of the fastest-growing airports in Europe, with more than 21 million passengers a year flying to over 170 places, mainly to the Continent. The only airline that currently flies to and from the US is business-class-only Eos, which flies from New York's JFK.

Opened in 1991, this airport is wonderfully airy, which makes up for the relative lack of shopping and eating opportunities. That said, you're not going to starve or die of boredom. Among the usual duty-free options (scent, alcohol, and cigarettes), you can also snap up classic British clothing at Hackett, beachwear at Quiksilver, toys at Hamley's, and high-street fashion from FCUK. Accessorize is a tempting place to browse for bags, beads, and sunhats, and Books etc has an excellent range of tomes for on-board entertainment.

As for sustenance, there's a Caviar House Seafood Bar for an indulgent pre-flight meal. In an Italian mood? There's Est Est Est for food, Est Bar Est for drinks, and Est-Presso for coffee.

Into Town By Taxi: STN is 35 miles northeast of London, and getting to London by road can be a lengthy process, especially in rush hour. The official Stansted taxi concession is Checker Cars (01279-661-111; checkercars.com), which has a reservation desk in the arrivals area.

Into Town By Train: Speed into London on the Stansted Express (0845-748-4950; stanstedexpress.com), which takes around 50 minutes to reach Liverpool Street Station, in the financial district.

Other Airports in the London Area

London City Airport (LCY) is only six miles from central London, close to the business district, and most of its two million travelers are business people heading to Europe or other parts of the UK. The Docklands Light Railway connects it to the Underground system, but you may prefer to take a taxi. londoncityairport.com

London Luton Airport (LTN) handles mainly low-cost scheduled services, carrying just under seven million people a year, and is 35 miles northwest of London. Trains run to central London throughout the day and night; for a taxi, expect to pay about £70 to £80. london-luton.co.uk

Getting to London: By Land

By Train: London is linked to continental Europe by Eurostar, a supremely useful train service that whisks you from Paris or Brussels under the English Channel to the center of London in under three hours. For tickets and schedules, call 0870-518-6186 or visit eurostar.com.

By Car: You can take a car from Europe into England two ways: under the Channel or over it. With Eurotunnel (0870-535-3535; eurotunnel.com), you drive your vehicle onto a special train at Calais in France, which then takes you to the port of Folkestone, where you drive off. It's then a two-hour drive to London. Otherwise, there are cross-Channel ferry services (go to ferrysavers.com).

London: Lay of the Land

Considering what a vast city it is, traveling around London is more straightforward than you might expect. The varied transport options include buses, Underground trains, speedy riverboats, various types of taxis, and, of course, walking. There are occasional hiccups, but on the whole the system works and is constantly being upgraded.

The city's postal codes offer some hint as to where a given venue is located, though it's a mistake to rely too heavily on their logic. N, E, SE, SW, W, and NW, along with EC (East Central) and WC (West Central) are all abbreviations for coordinates radiating out from the City. If the number following the coordinates is a 1, you can count on the venue being quite central. Beyond 1, the numbers could be anywhere in the city (and sequential numbers are not necessarily located next to each other). In this guide, the first portion of the postal code is included with addresses so that you can gain a sense of what part of the city they are in and identify places located within the same zone.

Getting Around London

By Subway: The Underground, or "the tube" as it's known, makes traveling around London a breeze once you've worked out the system. Maps are available free of charge from tube stations, airport information desks, and from Transport for London (020-7222-1234; tfl.gov.uk).

For transport purposes, London is divided into six concentric zones; most of the venues in this guide are located in the central area, Zone 1. On the map, each of the 12 tube lines (along with the privately owned Docklands Light Railway) gets a name and a color to distinguish it from the others; platforms will be signposted accordingly, so you may see "Northern Line Southbound" or "Central Line Westbound" with appropriate color-coding.

Fares depend on which zones you travel in; for instance, a single adult ticket in Zone 1 costs £3. If you're likely to explore further or use the tube and buses a few times in the day, you have several options. There's the One Day Travelcard, which can be bought from many newsagents as well as at stations. On weekdays, you'll pay £6.20 (Zones 1 and 2) if you're on the go before 9:30am; the Off-Peak card, on sale after 9:30am weekdays and any time on weekends, costs £4.90 (Zones 1 and 2). Three- and seven-day Travelcards can be bought in advance at tfl.gov.uk.

You may notice the locals using a bright blue smart card, called an Oyster Card. These are well worth getting. You'll need to ask at the ticket office for a form and pay a £3 administration fee. Once you've loaded it up using cash or your credit card, you can speed on your way, knowing you'll be saving time and money (with an Oyster Card a single adult ticket in Zone 1 costs £1.50 instead of £3).

You can look like a local in even more ways by remembering a few simple tube rules: People get rightly jumpy about unaccompanied baggage, so stay close to yours; carry water in hot weather, as it gets stuffy down there; and stand on the right on the escalators, so others can walk up or down on the left if they're feeling energetic. Remember, you may not be in a hurry, but you can be sure most of the people around you are.

The Underground runs from 5:30am Monday through Saturday and about 7:30am on Sunday, until around 12:30am (earlier on Sundays). The morning and evening rush hours run from about 7:30 to 9:15am and 5 to 6:30pm, and unless you really want to know how a canned sardine feels, you should avoid traveling then, especially with big bags.

By Bus: If the tube makes you feel like a bewildered rabbit, popping up out of the ground in different parts of town with no idea of what's in between, opt for London's bright red buses. Thanks to new dedicated bus lanes and the reduction in road traffic caused by the Congestion Charge (see By Car, below), it's a much speedier option than in the past. You can use your Oyster Card on buses (see p.192). Otherwise, you must buy a ticket before boarding from machines at the bus stop; unfortunately, these are unreliable, so purchase yours in books of six in advance (from most newsagents). If you have a Travelcard, it covers buses as well as the tube, or you can buy a One Day Bus Pass.

Taxi:	
Dial-A-Cab	020-7253-5000
Radio Taxis	020-7272-0272
Zingo (from cell phones only)	0870-070-0700

By Taxi: For convenience and comfort, not much beats the London cab. Before they're granted a license, drivers have to do "The Knowledge," which means spending an average of 34 months learning the best routes in a 12-mile circle of central London. Hail one in the street if its "for hire" sign is lit, pick one up outside your hotel, or call for one.

At busy times (rainy Friday evenings, for instance), you may have to opt for a minicab or "licensed private hire operator" (look for a disc on the windshield). The drivers are thoroughly vetted, but don't undergo the rigorous training of black-cab drivers, so they don't always know the way.

They don't have a meter, so check the price in advance. You should never hail a minicab in the street; avoid anyone who touts in this way, as they won't be legit. Ask locals for recommendations, or look on tfl.gov.uk.

By Cycle Rickshaw: For short journeys in fair weather, London's newest and most eye-catching option is the cycle rickshaw. The best-known firm is Bugbugs (020-7620-0500; bugbugs.co.uk), which has 60 pedicabs operating around the West End most nights. Amusing, and you're doing your bit to cut carbon emissions.

By Boat: Often overlooked, riverboats can be a practical and scenic way to travel between certain parts of town. You will find details of routes and operators at tfl.gov.uk; try Thames Clippers (0870-781-5049; thamesclippers.com), who connect several key attractions.

On Foot: London sprawls, but walking is still the best way to see it. The joy of it is that while you're getting from A to B, you'll see things you'd miss otherwise, such as tiny scraps of history or vignettes of modern life. Don't be shy about carrying a map, though. The discreet mini Geographers' A-Z tucks neatly into a pocket or purse and has an index; even Londoners use them. If you still need some help, don't bother asking how many blocks away somewhere is; the concept doesn't exist here.

By Car: Just don't. When a third of locals don't bother owning a car, you know there must be a reason. For a start, it's hideously expensive; gas prices are way higher than in the US, parking costs are breathtaking (see below); and there's the Congestion Charge, which means paying £8 for the day if you want to drive in central London. For visitors, there's also the "wrong side of the road" problem to negotiate, plus the fact that the narrow streets aren't laid out in a grid pattern, so navigating can be tricky. Save the driving for trips out of town.

Parking: If you thought driving was bad, wait until you try parking. Street parking in the center of town is at a premium, and expensive—as much as £1 for 15 minutes, with a maximum stay of two hours. Moreover, London's parking wardens are the most zealous in the world, so you can find yourself on the receiving end of a ticket, or being clamped or towed.

If you still insist on having your own wheels, the safest option is a garage, often multi-story, with an hourly or daily rate (where you pay either at the exit or buy a ticket for a specific amount of time in advance, which you then display behind your windshield). Various companies operate secure garages in central London, including National Car Parks (ncp.co.uk, 70 garages) and Masterpark (masterpark.org.uk, 18 garages). Here are some of their most useful 24-hour parking facilities.

Parking Garages

Covent Garden: **Drury Lane Car Park** (NCP), Parker St., WC2
City: **Thames Exchange Car Park** (NCP), Bell Wharf Ln., EC4
Marylebone: **Cavendish Square Car Park** (Masterpark), Cavendish Sq., W1
Marylebone: **Welbeck Street Car Park** (NCP), Welbeck St., W1
Knightsbridge: **Knightsbridge Car Park** (Masterpark), Kinnerton St., SW1
Soho: **Brewer St. Car Park** (NCP), Lexington St., W1
Soho: **Chinatown Car Park** (Masterpark), Newport Pl., WC2

Other Practical Information

Money Matters (Currency, Taxes, Tipping, and Service Charges): Britain uses pounds and pence (100 to the pound). For currency conversion rates, go to xe.com/ucc. The national sales tax is VAT (Value-Added Tax), which is charged at 17.5 percent on most items (among notable exceptions are food, books, newspapers, and children's clothes); prices in shops are quoted inclusive of VAT. Non-EU residents can claim back VAT on goods bought from retailers who are registered with the VAT Retail Export Scheme; they will issue a refund form, to be presented to customs on departure. For more information, download the leaflet "VAT Refunds for Travellers" at hmrc.gov.uk. There's no reliable rule for service charges; some restaurants add it on automatically, others don't. As always, it's best to ask. If nothing is included, 12.5 percent is a fair tip, and 15 percent is heading toward generous. For taxis, anything above 10 percent is fine. Hotel prices are usually quoted inclusive of taxes and service charges, though it's best to check. Leaving a tip of £1 to £2 a day in your room for the chambermaid has become standard practice.

Metric Conversion

From	To	Multiply by
Inches	Centimeters	2.54
Yards	Meters	0.91
Miles	Kilometers	1.60
US Gallons	Liters	3.79
Ounces	Grams	28.35
Pounds	Kilograms	0.45

Safety: London is a relatively safe city for visitors, and with a bit of care and common sense you should be fine. The standard urban rules apply: Use the hotel safe, don't carry lots of cash, be discreet with expensive toys like cameras, and take taxis home at night if you're not sure of the area. Frankly, you're more likely to have your pocket picked or cell phone stolen than anything more serious.

HIT THE GROUND

Numbers to Know (Hotlines)

Emergency, police, fire department, ambulance, and paramedics	999
Rape & Sexual Abuse Support Centre	0845-122-1331
24-Hour Mental Health / Suicide Prevention Helpline	0845-790-9090
24-Hour National Missing Persons Helpline	0500-700700
24-Hour US Consulate Emergency Helpline	020-7499-9000
Medical/Dental Referral Service (for nonemergencies) [NHS Direct will locate a Walk-in Centre, otherwise your hotel can locate a doctor for private care.]	0845-4647
Dental Emergency Care Service Mon-Fri 8:45am-3:30pm	020-7955-2186

24-hour emergency rooms:

• Charing Cross Hospital Fulham Palace Rd., W6; tube Hammersmith.	020-8846-1234
• Chelsea & Westminster Hospital 369 Fulham Rd., SW10; tube South Kensington, then bus #14 or 211.	020-8746-8000
• Guy's Hospital St. Thomas St., SE1; tube London Bridge.	020-7188-7188
• University College Hospital Grafton Way, WC1; tube Euston Square.	0845-155-5000

Late-night pharmacies:

• Bliss Chemists 5-6 Marble Arch, W1 9am to midnight, seven days a week Nearest Station: Marble Arch Tube	020-7723-6116
• Zafash 233 Old Brompton Road, SW5 London's only 24-hour pharmacy is open daily. Nearest Station: Earl's Court Tube	020-7373-2798

Gay and Lesbian Travel: London is widely acknowledged to be one of the world's most gay-friendly cities, with neighborhoods such as Soho having a particularly vibrant scene. You'll find a wealth of useful information at gaytoz.com. In the unlikely event of problems, there are two numbers you can call: London Lesbian & Gay Switchboard, (24/7) 020-7837-7324, llgs.org.uk; and London Friend, (7:30-10pm daily) 020-7837-3337, londonfriend.org.uk

Traveling with Disabilities: Visit tfl.gov.uk for transport information, artsline.org.uk for access to arts and entertainment venues, and radar.org.uk to order guides to days out and holidays in Britain.

Print Media: The UK has a range of national papers catering to most tastes and political opinions. London has only one local paper of similar stature to the nationals, the *Evening Standard* (thisislondon.com), with the first edition on sale starting at around 10am every weekday. Check out the glossy *ES* magazine, free with the *Standard* on Fridays, which is an entertaining lifestyle guide, covering everything from fashion and beauty to the latest hot bars and restaurants. Several of the national papers, notably the *Times*, *Independent,* and *Guardian*, have listings supplements with their Saturday editions. Otherwise, *Time Out* is a comprehensive weekly listings magazine for London with a slightly edgier appeal.

Radio Stations (a selection)

FM Stations

BBC Radio 2	89.1	MOR music and chat
BBC Radio 3	91.3	Classical
BBC Radio 4	93.5	News, spoken word
BBC London	94.9	Adult-oriented London life
Capital FM	95.8	Current charts
LBC	97.3	London phone-ins and chats
BBC Radio 1	98.8	Younger pop and rock
Kiss FM	100.0	Urban dance music
Classic FM	100.9	Classical
Smooth FM	102.2	Mellow music, some jazz
Magic	105.4	Easy listening
Virgin	105.8	Adult rock
Heart	106.2	Light music and entertainment

AM Stations

BBC Radio Five Live	909	Sport and news

Attire: London's not the buttoned-up city it used to be. Only the grandest places—or the merely pretentious—still insist on jacket and tie. That's not an excuse to waltz around in scruffy jeans and a baseball cap, however. The look you're going for is smart-casual and fashion-savvy. Londoners are great at quirky individuality, so allow yourself to be inspired. On a practical note, remember how unpredictable the weather is and adjust your outfit accordingly.

HIT THE GROUND

Size Conversion

Dress Sizes

UK	8	10	12	14	16	18
US	6	8	10	12	14	16
France	36	38	40	42	44	46
Italy	38	40	42	44	46	48
Europe	34	36	38	40	42	44

Women's Shoes

UK	4½	5	5½	6	6½	7
US	6	6½	7	7½	8	8½
Europe	38	38	39	39	40	41

Men's Suits

UK	36	38	40	42	44	46
US	36	38	40	42	44	46
Europe	46	48	50	52	54	56

Men's Shirts

UK	14½	15	15½	16	16½	17
US	14½	15	15½	16	16½	17
Europe	38	39	40	41	42	43

Men's Shoes

UK	7	7½	8½	9½	10½	11
US	8	8½	9½	10½	11½	12
Europe	41	42	43	44	45	46

Shopping Hours: There are no hard-and-fast rules, but central London shops are generally open from 9:30 or 10am until 6pm, Monday through Saturday, and for six hours on Sundays. Many West End shops stay open until 7 or 8pm on Thursday; in Knightsbridge, late-night shopping is on Wednesday.

When Drinking Is Legal: The legal drinking age is 18. If you're close to that or particularly youthful in appearance, it's worth carrying ID showing your date of birth. Otherwise, you're unlikely to be asked to prove your age.

Smoking: Smoking laws are currently under review. For now most bars and restaurants allow smoking, though many have no-smoking areas. Smoking is illegal on all public transport and in shops, however.

Drugs: Expect to do time in prison for possession, sale, use, import, or export of most controlled substances, including heroin, cocaine, and ecstasy. If you're caught in possession of a small amount of marijuana for personal use only, you might get away with a caution instead of jail—but don't bank on it.

Getting Into Clubs: London has a notoriously complicated system when it comes to getting into bars and clubs. The hierarchy is roughly as follows: Membership at some private members clubs is by word of mouth only, and they are famously hard to join. Given the near impossibility of visitors getting in, these types of venues are not covered in this guide. Other members bars allow guests at certain times. For instance, if you're dining at a restaurant or you're a guest at the hotel in which the bar is located, you may be allowed in the adjoining members-only bar. Other venues merely ask that you pay a pretty penny. For countless other nightspots—covered in this guide—it's simply a matter of calling ahead to get your name on the guest list. At others, it's advisable to call ahead to reserve a table. If it's important to call ahead, it's mentioned in the listing. Charm and/or dressing right can work their magic, but they don't guarantee anything. If you haven't lined anything up in advance, plenty of less exclusive bars just ask that you pay a cover charge, and these are included in the book.

Time Zone: London falls within the Greenwich mean time zone (GMT). A note on daylight savings time: Clocks are set ahead one hour at 1am on the last Sunday in March and back one hour at 1am on the last Sunday in October.

Additional Resources for Visitors

London Tourism Offices
Pick up brochures, maps, and destination advice. There's also a ticket agent, currency exchange, and internet lounge. Check online before you travel for useful downloads, including maps. You'll also find current offers on hotels, or you can call the accommodation booking service at 0845-64-43010. *Daily 8am-11pm.* 1 Lower Regent St., SW1 (St. James's), 020-7808-3801, visitlondon.com

Foreign Visitors
Entry: Americans and Canadians only need a valid passport to enter the UK.
US Embassy in London: 24 Grosvenor Sq. W1 (Mayfair), 020-7499-9000, usembassy.org.uk
Passport requirements: travel.state.gov/travel/tips/brochures/brochures_1229.html
Cell phones: The UK uses a 900MHz or 1,800MHz GSM system. It is illegal to use a mobile phone while driving, except with a hands-free adapter. To rent a phone, go to cellhire.co.uk.
Telephone Directory Assistance: 118-500
Electrical: UK standard is AC, 240 volts/50 cycles, with a plug of three flat pins in a triangular arrangement.

The Latest-Info Websites
Go to thisislondon.co.uk and timeout.com for events, restaurant reviews, and nightlife, and whatsonstage.com for the scoop on all things theatrical. Event Tickets: londontown.com
And of course, **pulseguides.com**.

Party Conversation—A Few Surprising Facts

- Although the BT Tower is one of London's tallest and most famous landmarks, until the mid-1990s it was officially not there. It was covered by the Official Secrets Act, which meant taking pictures of it was an offense, and it was omitted from Ordnance Survey maps.

- Gourmets rejoice: London has 36 Michelin-starred restaurants, including one with the full complement of three.

- Pall Mall, the main road in St. James's, is named for a favorite royal game called "paille-maille," like a cross between golf and croquet, played here in the early 17th century.

- The Tower of London has held many famous captives in its long history, but was last used as a prison in 1941 for Hitler's deputy Rudolph Hess.

- At the last count, there were 300 different languages regularly spoken in this multicultural city, from Amharic to Yoruba.

- The tube, as it has been known since it opened in 1890, is the oldest underground electric railway in the world, though the famous logo—a red circle crossed with a blue bar—didn't appear until 1913.

- Royalty has its privileges, but entering the City is not one of them; the Queen has to have the permission of the Lord Mayor to do so, a custom dating back nearly 800 years.

- The eye-catching outfits worn by London's kings and queens are decorated by thousands of buttons, arranged in traditional designs, and weigh up to 70 pounds.

- The first Globe Theatre burned to the ground in 1613, thanks to a misplaced cannon shot during a performance of Shakespeare's *Henry VIII*, which set fire to the thatched roof.

- London is the third-busiest filming production center in the world, behind only Los Angeles and New York. And the most popular location? The iconic London Eye.

The Cheat Sheet
(The Very Least You Ought to Know
About London)

There's no way you're going to learn everything about a city of seven million people on one visit, and even lifelong Londoners have their blind spots. However, there are a few scraps of knowledge that will make you sound as if you're on at least your second visit.

Neighborhoods

Chelsea may have swung in the '60s, but it has settled down into being a pleasant and prosperous neighborhood, with plenty of good places to eat, buy, and be merry, and some hot new spots.

The City is the site of the first Roman settlement and also the main financial district, resulting in a curious mix of soaring skyscrapers and ancient monuments.

Covent Garden has also had a facelift, and the old fruit-and-vegetable market and once-scruffy Victorian warehouses are now home to cafes, restaurants, and quirky shops.

Knightsbridge attracts the international mega-rich, who buy their groceries at Harrods department store and their clothes in the discreetly expensive shops nearby while the chauffeur waits outside.

Elegant **Mayfair** has long been the domain of the elegant rich, but its former rather stuffy image has been changed of late by the arrival of a host of hot new eateries and shops.

Notting Hill still has a bohemian vibe and its annual Carnival, but thanks to soaring property prices, the residents are increasingly as much chic as boho.

St. James's is London at its most traditional, with royal palaces, exclusive gentlemen's clubs, and old-world emporia that look as if they've been there for centuries—and they have.

Once-sleazy **Soho** has been cleaned up to emerge as one of London's liveliest— and most gay-friendly—areas, though still with a rakish edge.

South Kensington is a testament to the Victorian love of learning, with three of London's most famous museums and lots of other cultural institutions.

Westminster, where you'll find the Houses of Parliament and the famous Abbey, has been a political and religious powerhouse for a thousand years.

9 Thoroughfares

Bond Street is Mayfair's best known street, the perfect place to while away a few expensive hours in the sophisticated shops, galleries, and auction houses.

Broad Park Lane is more like a freeway than a lane, thanks to the fast-moving traffic; its salvation is Hyde Park on one side and several luxury hotels on the other.

Fleet Street used to be lined with newspaper offices. Although they have since moved to more spacious premises elsewhere, the name is still shorthand for the press.

The **King's Road** in Chelsea was where it was all happening in the '60s, and it's still an enjoyable spot for window-shopping.

Oxford Street is London's main shopping street, though not its ritziest, lined with chain stores and department stores, and to be avoided weekends and holidays.

Piccadilly separates Mayfair from St. James's, so no surprise that it is also home to some distinguished buildings, including the Ritz and the Royal Academy of Arts.

Elegant, curving **Regent Street** was designed in classical style in the early 19th century as a way of separating the rich swells in Mayfair from the poor folks in Soho.

Once lined with aristocratic palaces, **The Strand** is far less attractive or interesting nowadays, unless you're heading to the Savoy or Somerset House.

Whitehall is Westminster's main highway, a broad road flanked by palaces and government offices, often busy with visitors taking pictures of the mounted Horse Guards or heading between Parliament and Trafalgar Squares.

8 Performing Arts Centers

Cadogan Hall in Chelsea is London's newest concert space, offering state-of-the-art facilities in a fabulous faux-Byzantine church dating from the early 19th century.

The London Coliseum has been many things, including a greyhound track, but for nearly 40 years has been home to the marvelous English National Opera.

The Royal Albert Hall was inspired by the design of Roman amphitheaters, though thankfully feeding Christians to the lions is not on the entertainment list here.

The magnificent **Royal Opera House** has a long and venerable history, and thanks to recent refurbishment, it remains one of the world's top opera venues.

Sadler's Wells is heaven for dance enthusiasts, with a wide-ranging repertoire covering all the bases from mainstream contemporary dance to tango and flamenco.

St. John's Smith Square was originally used as a church, but nowadays visitors come to appreciate the fantastic acoustics as well as the elegant Baroque architecture.

The South Bank Centre consists of three performances halls of differing sizes housed in a 1950s geometric concrete structure that you either love or hate.

Wigmore Hall is a gem, a tiny but much-respected venue for song and chamber music performances; aficionados regard the Sunday morning "coffee concerts" as a particular joy.

Influential Architects

Sir **Charles Barry** rebuilt the Houses of Parliament in ancient style after a fire in 1834, with assistance from August Pugin. He also designed several of the suitably grand premises in St. James's still occupied by private gentleman's clubs.

Sir **Norman Foster** loves to push technology to the limits in his designs, whether they're glittering towers of glass such as the Swiss Re building or delicate metal structures such as the Millennium Bridge.

Nicholas Hawksmoor, a protégé of Christopher Wren's, also left his mark on London; several of its most elegant churches, such as St. George's Bloomsbury, are his work.

John Nash was the darling of Regency London and favored architect of the Prince Regent, responsible for such town-planning triumphs as Regent Street, Trafalgar Square, and Carlton House Terrace, among others.

August Pugin was a champion of the Gothic revival in Victorian times, best appreciated in his wonderful decorations and sculptures for the Houses of Parliament.

Sir **Richard Rogers** has given London some of its most cutting-edge structures, including the controversial "inside-out" office of Lloyds of London.

Sir **Christopher Wren** designed St. Paul's Cathedral, around 50 other graceful London churches, and other important public buildings, many of which have survived from the 17th century.

Landmarks

British Airways' London Eye is a modern engineering and design triumph, a vast gleaming Ferris wheel that has added a fabulous extra dimension to the skyline.

The BT Tower was the height of hi-tech design when it was built in the '60s, and the circular, top-heavy building still has a certain retro appeal.

Britain's tallest building, the **Canary Wharf Tower**, a steel-clad skyscraper with a distinctive pyramid-shaped roof, is the unmissable centerpiece to the new financial district in the former dock areas.

Nicknamed **The Gherkin**, master architect Sir Norman Foster's bulbous glass skyscraper for Swiss Re may be relatively young, but is already a much-praised addition to the downtown landscape.

The spiky outline of the **Houses of Parliament** in general, and the instantly recognizable clock tower of Big Ben in particular, are the classic image of London to many.

St. Paul's Cathedral, with its distinctive dome, was a technological triumph when it was built, and—narrowly escaping serious damage during the Blitz—remains a key feature at the western end of the City.

Central Parks

Just off Piccadilly, **Green Park** provides a leafy lunchtime retreat for local office workers on sunny days, when there are deck chairs for rent.

Hyde Park to the west of Mayfair is a focal point for Londoners, whether they're there for a large outdoor event or to make the most of the sporting and not-so-sporting activities on hand.

Divided from Hyde Park by an elongated lake, **Kensington Gardens** has several well-known attractions, from the not-entirely-successful Princess Diana Memorial Fountain to the never-dull Serpentine Gallery.

Regent's Park is the largest of the five inner-city green spaces, with room for a world-renowned zoo, an open-air theater, a rose garden, and an impressive range of sporting facilities.

St. James's Park was originally laid out in the 18th century by England's most fashionable landscape designer, Lancelot "Capability" Brown, and remains true to his vision.

Markets

Borough Market has become the hottest place in town to stock up on top-notch gourmet goodies, with loads of places to grab a bite or a coffee.

Columbia Road Flower Market is a Sunday morning joy, a whole street of stalls selling exotic blooms, unusual greenery, and more prosaic plant life to a mixed crowd of urbanites.

Portobello Road Market caters to Notting Hill trendies who can't resist the stalls offering everything from antiques and vintage clothing to cheese and olives.

Spitalfields Market marks the boundary between the City's glassy office blocks and one of London's most culturally diverse neighborhoods, and there's a similarly eclectic range of stalls and shops.

Department Stores

Everyone's heard of **Harrods**, which even sells its own brand souvenirs, but few Londoners will admit to having entered it—apart from the food halls, of course.

Harvey Nichols—Harvey Nicks to its fans—is designer heaven, with almost every famous label you can think of, and an in-house restaurant for ladies who lunch.

Selfridges is the most stylish and handsome store on bland Oxford Street. If you can't find your favorite luxury brand here, you're just not looking hard enough.

Mayors

The Lord Mayor has jurisdiction over a much smaller area, the City, but this ancient office does bring with it perks such as an annual parade and a ceremonial coach.

The Mayor of London is elected by Londoners to take responsibility for key areas such as transport, emergency services, and events in the Greater London area.

Singular Sensation

Savor a glass of champagne perched at the top of the **London Eye** at sunset.

Coffee (quick Stops for a java jolt)

Bar Italia A Soho institution serving up fortifying espressos all day and night. (p.111) 22 Frith St. (Soho), 020-7437-4520, baritaliasoho.co.uk

Books for Cooks Notting Hill's cult bookshop cum cafe serves a mean coffee and superb food. 4 Blenheim Crescent (Notting Hill), 020-7221-1992

Cafe Vergnano Set among used bookshops, this award-winning spot produces top-notch brews. 62 Charing Cross Rd. (Covent Garden), 020-8922-6308

Louis Patisserie A popular, long-running meeting place for Hampstead's intelligentsia. 32 Heath St. (Hampstead), 020-7435-9908

Maison Bertaux A well-established favorite for its superb coffee and irresistible pastries. (p.108) 28 Greek St. (Soho), 020-7437-6007

Monmouth Coffee Company Gourmet coffees and cozy wooden booths in which to linger. 27 Monmouth St. (Covent Garden), 020-7645-3560

Pâtisserie Valerie It has fabulous '50s décor, but it's the cakes that are the real draw. (p.108) 44 Old Compton St. (Soho), 0207-437-3466

The Poetry Café A literary crowd enjoys cafe fare by day and poetry readings by night. 22 Betterton St. (Covent Garden), 020-7420-9881

HIT THE GROUND

Just for Business and Conventions

As a major financial and trading center, London has plenty to offer the business traveler. The "old" financial district—usually called the City or Square Mile—has some excellent accommodations and a slew of fabulous restaurants, with sights such as St. Paul's Cathedral and the Museum of London a short stroll away. Eastwards, glittering developments such as Canary Wharf and the ExCeL conference center have helped bring new life and prosperity—not to mention ultramodern hotels and upscale eateries—to the old dock areas. Canary Wharf is home to the fascinating Museum in Docklands (0870-444-3857, museumindocklands.org.uk), while the Thames Barrier Park, with its views of London's futuristic flood defenses, is an easy walk from ExCeL. Even an hour or two of free time can be enough for a trip on a riverboat, a leisurely coffee at a waterside cafe, or a delicious meal.

Addresses to Know

Convention Centers

- Earls Court Conference Centre
  Warwick Rd., SW5
  020-7385-1200, eco.co.uk

- ExCeL London
  1 Western Gateway, Royal Victoria Dock, E16, 020-7069-5000, excel-london.co.uk

- Olympia
  Hammersmith Rd., W14
  020-7370-8009, eco.co.uk

City Information

- Britain & London Visitor Centre
  1 Regent St., SW1
  020-7808-3801, visitlondon.com

- City of London Information Centre
  St. Paul's Churchyard, EC4
  020-7332-1456,
  cityoflondon.gov.uk

- Visit London for Business
  020-7234-5833,
  visitlondon.com/business

Business and Convention Hotels

These hotels are close to ExCeL or the financial districts of the City or Canary Wharf, with plenty of facilities for the business traveler.

Apex City of London New upscale hotel, with contemporary décor and views of Tower Bridge. 1 Seething Ln., EC3, 0845-365-0000, apexhotels.co.uk

Crowne Plaza London Docklands Modern style and business-savvy facilities in this waterside hotel near the ExCeL conference center. Western Gateway, Royal Victoria Dock, E16, 0870-990-9692, crowneplazadocklands.co.uk

Four Seasons Canary Wharf Luxury with a business edge and attentive service. Westferry Circus, E14, 020-7510-1999, fourseasons.com

Marriott London West India Quay Contemporary comforts in waterside locale, handily placed for the new financial district and London City Airport. 22 Hertsmere Rd., E14, 020-7093-1000, marriott.com

196 Bishopsgate Clean-cut fully serviced apartments in the City, with no minimum stay, for independent-minded business types. 196 Bishopsgate, EC2, 020-7621-8788, 196bishopsgate.com

Threadneedles Boutique chic in an elegant former bank, located in the heart of the City. (p.61) 5 Threadneedle St., EC2, 020-7657-8080, theetoncollection.com

Business Entertaining

Strike that deal over drinks or a fabulous meal at one of these elegantly businesslike establishments in the financial district.

Aurora Impeccable modern British cuisine in one of London's finest dining rooms. 54 Great Eastern St., EC2, 020-7618-7000, great-eastern-hotel.co.uk

Bonds Sophisticated ambiance, European fare, and top-notch cocktails right in the City. (p.142) 5 Threadneedle St., EC2, 020-7657-8088, bonds-restaurant.com

Coq d'Argent A longtime favorite, with well-executed French food, excellent wines, and a terrace for fine days. 1 Poultry, EC2, 020-7395-5000, conran.com

Quadrato Imaginative Italian cuisine, smooth service, and stylish décor. 46 Westferry Circus, E14, 020-7510-1857, fourseasons.com

Rhodes Twenty-Four Traditional British cooking beautifully reinterpreted by one of Britain's best chefs—and superb vistas, too. (p.151) Tower 42, 25 Old Broad St., EC2, 020-7877-7703, rhodes24.com

Also see: **Best Fine Dining** (p.25)
              Best Power Lunches (p.37)

Ducking Out for a Half Day

You're in one of the world's major cities, so make time to see something of it.

Museum of London Historical facts, artifacts galore, and an excellent museum shop for highbrow spending—all a stone's throw from the financial district. (p.167) 150 London Wall, EC2, 0870-444-3852

St. Paul's Cathedral Wren's masterpiece is worth a few hours, especially as it's close to the financial district. Ludgate Hill, EC4, 020 7236 4128

Also see: **Best Modern Art Spaces** (p.35)
              Best Spas (p.46)

Gifts to Bring Home

Fortnum & Mason There's something for everyone at this classic department store famous for gourmet British foods. (p.164) 181 Piccadilly, W1, 020-7437-3278

Smythson Exquisite and contemporary leather and paper goods. (p.90) 40 New Bond St., W1, 020-7629-8558

HIT THE GROUND

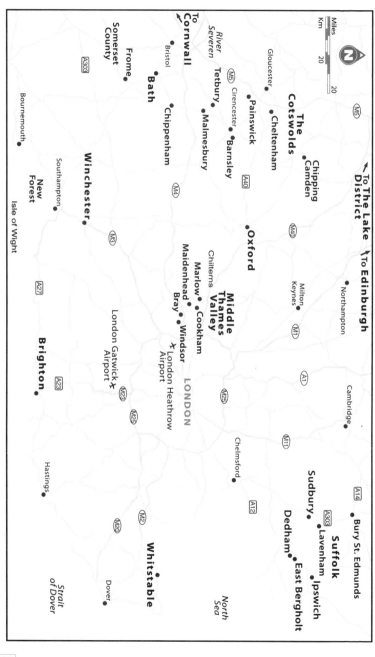

To The Lake District

To Edinburgh

To Cornwall

River Severn

Miles
Km
20
20

Gloucester

Bristol

Somerset County

A303

Frome

Bath

Tetbury

M5

Cirencester

Painswick

Barnsley

Malmesbury

Chippenham

The Cotswolds

Chipping Camden

Cheltenham

A40

M4

Bournemouth

Southampton

New Forest

Winchester

Isle of Wight

M3

A27

Oxford

M40

Milton Keynes

M1

Northampton

Chilterns

Middle Thames Valley

Marlow

Maidenhead

Bray

Cookham

Windsor

London Heathrow Airport

London Gatwick Airport

M23

A23

Brighton

A1

Cambridge

M25

M25

Chelmsford

M11

LONDON

M20

M2

Whitstable

Dover

Hastings

Strait of Dover

North Sea

A12

Sudbury

Dedham

East Bergholt

A303

Lavenham

Ipswich

Suffolk

A14

Bury St. Edmunds

LEAVING LONDON

If you want a break from the urban frenzy of London, a breathtaking variety of excursions is yours for the choosing. Whether you prefer to linger over decadent Michelin-starred meals in the bucolic English countryside, study centuries-old historic architecture, or party in a laid-back waterfront setting, the area around London's wide array of opportunities for relaxation, festivity, and indulgence means there's something for everyone.

LEAVING

Bath

Hot Tip: Weekends can be busy, especially in summer, so midweek visits make more sense.

The Lowdown: Few cities have the romance and elegance of Bath, with its Georgian squares and crescents creating an air of harmony and ease. A World Heritage Site, a status it shares with European cities such as Florence and Salzburg, it has welcomed wealthy visitors for centuries. The Romans came to bathe in the thermal waters, and the well-preserved remains of the baths complex can still be visited. Hundreds of years later, the restorative effects of Bath's spring waters were rediscovered, and Bath became England's most glamorous spa town for the Georgians, who came to socialize at least as much as for their health. Jane Austen captured the life of the city at the time in *Northanger Abbey,* and in the evening, when the light of the setting sun makes the sandstone houses glow like gold, you can almost see the ghosts of the past promenading in their finery. It would be easy, then, for Bath to become stuck in a rather agreeable time warp. Fortunately, that hasn't happened, though its pleasures are more classic good taste than out-there avant garde. Behind those restrained Palladian façades lie hotels that ooze luxury with a modern touch, with not a trace of pomposity, and some seriously accomplished kitchens catering to sophisticated tastes. Bath's most eagerly awaited new attraction, however, is a distinct homage to the city's past. The newly opened Thermae Bath Spa is Britain's only thermal spa, enabling a whole new generation of urban sophisticates to be pampered in ancient-and-modern style.

Best Attractions

Holburne Museum of Art Delightful small museum in a gem of a Georgian mansion holds a rich collection of fine art and artifacts, everything from English silver to several portraits by Gainsborough. £- Great Pulteney St., 01225-466669, bath.ac.uk/holburne

Museum of Costume Fascinating and ever-expanding collection dedicated to fashionable clothes in the elegant surroundings of the Georgian Assembly Rooms. £- Bennett St., 01225-477173, museumofcostume.co.uk

Number One Royal Crescent A showpiece of Palladian architecture, decorated and furnished to show how this grand residence might have appeared in the closing years of the 18th century. £- 1 Royal Crescent, 01225-428126, bath-preservation-trust.org.uk

Roman Baths Pump Room Roam where rich residents of Aquae Sulis used to preen, admire the Roman objects left as offerings to the goddess Minerva, and stop for a taste of the waters at the Georgian Pump Room afterwards. Stall St., 01225-477785, romanbaths.co.uk

Thermae Bath Spa Britain's only thermal spa. The Hetling Pump Room, Hot Bath St., 01225-335678, thermaebathspa.com

Best Restaurants

FishWorks Simple seafood restaurant below a fishmonger permanently busy with savvy locals who appreciate the fresher-than-fresh fish and shellfish, served without fuss. £ 6 Green St., 01225-448707, fishworks.co.uk

Lucknam Park Six miles from Bath, but worth the taxi ride for the setting—a fabulous Palladian mansion surrounded by parkland—and the inspired Modern British cooking. Try Sunday lunch or afternoon tea to appreciate it all in daylight. ££ Colerne, Chippenham, 01225-742777, lucknampark.co.uk

The Olive Tree Light, bright, and sharp basement offering a menu of sunny Mediterranean flavors to well-heeled locals and visitors alike. £- Russel St., 01225-447928, thequeensberry.co.uk

Pimpernel's Royal Crescent Hotel Not just a fine location, but impressive cooking, too, with fabulous updates on classic French cuisine and a suitably high-minded wine list. ££ 16 Royal Crescent, 01225-823333, royalcrescent.co.uk

Best Hotels

Babington House Babington Twelve miles south of Bath, the country outpost of London's private members club Soho House welcomes well-heeled visitors with a taste for cool 1970s James Bond décor and funky spa treatments. £££ Near Frome, Somerset, 01373-812266, babingtonhouse.co.uk

Charlton House Shepton Mallet Unfussily classic style and comfort in rolling countryside 18 miles south of Bath, with spacious grounds, highly acclaimed restaurant, and its own spa. £ Near Shepton Mallot, Somerset, 01749-342008, charltonhouse.com

The Queensbury Hotel A harmonious marriage of contemporary décor and Georgian architecture, secluded gardens, and a peaceful yet central location make this boutique hotel a stylish option. £ Russel St., Bath, 01225-447928, thequeensberry.co.uk

The Royal Crescent Hotel and Bath House Spa Antiques, fine art, and old-school luxury at its finest in this elegant Georgian mansion in the heart of the city. Inspired modern touches include the spa, with its signature water therapies. £££ 16 Royal Crescent, Bath, 01225-823333, royalcrescent.co.uk

Contacts

Bath Tourism Plus visitbath.co.uk; accommodation booking 0870-420-1278
Bath Tourist Information Centre Abbey Chambers, Abbey Church Yard

LEAVING

Getting There: Bath is 90 minutes by train from Paddington Station, or 15 miles from Bristol Airport.

Cornwall

Hot Tip: It is best to avoid the school summer holidays—mid-July to late August—when roads and beaches are unbearably busy.

The Lowdown: Cornwall has been a popular spot for seaside holidays for decades, but only recently has it acquired a reputation for the sort of rustic chic you usually only see in Ralph Lauren ads. The climate helps; thanks to the effect of the Gulf Stream on this southwesterly extremity of England, the winters are mild and summers reasonably warm without being scorching. That means all the most enjoyable fine-weather activities, like al fresco dining, sunset drinks at the beach, and lounging by the pool, are within driving distance; heaven for stressed-out urbanites who'd rather not join the migrating hordes heading to Europe. To cater to the whims of this new breed of traveler, whose idea of luxury is decidedly unstarchy, there are more and more clean-cut and mellow boutique hotels with laid-back spas. As for the food, the name Rick Stein is on everyone's lips; the opening of his first seafood restaurant at Padstow—sometimes jokingly referred to as "Padstein"—raised the culinary standards elsewhere and it's now possible to enjoy extraordinarily good food at rather less than London prices.

For those with the energy to leave the poolside, Cornwall has several worthwhile sights, from modern art galleries to exotic gardens of all sizes. There is the natural landscape, too, from the dramatic northern coastline littered with shipwrecks, to the pocket-sized wilderness of Bodmin Moor, whose haunting atmosphere Daphne du Maurier captured in print in *Jamaica Inn*. No wonder Cornwall acquired a reputation for being a bit different from the rest of England, something that now only adds to its charms.

Best Attractions

The Eden Project This former china-clay pit now houses Cornwall's contemporary tribute to all things botanical. Two vast greenhouse domes in impressively landscaped grounds contain tropical and temperate landscapes bursting with plants. £ Bodelva, St. Austell, 01726-811911, edenproject.com

Lost Gardens of Heligan An extraordinary grand Victorian garden full of rare specimens, neglected for more than 80 years, has been restored to its former lush gorgeousness. £- Pentewan, St. Austell, 01726-845100, heligan.com

Surfing Reef breaks, beach breaks, and swell for all ability levels make Cornwall home to the UK's surf scene. The British Surfing Association, based at Newquay, can give lessons and advise on local conditions. 01637-876474, britsurf.co.uk

Tate St. Ives The London gallery's far-west outpost provides a stylish home for abstract avant-garde works by St. Ives–school stalwarts such as Barbara Hepworth and Ben Nicholson. £- Porthmeor Beach, St. Ives, 01736-796226, tate.org.uk/stives

Best Restaurants and Nightlife

Beach Hut Bistro & Bar Join the hip surfing set for lazy lunches of fresh-caught fish or simple steaks, or linger for a chilled-out martini or cocktail as the sun goes down. £ The Beach, Watergate Bay, near Tregurrian, 01637-860877, watergatebay.co.uk

Hotel Tresanton On sunny days, a glamorous crowd packs the terrace for fine Mediterranean-influenced cuisine; the superb seafood is a highlight. ££ Lower Castle Rd., St. Mawes, 01326-270055, tresanton.com

Ripley's Rick Stein's former head chef, Paul Ripley, has earned a well-deserved Michelin star for his eponymous restaurant, where he serves up high-quality seasonal and local ingredients. £ St. Merryn, Padstow, 01841-520179

St. Ervan Manor Imaginative but sure-handed modern British cooking, using the best local ingredients, makes this a hot choice for dinner. Smart couples order one each of the two taster menus. £ St. Ervan, near Padstow, 01841-540255, stervanmanor.co.uk

Seafood Restaurant No prizes for guessing what's on the menu at the King of Padstow's showcase restaurant. Don't expect fancy garnishes or décor, just quality of the highest order. £ Riverside, Padstow, 01841-532700, rickstein.com

Best Hotels

Driftwood Hotel Calm uncluttered décor, sea views, and the cozy private cove and beach appeal to stressed-out urbanites. £ Rosevine, near Portscatho, 01872-580644, driftwoodhotel.co.uk

Hotel Tresanton Olga Polizzi's triumph of understated seaside chic attracts an A-list but unflashy crowd for year-round relaxation. ££ Lower Castle Rd., St. Mawes, 01326-270055, tresanton.com

Lugger Hotel Manages to be cool and romantic at the same time, thanks to spare but not stark interiors, a stunning setting, and a fabulous small spa. ££ Portloe, Truro, 01872-501322, luggerhotel.com

The Old Quay House A hip marriage of traditional architecture and 21st-century styling has helped create a boutique hotel with real flair. £ 28 Fore St., Fowey, 01726-833302, theoldquayhouse.com

Contacts

Visit Cornwall Pydar House, Pydar St., Truro, Cornwall, 01872-322900, cornwalltouristboard.co.uk

LEAVING

Getting There: Fly Ryanair (ryanair.com) from Stansted to Newquay, where rental cars are available. Alternatively, it's about six hours by train from Waterloo Station to Penzance.

The Cotswolds

Hot Tip: There's never really an off-season as such, but if you're looking for quiet, the crowds are definitely thinner in winter.

The Lowdown: Higgledy-piggledy stone cottages with roses around the door, in tiny villages with strange names like Upper Slaughter and Stow-on-the-Wold, apparently untouched by time, and surrounded by a gentle landscape of rolling hills and rippling rivers: It's this chocolate-box prettiness, rather than specific attractions, that has been luring visitors to the Cotswolds in droves for so many years. These days, however, there's a new incentive to head west from London: a clutch of fabulous new hotels and skillfully refurbished old ones. There's barely a 17th-century manor house in the whole area—which stretches all the way from north of Bath to south of Stratford-upon-Avon—that hasn't been given a dramatic facelift. Out has gone the chintz; in have come the flat-screen TVs, showerheads the size of dinner plates, funky furniture and contemporary antiques, and probably a cutting-edge spa as well. The restaurants have received similar treatment to cater to a new breed of visitor, the moneyed but design-conscious urbanite looking for indulgent downtime in restful surroundings. That means a wealth of places to eat, from gastropubs with open fires where there's no need to dress up to stylish and starry restaurants with a fine line in fine dining for a discreetly designer-clad clientele. It represents a new English glamour, a synthesis of the best of old and new, polished but informal.

Best Attractions

Cheltenham Art Gallery & Museum Technically just outside the Cotswolds, this enjoyable Arts and Crafts collection includes everything from furniture to jewelry and is recognized as being of international caliber. Clarence St., Cheltenham, 01242-237431, cheltenham.artgallery.museum

Hidcote Manor Garden Created in the last century in Arts and Crafts style as a series of "outdoor rooms" broken up by walls and hedges, Hidcote is impressive both for the fascinating selection of plants and the fine views. £- Hidcote Bartrim, near Chipping Campden, 01386-438333, nationaltrust.org.uk/hidcote

Painswick Rococo Garden An unusual 18th-century garden hidden in a Cotswold valley, notable for the flamboyant use of plants and the whimsical follies and garden buildings. £- Painswick, 01452-813204, rococogarden.co.uk

Best Restaurants and Nightlife

Juliana's Restaurant The more stylish of Cotswold House's two restaurants dishes up thoroughly modern fine food that uses impeccably sourced luxury ingredients in imaginative ways. £££ Cotswold House Hotel, Chipping Campden, 01386-840330, cotswoldhouse.com

Lords of the Manor Traditional-with-a-twist cuisine in a country-house setting that has attracted a loyal following in the area for many years. ££ Upper Slaughter, 01451-820243, lordsofthemanor.com

The Trouble House Inn This top-notch and easily overlooked gastropub has won plaudits for its food—simple modern staples prepared with great skill—but the relaxed atmosphere deserves an honorable mention, too. £ Cirencester Rd., Tetbury, 01666-502206, troublehouse.co.uk

The Village Pub This traditional Cotswold country pub owned by Barnsley House provides a more dressed-down option than its regular restaurant, although the standard of the food is just as high. £ Barnsley, Cirencester, Gloucestershire, 01285-740421, thevillagepub.co.uk

Whatley Manor Exceptional food, best described as modern eclectic, makes this a sophisticated choice for a memorable dinner accompanied by high-quality wines. £ Easton Grey, Malmesbury, 01666-822888, whatleymanor.com

Best Hotels

Barnsley House The former home of one of Britain's best-known gardeners has been transformed into a luxurious country retreat—but with chic modern styling, lots of electronic gizmos, and bathrooms to die for. ££ Barnsley, Cirencester, 01285-740000, barnsleyhouse.com

Cotswold House Restrained contemporary décor with all modern conveniences slotted elegantly behind a 17th-century façade in one of the Cotswolds' most adorable small towns. ££ The Square, Chipping Campden, 01386-840330, cotswoldhouse.com

Cowley Manor Funkadelic interior design meets stately-home architecture in this favorite with hip young and not-so-young Londoners and glossy magazine editors. Hunt them down in the spa or the spacious gardens. ££ Cowley, near Cheltenham, 01242-870900, cowleymanor.com

Whatley Manor A harmonious blend of old and new furnishings, a fabulous setting, and, above all, imaginative and thoughtful service make this a benchmark for understated luxury. Never mind the rain, there's an award-winning spa and a private cinema. ££ Easton Grey, Malmesbury, 01666-822888, whatleymanor.com

Contacts

Cotswold Tourist Board 01386-853790, cotswold.info

LEAVING

Getting There: Although it is possible to reach several parts of the Cotswolds by train and bus, renting a car—either in London or in, say, Oxford or Bath—gives much more flexibility.

Edinburgh, Scotland

Hot Tip: The liveliest time to visit is in August during the festivals, though you'll need to book accommodations well in advance (see p.181).

The Lowdown: What a difference a taste of independence can make. With England's northern neighbor being given more say in how it is governed of late and a spanking-new and shockingly over-budget Parliament building to show for it, the Scottish capital's confident, capital-city identity is even more obvious. Its beauty is of the slightly austere kind, with a dramatic setting that makes much of rocky crags and startling views. The medieval Old Town, for instance, is dominated by the castle that looms over it, and even the New Town's elegant Georgian squares and avenues are more restrained than in, say, Bath. Fortunately the residents are rather less austere, as evidenced by the exuberance with which they celebrate the New Year (see p.184). Plainly they are not averse to fine dining, either; in a country not noted for haute cuisine (deep-fried candy bars being one local specialty), Edinburgh now boasts two Michelin-starred eateries, and a whole host of other places where the food is worth the detour. As for the hotels, there has been a quiet revolution led by the Malmaison hotel group, which offers style without sky-high prices. There have always been plenty of reasons to tear yourself away from your room, from royal palaces to fine art collections, but there's also a thriving modern art scene, with independent and national galleries showing work from big names and the up-and-coming alike. Culturally, however, the highlight is the summer frenzy of the Edinburgh festivals, which feature everything from classical concerts to offbeat theater. Feeling sporty? This is the birthplace of golf, and all but the stuffiest clubs welcome voyaging players.

Best Attractions

The Fruitmarket Gallery One of Scotland's most interesting art spaces, featuring rotating exhibitions of work by new and established artists from Scotland and beyond. 45 Market St., Old Town, 0131-225-2383, fruitmarket.co.uk

Golf Courses There are 22 courses in Edinburgh itself, and more a short taxi ride away. Among the best are the championship-standard course at the Deer Park Golf & Country Club, exclusive Muirfield, and the links courses at Gullane Golf Club. Various venues, edinburgh.org/golf

National Galleries of Scotland Not one but four impressive collections: fine art at the National Gallery of Scotland and the Scottish National Portrait Gallery; 20th-century greats at the Scottish National Gallery of Modern Art; and Dadaism, Surrealism, and local boy Eduardo Paolozzi at the Dean Gallery. Various venues, 0131-624-6200, natgalscot.ac.uk

Palace of Holyroodhouse A lavishly furnished Baroque palace with a turbulent history: Mary Queen of Scots' lover Rizzio was brutally murdered here, and it was briefly home to the doomed Bonnie Prince Charlie. £- Royal Mile, 0131-556-5100, royalcollection.org.uk

Best Restaurants and Nightlife

Number One Restaurant Superb service, deservedly Michelin-starred modern European cooking, and a grand setting make this popular with Edinburgh's stylish set. Prepare to book a long way in advance. ££ The Balmoral, 1 Princes St., 0131-557-6727, thebalmoralhotel.com

Oloroso 33 Fabulous views, an eclectic menu of refined global fare, and a fashionable clientele make this one of the city's coolest hangouts. £- Castle St., 0131-226-7614, oloroso.co.uk

Rhubarb The dining room's as lavish as the rest of the hotel, though fortunately the food is less rich, emphasizing excellent local ingredients presented with flair. ££ Prestonfield, Priestfield Rd., 0131-225-7800, prestonfield.com

Rick's Flexible, all-day contemporary food makes this a hip hangout, but the chic bar with its cool cocktail list is the real draw, especially on weekends. £ 55a Frederick St., 0131-622-7800, ricksedinburgh.co.uk

The Witchery by the Castle Celebrity guests and romancing couples flock here for the modern British cuisine and theatrical setting; there are seven guest rooms if you can't bear to leave. £ 352 Castlehill, Royal Mile, 0131-225-5613, thewitchery.com

Best Hotels

The Balmoral Five-star luxury, oh-so-tasteful contemporary styling, and an impeccable position on Princes Street attract an A-list crowd to this Edinburgh landmark. £ 1 Princes St., 0131-556-2414, thebalmoralhotel.com

Howard For those who want a more intimate five-star experience, the 18-room Howard is an updated classic with superb levels of service, including a personal butler. ££ 34 Great King St., 0131-557-3500, thehoward.com

Prestonfield Forget minimalism: The look here is sumptuous and opulent, with rich colors and extravagant swaths of fabric. As for the guests, they're equally glamorous. ££ Priestfield Rd., 0131-225-7800, prestonfield.com

Rick's Cool, uncluttered, and yet incredibly cozy at the same time, Rick's proves that designer looks and hi-tech facilities don't have to come with a hefty price tag. £ 55a Frederick St., 0131-622-7800, ricksedinburgh.co.uk

Contacts

Tourist Information Centre 3 Princes St., 0845-225-5121, edinburgh.org

LEAVING

Getting There: Most convenient is the overnight Caledonian Sleeper train from London Euston Station, operated by First ScotRail (firstscotrail.com), or there are daily flights from several London airports. Flights take 85 minutes from Gatwick or Heathrow airports to Edinburgh.

250
miles
NW

The Lake District

Hot Tip: Spring and autumn offer scenic glory without the hordes; Wordsworth fans should come in early spring for the golden daffodils.

The Lowdown: No prizes for guessing how the Lake District acquired its name. However, this glorious piece of English countryside has not just 16 meres and waters but also five of the country's highest peaks, and while they're not particularly high, the scenery is romantic enough to have inspired poets and painters for several hundred years. Unfortunately, this popularity means that on summer weekends at Windermere and its neighbors you will certainly not be wandering lonely as a cloud, at least not in the middle of the day. Find your way to more secluded parts such as Eskdale and Buttermere, however, and the drama of the heather-covered hills and glittering lakes becomes apparent. Fortunately, the magnificence of the surroundings is no longer the only draw for visitors. A new generation of chefs has injected a much-needed dose of glamour into the local dining scene, and the prizes and plaudits have followed. Making much of local ingredients such as Herdwick lamb, Cumberland sausage, and freshwater fish from the lakes, they have attracted the attention of a new, moneyed clientele. They in turn have prompted a makeover of the region's hotels, so visitors are now spoiled for choice with everything from country-house luxury with built-in spa to quirky and informal modernity with a pub within strolling distance.

Best Attractions

Cartmel Village Shop Even macrobiotic celebrities have been known to succumb to Cumbria's famous sticky toffee pudding. Yes, you can find it in Fortnum & Mason, but this is its spiritual home. The Square, Cartmel, 01539-536280, stickytoffeepudding.co.uk

Dove Cottage The small cottage William Wordsworth shared with his wife and sister is now a small museum dedicated to his life and work, surrounded by the scenery that inspired him. £- Grasmere, 01539-435544, wordsworth.org.uk

Lake District National Park The Lake District National Park is the largest in England, and covers hundreds of square miles of unspoiled lakes, dales, and fells. Clearly marked routes for all fitness levels mean no one need miss out on the scenery. 01539-724555, lake-district.gov.uk

Best Restaurants and Nightlife

The Drunken Duck Inn & Restaurant Cleverly updated 400-year-old gastropub renowned for both its food—hearty Modern British—and the beer from the on-site brewery. Perfect for relaxed and cozy evenings by the fireside. £ Barngates, Ambleside, 01539-436347, drunkenduckinn.co.uk

Holbeck Ghyll Award-winning British cuisine with a distinctly French lilt showcasing the finest local produce, and scenery to match with views over Lake Windermere and the high peaks behind. ££ Holbeck Ln., Windermere, 01539-432375, holbeckghyll.com

L'Enclume Experimental but stunningly successful "molecular gastronomy," shown off to full effect in the tasting menus, in the unlikely surroundings of a refurbished old smithy. £££ Cavendish St., Cartmel, 01539-536362, lenclume.co.uk

The Samling Contemporary through and through, from the restrained elegance of the décor to the imaginative use of local produce and more recherché ingredients. ££ Ambleside Rd., Windermere, 01539-431922, thesamling.com

Sharrow Bay Internationally regarded modern British cuisine with big, rich flavors to match the magnificent setting by Lake Ullswater. It's a good idea to leave room for dessert if possible. ££££ Howtown, Ullswater, 01768-486301, sharrowbay.co.uk

Best Hotels

The Drunken Duck Inn & Restaurant Don't be put off by the uninspiring exterior; the inside is a haven of unpretentious comfort. There are 16 airy bedrooms, in a style that's neither jarringly modern nor stuffily old-fashioned. £ Barngates, Ambleside, 01539-436347, drunkenduckinn.co.uk

Holbeck Ghyll A former hunting lodge, and now one of the Lake District's finest country-house hotels, this is a classic example of how to do old-world luxury with style. £ Holbeck Ln., Windermere, 01539-432375, holbeckghyll.com

Linthwaite House Hotel Breathtaking views, fabulous grounds, and unfussy interiors make this a sound choice for a quiet retreat. £ Crook Rd., Windermere, 01539-488600, linthwaite.com

The Samling A hotel in the country, rather than a country-house hotel, as the owners are at pains to point out. A favorite celebrity haunt, thanks to its quirky modern style allied to fabulous service, food, and everything else. £ Ambleside Rd., Windermere, 01539-431922, thesamling.com

Sharrow Bay Hotel Opulent and luxurious, this is country-house style with a wonderfully old-fashioned slant and without any old-fashioned stuffiness, in an immaculate lakeside location. £ Howtown, Ullswater, 01768-486301, sharrow-bay.com

The Waterhead Hotel More townhouse than country house, in spite of its setting on the shores of Lake Windermere, with clean white interiors, modern art, and contemporary furnishings. £ Ambleside, 01539-432566, thewaterhead.co.uk

Contacts

Cumbria Tourist Board 01539-444444, cumbria-the-lake-district.co.uk

Getting There: Trains from Euston Station in London to Windermere take around four hours. However, local public transport is limited, especially outside the peak summer tourist season, so most people arrive by car—about four hours from London.

Suffolk

The idyllic scenery looks its best from May to early October, though the weather may be better from June onward.

The Lowdown: The timelessly serene countryside of Suffolk, especially the southern portion where it bumps against Essex, will be startlingly familiar for those with any knowledge of English landscape painting. The area around Flatford Mill, the star of several of John Constable's paintings, has hardly changed since he put oil to canvas. He would probably have little trouble recognizing other places such as Lavenham further north, where he attended school for a while. Once a thriving medieval wool center, it is now an extraordinarily quaint village of narrow lanes lined with wonky, half-timbered houses, miraculous survivors from medieval times. Suffolk also has bragging rights on another famous English painter, Thomas Gainsborough, whose portraits helped to put faces to many names of 18th-century high society. His family house in elegant Sudbury still contains excellent examples of his work. Even now, there's an "old money" feel to this part of the world, with far fewer chic new hotels than the Cotswolds, for instance. That said, there are several enjoyable options, whether you like the idea of lording it in style where marquises once slept or drifting off to sleep to the quiet babble of French voices after one of the best meals of your life. If you thrive on cutting-edge cool, this may not be your dream destination, but quiet good taste surely never really goes out of fashion.

Best Attractions

Flatford & Dedham Vale Familiar from many of Constable's paintings, the cute-as-anything cottages and surrounding water meadows are a serene vision of loveliness. £- East Bergholt, 01206-298260, nationaltrust.org.uk

Gainsborough's House The elegant townhouse where one of England's most famous 18th-century painters was born contains an important collection of his paintings, drawings, and prints. £- 46 Gainsborough St., Sudbury, 01787-372958, gainsborough.org

Ickworth House Eccentric former family home of the Earls of Bristol, built in 1795 to house the fourth Earl's international art collection, boasts a striking Italianate garden. Part is leased out as a hotel (see below). £- Horringer, Bury St. Edmunds, 01284-735270, nationaltrust.org

Lavenham Guildhall A magnificent timber-framed hall more than 400 years old, with a small museum dedicated to the medieval wool trade that made Lavenham so prosperous. £ Market Pl., Lavenham, 01787-247646, nationaltrust.org.uk

Best Restaurants

Fredericks Ambitious and intriguing modern European cuisine in impressive, stately surroundings, with an equally grand wine list. ££ The Ickworth, Horringer, Bury St. Edmunds, 01284-735350, ickworthhotel.com

The Great House Heavenly classic French food and wines in the heart of a quintessentially English village, served with flair and warmth. £ Market Pl., Lavenham, 01787-247431, greathouse.co.uk

Milsoms Clean-cut urban style in the heart of Constable Country at this inviting all-day eatery. Pick and choose from a mainly Mediterranean-inspired menu, but leave room for the delectable desserts. £ Stratford Rd., Dedham, Essex, 01206-322795, milsoms-hotel.com

The Sun Inn Cozy gastropub with eclectic furnishings, where a relaxed crowd feasts on expertly executed farmhouse cooking washed down by local ales or one of 15 wines by the glass. And there are four stylish bedrooms if you can't bear to leave. £ High St., Dedham, Essex, 01206-323351, thesuninndedham.com

Best Hotels

The Great House Just five bedrooms in a medieval house hidden behind a Georgian façade; the most romantic is the first-floor hideaway with four-poster bed. £ Market Pl., Lavenham, 01787-247431, greathouse.co.uk

Hintlesham Hall Gardens large enough for an 18-hole championship-length golf course surround an elegant small country hotel, packed to the rafters with fine art and antiques. £ Hintlesham, Ipswich, 01473-652334, hintleshamhall.com

The Ickworth State-house luxury with a contemporary twist, with funky old and new furnishings, an all-mod-cons spa, and acres of parkland to roam. £ Horringer, Bury St. Edmunds, 01284-735350, ickworthhotel.com

Lavenham Priory Antique-strewn, award-winning, and supremely restful bed and breakfast in a stunning historic priory dating from the 13th century. £ Water St., Lavenham, 01787-247404, lavenhampriory.co.uk

Contacts

East of England Tourist Board 0870-225-4800, visiteastofengland.com
Suffolk Tourism visit-suffolk.org.uk

LEAVING

Getting There: Trains from Liverpool Street Station go to Manningtree on the Suffolk/Essex border, a short bus ride from Dedham and Flatford Mill, or you can go to Bury St. Edmunds for infrequent bus connections to Lavenham. However, the best way of getting off the beaten track is to rent a car; it's only about 90 minutes by road from London.

Brighton

Hot Tip: For arty types, the Brighton Festival in May can throw up some inspiring moments, but this seaside spot is at its best in the summer.

The Lowdown: Not for nothing is Brighton routinely described as "London on Sea." True, it might not have quite the breathtaking number of restaurants, bars, and clubs of the nation's capital, but it certainly has more than its fair share.

Stressed-out Londoners have been flocking here for the sea air for more than 250 years, but it was the Prince Regent who put it on the map as a place for serious good fun. Today, it remains a liberal spot, with a youthful, alternative vibe and a sizable gay scene. Scan the boutiques and cafes in the narrow streets of Kemptown or the Lanes, two of Brighton's best-known areas, and you'll find plenty of evidence of the quirky tastes of its residents—including arty or media refugees from the big city and the occasional film star. The beach may not be anything special, but it's the place where Brighton's locals mingle on sunny days.

Best Attractions

Brighton Museum & Art Gallery Features innovative displays devoted to local history, fashion, and style, and 20th-century art and design. Royal Pavilion Gardens, 01273-290900, virtualmuseum.info

The Royal Pavilion The exterior of this ornate Oriental palace comes with gilded onion domes and minarets, but is positively plain compared to the extravagances inside. Royal Pavilion Gardens, 01273-292820, royalpavilion.org.uk

Best Restaurants

Blanch House Restaurant This restaurant serves delectable modern British food, with wicked cocktails in the bar to start or follow. ££ The Blanch House, 17 Atlingworth St., 01273-603504, blanchhouse.co.uk

Due South Sea views, locally sourced ingredients, and fresh, uncomplicated cooking. £ 139 King's Rd., Arches, 01273-821218, duesouth.co.uk

The Gingerman French-influenced dishes with a modern twist in either a relaxed bistro setting in a quiet backstreet, or the elegantly cool Drakes Hotel overlooking the sea. ££ 21a Norfolk Sq., 01273-326688 and Drakes Hotel, 44 Marine Parade, 01273-696934, gingermanrestaurants.com

One Paston Place Suave and sophisticated everything, from the modern European haute cuisine to the elegant surroundings and discreetly dressy customers. ££ 1 Paston Pl., 01273-606933, onepastonplace.co.uk

Contacts

Brighton Visitor Information Centre Bartholomew Sq., visitbrighton.com

Getting There: Brighton is around 50 minutes by train from Victoria Station.

Middle Thames Valley

30 miles W

Hot Tip: Late spring to early autumn is best for boating and waterside eating, though that sought-after table may be easier to get out of season.

The Lowdown: Londoners have always valued the scenic delights of the upstream section of the Thames that meanders around the southern tip of the Chilterns and down toward Windsor, with its famous castle. The lush riverside landscape isn't the only draw these days, however. The stylish 21st-century visitor is more likely to be heading for a date with a gastronomic experience of the highest level than a tour of the battlements. For around the sleepy riverside settlements of Bray and Marlow there's a cluster of world-class restaurants, including two with three Michelin stars. For those for whom even the best meal isn't enough of a draw, there is also the chance to mess about in boats—chartered, scheduled, or drive-your-own—in some of the loveliest scenery this close to the city.

Best Attractions

Cliveden Taplow A magnificent riverside hotel, with gorgeous gardens that are open to nonguests. Afternoon tea in the hotel makes a grand finale. £- Maidenhead, Berkshire, 01628-605069, nationaltrust.org.uk

Stanley Spencer Gallery Quirky gallery devoted to the work of Cookham's own visionary artist. £- King's Hall, High St., Cookham, 01628-471885, stanleyspencer.org.uk

Windsor Castle A royal residence worth visiting for its 900-year history, art-filled State Apartments, and St. George's Chapel. £ Windsor, 020-7766-7304

Best Restaurants

The Fat Duck Heston Blumenthal is the three-star chef of the moment for his novel techniques. ££££+ 1 High St., Bray, 01628-580333, fatduck.co.uk

The Market Bar and Dining Room Upmarket gastropub serving restrained, classy modern British food. £ Market Sq., Marlow, 01628-487661

Vanilla Pod This snug restaurant is permanently busy thanks to its perfect Anglo-French cuisine. £ 31 West St., Marlow, 01628-898101, thevanillapod.co.uk

The Waterside Inn It takes something special to hold three Michelin stars for nearly 20 years; from the French cuisine to the service, it all strikes the perfect, magical note. £££ Ferry Rd., Bray, 01628-620691, waterside-inn.co.uk

Contacts

Marlow Tourist Information Office 31 High St., Marlow, 01628-483597, marlowtown.co.uk

The Royal Borough of Windsor and Maidenhead 01753-743900, windsor.gov.uk

Getting There: Trains from Paddington and Waterloo stations take around 50 minutes to Windsor, and a little longer to Maidenhead and the smaller towns.

LEAVING

Oxford

Hot Tip: The university semesters are incredibly short, so to see student life in full summer flow the best month for a visit is May.

The Lowdown: Nicknamed "the city of dreaming spires," Oxford is dominated—physically and socially—by its famous university. It has more than 1,500 historic edifices classed as architecturally exceptional by English Heritage. But this is no mere open-air museum; there's also a thriving social scene, driven partly by the sophisticated tastes and fat purses of the parents who drop by to see their clever offspring, and partly by the wealthier of the undergraduates. That means excellent restaurants, hip cocktail bars, and interesting shops.

Best Attractions

Ashmolean An elegant building houses a fine array of classic antiquities and oriental art. Beaumont St., 01865-278000, ashmol.ox.ac.uk

Botanic Garden The oldest garden of its kind in Great Britain, known for its work in preserving rare plants. £- Rose Ln., 01865-286-690, botanic-garden.ox.ac.uk

Christ Church Picture Gallery One of Britain's most important private collections. £- Oriel Sq., 01865-276172, chch.ox.ac.uk

Modern Art Oxford A highly regarded modern and contemporary art space. 30 Pembroke St., 01865-722733, modernartoxford.org.uk

University of Oxford Centuries of history and architecture draw visitors to many of the 38 colleges and university buildings. 01865-270000, ox.ac.uk

Best Restaurants

Brown's Restaurant An Oxford institution, serving British classics in laid-back surroundings. £ 5-11 Woodstock Rd., 01865-511995, browns-restaurants.com

The Cherwell Boathouse Restaurant Boasting a superb riverside location, this long-standing favorite keeps its well-heeled regulars happy with modern British cuisine. £ Bardwell Rd., 01865-552746, cherwellboathouse.co.uk

The Lemon Tree Mediterranean and modern British cuisine, fabulous Moroccan-inspired décor, and the intimate ambiance make this a hit with Oxford's elegant set. £ 268 Woodstock Rd., 01865-311936, thelemontreeoxford.co.uk

Quod Bar and Grill See and be seen in the former banking hall that's now one of Oxford's hottest bars. £- 92-94 High St., 01865-202505, oldbank-hotel.co.uk

Contacts

Oxford City Council visitoxford.org
Oxford Information Centre 15-16 Broad St., 01865-726871

Getting There: "The Tube," a much-loved express coach service that runs 24/7 from just outside Victoria Station to the heart of Oxford, or train from Paddington Station.

Whitstable

Hot Tip: Visit in late July for the Oyster Festival and the best chance of fine weather.

The Lowdown: Quaint weatherboard cottages, the tang of salt in the air, and an unpolished charm have helped turn this fishing village, famous for its oyster trade, into one of England's hippest resorts of late. This is seaside life with a very British, very dressed-down flavor: The beach is pebbly, but backed by colorful beach huts, very in demand; the harbor is in use, and hasn't been gussied up as a tourist attraction; and the permanently busy seafood restaurants produce dishes to satisfy the most sophisticated gourmet. Even the shops on High Street and Harbour Street are an endearing mix of old-fashioned bakers, funky jewelry designers, and chic homeware boutiques. Between the main road and the shore lie tiny thoroughfares, lined with cute little houses that were once sailmakers' lofts and boatmakers' workshops.

Best Attractions

Somerset Maugham Gallery Just two rooms with a particularly impressive array of high-quality applied arts. 2 Horsebridge Arts & Community Centre, 11 Horsebridge Rd., 01227-281174, horsebridge-centre.co.uk

Thames Sailing Barge Relaxing and scenic day trips in a restored historic sailing barge. £ Greta Whitstable Harbour, 01795-534541, thamesbarges.co.uk

Whitstable Museum & Gallery Small eclectic display of everything from wicker oyster baskets to vintage snaps offering insights in the history of the town. £ Oxford St., 01227-276998, whitstable-museum.co.uk

Best Restaurants and Pubs

The Old Neptune Fabulous wood-paneled pub right on the beach, with tables outside for fine-weather drinks. £- Marine Terrace, 01227-272262

Wheelers Oyster Bar Tiny oyster bar, famous for super-fresh seafood; bring your own wine. £ 8 High St., 01227-273311, whitstable-shellfish.co.uk

Whitstable Oyster Fishery Company Famously fresh seafood, in a shabby-chic venue by the beach. £ The Royal Native Oyster Stores, 11 Horsebridge Rd., 01227-276856, oysterfishery.co.uk

Williams & Brown Tapas An exemplary selection of Spanish classics and delicious novelties in a minimalist setting. £ 48 Harbour St., 01227-273373

Contacts

Whitstable Information Centre 7 Oxford St., 01227-275482
Kent Tourism 01271-336020, kenttourism.co.uk

Getting There: Whitstable is about 90 minutes by train (South Eastern Trains, setrains.co.uk/setrains) from London's Victoria Station.

Winchester

Hot Tip: Food lovers will appreciate the Hampshire Food Festival in late June and early July.

The Lowdown: Had the course of history been a little different, this book would be dedicated to Winchester rather than London. This handsome Hampshire town, not the city on the Thames, was the capital of Alfred the Great's kingdom of Wessex, and it remained an important and powerful political and ecclesiastical center throughout the medieval period. Times change, however, and modern Winchester is a prosperous, sophisticated yet tranquil market town, though one blessed with far more historic monuments than others of similar size. Enjoy the atmosphere, which inspired such writers as John Keats and Jane Austen.

Best Attractions

The City Museum Learn all about the fascinating story of Winchester's changing fortunes. The Square, 01962-848269, winchester.gov.uk

The Great Hall and Round Table All that remains of Winchester's Norman Castle, the medieval Great Hall is home to the legendary Round Table of King Arthur fame—or, rather, a clever Tudor forgery. The Castle, 01962-846476, hants.gov.uk/discover/places/great-hall.html

Winchester Cathedral and Close One of Britain's greatest cathedrals, with 11th-century origins. 1 The Close, 01962-857200, winchester-cathedral.org.uk

Winchester College Founded nearly 700 years ago, this remains one of England's most prestigious private schools for boys. See six centuries of architectural styles on a guided tour. College St., 01962-621209, winchestercollege.co.uk

Best Restaurants

Chesil Rectory A local favorite for many years for both the quality of the food—British and European cuisine—and its riverside setting. £ 1 Chesil St., 01962-851555

The Forester Funky décor, great cocktails from the resident mixologists, and uncomplicated global cuisine pulls in a younger, hip crowd. £- 76a North Walls, 01962-861539, maverick-pubs.co.uk

Hotel du Vin & Bistro Classy but simple modern food with Mediterranean influences. £ 14 Southgate St., 01962-841414, hotelduvin.com

Loch Fyne Winchester Delectable seafood, available in the congenial surroundings of this historic barn. £ 18 Jewry St., 01962-872930, lochfyne.com

Contacts

Tourist Information Centre Guildhall, Broadway, 01962-840500
Winchester Tourism visitwinchester.co.uk

Getting There: The train from Waterloo Station to Winchester takes about an hour.

LONDON
BLACK BOOK

You're solo in the city—where's a singles-friendly place to eat? Is there a good lunch spot near the museum? Will the bar be too loud for easy conversation? Get the answers fast in the *Black Book*, a condensed version of every listing in our guide that puts all the essential information at your fingertips.

A quick glance down the page and you'll find the type of food, nightlife, or attractions you are looking for, the phone numbers, and which pages to turn to for more detailed information. How did you ever survive without it?

London Black Book

Hotels

NAME TYPE (ROOMS)	ADDRESS (TUBE STATION) WEBSITE	AREA PRICE	PHONE (020) 800 NUMBER	EXPERIENCE	PAGE
The Baglioni Trendy (68)	60 Hyde Park Gate, SW7 (High Street Ken.) baglionihotellondon.com	KE ££	7368-5700	Hot & Cool	57
The Berkeley Grand (214)	Wilton Pl., SW1 (Knightsbridge) the-berkeley.co.uk	KN £££	7235-6000	Hot & Cool	57
Blakes Hotel Trendy (45)	33 Roland Gdns., SW7 (Gloucester Road) blakeshotels.com	SK £££	7370-6701 800-926-3173	Hot & Cool	57
Brown's Hotel Modern (117)	33 Albemarle St., W1 (Green Park) brownshotel.com	MY £££	7493-6020	Classic	133
The Cadogan Timeless (50)	75 Sloane St., SW1 (Sloane Square) cadogan.com	KN ££	7235-7141	Classic	133
The Charlotte Street Hotel Timeless (52)	15 Charlotte St., W1 (Goodge Street) firmdalehotels.com	FI ££	7806-2000 800-553-6674	Hot & Cool	58
Claridge's Grand (263)	55 Brook St., W1 (Bond Street) claridges.co.uk	MY £££	7629-8860 800-637-2869	Classic	134
The Connaught Grand (92)	Carlos Pl., W1 (Green Park) theconnaughthotellondon.com	MY £££	7499-7070 800-637-2869	Classic	134
The Dorchester Grand (248)	Park Ln., W1 (Hyde Park Corner) thedorchester.com	MY ££££	7629-8888	Classic	134
Dukes Hotel Grand (89)	St. James's Pl., SW1 (Green Park) dukeshotel.co.uk	SJ £££	7491-4840	Classic	135
The Gore Hotel Grand (49)	190 Queen's Gate, SW7 (South Kensington) gorehotel.co.uk	SK ££	7584-6601	Classic	135
The Great Eastern Hotel Trendy (267)	Liverpool St., EC2 (Liverpool Street) great-eastern-hotel.co.uk	CT £££	7618-5000	Hip	99
Guesthouse West Modern (20)	163-165 Westbourne Grove, W11 (Notting Hill Gate) guesthousewest.com	NH £	7792-9800	Hip	99
The Halkin Timeless (41)	5 Halkin St., SW1 (Hyde Park Corner) halkin.co.uk	KN £££	7333-1000 888-425-5464	Hot & Cool	58
Hazlitt's Timeless (23)	6 Frith St., Soho Sq. W1 (Oxford Circus) hazlittshotel.com	SO ££	7434-1771	Classic	135
K West Hotel & Spa Modern (220)	Richmond Way, W14 (Shepherd's Bush) k-west.co.uk	KE ££	0870-027-4343	Hot & Cool	58

Neighborhood (Area) Key

BA = Bankside	HA = Hampstead	NH = Notting Hill
BL = Bloomsbury	HO = Holborn	PR = Primrose Hill
CH = Chelsea	HX = Hoxton	SJ = St. James's
CT = The City	HP = Hyde Park	SO = Soho
CL = Clerkenwell	IL = Islington	SB = South Bank
CO = Covent Garden	KE = Kensington	SK = South Kensington
DO = Docklands	KN = Knightsbridge	SP = Spitalfields
FI = Fitzrovia	MA = Marylebone	VA = Various
FU = Fulham	MY = Mayfair	WE = Westminster

NAME	ADDRESS (TUBE STATION)	AREA	PHONE (020)	EXPERIENCE	PAGE
TYPE (ROOMS)	WEBSITE	PRICE	800 NUMBER		
The Lanesborough	Hyde Park Corner, SW1 (Hyde Park Corner)	KN	7259-5599	Classic	136
Grand (95)	lanesborough.com	£££			
The Main House	6 Colville Rd., W11 (Notting Hill Gate)	NH	7221-9691	Hip	99
Modern (7)	themainhouse.co.uk	£			
Metropolitan London	19 Old Park Ln., W1 (Hyde Park Corner)	MY	7447-1047	Hot & Cool	59
Modern (150)	metropolitan.co.uk	£££			
The Milestone Hotel and Apts.	1 Kensington Court, W8 (High Street Ken.)	KE	7917-1000	Classic	136
Timeless (57)	milestonehotel.com	££			
Miller's Residence	111a Westbourne Gr., W2 (Notting Hill Gate)	NH	7243 -1024	Hip	100
Timeless (8)	millersuk.com	£			
myhotel Chelsea	35 Ixworth Pl., SW3 (South Kensington)	CH	7225-7500	Hip	100
Modern (45)	myhotels.co.uk	££			
No. 5 Cavendish Square	5 Cavendish Sq., W1 (Oxford Circus)	MA	7079-5000	Hot & Cool	59
Timeless (8)	no5ltd.com	££			
Number Eleven Cadogan Gdns.	11 Cadogan Gdns., SW3 (Sloane Square)	CH	7730-7000	Classic	137
Timeless (60)	number-eleven.co.uk	££			
One Aldwych	1 Aldwych, WC2 (Covent Garden)	CO	7300-1000	Hot & Cool	59
Modern (105)	onealdwych.co.uk	£££	800-223-6800		
The Pelham Hotel	15 Cromwell Pl., SW7 (South Kensington)	SK	7589-8288	Classic	137
Timeless (52)	pelhamhotel.co.uk	££			
The Portobello Hotel	22 Stanley Gdns., W11 (Notting Hill Gate)	NH	7727-2777	Hip	100
Timeless (24)	portobello-hotel.co.uk	£			
The Ritz Hotel	150 Piccadilly, W1 (Green Park)	MY	7493-8181	Classic	137
Grand (133)	theritzlondon.com	£££	877-748-9536		
The Rookery	Cowcross St., EC1 (Farringdon)	CL	7336-0931	Classic	138
Timeless (33)	rookeryhotel.com	££			
St. Martins Lane	45 St. Martin's Ln., WC2 (Leicester Sq.)	CO	7300-5500	Hot & Cool	60
Trendy (204)	stmartinslane.com	£££			
The Sanderson	50 Berners St., W1 (Oxford Circus)	FI	7300-1400	Hot & Cool	60
Trendy (154)	sandersonlondon.com	£££	800-697-1791		
The Savoy	The Strand, WC2 (Charing Cross)	CO	7836-4343	Classic	138
Timeless (263)	fairmont.com/savoy	£££	800-637-2869		
The Soho Hotel	4 Richmond Mews (Off Dean St.), W1	SO	7559-3000	Hot & Cool	61
Trendy (91)	(Tottenham Court Road) sohohotel.com	££	800-553-6674		
Threadneedles	5 Threadneedle St., EC2 (Bank)	CT	7657-8080	Hot & Cool	61
Modern (69)	theetoncollection.com	£££			
The Trafalgar	2 Spring Gdns., Trafalgar Sq., SW1	WE	7870-2900	Hot & Cool	61
Modern (129)	(Charing Cross) trafalgar.hilton.com	£££			
22 Jermyn Street	22 Jermyn St., SW1 (Piccadilly Circus)	SJ	7734-2353	Classic	138
Timeless (18)	22jermyn.com	££			
The Zetter	86-88 Clerkenwell Rd., EC1 (Farringdon)	CL	7324-4444	Hip	101
Modern (59)	thezetter.com	£			

BLACK BOOK

Restaurants

NAME TYPE	ADDRESS (TUBE STATION) WEBSITE	AREA PRICE	PHONE (020) SINGLES/NOISE	EXPERIENCE 99 BEST	PAGE PAGE
The Admiralty	Somerset House, The Strand, WC2 (Temple)	CO	7845-4646	Classic	139
French	somerset-house.org.uk	££	- =		
Alastair Little	49 Frith St., W1 (Leicester Square)	SO	7734-5183	Classic	139
British		££	- –		
Allium	Dolphin Sq., Chichester St., SW1 (Pimlico)	VA	7798-6888	Classic	139
French	allium.co.uk	££	- –		
Amaya	Halkin Arcade, Motcomb St., SW1	KN	7823-1166	Hot & Cool	*54*, 62
Indian	(Knightsbridge) realindianfood.com	££	- =	Indian Rests.	31
Anchor & Hope	36 The Cut, SE1 (Southwark)	SB	7928-9898	Hot & Cool	*51*, 62
Gastropub		£-	- ≡	Gastropubs	27
Angela Hartnett	16 Carlos Pl., W1 (Bond Street)	MY	7592-1222	Classic	139
Italian	gordonramsay.com	££	- =		
Asia dè Cuba	45 St. Martin's Ln., WC2 (Leicester Square)	CO	7300-5588	Hot & Cool	*52*, 62
Fusion	chinagrillmgt.com	££	- ≡		
Aubergine	11 Park Walk, SW10 (Gloucester Road)	CH	7352-3449	Classic	140
French (G)	atozrestaurants.com	££	- =		
Automat	33 Dover St., W1 (Bond Street)	MY	7499-3033	Classic	140
American	automat-london.com	££	- =		
The Avenue	7-9 St. James's St., SW1 (Green Park)	SJ	7321-2111	Classic	140
British	egami.co.uk	£	- =		
Babylon	99 Kensington High St., the Roof Gardens, 7th Fl., W8				
	(High Street Kensington)	KE	7368-3993	Hot & Cool	*54*, 62
Modern European	roofgardens.com	£	- ≡		
Baltic*	74 Blackfriars Rd., SE1 (Southwark)	SB	7928-1111	Hot & Cool	*51*, 63
East European	balticrestaurant.co.uk	£-	[B] =	Restaurant Lounges	40
Bar Italia*	22 Frith St., W1 (Leicester Square)	SO	7437-4520	Hip	102
Cafe	baritaliasoho.co.uk	£-	- ≡		
The Belvedere	Holland Park House, off Abbotsbury Rd., W8	VA	7602-1238	Classic	140
French	(Holland Park) whitestarline.org.uk	££	- –	Romantic Dining	41
Benares	12 Berkeley Sq. , W1 (Green Park)	MY	7629-8886	Hot & Cool	*53*, 63
Indian	benaresrestaurant.com	££	- –		
Bentley's Oyster Bar & Grill*	11-13 Swallow St., W1 (Piccadilly Circus)	SJ	7734-4756	Classic	141
Seafood	bentleysoysterbarandgrill.co.uk	££	- –		
Bermondsey Kitchen	194 Bermondsey St., SE1 (London Bridge)	BA	7407-5719	Hip	*94*, 102
British	bermondseykitchen.co.uk	£	- =		

Restaurant and Nightlife Symbols

Restaurants
Singles Friendly (eat and/or meet)
[ ] = Communal table
[B] = Food served at bar

(G) = Gourmet destination

Nightlife
Price Warning
[C] = Cover or ticket charge

Restaurant + Nightlife
Prime time noise levels
– = Quiet
= = A buzz, but still conversational
≡ = Loud
– ≡ = Various

Venues followed by an * are those we recommend as both a restaurant and a destination bar.

Note regarding page numbers: Italic = itinerary listing; Roman *= description in theme chapter listing.*

NAME	ADDRESS (TUBE STATION)	AREA	PHONE (020)	EXPERIENCE	PAGE
TYPE	WEBSITE	PRICE	SINGLES/NOISE	99 BEST	PAGE
Bevis Marks Restaurant	Bevis Marks, EC3 (Liverpool Street)	CT	7283-2220	Classic	141
Kosher	bevismarkstherestaurant.com	£	-	—	
Bibendum	81 Fulham Rd., SW3 (South Kensington)	CH	7581-5817	Classic	141
French	bibendum.co.uk	££	-	=	
Bistrotheque*	23-27 Wadeson St., E2 (Bethnal Green)	HX	8983-7900	Hip	93, 102
French	bistrotheque.com	£	-	=	Trendy Tables	48
Blue Elephant	3-6 Fulham Broadway, SW6	FU	7385-6595	Classic	141
Thai	(Fulham Broadway) blueelephant.com	£	-	≡	
Bluebird Dining Rooms	350 King's Rd., SW3 (Sloane Square)	CH	7559-1129	Classic	130, 142
British	conran.com	££	-	—	
Bonds*	Threadneedles, 5 Threadneedle St., EC2	CT	7657-8088	Classic	142
European	(Bank) bonds-restaurant.com	££	-	=	
Boxwood Café	Wilton Pl., SW1 (Knightsbridge)	KN	7235-1010	Hot & Cool	63
American	gordonramsay.com	££	-	=	
Brick Lane Beigel Bake	159 Brick Ln., E1 (Liverpool Street)	SP	7729-0616	Hip	96, 102
Bagels		£-	-	=	
Café Corfu	7 Pratt St., NW1 (Camden Town)	VA	7267-8088	Hip	102
Greek	cafecorfu.com	£	-	≡	
Cambio de Tercio	163 Old Brompton Rd., SW5	SK	7244-8970	Classic	142
Spanish	(Gloucester Rd.) cambiodetercio.co.uk	£	-	=	
Canteen	Unit 2, Crispin Pl., E1 (Liverpool Street)	CT	0845-686-1122	Hip	96, 103
British	canteen.co.uk	£	-	=	
The Capital	22-24 Basil St., SW3 (Knightsbridge)	KN	7589-5171	Classic	130, 142
French (G)	capitalhotel.co.uk	££	-	—	
Champor-Champor	62-64 Weston St., SE1 (London Bridge)	BA	7403-4600	Hip	103
Malaysian	champor-champor.com	£	-	=	
Chez Bruce	2 Bellevue Rd., SW17 (Balham)	VA	8672-0114	Classic	143
Modern British (G)	chezbruce.co.uk	£	-	=	Famous Chefs	24
China Tang	53 Park Ln., W1 (Hyde Park Corner)	MY	7629-9988	Classic	129, 143
Chinese	thedorchester.com	£££	-	=	
The Cinnamon Club*	The Old Westminster Library, Great Smith St.	WE	7222-2555	Hot & Cool	63
Indian	(St. James's/Westmin.) cinnamonclub.com	££	-	=	Restaurant Lounges 40
Cipriani	23-25 Davies St., W1 (Bond Street)	MY	7399-0500	Classic	143
Italian	cipriani.com	££	-	≡	
Clarke's	124 Kensington Church St., W8	KE	7221-9225	Hip	103
International (G)	(Notting Hill Gate) sallyclarke.com	£	-	—	
Club Gascon	57 West Smithfield, EC1 (Farringdon)	CT	7796-0600	Hip	103
French (G)		£	-	=	
Cow Dining Room*	89 Westbourne Park Rd., W2	NH	7221-0021	Hip	95, 104
Gastropub	(Westbourne Park)	£	-	=	Gastropubs	27
Daphne's	112 Draycott Ave., SW3 (South Kensington)	CH	7589-4257	Classic	130, 143
Italian	daphnes-restaurant.co.uk	££	-	=	
Deep	The Boulevard, Imperial Wharf, SW6	FU	7736-3337	Hot & Cool	64
Seafood	(Fulham Broadway) deeplondon.co.uk	£	-	=	

BLACK BOOK

Restaurants (cont.)

NAME TYPE	ADDRESS (TUBE STATION) WEBSITE	AREA PRICE	PHONE (020) SINGLES/NOISE	EXPERIENCE 99 BEST	PAGE PAGE
Delfina Fusion	50 Bermondsey St., SE1 (London Bridge) delfina.org.uk	BA £	7357-0244 - ≡	Hip	*94*, 104
E & O* Pan-Asian	14 Blenheim Crescent, W11 (Ladbroke Grove) eando.nu	NH £	7229-5454 Ⓑ ≈	Hip Trendy Tables	*96*, 104 48
Eagle Gastropub	159 Farringdon Rd., EC1 (Farringdon)	CL £	7837-1353 - ≡	Hip	*94*, 104
Eagle Bar Diner American	3-5 Rathbone Pl., W1 (Tottenham Court Rd.) eaglebardiner.com	BL £	7637-1418 - ≡	Hip	*94*, 105
Eight Over Eight Chinese	392 King's Rd., SW3 (Sloane Square) eightovereight.nu	CH £	7349-9934 Ⓑ ≈	Hip Oriental Rests.	105 36
1880 French	Harrington Gdns., SW7 (Gloucester Road) thebentley-hotel.com	SK £££	7244-5555 - ⌐	Classic	143
Electric Brasserie* British	191 Portobello Rd., W11 (Ladbroke Grove) the-electric.co.uk	NH £	7908-9696 - ≡	Hip	*96*, 105
Elena's L'Étoile French	30 Charlotte St., W1 (Goodge Street)	FI £	7636-7189 - ⌐	Classic	144
Emporio Armani Caffe Italian	191 Brompton Rd., SW3 (Knightsbridge)	KN £	7823-8818 - ⌐	Hot & Cool	64
Fifteen Italian	15 Westland Pl., N1 (Old Street) fifteenrestaurant.com	CT ££	0871-330-1515 - ≈	Hip Famous Chefs	*93*, 105 24
Fino Tapas	33 Charlotte St., W1 (Tottenham Court Rd.) finorestaurant.com	BL £	7813-8010 - ≡	Hot & Cool	64
Food @ the Muse Fusion	269 Portobello Rd., W11 (Ladbroke Grove) themuseat269.com/foodatthemuse.php	NH £	7792-1111 ⌐	Hip	*95*, 106
1492 Latin American	404 North End Rd., SW6 (Fulham Bdwy.) 1492restaurant.com	FU £	7381-3810 - ≡	Hip	106
Frankie's Italian Bar & Grill American	3 Yeoman's Row, SW3 (Knightsbridge) frankiesitalianbarandgrill.com	KN £	7590-9999 - ≈	Hot & Cool	64
Galvin Bistrot de Luxe French	66 Baker St., W1 (Baker Street) galvinbistrotdeluxe.co.uk	MA £	7935-4007 - ≈	Classic	144
Garden Café British	Inner Circle Regents Park, NW1 (Regent's Park) thegardencafe.co.uk	VA £	7935-5729 - ≈	Hip Al Fresco Dining	106 16
Glas Swedish	3 Park St., SE1 (London Bridge) glasrestaurant.com	SB £-	7357-6060 - ≈	Hot & Cool	*53*, 65
Gordon Ramsay French (G)	68 Royal Hospital Rd., SW3 (Sloane Square) gordonramsay.com	CH £££	7352-4441 - ⌐	Classic Fine Dining	144 25
Gordon Ramsay at Claridge's Modern European (G)	55 Brook St., W1 (Bond Street) gordonramsay.com	MY ££	7499-0099 - ⌐	Classic	*130*, 144
Green's British	36 Duke St., SW1 (Green Park) greens.org.uk	SJ £££	7930-4566 - ⌐	Classic	145
The Greenhouse French	27A Hay's Mews, W1 (Green Park) greenhouserestaurant.co.uk	MY £	7499-3331 - ≈	Classic	145
Gun Gastropub	27 Coldharbour, Isle of Dogs, E14 (South Quay) thegundocklands.com	DO £	7515-5222 - ≈	Hot & Cool Gastropubs	65 27

NAME	ADDRESS (TUBE STATION)	AREA	PHONE (020)	EXPERIENCE	PAGE
TYPE	WEBSITE	PRICE	SINGLES/NOISE	99 BEST	PAGE
Hakkasan*	8 Hanway Pl., W1 (Tottenham Court Road)	BL	7907-1888	Hot & Cool	*52*, 65
Chinese		££	B♥ ≡	Always-Hot Rests.	17
Hoxton Apprentice	16 Hoxton Sq., N1 (Old Street)	HX	7734-2828	Hip	*96*, 106
Mediterranean	hoxtonapprentice.com	£-	- ≡		
Inc Bar & Restaurant*	7 College Approach, SE10	VA	8858-6721	Hip	107
British	(Cutty Sark DLR)	£	B ≡		
Inn the Park	St. James's Park, SW1 (St. James's Park)	WE	7451-9999	Hot & Cool	*54*, 65
British	innthepark.com	£	- ≡	Al Fresco Dining	16
The Ivy	1-5 West St., WC2 (Leicester Square)	CO	7836-4751	Classic	*127*, 145
British	the-ivy.co.uk	£	- ≡	Celeb Haunts	21
J Sheekey	28-32 St. Martin's Ct., WC2	CO	7240-2565	Classic	*128*, 145
British	(Leicester Square) j-sheekey.co.uk	£	- ≡		
Kai Mayfair	65 South Audley St., W1 (Bond Street)	MY	7493-8988	Classic	146
Chinese (G)	kaimayfair.com	£££	- ≡		
Kaya	42 Albemarle St., W1 (Green Park)	MY	7499-0622	Classic	146
Korean		£	- ≡		
La Fromagerie	2-4 Moxon St., W1 (Baker Street)	MA	7935-0341	Hip	107
Mediterranean	lafromagerie.co.uk	£	- ≡		
Ladurée	Harrods, 87-135 Brompton Rd., Door 1B	KN	3155-0111	Classic	146
Tea Room	SW1 (Knightsbridge) laduree.com	£	- ≡		
Le Caprice	Arlington House, Arlington St., SW1	MY	7629-2239	Classic	146
British	(Green Park) le-caprice.co.uk	£	- —	Celeb Haunts	21
Le Cercle	1 Wilbraham Pl., SW1 (Sloane Square)	CH	7901-9999	Hot & Cool	66
French		£	B ≡		
L'Escargot	48 Greek St., W1 (Leicester Square)	SO	7437-2679	Classic	146
French	whitestarline.org.uk	££	- —		
Le Gavroche	43 Upper Brook St., W1 (Marble Arch)	MY	7408-0881	Classic	*128*, 147
French (G)	le-gavroche.co.uk	£££	≡	Fine Dining	25
Le Pont de la Tour	Butlers Wharf Bldg, 36D Shad Thames,	BA	7403-8403	Classic	147
French	SE1 (London Bridge) conran.com	£	- ≡		
The Ledbury	127 Ledbury Rd., W11 (Westbourne Park)	NH	7792-9090	Hot & Cool	66
French	theledbury.com	££	- ≡		
Les Trois Garcons	1 Club Row , E1 (Shoreditch)	HX	7613-1924	Hip	*93*, 107
French	lestroisgarcons.com	££	B ≡	Trendy Tables	48
Lindsay House	21 Romilly St., W1 (Leicester Square)	SO	7439-0450	Classic	147
Irish	lindsayhouse.co.uk	£	- —		
Little Earth Café	6 Erskine Rd., NW3 (Chalk Farm)	PR	7449-0700	Hip	107
Raw Food		£-	- —		
Locanda Locatelli	8 Seymour St., W1 (Marble Arch)	MA	7935-9088	Hot & Cool	66
Italian	locandalocatelli.com	££	- ≡		
Luciano	72-73 St. James's St., SW1 (Green Park)	MY	7408-1440	Classic	147
Italian	lucianorestaurant.co.uk	£	- ≡		
Maison Bertaux	28 Greek St., W1 (Tottenham Court Road)	SO	7437-6007	Hip	108
French		£-	- —		

Restaurants (cont.)

NAME	ADDRESS (TUBE STATION)	AREA	PHONE (020)	EXPERIENCE	PAGE
TYPE	WEBSITE	PRICE	SINGLES/NOISE	99 BEST	PAGE
Matsuri	71 High Holborn, WC1 (Holborn)	HO	7430-1970	Classic	*128*, 148
Sushi	matsuri-restaurant.com	£	- ⬛	Sushi	47
Maze	10-13 Grosvenor Sq., W1 (Bond Street)	MY	7107-0000	Hot & Cool	*53*, 66
French/Pan-Asian	gordonramsay.com	£	Ⓑ ⬛		
Medcalf	40 Exmouth Market, EC1 (Farringdon)	CI	7833-3533	Hip	108
British	medcalfbar.co.uk	£	- ⬛		
Mirabelle	56 Curzon St., W1 (Green Park)	MY	7499-4636	Classic	148
French	whitestarline.org.uk	££	- ⬛		
Mr. Chow	151 Knightsbridge, SW1 (Knightsbridge)	KN	7589-7347	Classic	*130*, 148
Chinese	mrchow.com	££	- ⬛		
Momo	25 Heddon St., W1 (Piccadilly Circus)	MY	7434-4040	Hot & Cool	67
Moroccan	momoresto.com	£	Ⓑ ⬛	Romantic Dining	41
Morgan M	489 Liverpool Rd., N7 (Highbury & Islington)	IL	7609-3560	Classic	148
French	morganm.com	££	- ⬛		
Moro	34-36 Exmouth Market (Farringdon)	CL	7833-8336	Hot & Cool	67
Moorish	moro.co.uk	£	- ⬛		
Nahm	5 Halkin St., SW1 (Hyde Park Corner)	KN	7333-1234	Classic	148
Thai	halkin.co.uk	££	- ⬛		
Nicole's	158 New Bond St., W1 (Bond Street)	MY	7499-8408	Hot & Cool	67
British	nicolefarhi.com	£	Ⓑ ⬛		
Nipa	Lancaster Terrace, W2 (Lancaster Gate)	MA	7551-6039	Classic	149
Thai	niparestaurant.co.uk	£	- ⬛		
Nobu	19 Old Park Ln., W1 (Hyde Park Corner)	MY	7447-4747	Hot & Cool	*52*, 67
Japanese (G)	noburestaurants.com	££	- ⬛	Oriental Rests.	36
Nobu Berkeley*	15 Berkeley St., W1 (Green Park)	MY	7290-9222	Hot & Cool	68
Japanese	noburestaurants.com	££	Ⓑ ⬛		
Notting Hill Brasserie	92 Kensington Park Rd., W11	NH	7229-4481	Hip	*96*, 108
French	(Notting Hill Gate)	£	- ⬛		
Occo*	58 Crawford St., W1 (Edgeware Road)	MA	7724-4991	Hot & Cool	68
Moroccan	occo.co.uk	£	Ⓑ ⬛		
1 Lombard Street*	1 Lombard St., EC3 (Bank)	CT	7929-6611	Classic	149
British	1lombardstreet.com	£	- ⬛		
Origin	The Hospital, 24 Endell St., WC2	CO	7170-9200	Classic	149
British	(Covent Garden) origin-restaurant.com	££	Ⓑ ⬛		
Ottolenghi	63 Ledbury Rd., W11 (Notting Hill Gate)	NH	7727-1121	Hip	*95*, 108
Cafe	ottolenghi.co.uk	£-	⓪ ⬛		
Palm Court	The Ritz Hotel, 150 Piccadilly, W1	MY	7493-8181	Classic	149
Tea Room	(Green Park) theritzlondon.com	££££	- ⬛		
Pasha	1 Gloucester Rd. (Gloucester Road)	KE	7589-7969	Classic	150
Moroccan	pasha-restaurant.co.uk	£	- ⬛		
Patara	15 Greek St., W1 (Tottenham Court Road)	SO	7437-1071	Classic	150
Thai		£	- ⬛		
Pâtisserie Valerie	44 Old Compton St., W1 (Leicester Square)	SO	7437-3466	Hip	108
Cafe	patisserie-valerie.co.uk	£-	⬛		

NAME	ADDRESS (TUBE STATION)	AREA	PHONE (020)	EXPERIENCE	PAGE
TYPE	WEBSITE	PRICE	SINGLES/NOISE	99 BEST	PAGE
Pearl Bar & Restaurant*	252 High Holborn, WC1 (Holborn)	HO	7829-7000	Hot & Cool	68
French	pearl-restaurant.com	££	-	≈	Restaurant Lounges 40
Pétrus	Wilton Pl., SW1 (Knightsbridge)	KN	7235-1200	Classic	128, 150
French (G)	gordonramsay.com	£££	-	≈	Power Lunches 37
Pied à Terre	34 Charlotte St., W1 (Goodge Street)	BL	7636-1178	Classic	128, 150
French (G)	pied-a-terre.co.uk	££	-	≈	Power Lunches 37
Plateau	Canada Pl., Canada Sq., E14	DO	7715-7100	Hot & Cool	68
French	(Canary Wharf) conran.com	££	⬛	≈	
Princess	76 Paul St., EC2 (Old Street)	HX	7729-9270	Hip	109
Gastropub		£	⬛	≈	
The Providores & Tapa Room	109 Marylebone High St., W1 (Bond Street)	MA	7935-6175	Hot & Cool	52, 69
Tapas	theprovidores.co.uk	££	⬛	≈	
Quaglino's	16 Bury St., SW1 (Green Park)	SJ	7930-6767	Classic	151
European	quaglinos.co.uk	£	⬛	≈	
Racine	239 Brompton Rd., SW3	KN	7584-4477	Classic	151
French	(South Kensington)	£	-	≈	
Rasoi Vineet Bhatia	10 Lincoln St., SW3 (Sloane Square)	CH	7225-1881	Classic	151
Indian	vineetbhatia.com	£££	-	—	Indian Rests. 31
The Real Greek	15 Hoxton Market, N1 (Old Street)	HX	7739-8212	Hip	109
Greek	therealgreek.co.uk	£	-	≈	
Rhodes Twenty-Four	Tower 42, 25 Old Broad St., 24th Fl., EC2	CT	7877-7703	Classic	151
British	(Bank) rhodes24.co.uk	£	-	≈	
The Rib Room & Oyster Bar	The Carlton Tower, Cadogan Pl., SW1	KN	7858-7053	Classic	129, 152
British	(Knightsbridge) carltontower.com	££	-	≈	
River Café	Thames Wharf, Rainville Rd., W6	VA	7386-4200	Hot & Cool	69
Italian (G)	(Hammersmith) rivercafe.co.uk	££	-	≈	Al Fresco Dining 16
Roast	The Floral Hall, Borough Market, SE1	BA	7940-1300	Hot & Cool	53, 69
British	(London Bridge) roast-restaurant.com	££	⬛	≈	
Roka	37 Charlotte St., W1 (Goodge Street)	BL	7580-6464	Hot & Cool	70
Sushi	rokarestaurant.com	££	⬛	≡	Sushi 47
Roussillon	16 St. Barnabas St., SW1 (Sloane Square)	CH	7730-5550	Classic	152
French (G)	roussillon.co.uk	££	-	≈	
Royal China Queensway	13 Queensway, W2 (Queensway)	KE	7221-2535	Classic	152
Dim Sum	royalchinagroup.co.uk	£-	-	≡	
Rules	35 Maiden Ln., WC2 (Covent Garden)	CO	7836-5314	Classic	152
British	rules.co.uk	£	-	≈	
St. John	26 St. John St. EC1 (Farringdon)	CL	7251-0848	Classic	129, 152
British	stjohnrestaurant.com	£	-	≈	Famous Chefs 24
San Lorenzo	22 Beauchamp Pl., SW3 (Knightsbridge)	KN	7584-1074	Hot & Cool	70
Italian	sanlorenzo.com	££	-	≈	Celeb Haunts 21
Sardo	45 Grafton Way, W1 (Warren Street)	FI	7387-2521	Hot & Cool	70
Sardinian	sardo-restaurant.com	£	-	≈	
Savoy Grill	The Strand, WC2 (Charing Cross)	CO	7592-1600	Classic	127, 153
British	savoy-group.com	££	-	≈	Power Lunches 37

BLACK BOOK

Restaurants (cont.)

NAME TYPE	ADDRESS (TUBE STATION) WEBSITE	AREA PRICE	PHONE (020) SINGLES/NOISE	EXPERIENCE 99 BEST	PAGE PAGE
Shanghai Blues Chinese	193-197 High Holborn, WC1 (Holborn) shanghaiblues.co.uk	CO £	7404-1668 - =	Classic	153
Sketch* International	9 Conduit St., W1 (Oxford Circus) sketch.uk.com	MY £££	0870-777-4488 B =	Hot & Cool Always-Hot Rests.	*53*, 70 17
Smiths of Smithfield European	67-77 Charterhouse St., EC1 (Farringdon) smithsofsmithfield.co.uk	CL ££	7251-7950	Hip	109
Spoon at Sanderson Fusion	50 Berners St., W1 (Oxford Circus) spoon-restaurant.com	FI ££	7300-1444 B =	Hot & Cool	71
The Square French	6-10 Bruton St., W1 (Bond Street) squarerestaurant.com	MY ££	7495-7100 - =	Classic	153
Story Deli Deli	91 Brick Ln., E1 (Liverpool Street)	SP £-	7247-3137 D =	Hip	109
Sugar Hut Thai	374 North End Rd., SW6 (Fulham Broadway) sugarhutfulham.com	FU £	7386-8950 - ≡	Hot & Cool	71
Sumosan Japanese	26 Albemarle St., W1 (Green Park) sumosan.com	MY ££	7495-5999 B =	Hot & Cool Sushi	71 47
Tamarind Indian	20 Queen St., W1 (Green Park) tamarindrestaurant.com	MY ££	7629-3561 =	Classic Indian Rests.	153 31
Tapas Brindisa Tapas	18-20 Southwark St., SE1 (London Bridge)	BA £-	7357-8880 - =	Hip	110
Tom Aikens French	43 Elystan St., SW3 (South Kensington) tomaikens.co.uk	CH ££	7584-2003 - =	Classic Fine Dining	154 25
Tom's Delicatessen British	226 Westbourne Grove, W11 (Notting Hill Gate)	NH £-	7221-8818 - =	Hip	110
Tugga Portuguese	312 King's Rd., SW3 (South Kensington) tugga.com	CH £	7351-0101 - ≡	Hot & Cool	71
Umu Japanese	14-16 Bruton Pl., W1 (Green Park)	MY £££	7499-8881 - =	Hot & Cool Oriental Rests.	72 36
Vingt Quatre* Late-Night Restaurant	325 Fulham Rd., SW10 (Gloucester Road)	CH £	7376-7224	Classic	154
Wapping Food British	Wapping Hydraulic Power Station, Wapping Wall (Wapping)	DO £	7680-2080 - =	Hip	*94*, 110
Wiltons British	55 Jermyn St., SW1 (Green Park) wiltons.co.uk	SJ ££	7629-9955 - ≡	Classic	154
Wizzy Korean	616 Fulham Rd., SW6 (Parsons Green)	FU £	7736-9171 - =	Hot & Cool	72
The Wolseley Cafe	160 Piccadilly, W1 (Green Park) thewolseley.com	SJ £	7499-6996 - =	Classic	*128*, 154
Yauatcha Dim Sum	15 Broadwick St, W1 (Oxford Circus)	SO ££	7494-8888 - =	Hot & Cool	*52*, 72
Zafferano Italian (G)	15 Lowndes St., SW1 (Knightsbridge) zafferanorestaurant.com	KN ££	7235-5800 - =	Classic	*129*, 154
Zaika Indian	1 Kensington High St., W8 (High Street Kensington) zaika-restaurant.co.uk	KE ££	7795-6533 B =	Hot & Cool Romantic Dining	72 41

| NAME | ADDRESS (TUBE STATION) | AREA | PHONE (020) | EXPERIENCE | PAGE |
TYPE	WEBSITE	PRICE	SINGLES/NOISE	99 BEST	PAGE
Zetter	86-88 Clerkenwell Rd., EC1 (Farringdon)	CL	7324-4444	Hot & Cool	73
Italian	thezetter.com	£	-	─	
Zuma*	5 Raphael St., SW7 (Knightsbridge)	KN	7584-1010	Hot & Cool	54, 73
Japanese	zumarestaurant.com	££	B =	Always-Hot Rests.	17

Nightlife

| NAME | ADDRESS (TUBE STATION) | AREA | PHONE (020) | EXPERIENCE | PAGE |
TYPE	WEBSITE	COVER	NOISE	99 BEST	PAGE
Ain't Nothin But The Blues	20 Kingly St., W1 (Oxford Circus)	SO	7287-0514	Hip	111
Bar Blues Bar	aintnothinbut.co.uk	C	≡		
Aka	18 West Central St., WC1	CO	7836-0110	Hot & Cool	54, 74
DJ Bar	(Tottenham Court Road) akalondon.com	C	≡		
Akbar	Red Fort, 77 Dean St., W1	SO	7437-2525	Hot & Cool	74
Restaurant Bar	(Tottenham Court Road) redfort.co.uk	-	_ ≡		
Albannach	66 Trafalgar Sq., WC2 (Charing Cross)	WE	7930-0066	Classic	128, 155
Restaurant Bar	albannach.co.uk	-	_ ≡		
The Almeida	30 Almeida St., N1 (Highbury & Islington)	IL	7359-4404	Hot & Cool	74
Theater	almeida.co.uk	C	≡		
The American Bar	The Strand, WC2 (Charing Cross)	CO	7836-4343	Classic	155
Hotel Bar	savoy-group.com	-	_		
Annex 3	6 Little Portland St., W1 (Oxford Circus)	MA	7631-0700	Hip	94, 111
Restaurant Bar	loungelover.co.uk	-	_ ≡		
Baltic*	74 Blackfriars Rd., SE1 (Southwark)	SB	7928-1111	Hot & Cool	74
Restaurant Bar	balticrestaurant.co.uk	-	_ ≡		
Bar Italia*	22 Frith St., W1 (Leicester Square)	SO	7437-4520	Hip	95, 111
Cafe	baritaliasoho.co.uk	-	_	Late-Night Haunts	32
Bar Kick	127 Shoreditch High St., E1 (Old Street)	HX	7739-8700	Hip	111
Bar	barkick.co.uk	-	≡		
Below 54	54-56 Great Eastern St. EC2 (Old Street)	HX	7613-4545	Hot & Cool	75
Restaurant Bar	greateasterndining.co.uk	-	≡		
Below Zero & Absolut Ice Bar	31-33 Heddon St., W1 (Oxford Street)	MY	7478-8910	Hot & Cool	53, 75
Bar	belowzerolondon.com	C	≡		
Bentley's Oyster Bar & Grill*	11-13 Swallow St., W1 (Piccadilly Circus)	SJ	7734-4756	Classic	155
Restaurant Bar	bentleysoysterbarandgrill.co.uk	-	_		
Big Chill Bar	Dray Walk, off Brick Ln., E1 (Liverpool St.)	HX	7392-9180	Hip	96, 111
DJ Bar	bigchill.net	-	≡		
Bistrotheque *	23-27 Wadeson St., E2 (Bethnal Green)	HX	8983-7900	Hip	93, 112
Bar	bistrotheque.com	-	_ ≡		
The Blue Bar	Wilton Place, SW1 (Knightsbridge)	KN	7235-6000	Classic	129, 155
Hotel Bar	the-berkeley.co.uk	-	_	Hotel Bars	30
Bonds*	5 Threadneedle St., EC2 (Bank)	CT	7657-8088	Classic	155
Hotel Bar	bonds-restaurant.com	-	=		

BLACK BOOK

Nightlife (cont.)

NAME TYPE	ADDRESS (TUBE STATION) WEBSITE	AREA COVER	PHONE (020) NOISE	EXPERIENCE 99 BEST	PAGE PAGE
Café de Paris Nightclub	4 Coventry St., W1 (Piccadilly Circus) cafedeparis.com	SO Ⓒ	7734-7700 ≡	Classic	156
Candy Bar Lesbian Bar	4 Carlisle St., W1 (Tottenham Court Road) thecandybar.co.uk	SO Ⓒ	7494-4041 ≡	Hip Gay Bars & Clubs	112 28
Cargo Nightclub	83 Rivington St., Kingsland Viaduct, EC2 (Old Street) cargolondon.com	HX Ⓒ	7749-7840 ≡	Hip Live-Music Venues	*94*, 112 33
Cellar Gascon Restaurant Bar	59 West Smithfield, EC1 (Farringdon)	CT -	7796-0600 ≡	Classic	156
Chinawhite Nightclub	6 Air St., W1 (Piccadilly Circus) chinawhite.com	SO Ⓒ	7343-0040 ≡	Hot & Cool	75
The Cinnamon Club* Restaurant Bar	Old Westminster Library, Great Smith St. (St. James's/Westmin.) cinnamonclub.com	WE -	7222-2555 ≡	Hot & Cool	75
Claridge's Bar Hotel Bar	55 Brook St., W1 (Bond Street) claridges.co.uk	MY -	7629-8860 _ ≡	Classic Hotel Bars	*128*, 156 30
Cocoon Restaurant Bar	65 Regent St., W1 (Piccadilly Circus) cocoon-restaurants.com	SO -	7494-7600 ≡	Hot & Cool Cocktails	75 22
Comedy Store Comedy Club	1 Oxendon St., SW1 (Leicester Square) thecomedystore.co.uk	SO Ⓒ	7344-0234 ≡	Hip	112
Counting House Pub	50 Cornhill, EC3 (Bank)	CT -	7283-7123 ≡	Classic	156
Cow Dining Room* Gastropub	89 Westbourne Park Rd., W2 (Westbourne Park)	NH -	7221-0021 ≡	Hip	*95*, 112
Crazy Bear Bar	26-28 Whitfield St., W1 (Goodge Street) crazybeargroup.co.uk	FI -	7631-0088 ≡	Hot & Cool See-and-be-Seen	*52*, 76 42
CVO Firevault Bar	36 Great Titchfield St., W1 (Oxford Circus) cvo.co.uk	FI -	7636-2091 _	Hot & Cool	76
Donmar Warehouse Theater	41 Earlham St., WC2 (Covent Garden) donmarwarehouse.com	CO Ⓒ	7240-4882 ≡	Hip	113
Dover Street Restaurant & Jazz Bar Jazz Club	8-10 Dover St., W1 (Green Park) doverst.co.uk	MY -	7491-7509 ≡	Classic	*130*, 156
Dragon Bar Bar	5 Leonard St., EC2 (Old Street)	HX -	7490-7110 ≡	Hip	113
Duke of Cambridge Gastropub	30 St. Peter's St., N1 (Angel) singhboulton.co.uk	IL -	7359-3066 ≡	Hip	113
Dukes Bar Hotel Bar	St. James's Place, SW1 (Green Park) dukeshotel.co.uk	SJ Ⓒ	7491-4840 _	Classic	157
E & O* Restaurant Bar	14 Blenheim Crescent, W11 (Ladbroke Grove) eando.nu	NH -	7229-5454 ≡	Hip	113
Eclipse Bar	111-113 Walton St., SW3 (South Ken.) eclipse-ventures.com	CH -	7581-0123 ≡	Hot & Cool	*54*, 76
Egg Nightclub	200 York Way, N7 (Kings Cross) egglondon.net	VA Ⓒ	7609-8364 ≡	Hip	113
Electric Brasserie* Restaurant Bar	191 Portobello Rd., W11 (Ladbroke Grove) the-electric.co.uk	NH -	7908-9696 _ ≡	Hip	113

NAME	ADDRESS (TUBE STATION)	AREA	PHONE (020)	EXPERIENCE	PAGE
TYPE	WEBSITE	COVER	NOISE	99 BEST	PAGE
Embassy	29 Old Burlington St., W1 (Oxford Circus)	MY	7851-0956	Hot & Cool	76
Nightclub	theembassygroup.co.uk	-	≡		
The End	18 West Central St., WC1	CO	7419-9199	Hot & Cool	54, 76
Nightclub	(Tottenham Court Road) endclub.com	C	≡	Dance Clubs	23
The Endurance	90 Berwick St., W1 (Oxford Circus)	SO	7437-2944	Hip	114
Gastropub		-	_ ≡		
The Engineer	65 Gloucester Ave., NW1 (Chalk Farm)	PR	7722-0950	Classic	157
Gastropub	the-engineer.com	-	_ ≡		
Fabric	77a Charterhouse St., EC1 (Farringdon)	CT	7336-8898	Hip	95, 114
Nightclub	fabriclondon.com	C	≡	Dance Clubs	23
Floridita	100 Wardour St., W1 (Oxford Circus)	SO	7314-4000	Classic	130, 157
Restaurant Bar	floriditalondon.com	-	≡		
Freedom	66 Wardour St., W1 (Oxford Circus)	SO	7734-0071	Hot & Cool	77
Gay Bar		C	≡		
French House	49 Dean St., W1 (Leicester Square)	SO	7437-2799	Classic	157
Pub		-	≡		
Freud	198 Shaftesbury Ave., WC2	CO	7240-9933	Hip	114
Cocktail Bar	(Covent Garden) freudliving.co.uk	-	≡	Cocktails	22
G-A-Y Bar	30 Old Compton St., W1 (Leicester Square)	SO	7494-2756	Hip	114
Gay Bar	g-a-y.co.uk	-	≡		
The George Inn	The George Inn Yard, 77 Borough High St., Southwark. SE1				
	(London Bridge)	BA	7407-2056	Classic	157
Pub	pubs.com/george1.htm	-	_ ≡		
Ghetto	Falconberg Court, behind the Astoria, W1	SO	7287-3726	Hip	114
Gay Bar	(Tottenham Court Rd.) ghetto-london.co.uk	C	≡		
Gordon's Wine Bar	47 Villiers St., WC2 (Embankment)	WE	7930-1408	Classic	158
Wine Bar	gordonswinebar.com	-	_ ≡		
Grill Room at Café Royale	68 Regent St., W1 (Oxford Circus)	SO	7439-1865	Hip	115
Nightclub		-	≡		
Guanabara	Parker St., WC2 (Holborn)	CO	7242-8600	Hip	95, 115
Nightclub	guanabara.co.uk	C	≡	Dance Clubs	23
Harlem	78 Westbourne Grove, W2 (Westbourne Pk.)	NH	7985-0900	Hip	115
Restaurant Bar	harlemsoulfood.com	-	_ ≡		
Heaven	Villiers St., Under the Arches, WC2	CO	7930-2020	Hot & Cool	77
Gay Club	(Charing Cross) heaven-london.com	C	≡	Gay Bars & Clubs	28
Herbal	10-14 Kingsland Rd., E2 (Old Street)	HX	7613-4462	Hip	115
Nightclub	herbaluk.com	C	≡		
The Holly Bush	22 Holly Mount, NW3 (Hampstead)	HA	7435-2892	Classic	158
Pub		-	≡	Pubs	38
Hush	8 Lancashire Ct., Brook St., W1 (Bond St.)	MY	7659-1500	Classic	158
Restaurant Bar	strictlyhush.com		≡		
ICA Bar	ICA, The Mall, SW1 (Charing Cross)	SJ	7930-3647	Hip	94, 115
Bar	ica.org.uk	C	_ ≡		
Inc Bar & Restaurant*	7 College Approach, SE10 (Cutty Sark DLR)	VA	8858-6721	Hip	116
Restaurant Bar		-	≡		

Nightlife (cont.)

Nightlife (cont.)

NAME	ADDRESS (TUBE STATION)	AREA	PHONE (020)	EXPERIENCE	PAGE
TYPE	WEBSITE	COVER	NOISE	99 BEST	PAGE
Itsu	118 Draycott Ave., SW3 (South Kensington)	CH	7590-2400	Hot & Cool	77
Restaurant Bar	itsu.co.uk	-	≈		
The Jamaica Wine House	St. Michael's Alley, Cornhill, EC3 (Bank)	CT	7929-6972	Classic	158
Pub	massivepub.com	-	≈		
Jazz Café	5 Parkway, NW1 (Camden Town)	VA	7534-6955	Hot & Cool	77
Jazz Club	jazzcafe.co.uk	C	≡	Live-Music Venues	33
Jerusalem Tavern	55 Briton St., EC1 (Farringdon)	CT	7490-4281	Classic	129, 158
Pub	stpetersbrewery.co.uk	-	≈	Pubs	38
Kabaret's Prophecy	16-18 Beak St., W1 (Oxford Circus)	SO	7439-2229	Hot & Cool	53, 77
Nightclub	kabaretsprophecy.com	C	≡	Bar Interiors	19
Kensington Roof Gardens	99 Derry St., W8 (High Street Kensington)	KE	7937-7994	Hot & Cool	53, 78
Nightclub	roofgardens.com	C	≈ ≡		
The Key	Kings Cross Freight Depot, N1 (Kings Cross)	VA	7837-1027	Hip	96, 116
Nightclub	thekeylondon.com	C	≡	Late-Night Haunts	32
Kilo	3-5 Mill St., W1 (Oxford Circus)	MY	7629-8877	Hot & Cool	78
Nightclub	kilo-mayfair.co.uk	-	≈		
King William IV	77 Hampstead High St., NW3 (Hampstead)	HA	7435-5747	Classic	159
Pub	kw4.co.uk	-	≈ ≡	Gay Bars & Clubs	28
Lab	12 Old Compton St., W1 (Leicester Square)	SO	7437-7820	Hip	116
Cocktail Bar	lab-townhouse.com	-	≈		
The Lansdowne	90 Gloucester Ave., NW1 (Chalk Farm)	PR	7483-0409	Hot & Cool	78
Pub		-	≈	Pubs	38
Library at the Lanesborough	Hyde Park Corner, W1 (Hyde Park Corner)	KN	7259-5599	Classic	129, 159
Hotel Bar	lanesborough.com	-	≈		
Light Bar	45 St. Martin's Ln., WC2 (Leicester Square)	CO	7300-5500	Hot & Cool	53, 78
Hotel Bar	stmartinslane.com	-	≈ ≡		
Ling Ling at Hakkasan*	8 Hanway Pl., W1 (Tottenham Court Road)	BL	7907-1888	Hot & Cool	52, 79
Restaurant Bar		≡		See-and-be-Seen	42
Lobby Bar	1 Aldwych, WC2 (Covent Garden)	CO	7300-1000	Hot & Cool	79
Hotel Bar	onealdwych.co.uk	-	≈ ≡		
The Lock Tavern	35 Chalk Farm Rd., NW1 (Chalk Farm)	VA	7482-7163	Hip	116
Pub	lock-tavern.co.uk	-	≈		
Long Bar	50 Berners St., W1 (Oxford Circus)	FI	7300-1496	Hot & Cool	52, 79
Hotel Bar	sandersonlondon.com	-	≈	Single Scenes	44
The Lonsdale	44-48 Lonsdale Rd., W11 (Westbourne Pk.)	NH	7727-4080	Hot & Cool	79
Cocktail Bar	thelonsdale.co.uk	-	≈ ≡		
Loungelover	1 Whitby St., E1 (Liverpool Street)	HX	7012-1234	Hip	93, 116
Cocktail Bar	loungelover.co.uk	-	≈	Bar Interiors	19
Lucky Voice	52 Poland St., W1 (Oxford Circus)	SO	7439-3660	Hip	95, 117
Karaoke Bar	luckyvoice.co.uk	-	≈ ≡		
The Mandarin Bar	66 Knightsbridge, SW1 (Knightsbridge)	KN	7235-2000	Classic	129, 159
Hotel Bar	mandarinoriental.com	-	≈	Hotel Bars	30
Market Place	11-13 Market Pl., W1 (Oxford Circus)	FI	7079-2020	Hip	117
DJ Bar	marketplace-london.com	-	≈		

NAME TYPE	ADDRESS (TUBE STATION) WEBSITE	AREA COVER	PHONE (020) NOISE	EXPERIENCE 99 BEST	PAGE PAGE
Mash Restaurant Bar	19-21 Great Portland St., W1 (Oxford Circus) mashbarandrestaurant.com	FI -	7637-5555	Hot & Cool	52, 79
Match Bar	37-38 Margaret St., W1 (Oxford Circus) matchbar.com	MA -	7499-3443 ≡	Hot & Cool	80
The Medicine Bar DJ Bar	89 Great Eastern St., EC2 (Old Street) medicinebar.net	HX -	7739-5173 ⊐≡	Hip	117
Met Bar Members Bar	18-19 Old Park Ln., W1 (Hyde Park Corner) metropolitan.co.uk	MY -	7447-1000 _≡	Hot & Cool	80
Milk and Honey Members Bar	61 Poland St., W1 (Oxford Circus) mlkhny.com	SO -	070-0065-5469 ≡	Classic Cocktails	159 22
Ministry of Sound Nightclub	103 Gaunt St., SE1 (Elephant and Castle) ministryofsound.com	SB C	0870-060-0010 ≡	Hot & Cool	80
Mo Tea Room Restaurant Bar	23 Heddon St., W1 (Piccadilly Circus) momoresto.com/momo.html	MY -	7434-4040 ≡	Hip Bar Interiors	117 19
Movida Nightclub	8-9 Argyll St., W1 (Oxford Circus) movida-club.com	SO C	7734-5776 ≡	Hot & Cool	52, 80
Nectar Bar	562 Kings Rd., SW6 (Sloane Square) nectarbar.co.uk	CH -	7326-7450 ≡	Hot & Cool	81
Neighbourhood Nightclub	12 Acklam Rd., W10 (Ladbroke Grove) neighbourhoodclub.net	NH C	7524-7979 ≡	Hip	117
93 Feet East Nightclub	150 Brick Ln., E1 (Liverpool Street) 93feeteast.co.uk	HX C	7247-3293 ≡	Hip	118
No. 5 Cavendish Square Bar	5 Cavendish Sq., W1 (Oxford Circus) no5ltd.com	MA -	7079-5000 _≡	Classic	160
Nobu Berkeley* Restaurant Bar	15 Berkeley St., W1 (Green Park) noburestaurants.com	MY -	7290-9222 ≡	Hot & Cool	81
Notting Hill Arts Club Nightclub	21 Notting Hill Gate, W11 (Notting Hill Gate) nottinghillartsclub.com	NH C	7460-4459 ≡	Hip	96, 118
Occo* Restaurant Bar	58 Crawford St., W1 (Edgeware Road) occo.co.uk	MA -	7724-4991 ≡	Hot & Cool	81
1 Lombard Street * Restaurant Bar	1 Lombard St., EC3 (Bank) 1lombardstreet.com	CT -	7929-6611 _≡	Classic	160
Opal Restaurant Bar	36 Gloucester Rd., SW7 (Gloucester Road) etranger.co.uk	SK -	7584-9719 _≡	Hot & Cool	81
Opium Nightclub	1a Dean St., W1 (Tottenham Court Road) opium-bar-restaurant.com	SO C	7287-9608 _≡	Hot & Cool	53, 81
Oscar Hotel Bar	15-17 Charlotte St., London W1 (Tottenham Court Road) charlottestreethotel.com	FI -	7806-2000 _≡	Classic	160
Pacha Nightclub	Terminus Pl., SW1 (Victoria) pachalondon.com	SJ C	7833-3139 ≡	Hot & Cool	81
Pangaea Nightclub	85 Piccadilly, W1 (Green Park) pangaeauk.com	MY C	7495-2595 ≡	Hot & Cool Single Scenes	54, 82 44
Pearl Bar & Restaurant* Restaurant Bar	252 High Holborn, WC1 (Holborn) pearl-restaurant.com	HO -	7829-7000 ≡	Hot & Cool	82

BLACK BOOK

Nightlife (cont.)

NAME	ADDRESS (TUBE STATION)	AREA	PHONE (020)	EXPERIENCE	PAGE
TYPE	WEBSITE	COVER	NOISE	99 BEST	PAGE
The Perseverance	63 Lamb's Conduit St., WC1	BL	7405-8278	Hip	118
Gastropub	(Russell Square)	-	≈		
Pizza on the Park	11 Knightsbridge, SW1 (Hyde Park Corner)	KN	7235-5273	Classic	160
Restaurant Bar	pizzaonthepark.co.uk	Ⓒ	≈		
Plastic People	147-149 Curtain Rd., EC2 (Old Street)	HX	7739-6471	Hip	118
Nightclub	plasticpeople.co.uk	Ⓒ	≡		
The Player	8 Broadwick St., W1 (Tottenham Court Rd.)	SO	7494-9125	Hot & Cool	82
Cocktail Bar	thplyr.com	-	≈		
Purple Bar	50 Berners St., W1 (Oxford Circus)	FI	7300-1496	Hot & Cool	52, 82
Hotel Bar	sandersonlondon.com	Ⓒ	_|≡		
Refuel	4 Richmond Mews, W1	SO	7559-3000	Hot & Cool	82
Hotel Bar	(Tottenham Court Road) sohohotel.com	Ⓒ	≈		
The Rivoli Bar	150 Piccadilly, W1 (Green Park)	SJ	7493-8181	Classic	130, 160
Hotel Bar	theritzlondon.com	-	≈		
Rockwell Bourbon Bar	2 Spring Gdns., SW1 (Charing Cross)	WE	7870-2959	Hot & Cool	82
Hotel Bar	trafalgar.hilton.com	-	≈		
Ronnie Scott's	47 Frith St., W1 (Tottenham Court Road)	SO	7439-0747	Classic	128, 160
Jazz Club	ronniescotts.co.uk	Ⓒ	≈|	Live-Music Venues	33
The Royal Opera House	Royal Opera House, Bow St., WC2	CO	7304-4000	Classic	161
Theater	(Covent Garden) royaloperahouse.org	Ⓒ	-		
Ruby Lo	23 Orchard St., W1 (Marble Arch)	MY	7486-3671	Hip	119
DJ Bar	ruby.uk.com	Ⓒ	≡	Single Scenes	44
Salvador and Amanda	8 Great Newport St., WC2 (Leicester Sq.)	CO	7240-1551	Hip	119
Bar	salvadorandamanda.com	-	≈		
Shochu Lounge	37 Charlotte St., Fitzrovia, W1 (Goodge St.)	FI	7580-6464	Hot & Cool	83
Cocktail Bar	shochulounge.com	-	_|≡		
Sketch*	9 Conduit St., W1 (Oxford Circus)	MY	0870-777-4488	Hot & Cool	53, 83
Restaurant Bar	sketch.uk.com	-	≈		
The Social	5 Little Portland St., W1 (Oxford Circus)	FI	7434-0620	Hip	119
DJ Bar	thesocial.com	-	≡		
Sosho	2 Tabernacle St., EC2 (Old Street)	HX	7920-0701	Hot & Cool	83
DJ Bar	sosho3am.com	Ⓒ	_|≡		
Taman Gang	141 Park Ln., W1 (Marble Arch)	MY	7518-3160	Hot & Cool	54, 83
Bar	tamangang.com	-	≈	See-and-be-Seen	42
The Tenth Bar	2-24 Kensington High St., W8 (High Street	KE	7361-1910	Classic	130, 161
Hotel Bar	Kensington) royalgardenhotel.co.uk	-	_|	Bars with a View	20
333 and Mother Bar	333 Old St., EC1 (Old Street)	HX	7739-5949	Hip	94, 119
Nightclub	333mother.com	Ⓒ	≈		
Trader Vic's	22 Park Ln., W1 (Hyde Park Corner)	MY	7208-4113	Classic	161
Restaurant Bar	tradervics.com	-	_|		
Trailer Happiness	177 Portobello Rd., W11 (Notting Hill Gate)	NH	7727-2700	Hip	95, 119
Cocktail Bar	trailerhappiness.com	-	_|≡		
The Troubadour	263-267 Old Brompton Rd., SW5	CH	7370-1434	Classic	161
Bar	(West Brompton) troubadour.co.uk	-	_|≡		

NAME	ADDRESS (TUBE STATION)	AREA	PHONE (020)	EXPERIENCE	PAGE
TYPE	WEBSITE	COVER	NOISE	99 BEST	PAGE
Turnmills	63B Clerkenwell Rd., EC1 (Farringdon)	CT	7250-3409	Hip	120
Nightclub	turnmills.co.uk	☺	≡		
Umbaba	15-21 Ganton St., W1 (Oxford Circus)	SO	7734-6696	Hot & Cool	84
Nightclub	umbaba.co.uk	☺	≡		
Under the Westway	242 Acklam Rd., W10 (Ladbroke Grove)	NH	7575-3123	Hip	*95*, 120
Bar	barworks.com	-	_ ≡		
Vertigo 42	Tower 42, 25 Old Broad. St., EC2 (Bank)	CT	7877-7842	Classic	162
Champagne Bar	vertigo42.co.uk	-	_	Bars with a View	20
Vingt Quatre*	325 Fulham Rd., SW10 (Gloucester Road)	CH	7376-7224	Classic	*129*, 162
Late-Night Restaurant		-	≡	Late-Night Haunts	32
The Westbourne	101 Westbourne Park Villas, W2	NH	7221-1332	Hip	120
Gastropub	(Westbourne Park)	-	_ ≡		
Windows at the Hilton	22 Park Ln., W1 (Hyde Park Corner)	MY	7493-8000	Classic	*128*, 162
Hotel Bar	hilton.co.uk	-	_	Bars with a View	20
Windsor Castle	114 Campden Hill Rd., W8 (Notting Hill	KE	7243-9551	Classic	162
Pub	Gate) windsor-castle-pub.co.uk	-	_ ≡		
Woody's	41-43 Woodfield Rd., W9 (Westbourne Pk.)	NH	7266-3030	Hot & Cool	84
Bar	woodysclub.com	☺	_ ≡		
Ye Olde Mitre	1 Ely Court, Ely Pl. (off 8 Hatton Gdns.) EC1	CT	7405-4751	Classic	162
Pub	(Chancery Lane)	-	_		
Zander	45 Buckingham Gate, SW1 (St. James's)	SJ	7379-9797	Hot & Cool	84
Restaurant Bar	bankrestaurants.com	-	_ ≡		
Zeta	25 Hertford St., W1 (Knightsbridge)	KN	7208-4067	Hot & Cool	84
Nightclub	zeta-bar.com	-	≡		
Zigfrid	11 Hoxton Sq., N1 (Old Street)	HX	7613-3105	Hip	*93*, 120
DJ Bar	zigfrid.com	-	≡		
Zuma*	5 Raphael St., SW7 (Knightsbridge)	KN	7584-1010	Hot & Cool	84
Sake Bar	zumarestaurant.com	-	≡		

Attractions

NAME	ADDRESS (TUBE STATION)	AREA	PHONE (020)	EXPERIENCE	PAGE
TYPE	WEBSITE	PRICE		99 BEST	PAGE
Agua Bathhouse Spa	50 Berners St., W1 (Oxford Circus)	FI	7300-1414	Hot & Cool	85
Spa	sandersonlondon.com	££££		Spas	46
Aime	32 Ledbury Rd, W11 (Notting Hill Gate)	NH	7221-7070	Hot & Cool	85
Shop	aimelondon.com	-			
Asprey	167 New Bond St., W1 (Green Park)	MY	7493-6767	Classic	163
Shop	asprey.com				
Benjamin Franklin House	36 Craven St., WC2 (Charing Cross)	WE	7930-6601	Classic	163
Historic Home	benjaminfranklinhouse.org	£-			
Berry Bros & Rudd	3 St. James's St., SW1 (Green Park)	SJ	7396-9600	Classic	163
Shop	bbr.com				

Attractions (cont.)

NAME	ADDRESS (TUBE STATION)	AREA	PHONE (020)	EXPERIENCE	PAGE
TYPE	WEBSITE	PRICE		99 BEST	PAGE
Borough Market	Southwark St., SE1 (London Bridge)	BA	7407-1002	Hot & Cool	*53*, 85
Market	boroughmarket.org.uk	-		Markets	34
The British Museum	Great Russell St., WC1 (Russell Square)	BL	7323-8299	Classic	*128*, 163
Art Museum	thebritishmuseum.ac.uk	£-			
British Airways London Eye	Next to County Hall, Westminster Bridge Rd.,	SB	0870-500-0600	Hot & Cool	*51*, 85
Sight	SE1 (Westminster) ba-londoneye.com	££			
Broadgate Ice	Broadgate Cir., Eldon St., EC4 (Liverpool St.)	CT	7505-4068	Hot & Cool	85
Sports	broadgateice.co.uk	£-		Fresh Air Exp.	26
Cath Kidston	51 Marylebone High St., W1 (Bond Street)	MA	7935-6555	Hot & Cool	86
Shop	cathkidston.co.uk	-			
Chelsea Physic Garden	66 Royal Hospital Rd., SW3 (Sloane Sq.)	CH	7352-5646	Classic	164
Garden	chelseaphysicgarden.co.uk	£-		Green Spaces	29
The Circus Space	Coronet St., N1 (Old Street)	HX	7613-4141	Hip	121
Activity	thecircusspace.co.uk	££££			
Clarence House	Stableyard Rd., SW1 (Green Park)	SJ	7766-7303	Classic	164
Historic Home	royal.gov.uk	-			
Coco de Mer	23 Monmouth St., WC2 (Covent Garden)	CO	7836-8882	Hip	121
Shop	coco-de-mer.co.uk	-			
Columbia Rd. Flower Market	Columbia Rd., E2 (Shoreditch)	SP	-	Hip	121
Market	columbia-flower-market.freespace.com	-			
Contemporary Applied Arts	2 Percy St., W1 (Tottenham Court Road)	FI	7436-2344	Hot & Cool	86
Art Gallery	caa.org.uk	-			
Cork Street	Cork St., W1 (Green Park)	MY	-	Hot & Cool	86
Art Galleries		-			
Cowshed	119 Portland Rd., W11 (Holland Park)	VA	7078-1944	Hip	*95*, 121
Spa	cowshedclarendoncross.com	££		Spas	46
Dalí Universe	County Hall Gallery, Westminster Bridge	SB	7620-2720	Hot & Cool	86
Art Museum	Rd., SE1 (Westminster) daliuniverse.com	£-			
Dennis Severs' House	18 Folgate St., E1 (Liverpool Street)	SP	7247-4013	Classic	164
Historic Home	dennissevershouse.co.uk	£-			
Design Museum	Shad Thames, SE1 (London Bridge)	BA	0870-909-9009	Hot & Cool	*53*, 87
Museum	designmuseum.org	£-			
Diverse	294 Upper St., N1 (Angel)	IL	7359-8877	Hot & Cool	87
Shop	diverseclothing.com	-			
Elemis day-spa	2-3 Lancashire Court, W1 (Bond Street)	MY	0870-410-4995	Hot & Cool	*54*, 87
Spa	elemis.com	££££		Spas	46
Estorick Collection of Modern	39a Canonbury Sq, N1 (Highbury &	IL	7704-9522	Hot & Cool	87
Italian Art Art Museum	Islington) estorickcollection.com	£-			
Fashion & Textile Museum	83 Bermondsey St., SE1 (London Bridge)	BA	7403-0222	Hip	*94*, 122
Museum	ftmlondon.org	£-			
Feliks Topolski's Memoir of	Hungerford Bridge Arches,				
the Century	Concert Hall Approach, SE1 (Waterloo)	SB	-	Hip	122
Art Museum	felikstopolski.com/memoir.htm	£-			
Fortnum & Mason	181 Piccadilly, W1 (Green Park)	SJ	7734-8040	Classic	*130*, 164
Shop	fortnumandmason.com	-			

NAME	ADDRESS (TUBE STATION)	AREA	PHONE (020)	EXPERIENCE	PAGE
TYPE	WEBSITE	PRICE		99 BEST	PAGE
The Foundling Museum	40 Brunswick Sq., WC1 (Russell Square)	BL	7841-3600	Classic	164
Art Museum	foundlingmuseum.org.uk	£-		Small Museums	45
Getty Images Gallery	46 Eastcastle St., W1 (Goodge Street)	FI	7291-5380	Hot & Cool	87
Art Museum	hultongetty.com	-			
Hampstead Heath and	NW3 and NW5 (Hampstead)	HA	-	Classic	130, 165
Parliament Hill Park	cityoflondon.gov.uk	-		Green Spaces	29
Handel House Museum	25 Brook St., W1 (Bond Street)	MY	7495-1685	Classic	165
Museum	handelhouse.org	£-		Small Museums	45
Haunch of Venison	6 Haunch of Venison Yd., W1 (Bond Street)	MY	7495-5050	Hip	122
Art Gallery	haunchofvenison.com	-			
Hayward Gallery	Belvedere Rd., SE1 (Waterloo)	SB	7921-0813	Hot & Cool	52, 88
Art Museum	hayward.org.uk	£-		Modern Art Spaces	35
Hyde Park Stables	63 Bathurst Mews, W2 (Marble Arch)	HP	7723-2813	Classic	130, 165
Activity	hydeparkstables.com	££££		Fresh Air Exp.	26
Imperial War Museum	Lambeth Rd., SE1 (Lambeth North)	SB	7416-5320	Classic	165
Museum	iwm.org.uk	£-			
Institute of Contemporary	The Mall, SW1 (Charing Cross)	SJ	7930-3647	Hip	94, 122
Arts Art Museum	ica.org.uk	£-			
Jerwood Space	171 Union St., SE1 (Southwark)	BA	7654-0171	Hip	122
Art Museum	jerwoodspace.co.uk	£-			
Karma Kars	Various	VA	8964-0700	Hip	95, 123
Tour	karmakabs.com	££££			
Kensington Palace	Kensington Gdns., W8 (High Street Ken.)	KE	0870-751-5170	Classic	166
Historic Home	hrp.org.uk	£			
Kenwood House	Hampstead Ln., NW3 (Hampstead)	HA	8348-1286	Classic	130, 166
Historic Home	english-heritage.org	£-		Aristocratic Mns.	18
Leighton House	12 Holland Park Rd, W14 (High Street Ken.)	KE	7602-3316	Classic	166
Historic Home	rbkc.gov.uk/leightonhousemuseum	£-		Aristocratic Mns.	18
Liberty	214 Regent St., W1 (Oxford Circus)	SO	7734-1234	Classic	166
Shop	liberty.co.uk	-			
Lincoln's Inn	WC2 (Holborn)	HO	7405-1393	Classic	129, 167
Sight	lincolnsinn.org.uk	£-			
Lisson Gallery	29 & 52-54 Bell St., NW1 (Edgeware Road)	MA	7724-2739	Hot & Cool	88
Art Gallery	lisson.co.uk	-			
London Silver Vaults	53-64 Chancery Ln., WC2 (Chancery Lane)	HO	-	Classic	129, 167
Shopping	thesilvervaults.com				
London Walks	Various	VA	7624-3978	Classic	167
Tour	walks.com	£-			
Magma	8 Earlham St., WC2 (Covent Garden)	CO	7240-8498	Hip	123
Shop	magmabooks.com				
Millennium Bridge	across Thames between Bankside and City	CT	-	Hot & Cool	88
Sight	(Blackfriars) arup.com/millenniumbridge	-			
Moss Bros	27-28 King St., WC2 (Covent Garden)	CO	7632-9700	Classic	167
Service	mossbros.co.uk	££££			

Attractions (cont.)

NAME	ADDRESS (TUBE STATION)	AREA	PHONE (020)	EXPERIENCE	PAGE
TYPE	WEBSITE	PRICE		99 BEST	PAGE
Museum of London Museum	150 London Wall, EC2 (Barbican) museumoflondon.org.uk	CT £-	0870-444-3852	Classic	167
My Chocolate Activity	41a Linden Gardens, Notting Hill Gate, W2 (Notting Hill Gate) mychocolate.co.uk	NH ££££	7792-6865	Hot & Cool	88
National Film Theatre Film Center	Belvedere Rd., SE1 (Waterloo) bfi.org.uk	SB £-	7928-3232	Hip Rainy Day Activities	*94*, 123 39
National Gallery Art Museum	Trafalgar Sq., WC2 (Charing Cross) nationalgallery.org.uk	WE £-	7747-2885	Classic	*127*, 168
National Portrait Gallery Art Museum	2 St. Martin's Place, WC2 (Charing Cross) npg.org.uk	WE £-	7306-0055	Classic	168
Oxo Tower Wharf Shopping	Bargehouse St., SE1 (Blackfriars) oxotower.co.uk	SB -	7401-2255	Hot & Cool	*54*, 89
Ozwald Boateng Shop	9 Vigo St., W1 (Piccadilly Circus) ozwaldboateng.co.uk	MY -	7437-0620	Hot & Cool	89
Percival David Foundation of Chinese Art Museum	53 Gordon Sq., WC1 (Euston Square) pdfmuseum.org.uk	BL £-	7387-3909	Classic	168
The Photographers' Gallery Art Gallery	5 & 8 Great Newport St., WC2 (Leicester Sq.) photonet.org.uk	CO	7831-1772	Hot & Cool	89
Portobello Market Market	Portobello Rd., W11 (Notting Hill Gate) portobelloroad.co.uk	NH -	7375-0441	Hip Markets	*95*, 123 34
Prescott & Mackay Activity	74 Broadway Market, E8 (Bond Street) prescottandmackay.co.uk	MY ££££	7923-9450	Hot & Cool	89
The Queen's Gallery Art Museum	Buckingham Gate, SW1 (Victoria) royal.gov.uk	SJ £-	7766-7301	Classic	168
Riflemaker Art Gallery	79 Beak St., W1 (Oxford Circus) riflemaker.org	SO -	7439-0000	Hip	123
Rollerstroll Activity	Hyde Park, W1 (Hyde Park Corner) rollerstroll.com	HP -	-	Hot & Cool Fresh Air Exp.	*54*, 89 26
Royal Academy of Arts Art Museum	Burlington House, Piccadilly, W1 (Green Park) royalacademy.org.uk	MY -	7300-8000	Hot & Cool	90
Royal Botanic Gardens Garden	Kew, Richmond (Kew Gardens) rbgkew.org.uk	VA £-	8940-1171	Classic Green Spaces	169 29
St. Martin-in-the-Fields Sight	Trafalgar Sq., WC2 (Charing Cross) smitf.org	WE £-	7766-1100	Classic	169
St. Paul's Cathedral Sight	Ludgate Hill, EC4 (St. Paul's) stpauls.co.uk	CT £-	7236-4128	Classic	*127*, 169
Serpentine Boating Lake Activity	The Boat House, Serpentine Rd., Hyde Park, W2 (Knightsbridge) royalparks.gov.uk	HP £-	7262-1330	Classic	*130*, 169
Serpentine Gallery Art Museum	Kensington Gdns., W2 (Knightsbridge) serpentinegallery.org	HP -	7402-6075	Hip	124
Shakespeare's Globe Sight/Museum	21 New Globe Walk, SE1 (Southwark) shakespeares-globe.org	BA £-	7902-1500	Classic	170
Sir John Soane's Museum Museum/Historic Home	13 Lincoln's Inn Fields, W2 (Holborn) soane.org	HO £-	7405-2107	Classic Small Museums	*128*, 170 45

NAME TYPE	ADDRESS (TUBE STATION) WEBSITE	AREA PRICE	PHONE (020)	EXPERIENCE 99 BEST	PAGE PAGE
Skandium Shop	86 Marylebone High St., W1 (Bond Street) skandium.com	MA -	7935-2077	Hot & Cool	90
Smythson Shop	40 New Bond St., W1 (Bond Street) smythson.co.uk	MY -	7629-8558	Hot & Cool	90
Somerset House Sight/Art Museum	The Strand, WC2 (Temple) somerset-house.org.uk	CO £-	7845-4600	Hot & Cool	*52*, 90
The Spa at the Dorchester Spa	Park Ln., W1 (Hyde Park Corner) thedorchester.com	MY ££££	7495-7335	Classic	*130*, 170
Spencer House Historic Home	27 St. James's Pl., SW1 (Green Park) spencerhouse.co.uk	SJ £-	7499-8620	Classic Aristocratic Mns.	*130*, 170 18
Spitalfields Market Market	Commercial St., E1 (Liverpool Street) spitalfields.org	SP -	7247-8556	Hip Markets	*96*, 124 34
Tate Britain Art Museum	Millbank, SW1 (Pimlico) tate.org.uk	VA £-	7887-8888	Classic	170
Tate Modern Art Museum	Bankside, SE1 (Southwark) tate.org.uk	BA £-	7887-8888	Hot & Cool Modern Art Spaces	*51*, 91 35
Tate to Tate Service/Activity	Bet.. Millbank Pier and Bankside (Pimlico/Southwark) tate.org.uk	BA £-	7887-8888	Hot & Cool	91
Tea at the Ritz Activity	150 Piccadilly, W1 (Green Park) theritzlondon.com	MY ££££	7493-8181	Classic Rainy Day Activities	*130*, 171 39
Tower of London Sight	Tower Hill, EC3 (Tower Hill) hrp.org.uk	CT £	0870-756-6060	Classic	171
Triyoga Sports	6 Erskine Rd., NW3 (Chalk Farm) triyoga.co.uk	PR £-	7483-3344	Hip	124
2 Willow Road Historic Home	2 Willow Rd., NW3 (Hampstead) nationaltrust.org.uk	HA	7435-6166	Hot & Cool	91
Urban Golf Sports	33 Great Pulteney St., W1 (Oxford Circus) urbangolf.co.uk	SO £	7434-4300	Hip Rainy Day Activities	*94*, 124 39
Vertical Chill Sports	Tower House, 3-11 Southampton St., WC2 (Covent Garden) ellis-brigham.com	CO ££	7395-1010	Hip	125
Victoria & Albert Museum Museum	Cromwell Rd, SW7 (South Kensington) vam.ac.uk	SK £-	7942-2000	Classic	*129*, 171
Vivienne Westwood Shop	44 Conduit St., W1 (Oxford Circus) viviennewestwood.co.uk	MY -	7439-1109	Classic	171
Wallace Collection Art Museum	Hertford House, Manchester Sq., W1 (Bond Street) wallacecollection.org	MA £-	7563-9500	Classic	172
Westminster Abbey Sight	20 Dean's Yard, SW1 (Westminster) westminster-abbey.org	WE £-	7222-5152	Classic	172
White Cube Art Gallery	48 Hoxton Sq., N1 (Old Street) whitecube.com	HX -	7930-5373	Hip	125
Whitechapel Art Gallery Art Gallery	80-82 Whitechapel High St., E1 (Aldgate East) whitechapel.org	CT £-	7522-7888	Hip Modern Art Spaces	*96*, 125 35

BLACK BOOK

London Black Book By Neighborhood

Bankside (BA)

R	Bermondsey Kitchen		102
	Champor-Champor		103
	Delfina		104
	Le Pont de la Tour		147
	Roast		69
	Tapas Brindisa		110
N	The George Inn		157
A	Borough Market	34	85
	Design Museum		87
	Fashion & Textile Museum		122
	Jerwood Space		122
	Shakespeare's Globe		170
	Tate Modern	35	91
	Tate to Tate		91

Bloomsbury (BL)

R	Eagle Bar Diner		105
	Fino		64
	Hakkasan*	17	65
	Pied à Terre	37	150
	Roka	47	70
N	Ling Ling at Hakkasan*	42	79
	The Perseverance		118
A	The British Museum		163
	The Foundling Museum	45	164
	Percival David Foundation of Chinese Art		168

Chelsea (CH)

H	myhotel Chelsea		100
	Number Eleven Cadogan Gardens		137
R	Aubergine		140
	Bibendum		141
	Bluebird Dining Rooms		142
	Daphne's		143
	Eight Over Eight	36	105
	Gordon Ramsay	25	144
	Le Cercle		66
	Rasoi Vineet Bhatia	31	151
	Roussillon		152
	Tom Aikens	25	154
	Tugga		71

R	Vingt Quatre*		154
N	Eclipse		76
	Itsu		77
	Nectar		81
	The Troubadour		161
	Vingt Quatre*	32	162
A	Chelsea Physic Garden	29	164

The City (CT)

H	The Great Eastern Hotel		99
	Threadneedles		61
R	Bevis Marks Restaurant		141
	Bonds*		142
	Canteen		103
	Club Gascon		103
	Fifteen	24	105
	1 Lombard Street*		149
	Rhodes Twenty-Four		151
N	Bonds*		155
	Cellar Gascon		156
	Counting House		156
	Fabric	23	114
	The Jamaica Wine House		158
	Jerusalem Tavern	38	158
	1 Lombard Street *		160
	Turnmills		120
	Vertigo 42	20	162
	Ye Olde Mitre		162
A	Broadgate Ice	26	85
	Millennium Bridge		88
	Museum of London		167
	St. Paul's Cathedral		169
	Tower of London		171
	Whitechapel Art Gallery	35	125

Clerkenwell (CL)

H	The Rookery		138
	The Zetter		101
R	Eagle		104
	Medcalf		108
	Moro		67
	St. John	24	152
	Smiths of Smithfield		109

Code: H-Hotels; R-Restaurants; N-Nightlife; A-Attractions. *Blue page numbers denote listings in 99 Best. Black page numbers denote listings in theme chapters. The London Neighborhoods Map is on p.255.*

R Zetter   73

Covent Garden (CO)
H One Aldwych   59
  The Savoy   138
  St. Martin's Lane   60
R The Admiralty   139
  Asia de Cuba   62
  The Ivy   21 145
  J Sheekey   145
  Origin   149
  Rules   152
  Savoy Grill   37 153
  Shanghai Blues   153
N Aka   74
  The American Bar   155
  Donmar Warehouse   113
  The End   23 76
  Freud   22 114
  Guanabara   23 115
  Heaven   28 77
  Light Bar   78
  Lobby Bar   79
  The Royal Opera House   161
  Salvador and Amanda   119
A Coco de Mer   121
  Magma   123
  Moss Bros   167
  The Photographers' Gallery   89
  Somerset House   90
  Vertical Chill   125

Docklands (DO)
R Gun   27 65
  Plateau   68
  Wapping Food   110

Fitzrovia (FI)
H The Charlotte Street Hotel   58
  The Sanderson   60
R Elena's L'Étoile   144
  Sardo   70
  Spoon at Sanderson   71
N Crazy Bear   42 76
  CVO Firevault   76
  Long Bar   44 79
  Market Place   117

N Mash   79
  Oscar   160
  Purple Bar   82
  Shochu Lounge   83
  The Social   119
A Agua Bathhouse Spa   46 85
  Contemporary Applied Arts   86
  Getty Images Gallery   87

Fulham (FU)
R Blue Elephant   141
  Deep   64
  1492   106
  Sugar Hut   71
  Wizzy   72

Hampstead (HA)
N The Holly Bush   38 158
  King William IV   28 159
A Hampstead Heath and
    Parliament Hill   29 165
  Kenwood House   18 166
  2 Willow Road   91

Holborn (HO)
R Matsuri   47 148
  Pearl Bar & Restaurant*   40 68
N Pearl Bar & Restaurant*   82
A Lincoln's Inn   167
  London Silver Vaults   167
  Sir John Soane's Museum   45 170

Hoxton (HX)
R Bistrotheque*   48 102
  Hoxton Apprentice   106
  Les Trois Garçons   48 107
  Princess   109
  The Real Greek   109
N Bar Kick   111
  Below 54   75
  Big Chill Bar   111
  Bistrotheque*   112
  Cargo   33 112
  Dragon Bar   113
  Herbal   115
  Loungelover   19 116
  The Medicine Bar   117

BLACK BOOK

Hoxton (HX) (cont.)

N 93 Feet East 118
Plastic People 118
Sosho 83
333 and Mother Bar 119
Zigfrid 120
A The Circus Space 121
White Cube 125

Hyde Park (HP)

A Hyde Park Stables 26 165
Rollerstroll 26 89
Serpentine Boating Lake 169
Serpentine Gallery 124

Islington (IL)

R Morgan M 148
N The Almeida 74
Duke of Cambridge 113
A Diverse 87
Estorick Collection of Modern
Italian Art 87

Kensington (KE)

H The Baglioni 57
K West Hotel & Spa 58
The Milestone Hotel and
Apartments 136
R Babylon 62
Clarke's 103
Pasha 150
Royal China Queensway 152
Zaika 41 72
N Kensington Roof Gardens 78
The Tenth Bar 20 161
Windsor Castle 162
A Kensington Palace 166
Leighton House 18 166

Knightsbridge (KN)

H The Berkeley 57
The Cadogan 133
The Halkin 58
The Lanesborough 136
R Amaya 31 62
Boxwood Café 63
The Capital 142

R Emporio Armani Caffe 64
Frankie's Italian Bar & Grill 64
Ladurée 146
Mr. Chow 148
Nahm 148
Pétrus 37 150
Racine 151
The Rib Room & Oyster Bar 152
San Lorenzo 21 70
Zafferano 154
Zuma* 17 73
N The Blue Bar 30 155
Library at the Lanesborough 159
The Mandarin Bar 30 159
Pizza on the Park 160
Zeta 84
Zuma* 84

Marylebone (MA)

H No. 5 Cavendish Square 59
R Galvin Bistrot de Luxe 144
La Fromagerie 107
Locanda Locatelli 66
Nipa 149
Occo* 68
The Providores & Tapa Room 69
N Annex 3 111
Match 80
No. 5 Cavendish Square 160
Occo* 81
A Cath Kidston 86
Lisson Gallery 88
Skandium 90
Wallace Collection 172

Mayfair (MY)

H Brown's Hotel 133
Claridge's 134
The Connaught 134
The Dorchester 134
Metropolitan London 59
The Ritz Hotel 137
R Angela Hartnett 139
Automat 140
Benares 63
China Tang 143
Cipriani 143

R	Gordon Ramsay at Claridge's	144
	The Greenhouse	145
	Kai Mayfair	146
	Kaya	146
	Le Caprice	21 146
	Le Gavroche	25 147
	Luciano	147
	Maze	66
	Mirabelle	148
	Momo	41 67
	Nicole's	67
	Nobu	36 67
	Nobu Berkeley*	68
	Palm Court	149
	Sketch*	17 70
	The Square	153
	Sumosan	47 71
	Tamarind	31 153
	Umu	36 72
N	Below Zero/Absolut Ice Bar	75
	Claridge's Bar	30 156
	Dover Street Restaurant &	
	Jazz Bar	156
	Embassy	76
	Hush	158
	Kilo	78
	Met Bar	80
	Mo Tea Room	19 117
	Nobu Berkeley*	81
	Pangaea	44 82
	Ruby Lo	44 119
	Sketch*	83
	Taman Gang	42 83
	Trader Vic's	161
	Windows at the Hilton	20 162
A	Asprey	163
	Cork Street	86
	Elemis day-spa	46 87
	Handel House Museum	45 165
	Haunch of Venison	122
	Ozwald Boateng	89
	Prescott & Mackay	89
	Royal Academy of Arts	90
	Smythson	90
	The Spa at the Dorchester	170
	Tea at the Ritz	39 171
	Vivienne Westwood	171

Notting Hill (NH)

H	Guesthouse West	99
	The Main House	99
	Miller's Residence	100
	The Portobello Hotel	100
R	Cow Dining Room*	27 104
	E & O*	48 104
	Electric Brasserie*	105
	Food @ the Muse	106
	The Ledbury	66
	Notting Hill Brasserie	108
	Ottolenghi	108
	Tom's Delicatessen	110
N	Cow Dining Room*	112
	E & O*	113
	Electric Brasserie*	113
	Harlem	115
	The Lonsdale	38 78
	Neighbourhood	117
	Notting Hill Arts Club	118
	Trailer Happiness	119
	Under the Westway	120
	The Westbourne	120
	Woody's	84
A	Aime	85
	My Chocolate	88
	Portobello Market	34 123

Primrose Hill (PR)

R	Little Earth Café	107
N	The Engineer	157
	The Lansdowne	38 78
A	Triyoga	124

St. James's (SJ)

H	Dukes Hotel	135
	22 Jermyn Street	138
R	The Avenue	140
	Bentley's Oyster Bar & Grill*	141
	Green's	145
	Quaglino's	151
	Wiltons	154
	The Wolseley	154
N	Bentley's Oyster Bar & Grill*	155
	Dukes Bar	157
	ICA Bar	115
	Pacha	81

BLACK BOOK

St. James's (SJ) (cont.)

N	The Rivoli Bar	160
	Zander	84
A	Berry Bros & Rudd	163
	Clarence House	164
	Fortnum & Mason	164
	Institute of Contemporary Arts	122
	The Queen's Gallery	168
	Spencer House	18 170

Soho (SO)

H	Hazlitt's	135
	The Soho Hotel	61
R	Alastair Little	139
	Bar Italia*	102
	L'Escargot	146
	Lindsay House	147
	Maison Bertaux	108
	Patara	150
	Pâtisserie Valerie	108
	Yauatcha	72
N	Ain't Nothin But The Blues Bar	111
	Akbar	74
	Bar Italia*	32 111
	Café de Paris	156
	Candy Bar	28 112
	Chinawhite	75
	Cocoon	22 75
	Comedy Store	112
	The Endurance	114
	Floridita	157
	Freedom	77
	French House	157
	G-A-Y Bar	114
	Ghetto	114
	Grill Room at Café Royale	115
	Kabaret's Prophecy	19 77
	Lab	116
	Lucky Voice	117
	Milk and Honey	22 159
	Movida	80
	Opium	81
	The Player	82
	Refuel	82
	Ronnie Scott's	33 160
	Umbaba	84
A	Liberty	166

A	Riflemaker	123
	Urban Golf	39 124

South Bank (SB)

R	Anchor & Hope	27 62
	Baltic*	40 63
	Glas	65
N	Baltic*	74
	Ministry of Sound	80
A	British Airways London Eye	85
	Dalí Universe	86
	Feliks Topolski's Memoir of the Century	122
	Hayward Gallery	35 88
	Imperial War Museum	165
	National Film Theatre	39 123
	Oxo Tower Wharf	89

South Kensington (SK)

H	Blakes Hotel	57
	The Gore Hotel	135
	The Pelham Hotel	137
R	Cambio de Tercio	142
	1880	143
N	Opal	81
A	Victoria & Albert Museum	171

Spitalfields (SP)

R	Brick Lane Beigel Bake	102
	Story Deli	109
A	Columbia Road Flower Market	121
	Dennis Severs' House	164
	Spitalfields Market	34 124

Westminster (WE)

H	The Trafalgar	61
R	The Cinnamon Club*	40 63
	Inn the Park	16 65
N	Albannach	155
	The Cinnamon Club*	75
	Gordon's Wine Bar	158
	Rockwell Bourbon Bar	82
A	Benjamin Franklin House	163
	National Gallery	168
	National Portrait Gallery	168
	St. Martin-in-the-Fields	170
	Westminster Abbey	172

London Unique Shopping Index

NAME	(020) PHONE	AREA	PRODUCTS	PAGE
Aime	7221-7070	NH	French women's apparel and décor	56, 85
Asprey	7493-6767	MY	Housewares and accessories	132, 163
Berry Bros & Rudd	7396-9600	SJ	Wines and spirits	132, 163
Beyond Retro	7613-3636	SP	Vintage clothing	98
Beyond the Valley	7437-0199	SO	Concept shop focusing on art	98
Bond International	7437-0199	SO	Stylish men's apparel	98
Burberry	7839-5222	MY	Classic British fashion label	132
Burlington Arcade	-	MY	Shops selling cashmere, antiques, gifts	132
Cath Kidston	7935-6555	MA	Home décor in British florals	56, 86
Chanel	7581-8620	KN	Huge branch of fashion giant	132
Church's Shoes	7930-8210	SJ	Classic leather footwear	132
Cinch	7287-4941	SO	Vintage clothing and shoes	98
Cloud Cuckoo Land	7935-2077	IL	Vintage clothing and accessories	56
Coco de Mer	7836-8882	CO	High-end lingerie and erotica	98, 121
Conran Shop	7589-7401	KN	Classic modernist home designs	132
The Dispensary	7287-8145	SO	Edgy women's apparel	98
Diverse	7350-8877	IL	Colorful men's, and women's apparel	56, 87
Emma Hope's Shoes	7313-7490	NH	Fancy footwear for women	56
Fortnum & Mason	7734-8040	SJ	Dept. store famous gourmet food	132, 164
Ginka	7589-4866	KN	Prints, stationery, and fashion	132
J Floris	0845-702-3239	SJ	Fragrances and soaps	132
Jess James	7437-0199	SO	Contemporary jewelry	98
Joseph	7225-3335	KN	Classic womenswear	132
Koh Samui	7240-4280	CO	Sexy women's apparel	98
Labour and Wait	7729-6253	SP	Retro home décor and accessories	98
Liberty	7734-1234	SO	One of London's premier dept. stores	166
London Silver Vaults	-	HO	Assorted shops specializing in silver	167
Magma	7240-8498	CO	Art and design bookshop	98, 123
Mimi	7729-6699	SP	Edgy handbags and leather goods	98
Oxo Tower Wharf	7401-2255	SB	Studios and shops with varied crafts	89
Ozwald Boateng	7437-0620	MY	High-end menswear	89
Paul Smith	7727-3553	NH	British designer apparel	56
Poste Mistress	7379-4040	CO	Women's shoe shop	98
Sefton	7226-9822	IL	High-end men's and women's apparel	56
Shelf	7739-9444	SP	Art and creative gifts	98
Skandium	7935-2077	MA	Scandinavian home décor	56, 90
Smythson	7629-8558	MY	High-end stationery, leather goods	56, 90
Solane Azagury-Partridge	7792-0197	NH	Fine jewelry with a modern twist	56
Space.NK	7486-8791	MA	Beauty shop	56
Stella Cadente	7359-8015	IL	Fanciful women's apparel	56
Stussy	7836-9418	CO	Designer menswear	98
Thomas Pink	7498-3882	SJ	Luxury shirtmaker	132
Vivienne Westwood	7439-1109	MY	Designer/punk women's apparel	56, 171

For Neighborhood (Area) Key, see p.228.

BLACK BOOK

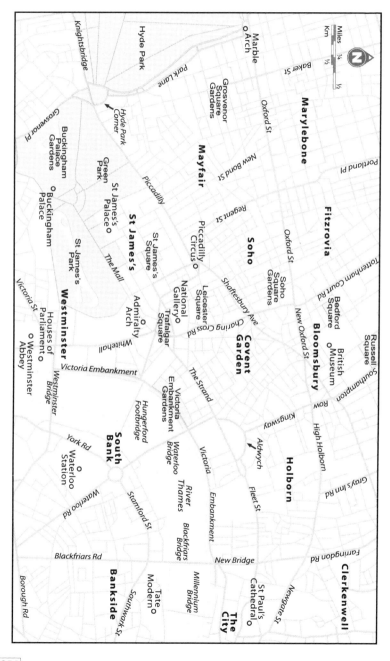

Map of London Neighborhoods

Notting Hill
Ladbroke Grove
Notting Hill Gate
Kensington Palace
Kensington High St
Kensington
South Kensington
Fulham
New King's Rd
King's Rd
Battersea Bridge
Albert Bridge
Battersea Park
Chelsea Bridge
River Thames
Chelsea
Wandsworth Rd
Clapham Rd
Albany Rd
Old Kent Rd
Camberwell New Rd
Knightsbridge
Royal Albert Hall
Victoria and Albert Museum
Sloane St
The Serpentine
Round Pond
Hyde Park
Bayswater Rd
Westway
Edgware Rd
Maida Vale
Park Rd
Regent's Park
Boating Lake
Primrose Hill
To Hampstead
Camden St
Eversholt St
Euston Rd
Marylebone
Baker St
Oxford St
Park Lane
Mayfair
Green Park
Piccadilly
St James's Park
Palace Gardens
Victoria St
Victoria Station
Tate
Lambeth Bridge
Vauxhall Bridge
Westminster
National Gallery
St James's
Soho
Covent Garden
Fitzrovia
Bloomsbury
Holborn
Gray's Inn Rd
Clerkenwell
City Road
Islington
Hoxton
Kingsland Rd
Hackney Rd
Commercial Rd
Victoria Park
Grove Rd
South Bank
Waterloo Station
Blackfriars Bridge
Blackfriars Rd
Newgate St
Bankside
Tate Modern
London Bridge
The City
Bishopsgate
Spitalfields
Whitechapel Rd
Great Dover
Tower Bridge Rd
Tower Bridge
Tower of London
Jamaica Rd
Southwark Park
River Thames
Lower Rd
Greenland Dock
Docklands
Salter Rd
Miles
Kilometers

N

It's New. It's You.
Night+Day online
@ pulseguides.com

a travel web site designed to
complement your lifestyle

Today's urbane, sophisticated traveler knows
how fast things change in the world. What's hot,
and what's not? Now you have access to the
insider information you need, whenever you
need it **Night+Day**—at pulseguides.com.

We're committed to providing the latest, most
accurate information on the hottest, hippest,
coolest and classiest venues around the world,
which means keeping our listings current—
even after you've purchased one of our
Night+Day guides.

Visit pulseguides.com and browse your way to any
destination to view or download the most recent
updates to the **Night+Day** guide of your choice.

Online and in print, **Night+Day** offers independent travel advice tailored to suit your lifestyle,
capturing the unique personality of each city.
From uptown chic to downtown cool, our guides
are packed with opinionated tips, and selective,
richly detailed descriptions geared toward the
discerning traveler.

Enhance your travel experience online:
- Zero in on hot restaurants, classic
  attractions and hip nightlife
- Print out your favorite itinerary to keep
  in your purse or pocket as you travel
- Update your **Night+Day** guide with
  what's new
- Read news and tips from around the world
- Get great deals on all the titles in our Cool
  Cities series

Night+Day—online now at pulseguides.com .

"Perfect for the
business person
or jet-setter."
—*Sacramento Bee*

"Focus[es] their
information to attract
vacationers who don't
want cookie-cutter
itineraries."
—*Wall Street Journal*

"Delivers pithy
comments and
frank opinions."
—*Salt Lake Tribune*

"Count on trendy,
hip, and hot tips,
smart clubs, and
fashionable fun."
—*Physicians Travel
Monthly*

"Refreshingly
different ... It's amazing
how much information
is crammed into a
handy 230-page
paperback format."
—*Anthony Dias Blue,
KCBS Radio*